This orange (its color faded ages ago) mechanical pencil, long missing its cap, was a faithful friend that put in countless hours of good work. When I was finishing up the last part of the final chapter, its eraser finally fell apart and clogged up the end. I can no longer put new lead into it. Thank you for everything you gave me, my old friend...

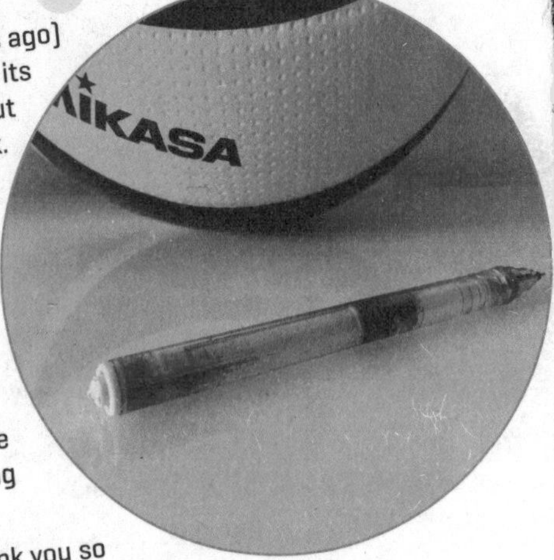

Obviously, I'm going to dig the eraser bits out and keep using it though...

This is the final volume. Thank you so much for everything! Look at all the muscle eight and a half years of *Haikyu!!* has built!

HARUICHI FURUDATE began his manga career when he was 25 years old with the one-shot *Ousama Kid* (King Kid), which won an honorable mention for the 14th Jump Treasure Newcomer Manga Prize. His first series, *Kiben Gakuha, Yotsuya Sensei no Kaidan* (Philosophy School, Yotsuya Sensei's Ghost Stories), was serialized in *Weekly Shonen Jump* in 2010. In 2012, he began serializing *Haikyu!!* in *Weekly Shonen Jump*, where it became his most popular work to date.

HAIKYU!!
VOLUME 45
SHONEN JUMP Manga Edition

Story and Art by
HARUICHI FURUDATE

Translation ■ **ADRIENNE BECK**
Touch-Up Art & Lettering ■ **ERIKA TERRIQUEZ**
Design ■ **JULIAN [JR] ROBINSON**
Editor ■ **MARLENE FIRST**

HAIKYU!! © 2012 by Haruichi Furudate
All rights reserved.
First published in Japan in 2012 by SHUEISHA Inc., Tokyo.
English translation rights arranged by SHUEISHA Inc.

The stories, characters and incidents mentioned
in this publication are entirely fictional.

Printed in Canada

Published by VIZ Media, LLC
P.O. Box 77010
San Francisco, CA 94107

10 9 8 7 6 5 4 3 2 1
First printing, August 2021

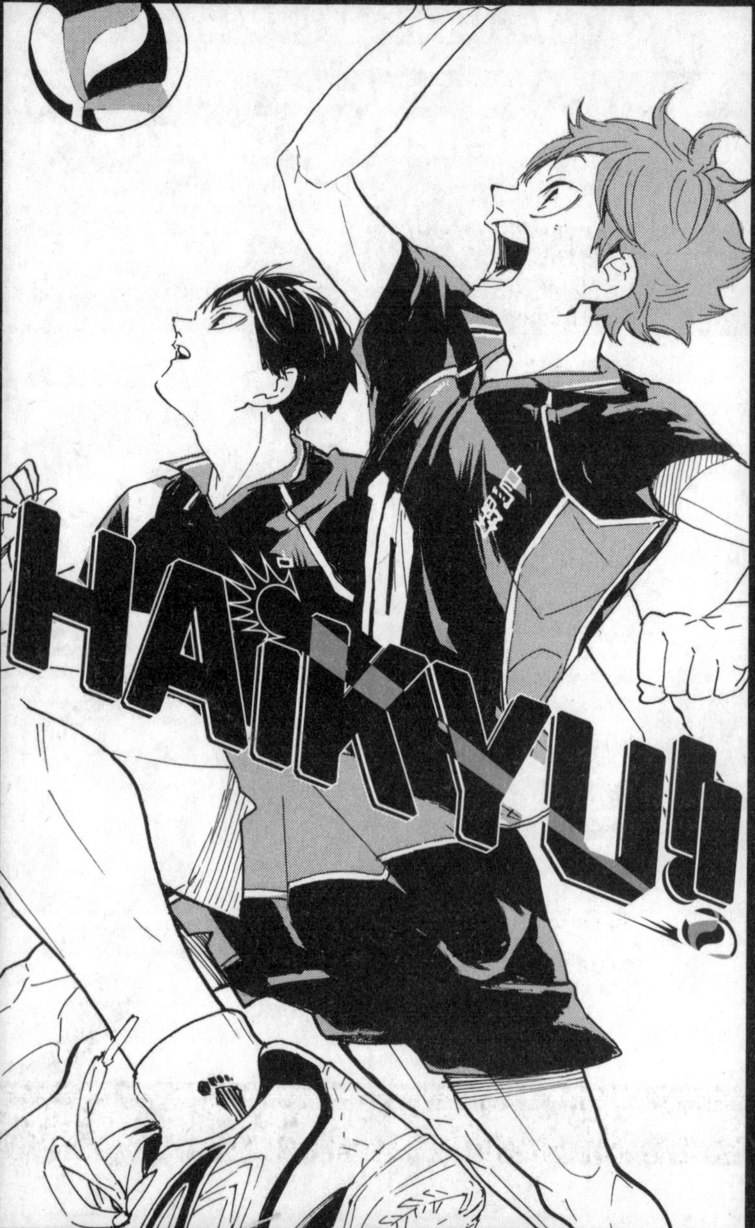
HAIKYU!!

HARUICHI
FURUDATE

CHALLENGERS 45

CHARACTERS

2018 - 2019 Season

V.LEAGUE MEN'S Division 1

SCHWEIDEN ADLERS Vs MSBY BLACK JACKALS

in SENDAI

MSBY BLACKJACKALS

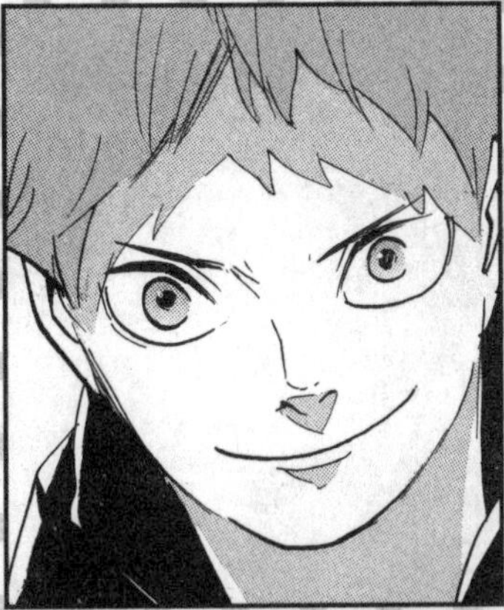

SHOYO HINATA (22)

OP / 5'7"

Trained in beach volleyball in Brazil before joining the V.League in Japan.

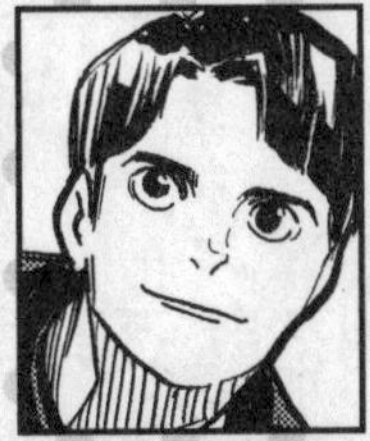

ADRIAH THOMAS (27)

MB / 6'7"

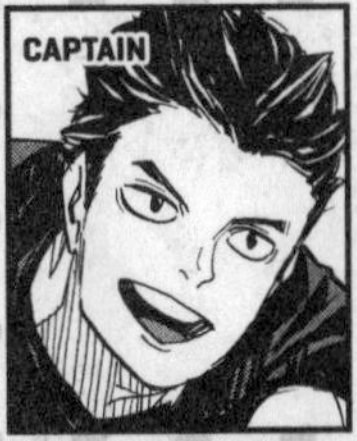
CAPTAIN

SHUGO MEIAN (29)

MB / 6'5"

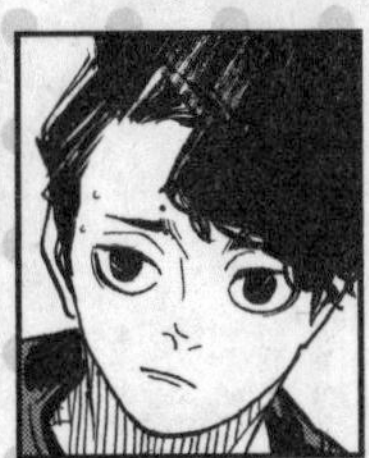

KIYOOMI SAKUSA (22)

OH / 6'4"

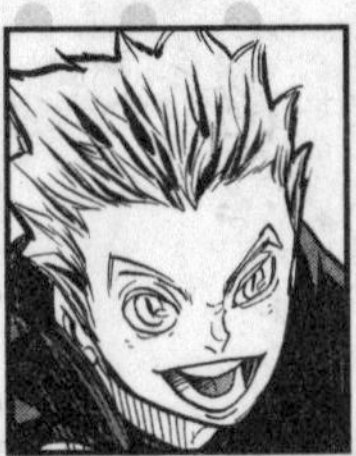

KOTARO BOKUTO (24)

OH / 6'3"

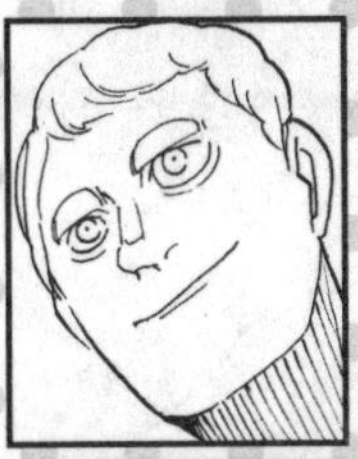

SAMSON FOSTER (43)

HEAD COACH

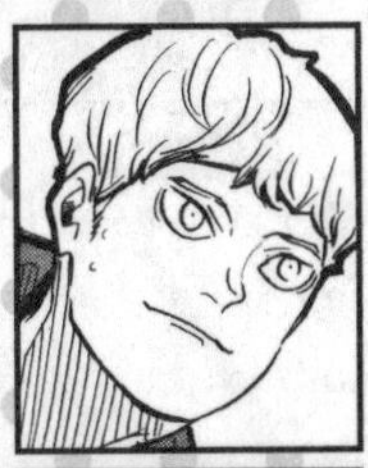

SHION INUNAKI (26)

L / 5'9"

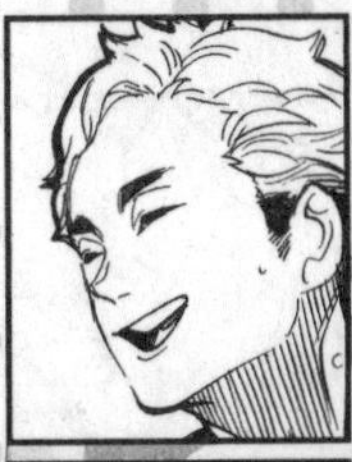

ATSUMU MIYA (23)

S / 6'2"

Schweiden ADLERS

NICOLAS ROMERO (30)

OH / 6'3"

TATSUTO SOKOLOV (25)

MB / 6'7"

CAPTAIN

FUKURO HIRUGAMI (29)

MB / 6'6"

WAKATOSHI USHIJIMA (24)

OP / 6'4"

KORAI HOSHIUMI (23)

OH / 5'8"

TOBIO KAGEYAMA (21)

S / 6'2"

He advanced straight into the
V.League after graduation, putting up
eye-popping stats as a teenage rookie.

BANJO SUZAKU (46)

HEAD COACH

TOSHIRO HEIWAJIMA (28)

L / 5'9"

Ever since he saw the legendary player known as "the Little Giant" compete at the national volleyball finals, Shoyo Hinata has been aiming to be the best volleyball player ever! He decides to join the volleyball club at his middle school and gets to play in an official tournament during his third year. His team is crushed by a team led by volleyball prodigy Tobio Kageyama, also known as "the King of the Court." Swearing revenge on Kageyama, Hinata graduates middle school and enters Karasuno High School, the school where the Little Giant played. However, upon joining the club, he finds out that Kageyama is there too! The two of them bicker constantly, but they bring out the best in each other's talents and become a powerful combo. Six years later, Hinata and Kageyama finally go head-to-head, in V.League Division 1! Kageyama, who has become the King of the Court in both name and attitude, acknowledges Hinata as his greatest opponent. Atsumu Miya has now mastered three types of serves, while Bokuto has harnessed the power of being "normal" and Hoshiumi has taken command of the skies. With incredible play after incredible play, which team will take the win?!

HAIKYU!!

45 CHALLENGERS

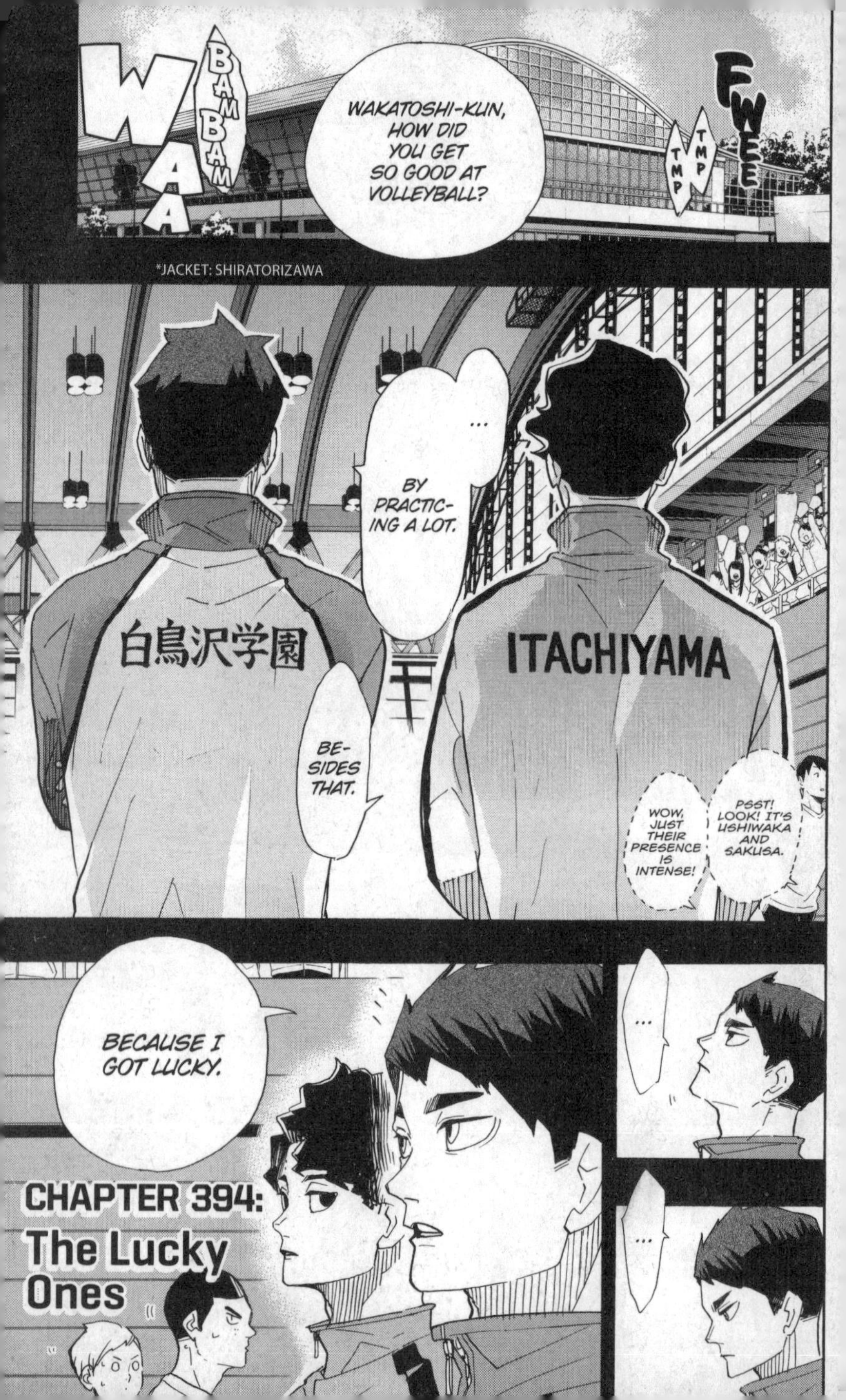
FWEE
TMP TMP
WAKATOSHI-KUN, HOW DID YOU GET SO GOOD AT VOLLEYBALL?
BAM BAM
WAA
*JACKET: SHIRATORIZAWA
...
BY PRACTICING A LOT.
ITACHIYAMA
白鳥沢学園
BESIDES THAT.
PSST! LOOK! IT'S USHIWAKA AND SAKUSA.
WOW, JUST THEIR PRESENCE IS INTENSE!
...
...
BECAUSE I GOT LUCKY.
CHAPTER 394: The Lucky Ones

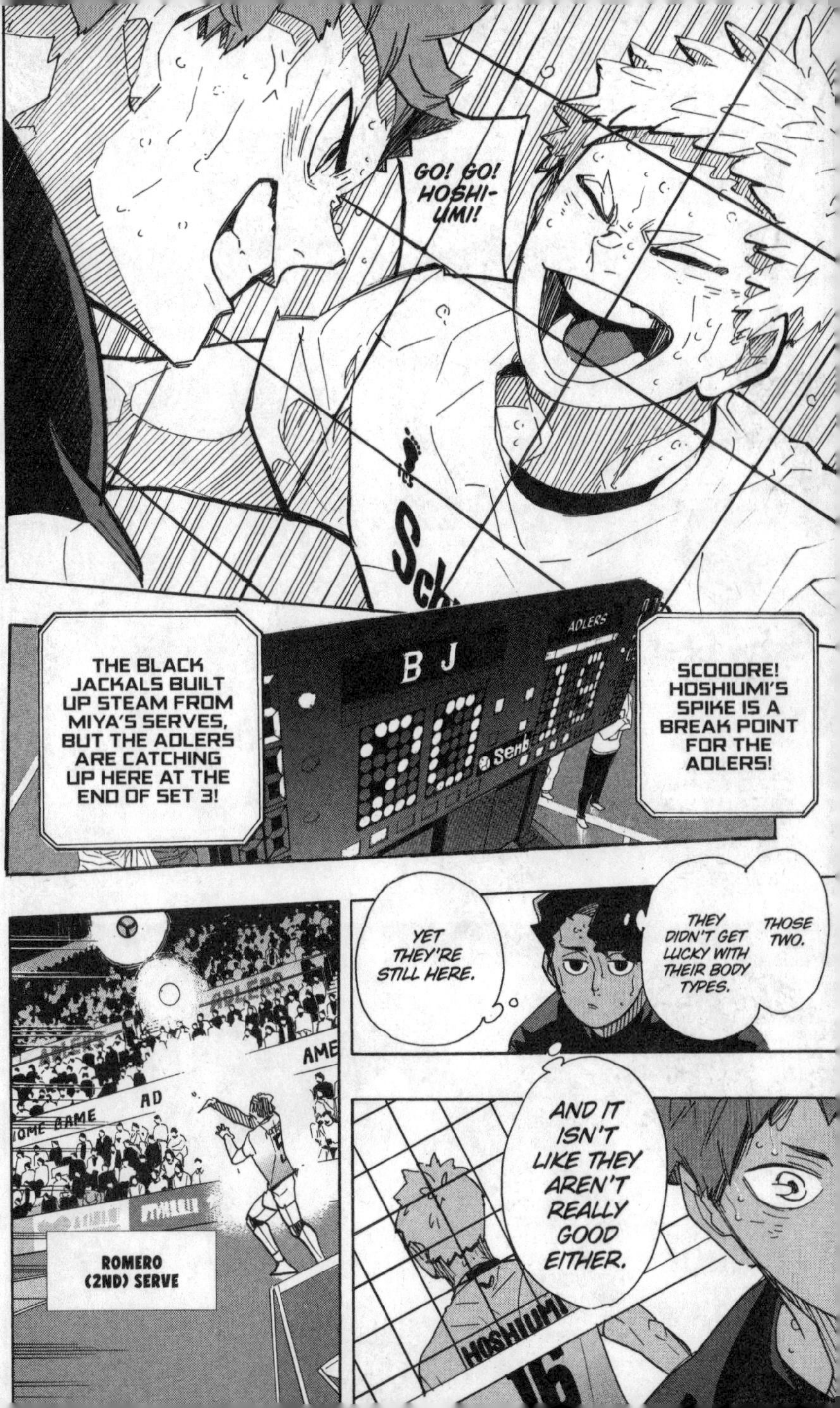
GO! GO! HOSHIUMI!
SCOOORE! HOSHIUMI'S SPIKE IS A BREAK POINT FOR THE ADLERS!
THE BLACK JACKALS BUILT UP STEAM FROM MIYA'S SERVES, BUT THE ADLERS ARE CATCHING UP HERE AT THE END OF SET 3!
THOSE TWO.
THEY DIDN'T GET LUCKY WITH THEIR BODY TYPES.
YET THEY'RE STILL HERE.
AND IT ISN'T LIKE THEY AREN'T REALLY GOOD EITHER.
HOSHIUMI
ROMERO (2ND) SERVE

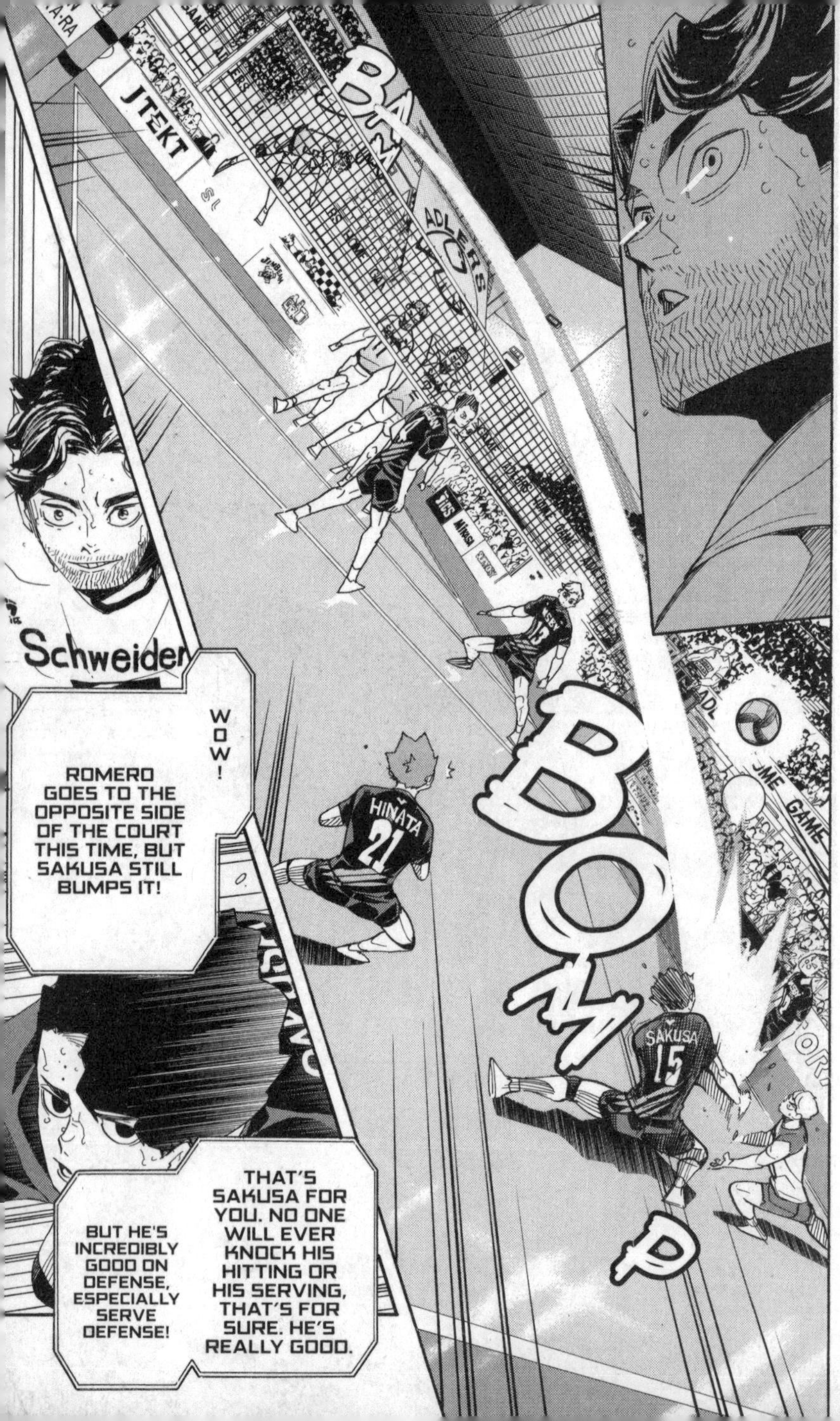

BOMP
Schweiden
WOW!
ROMERO GOES TO THE OPPOSITE SIDE OF THE COURT THIS TIME, BUT SAKUSA STILL BUMPS IT!
THAT'S SAKUSA FOR YOU. NO ONE WILL EVER KNOCK HIS HITTING OR HIS SERVING, THAT'S FOR SURE. HE'S REALLY GOOD.
BUT HE'S INCREDIBLY GOOD ON DEFENSE, ESPECIALLY SERVE DEFENSE!

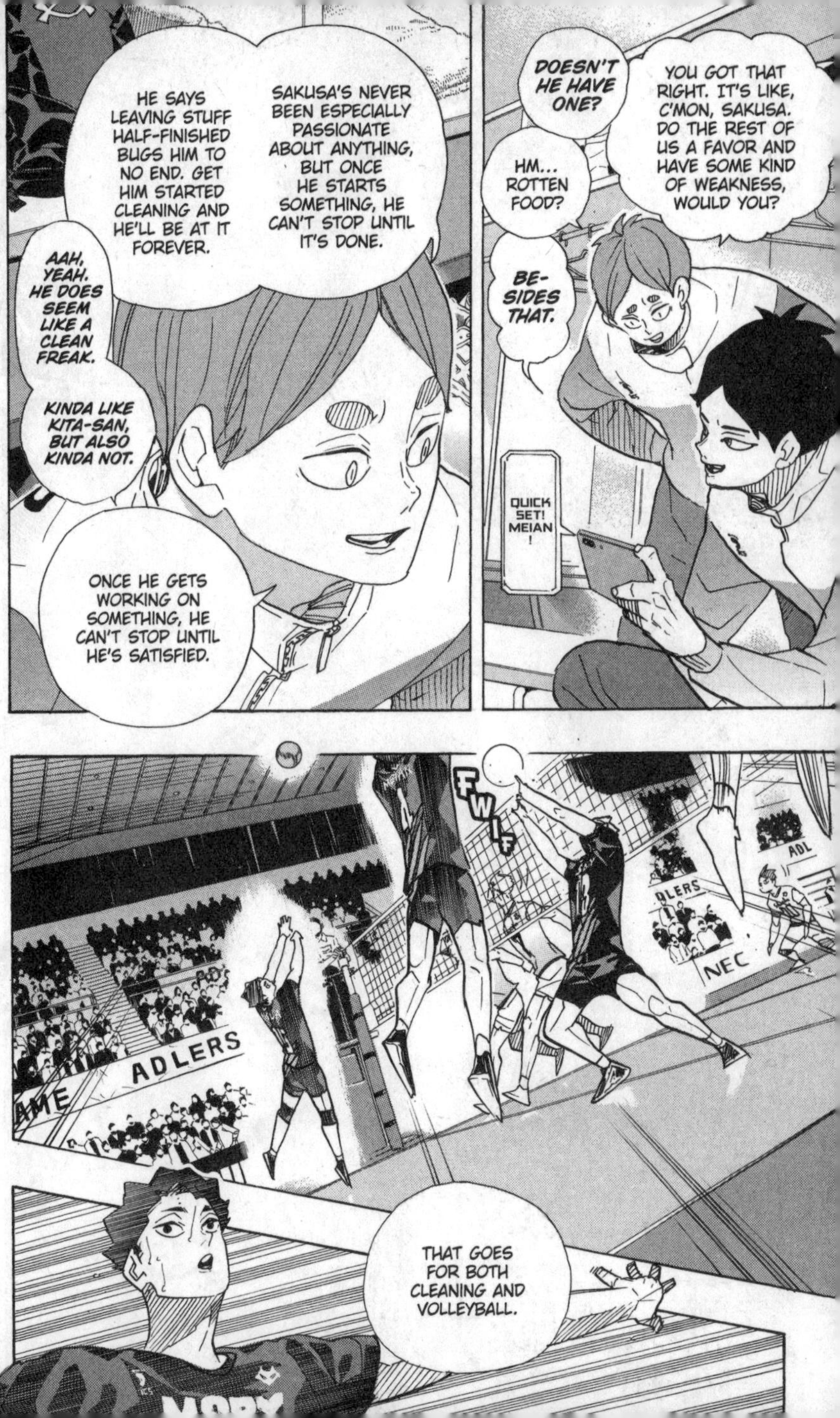
YOU GOT THAT RIGHT. IT'S LIKE, C'MON, SAKUSA. DO THE REST OF US A FAVOR AND HAVE SOME KIND OF WEAKNESS, WOULD YOU?
DOESN'T HE HAVE ONE?
HM... ROTTEN FOOD?
BE-SIDES THAT.
QUICK SET! MEIAN!
SAKUSA'S NEVER BEEN ESPECIALLY PASSIONATE ABOUT ANYTHING, BUT ONCE HE STARTS SOMETHING, HE CAN'T STOP UNTIL IT'S DONE.
HE SAYS LEAVING STUFF HALF-FINISHED BUGS HIM TO NO END. GET HIM STARTED CLEANING AND HE'LL BE AT IT FOREVER.
AAH, YEAH. HE DOES SEEM LIKE A CLEAN FREAK.
KINDA LIKE KITA-SAN, BUT ALSO KINDA NOT.
ONCE HE GETS WORKING ON SOMETHING, HE CAN'T STOP UNTIL HE'S SATISFIED.
FWIF
NEC
ADLERS
THAT GOES FOR BOTH CLEANING AND VOLLEYBALL.

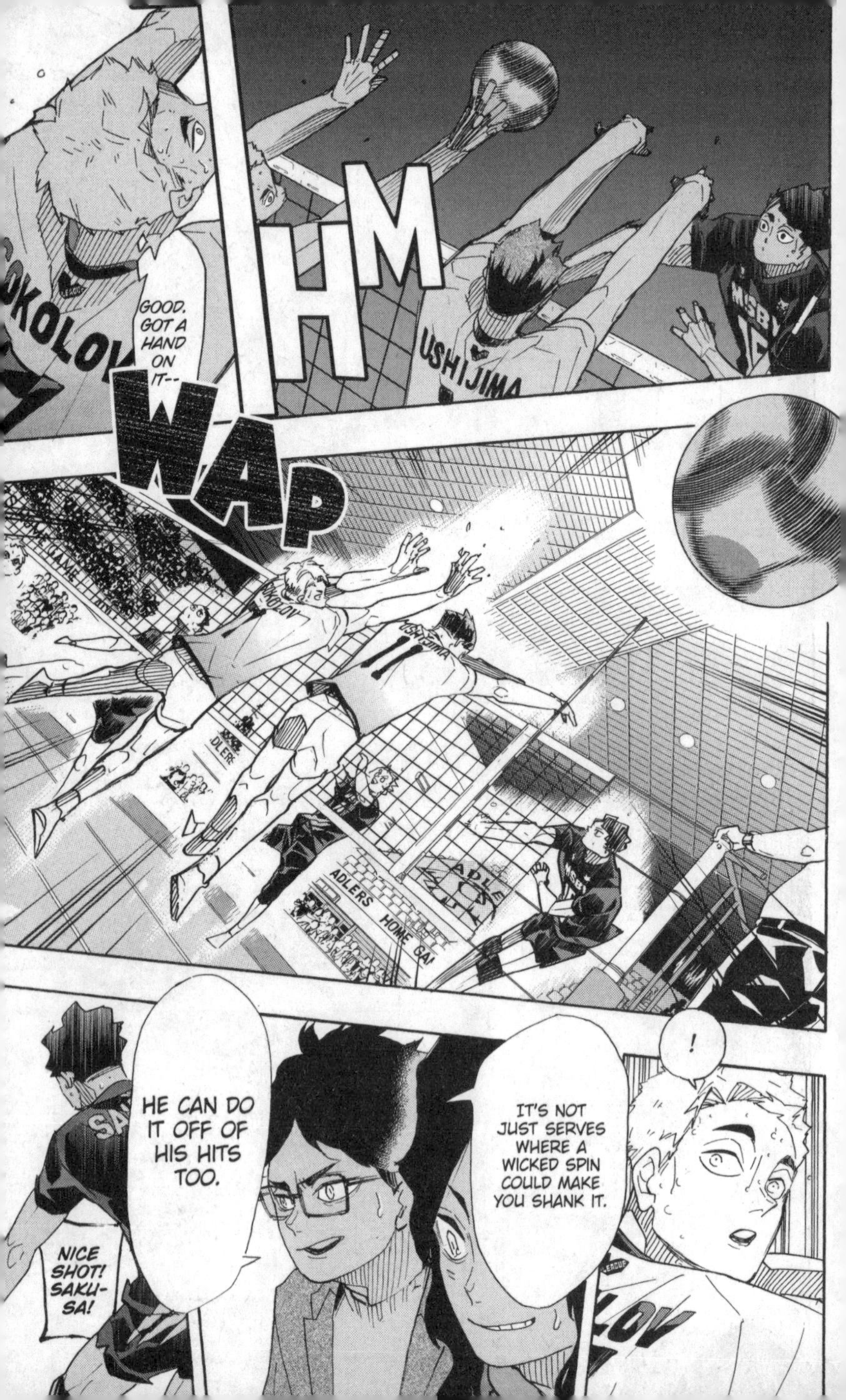
HM
GOOD. GOT A HAND ON IT--
WAP
!
IT'S NOT JUST SERVES WHERE A WICKED SPIN COULD MAKE YOU SHANK IT.
HE CAN DO IT OFF OF HIS HITS TOO.
NICE SHOT! SAKU-SA!

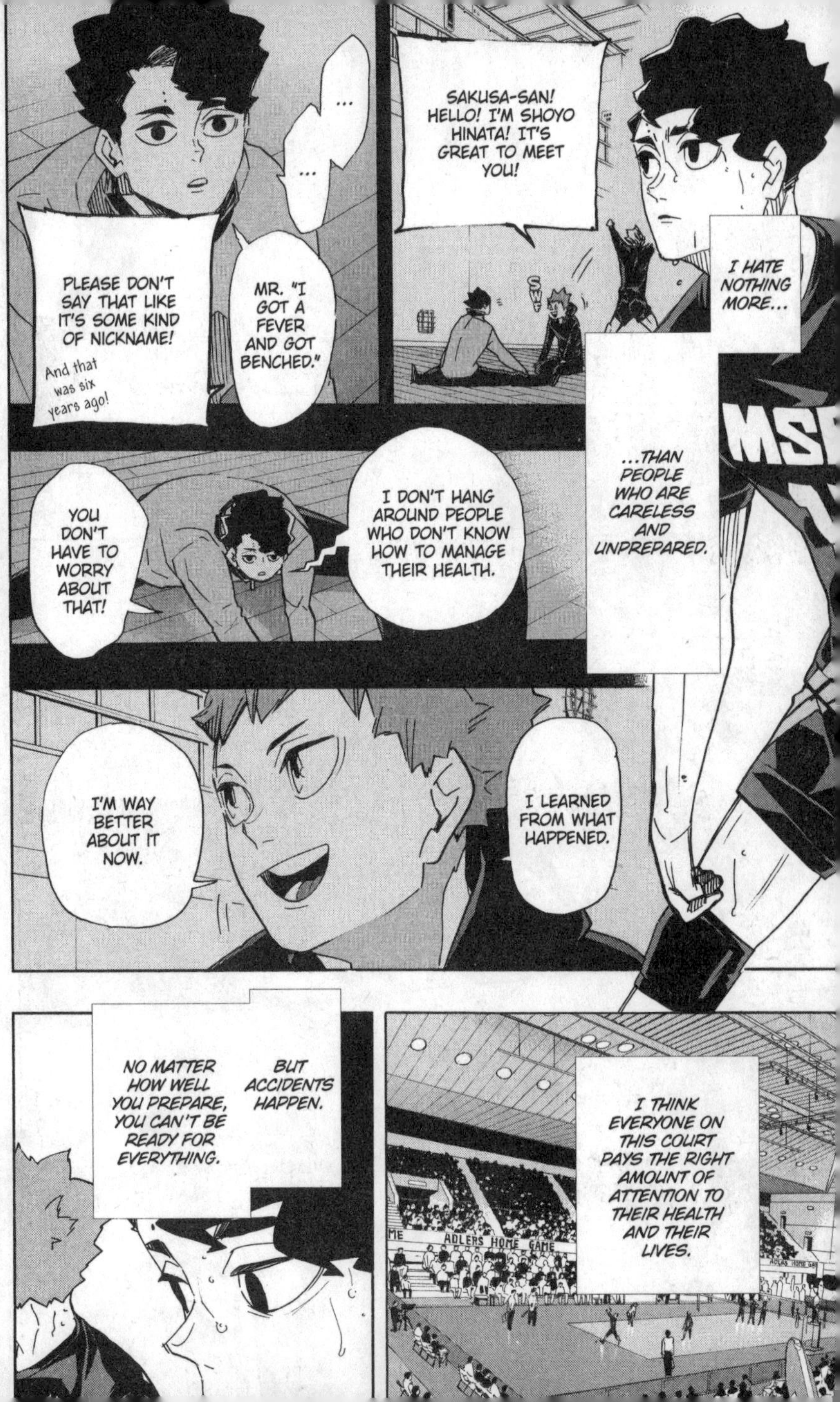
I HATE NOTHING MORE...
...THAN PEOPLE WHO ARE CARELESS AND UNPREPARED.
SAKUSA-SAN! HELLO! I'M SHOYO HINATA! IT'S GREAT TO MEET YOU!
SWT
...
...
MR. "I GOT A FEVER AND GOT BENCHED."
PLEASE DON'T SAY THAT LIKE IT'S SOME KIND OF NICKNAME!
And that was six years ago!
I DON'T HANG AROUND PEOPLE WHO DON'T KNOW HOW TO MANAGE THEIR HEALTH.
YOU DON'T HAVE TO WORRY ABOUT THAT!
I LEARNED FROM WHAT HAPPENED.
I'M WAY BETTER ABOUT IT NOW.
ADLERS HOME GAME
I THINK EVERYONE ON THIS COURT PAYS THE RIGHT AMOUNT OF ATTENTION TO THEIR HEALTH AND THEIR LIVES.
BUT ACCIDENTS HAPPEN.
NO MATTER HOW WELL YOU PREPARE, YOU CAN'T BE READY FOR EVERYTHING.

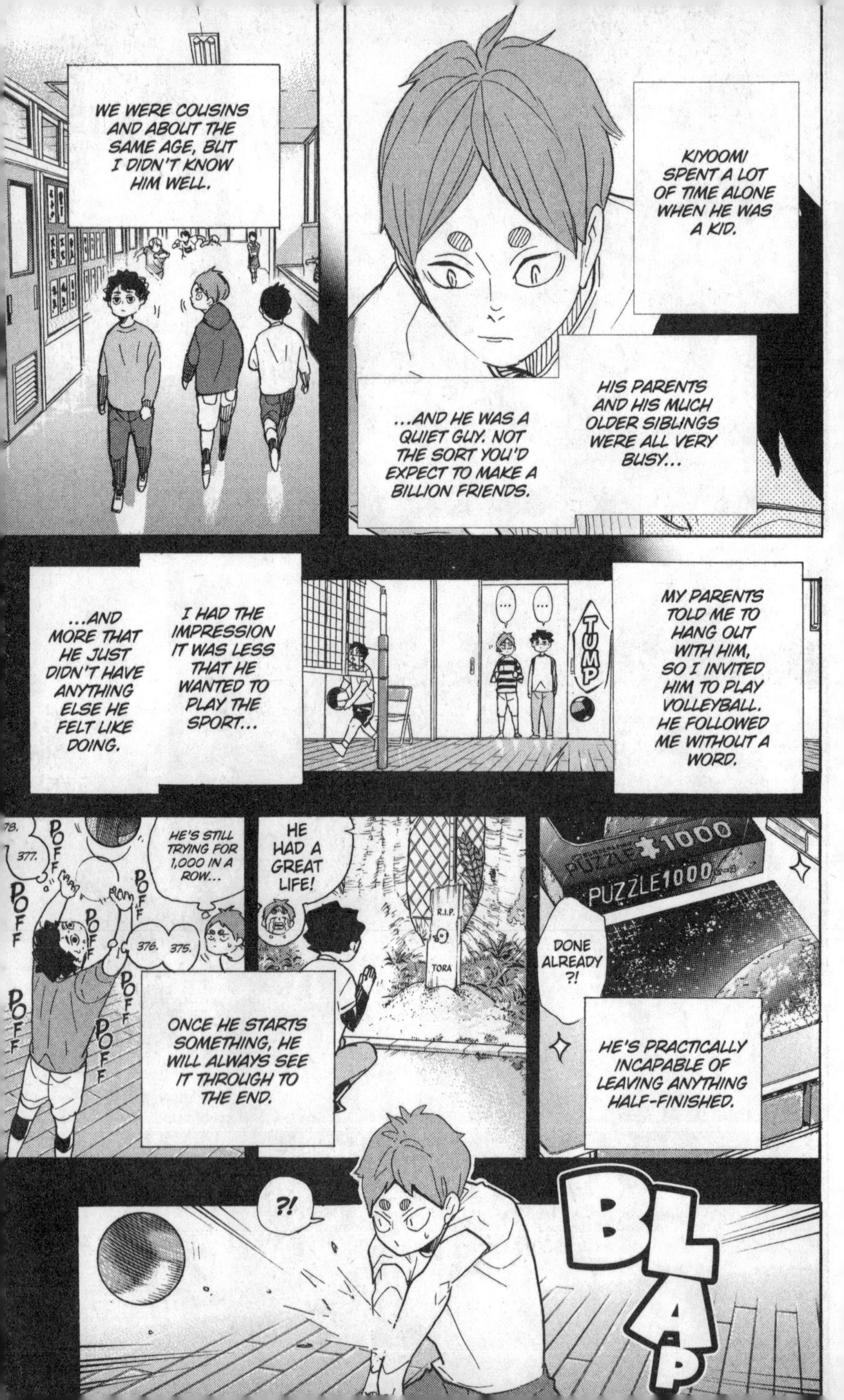

KIYOOMI SPENT A LOT OF TIME ALONE WHEN HE WAS A KID.
HIS PARENTS AND HIS MUCH OLDER SIBLINGS WERE ALL VERY BUSY...
...AND HE WAS A QUIET GUY. NOT THE SORT YOU'D EXPECT TO MAKE A BILLION FRIENDS.
WE WERE COUSINS AND ABOUT THE SAME AGE, BUT I DIDN'T KNOW HIM WELL.
MY PARENTS TOLD ME TO HANG OUT WITH HIM, SO I INVITED HIM TO PLAY VOLLEYBALL. HE FOLLOWED ME WITHOUT A WORD.
TUMP
...
...
I HAD THE IMPRESSION IT WAS LESS THAT HE WANTED TO PLAY THE SPORT...
...AND MORE THAT HE JUST DIDN'T HAVE ANYTHING ELSE HE FELT LIKE DOING.
PUZZLE1000
PUZZLE1000
DONE ALREADY ?!
HE'S PRACTICALLY INCAPABLE OF LEAVING ANYTHING HALF-FINISHED.
HE HAD A GREAT LIFE!
R.I.P.
TORA
HE'S STILL TRYING FOR 1,000 IN A ROW...
78.
377.
376.
375.
POFF
POFF
POFF
POFF
POFF
POFF
POFF
ONCE HE STARTS SOMETHING, HE WILL ALWAYS SEE IT THROUGH TO THE END.
?!
BLAP

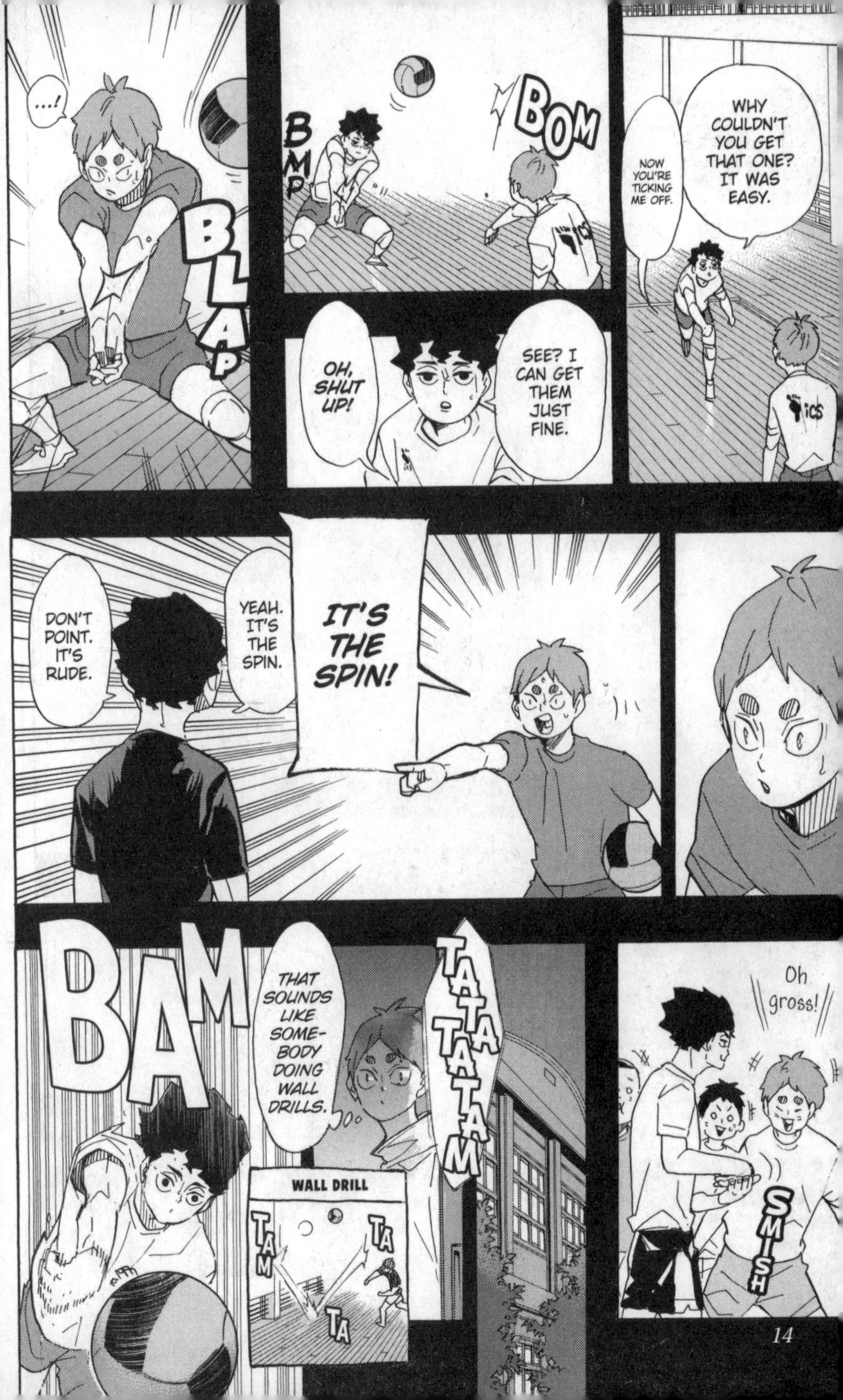
WHY COULDN'T YOU GET THAT ONE? IT WAS EASY.
NOW YOU'RE TICKING ME OFF.
BOM
BMP
SEE? I CAN GET THEM JUST FINE.
OH, SHUT UP!
...!
BLAP
IT'S THE SPIN!
YEAH. IT'S THE SPIN.
DON'T POINT. IT'S RUDE.
Oh gross!
SMISH
TATATATAM
THAT SOUNDS LIKE SOMEBODY DOING WALL DRILLS.
WALL DRILL
TA
TAM
TA
BAM

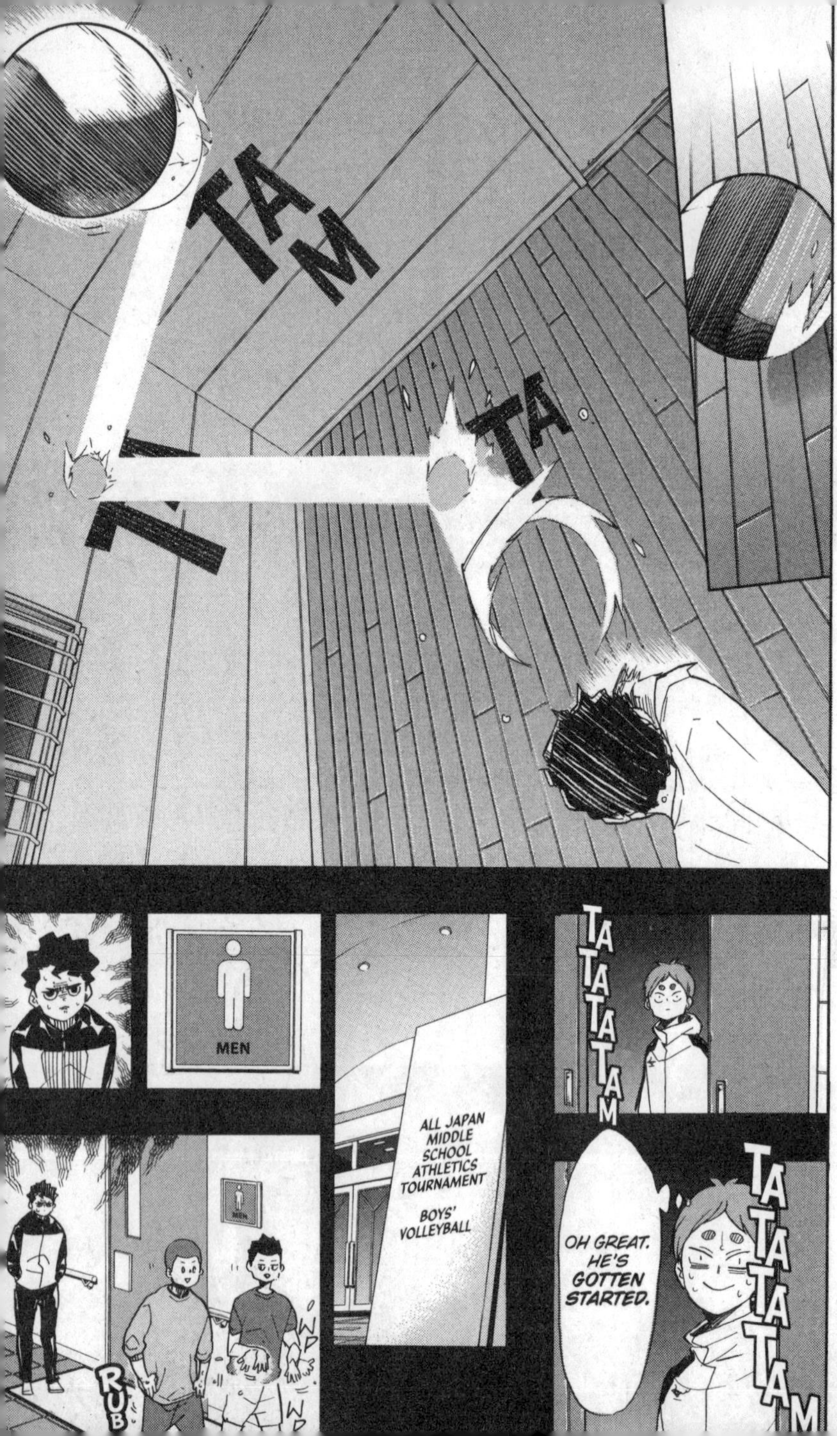
TAM
TA
TA
TATATATAM
OH GREAT. HE'S GOTTEN STARTED.
TATATATATAM
ALL JAPAN MIDDLE SCHOOL ATHLETICS TOURNAMENT
BOYS' VOLLEYBALL
MEN
MEN
WD
WD
RUB

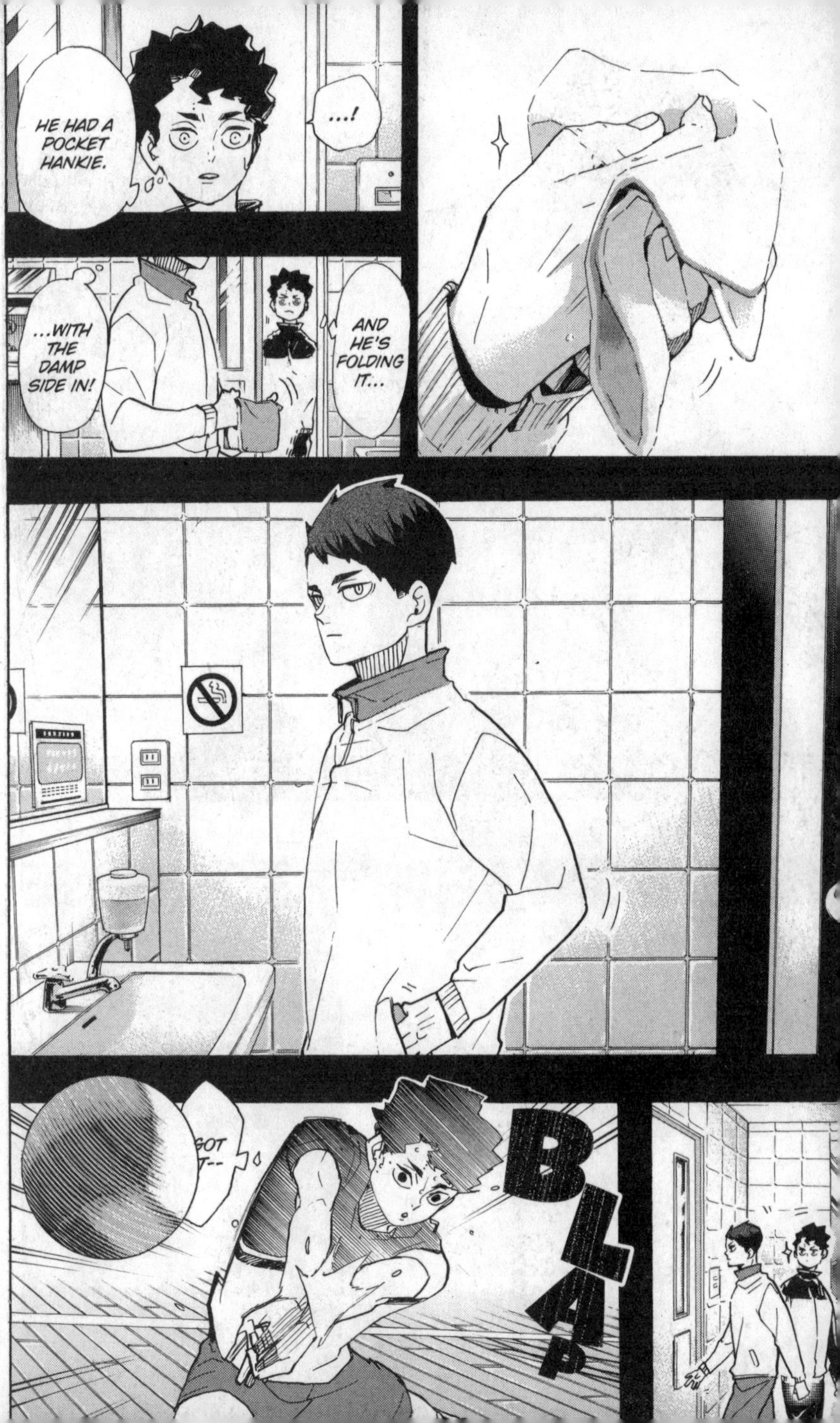
...!
HE HAD A POCKET HANKIE.
AND HE'S FOLDING IT...
...WITH THE DAMP SIDE IN!
BLAP
GOT

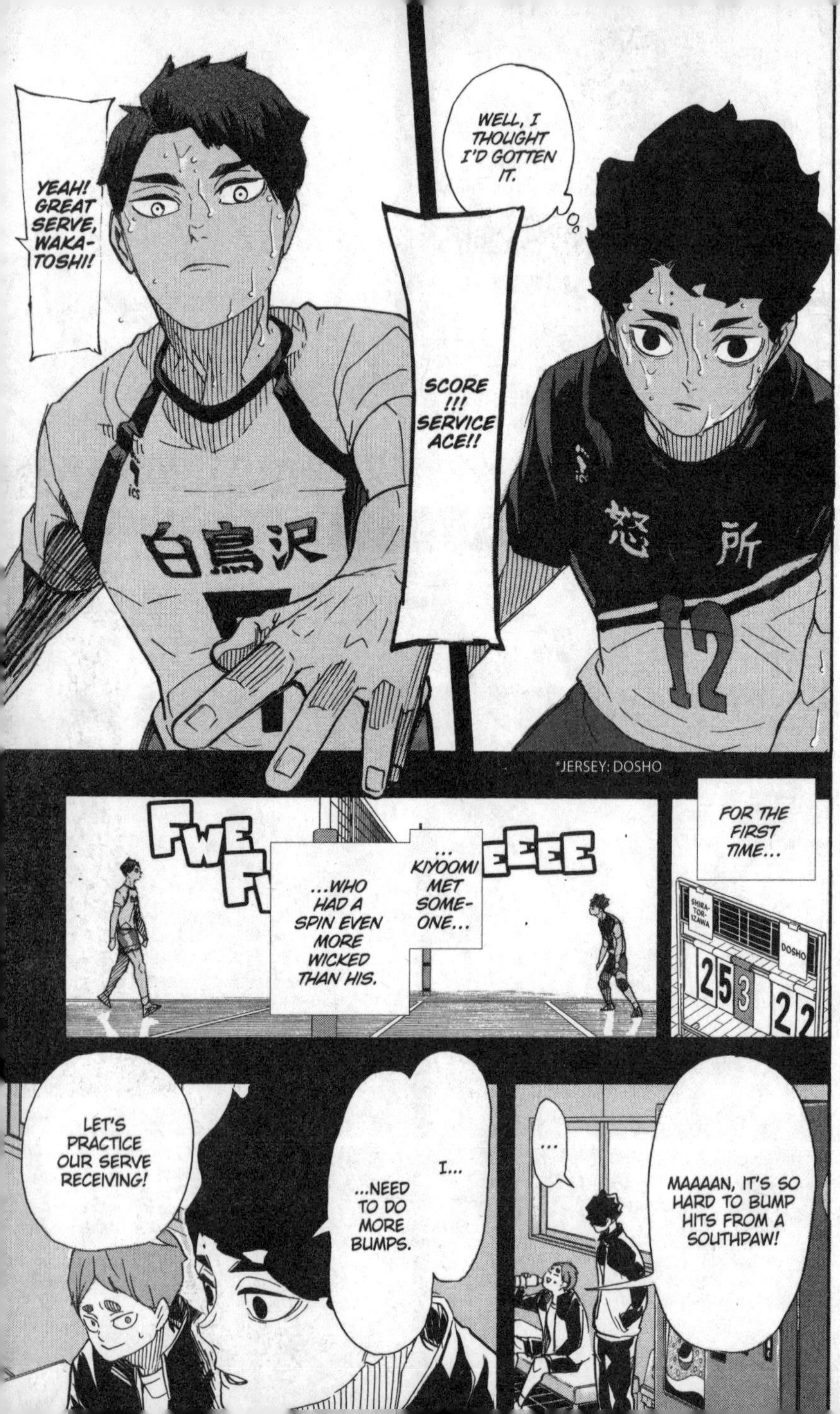
WELL, I THOUGHT I'D GOTTEN IT.
SCORE!!! SERVICE ACE!!
YEAH! GREAT SERVE, WAKA-TOSHI!!
*JERSEY: DOSHO
FOR THE FIRST TIME...
SHIRA-TORI-ZAWA
DOSHO
FWEEEEEE
... KIYOOMI MET SOME-ONE...
...WHO HAD A SPIN EVEN MORE WICKED THAN HIS.
MAAAAN, IT'S SO HARD TO BUMP HITS FROM A SOUTHPAW!
...
I...
...NEED TO DO MORE BUMPS.
LET'S PRACTICE OUR SERVE RECEIVING!

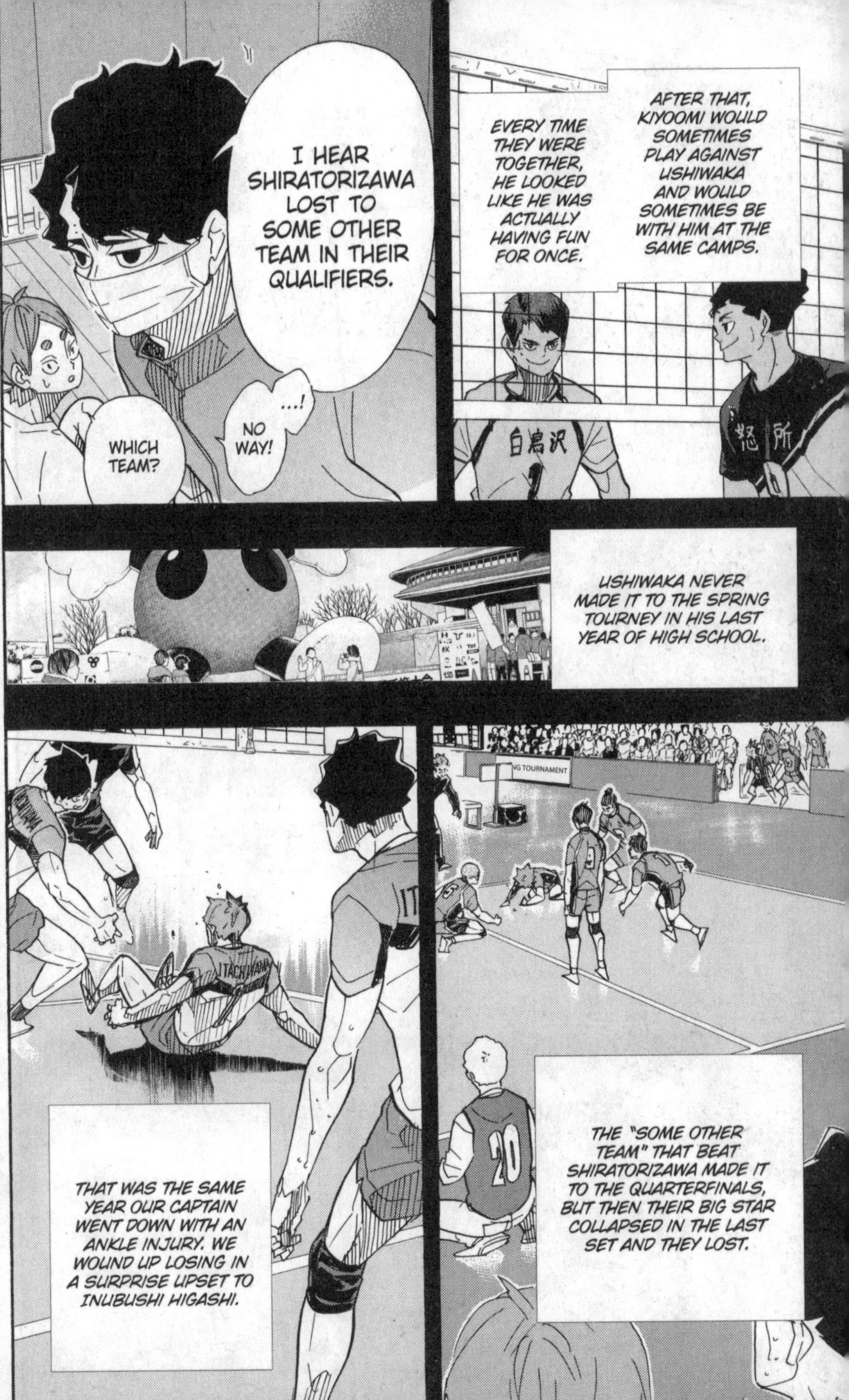
AFTER THAT, KIYOOMI WOULD SOMETIMES PLAY AGAINST USHIWAKA AND WOULD SOMETIMES BE WITH HIM AT THE SAME CAMPS.
EVERY TIME THEY WERE TOGETHER, HE LOOKED LIKE HE WAS ACTUALLY HAVING FUN FOR ONCE.
I HEAR SHIRATORIZAWA LOST TO SOME OTHER TEAM IN THEIR QUALIFIERS.
...!
NO WAY!
WHICH TEAM?
USHIWAKA NEVER MADE IT TO THE SPRING TOURNEY IN HIS LAST YEAR OF HIGH SCHOOL.
NG TOURNAMENT
THE "SOME OTHER TEAM" THAT BEAT SHIRATORIZAWA MADE IT TO THE QUARTERFINALS, BUT THEN THEIR BIG STAR COLLAPSED IN THE LAST SET AND THEY LOST.
THAT WAS THE SAME YEAR OUR CAPTAIN WENT DOWN WITH AN ANKLE INJURY. WE WOUND UP LOSING IN A SURPRISE UPSET TO INUBUSHI HIGASHI.

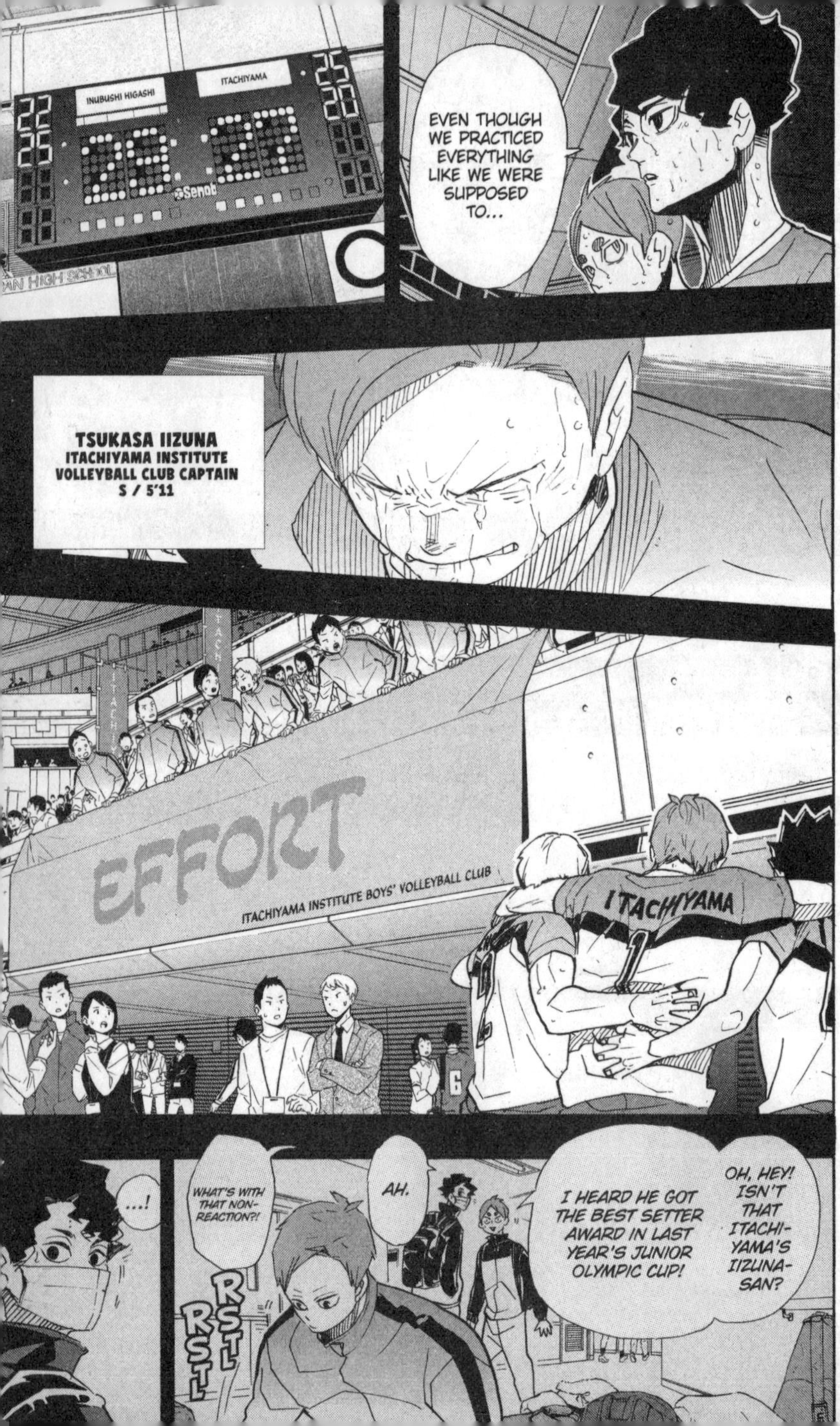
EVEN THOUGH WE PRACTICED EVERYTHING LIKE WE WERE SUPPOSED TO...
INUBUSHI HIGASHI
ITACHIYAMA
TSUKASA IIZUNA
ITACHIYAMA INSTITUTE
VOLLEYBALL CLUB CAPTAIN
S / 5'11
EFFORT
ITACHIYAMA INSTITUTE BOYS' VOLLEYBALL CLUB
ITACHIYAMA
OH, HEY! ISN'T THAT ITACHIYAMA'S IIZUNA-SAN?
I HEARD HE GOT THE BEST SETTER AWARD IN LAST YEAR'S JUNIOR OLYMPIC CUP!
AH.
WHAT'S WITH THAT NON-REACTION?!
RSTL
RSTL
...!

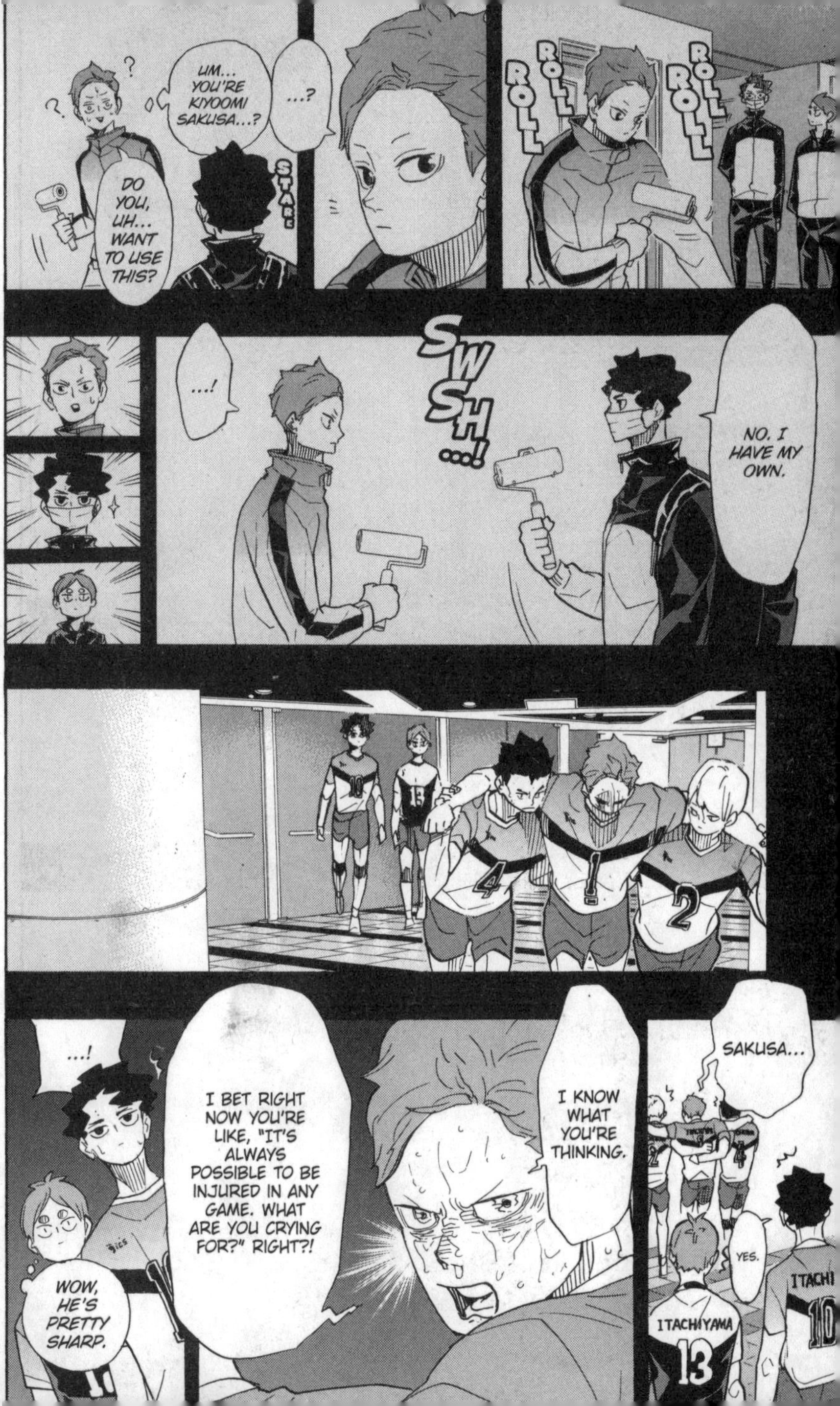
ROLL ROLL
ROLL ROLL
...?
UM... YOU'RE KIYOOMI SAKUSA...?
STARE
DO YOU, UH... WANT TO USE THIS?
NO. I HAVE MY OWN.
SWSH...!
...!
SAKUSA...
YES.
ITACHI
ITACHIYAMA
I KNOW WHAT YOU'RE THINKING.
I BET RIGHT NOW YOU'RE LIKE, "IT'S ALWAYS POSSIBLE TO BE INJURED IN ANY GAME. WHAT ARE YOU CRYING FOR?" RIGHT?!
...!
WOW, HE'S PRETTY SHARP.

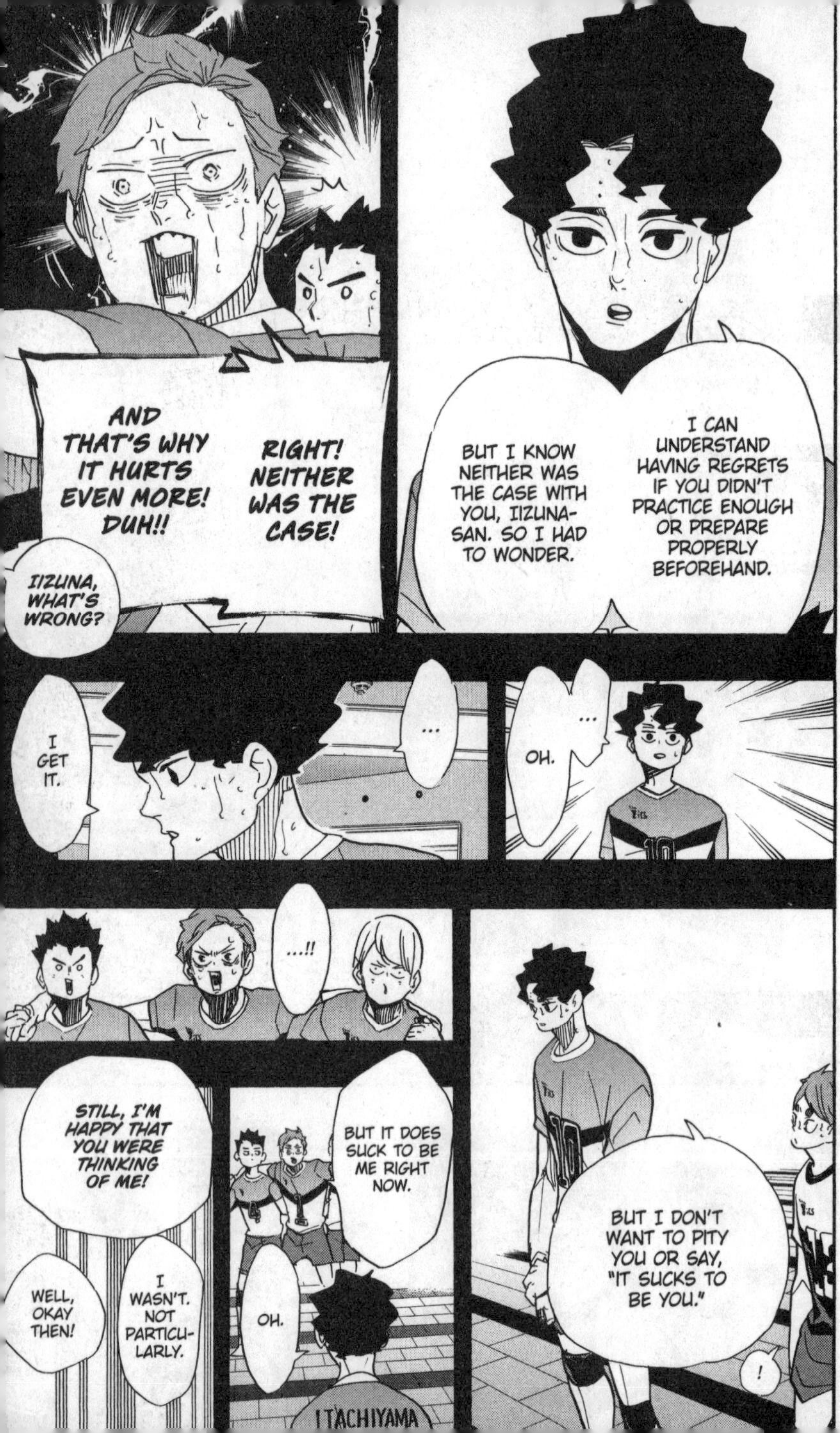
I CAN UNDERSTAND HAVING REGRETS IF YOU DIDN'T PRACTICE ENOUGH OR PREPARE PROPERLY BEFOREHAND.
BUT I KNOW NEITHER WAS THE CASE WITH YOU, IIZUNA-SAN. SO I HAD TO WONDER.
RIGHT! NEITHER WAS THE CASE!
AND THAT'S WHY IT HURTS EVEN MORE! DUH!!
IIZUNA, WHAT'S WRONG?
...
OH.
...
I GET IT.
BUT I DON'T WANT TO PITY YOU OR SAY, "IT SUCKS TO BE YOU."
!
...!!
BUT IT DOES SUCK TO BE ME RIGHT NOW.
OH.
ITACHIYAMA
STILL, I'M HAPPY THAT YOU WERE THINKING OF ME!
I WASN'T. NOT PARTICULARLY.
WELL, OKAY THEN!

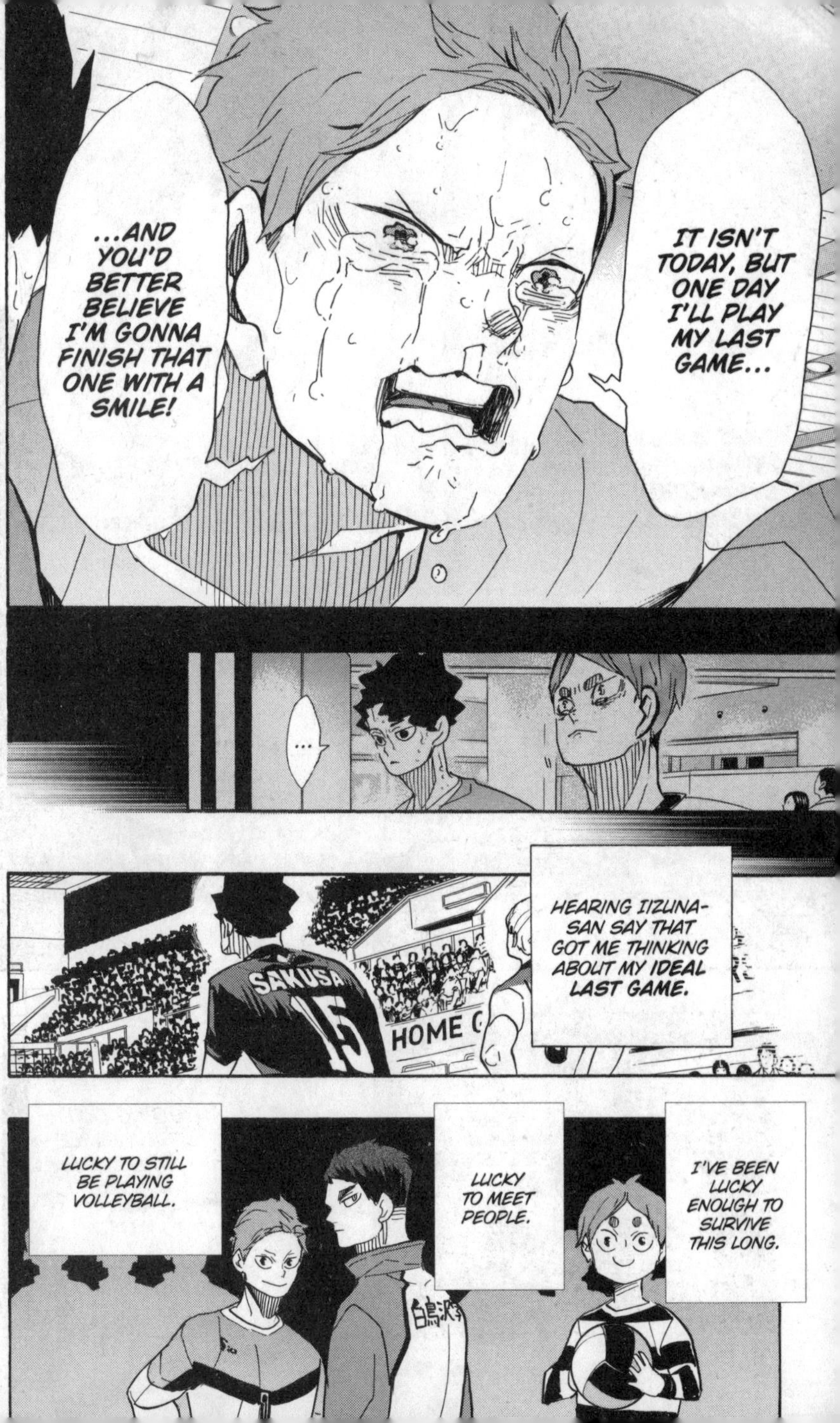
IT ISN'T TODAY, BUT ONE DAY I'LL PLAY MY LAST GAME...
...AND YOU'D BETTER BELIEVE I'M GONNA FINISH THAT ONE WITH A SMILE!
...
HEARING IIZUNA-SAN SAY THAT GOT ME THINKING ABOUT MY IDEAL LAST GAME.
SAKUSA
15
HOME G
I'VE BEEN LUCKY ENOUGH TO SURVIVE THIS LONG.
LUCKY TO MEET PEOPLE.
LUCKY TO STILL BE PLAYING VOLLEYBALL.

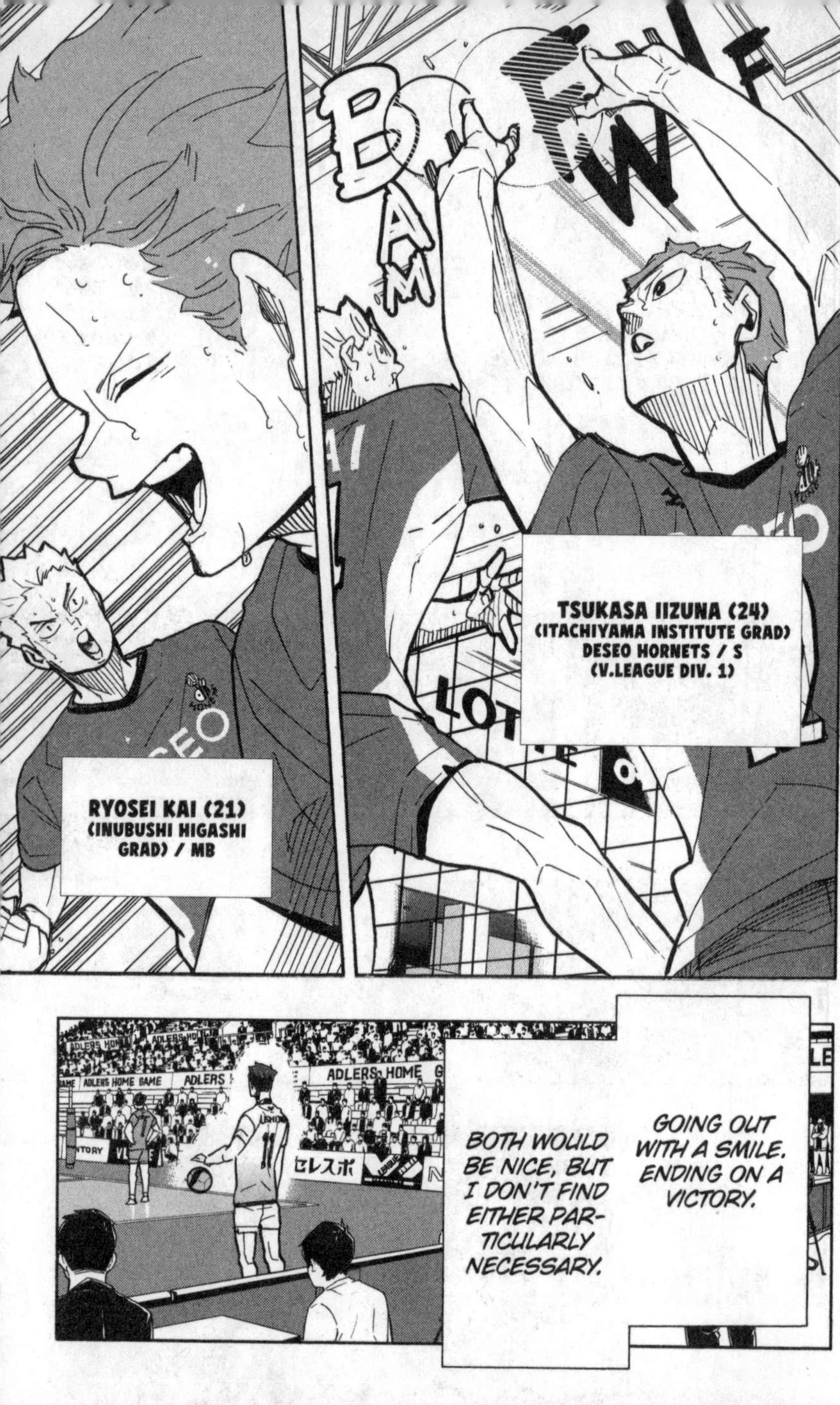
BAM
TSUKASA IIZUNA (24)
(ITACHIYAMA INSTITUTE GRAD)
DESEO HORNETS / S
(V.LEAGUE DIV. 1)
RYOSEI KAI (21)
(INUBUSHI HIGASHI GRAD) / MB
ADLERS HOME GAME
GOING OUT WITH A SMILE. ENDING ON A VICTORY.
BOTH WOULD BE NICE, BUT I DON'T FIND EITHER PARTICULARLY NECESSARY.

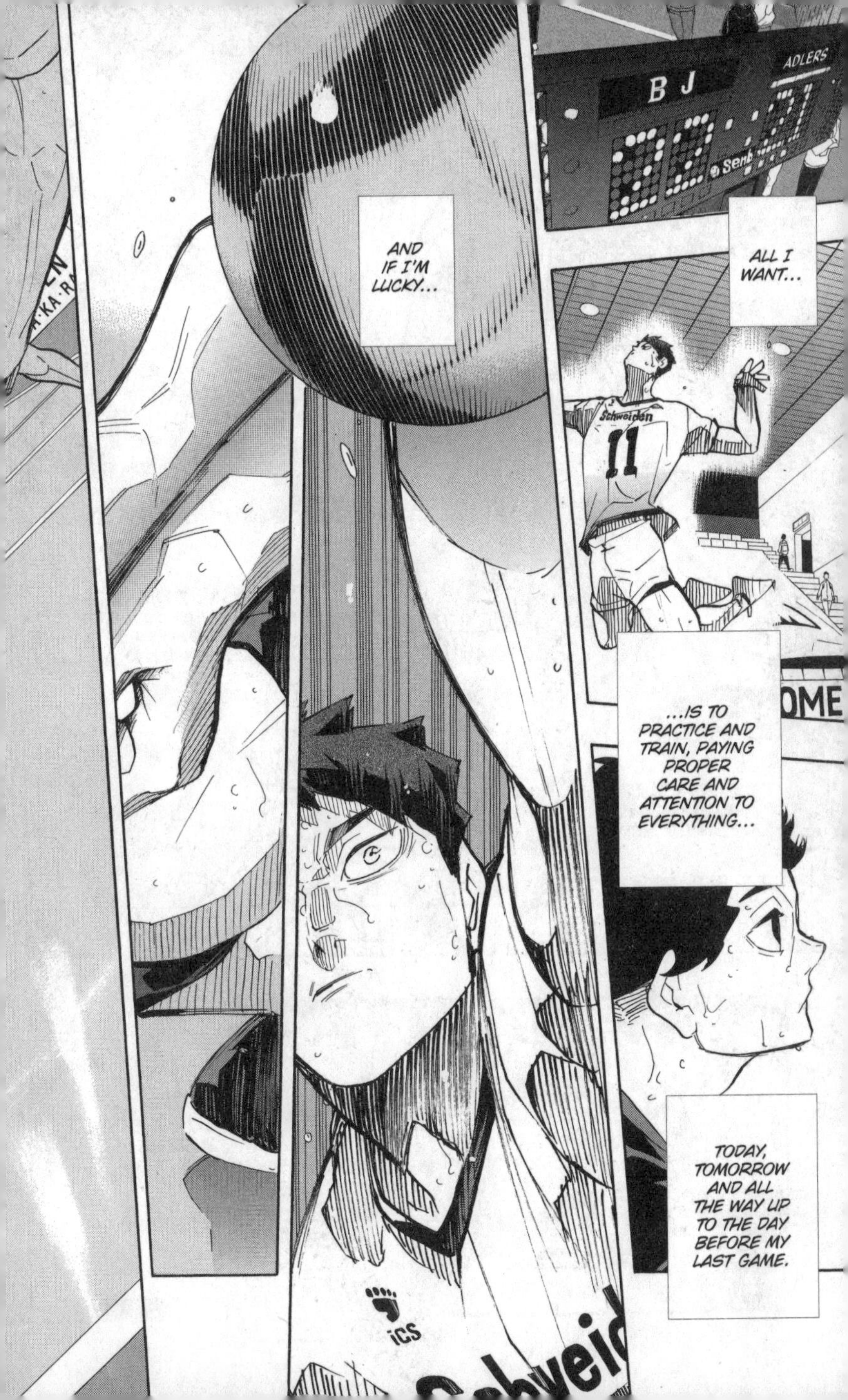

B J
ADLERS
ALL I WANT...
Schweiden
11
...IS TO PRACTICE AND TRAIN, PAYING PROPER CARE AND ATTENTION TO EVERYTHING...
TODAY, TOMORROW AND ALL THE WAY UP TO THE DAY BEFORE MY LAST GAME.
AND IF I'M LUCKY...

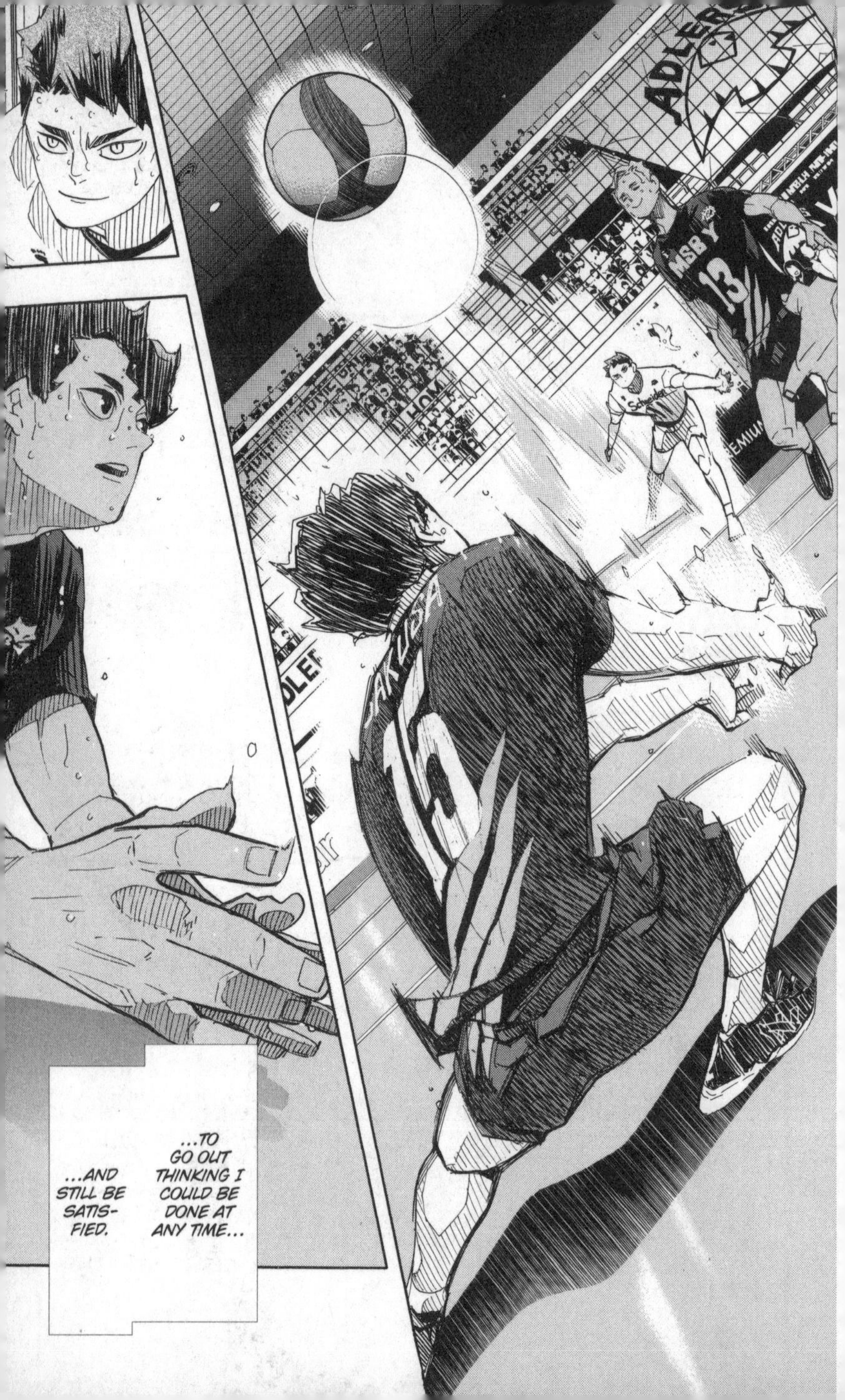
...TO GO OUT THINKING I COULD BE DONE AT ANY TIME...
...AND STILL BE SATIS-FIED.

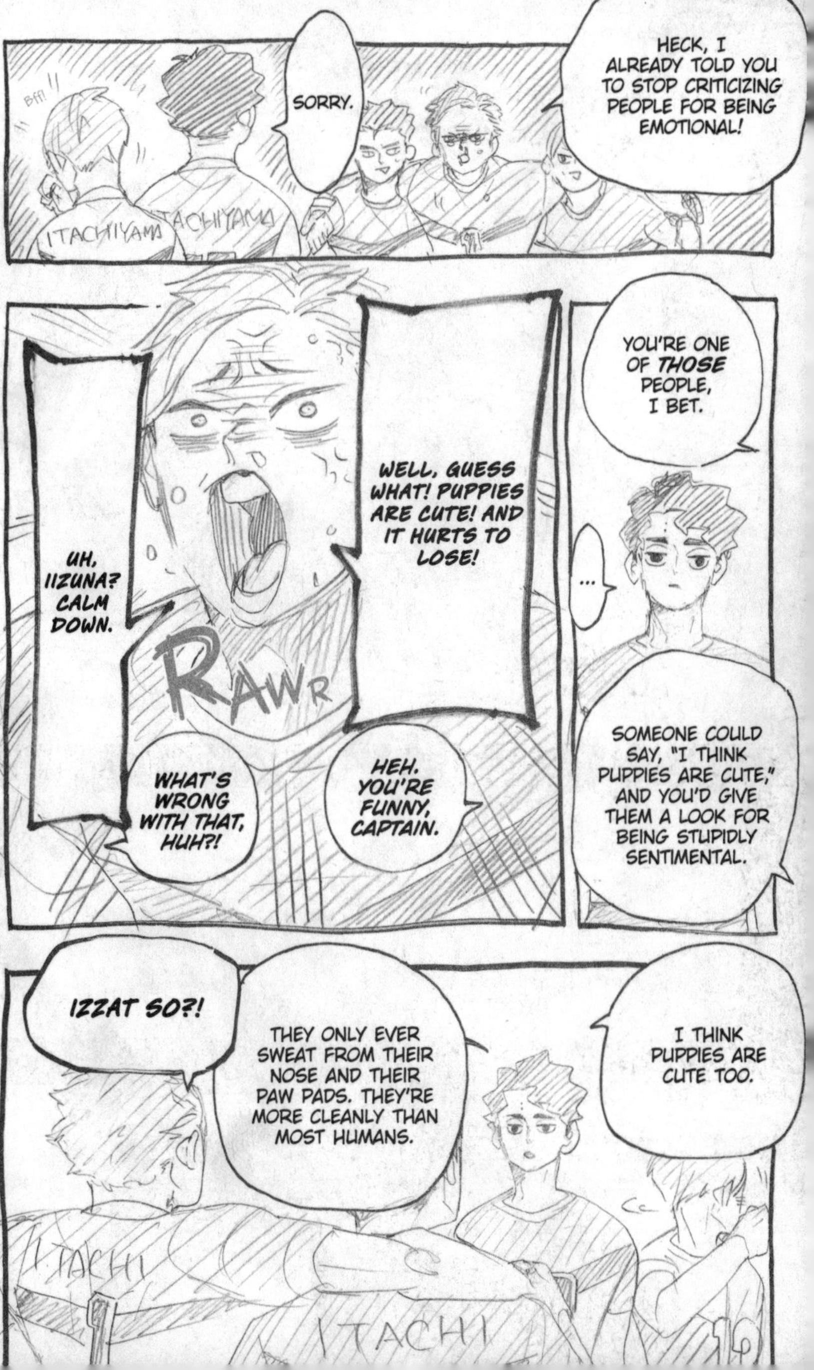
HECK, I ALREADY TOLD YOU TO STOP CRITICIZING PEOPLE FOR BEING EMOTIONAL!
SORRY.
ITACHIYAMA
ITACHIYAMA
YOU'RE ONE OF THOSE PEOPLE, I BET.
...
SOMEONE COULD SAY, "I THINK PUPPIES ARE CUTE," AND YOU'D GIVE THEM A LOOK FOR BEING STUPIDLY SENTIMENTAL.
WELL, GUESS WHAT! PUPPIES ARE CUTE! AND IT HURTS TO LOSE!
UH, IIZUNA? CALM DOWN.
RAWR
HEH. YOU'RE FUNNY, CAPTAIN.
WHAT'S WRONG WITH THAT, HUH?!
I THINK PUPPIES ARE CUTE TOO.
THEY ONLY EVER SWEAT FROM THEIR NOSE AND THEIR PAW PADS. THEY'RE MORE CLEANLY THAN MOST HUMANS.
IZZAT SO?!
ITACHI
ITACHI

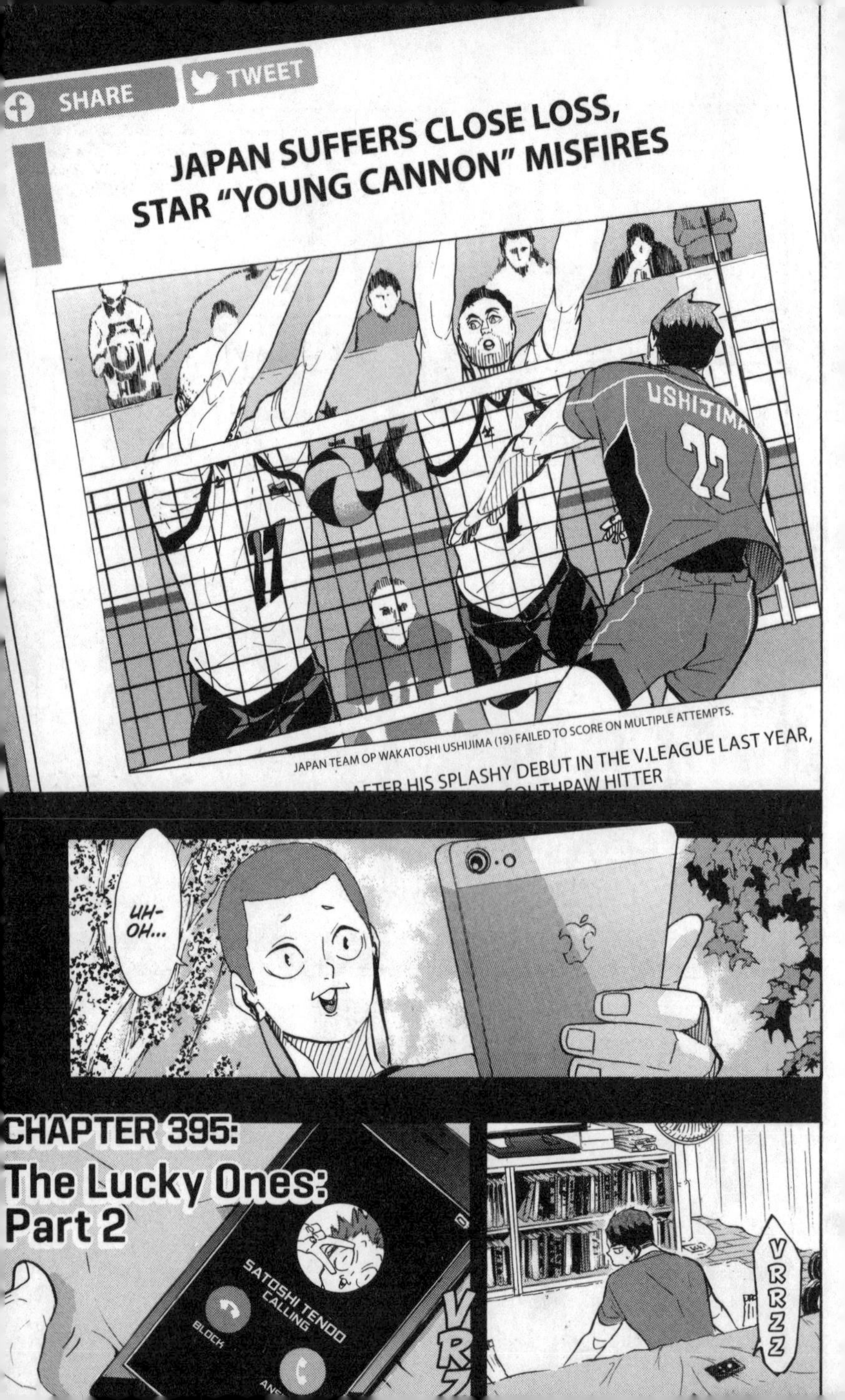
SHARE
TWEET
JAPAN SUFFERS CLOSE LOSS, STAR "YOUNG CANNON" MISFIRES
USHIJIMA 22
JAPAN TEAM OP WAKATOSHI USHIJIMA (19) FAILED TO SCORE ON MULTIPLE ATTEMPTS.
AFTER HIS SPLASHY DEBUT IN THE V.LEAGUE LAST YEAR,
HITTER
UH-OH...
VRRZZ
CHAPTER 395:
The Lucky Ones: Part 2
SATOSHI TENDO CALLING
BLOCK

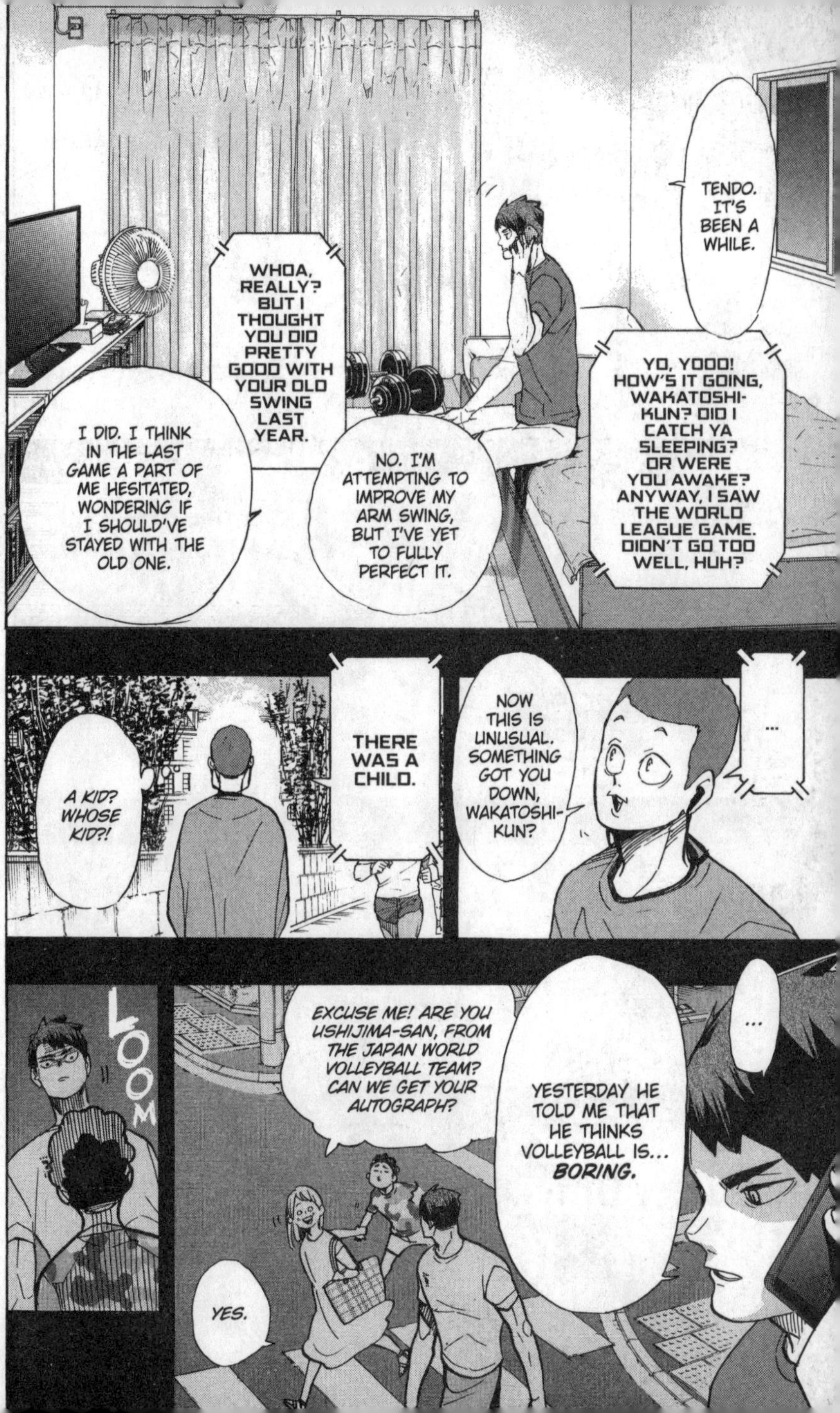
TENDO. IT'S BEEN A WHILE.
YO, YOOO! HOW'S IT GOING, WAKATOSHI-KUN? DID I CATCH YA SLEEPING? OR WERE YOU AWAKE? ANYWAY, I SAW THE WORLD LEAGUE GAME. DIDN'T GO TOO WELL, HUH?
NO. I'M ATTEMPTING TO IMPROVE MY ARM SWING, BUT I'VE YET TO FULLY PERFECT IT.
WHOA, REALLY? BUT I THOUGHT YOU DID PRETTY GOOD WITH YOUR OLD SWING LAST YEAR.
I DID. I THINK IN THE LAST GAME A PART OF ME HESITATED, WONDERING IF I SHOULD'VE STAYED WITH THE OLD ONE.
...
NOW THIS IS UNUSUAL. SOMETHING GOT YOU DOWN, WAKATOSHI-KUN?
THERE WAS A CHILD.
A KID? WHOSE KID?!
...
YESTERDAY HE TOLD ME THAT HE THINKS VOLLEYBALL IS... **BORING.**
EXCUSE ME! ARE YOU USHIJIMA-SAN, FROM THE JAPAN WORLD VOLLEYBALL TEAM? CAN WE GET YOUR AUTOGRAPH?
YES.
LOOM

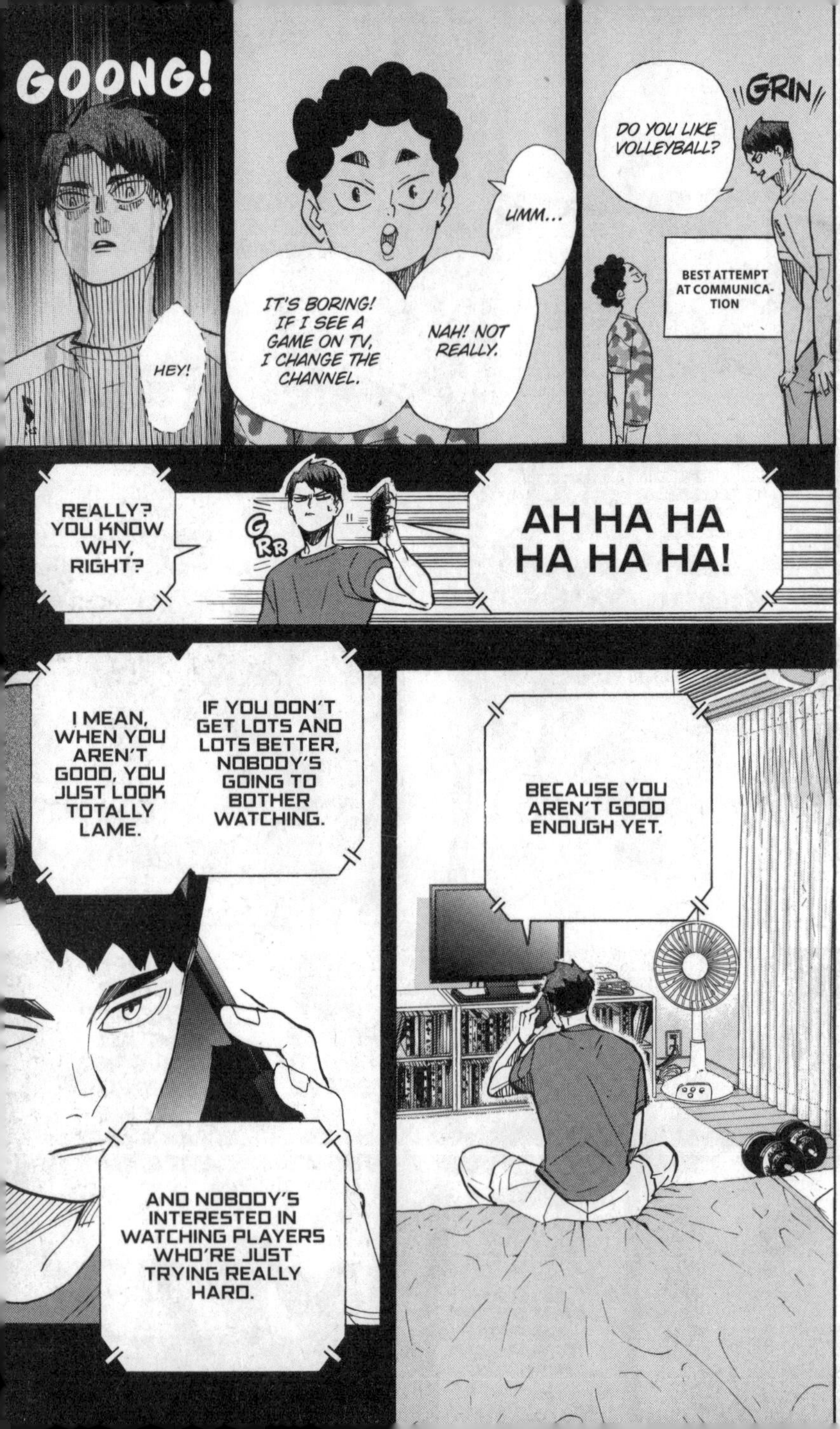
GRIN
DO YOU LIKE VOLLEYBALL?
BEST ATTEMPT AT COMMUNICATION
UMM...
NAH! NOT REALLY.
IT'S BORING! IF I SEE A GAME ON TV, I CHANGE THE CHANNEL.
GOONG!
HEY!
AH HA HA HA HA HA!
GRR
REALLY? YOU KNOW WHY, RIGHT?
BECAUSE YOU AREN'T GOOD ENOUGH YET.
IF YOU DON'T GET LOTS AND LOTS BETTER, NOBODY'S GOING TO BOTHER WATCHING.
I MEAN, WHEN YOU AREN'T GOOD, YOU JUST LOOK TOTALLY LAME.
AND NOBODY'S INTERESTED IN WATCHING PLAYERS WHO'RE JUST TRYING REALLY HARD.

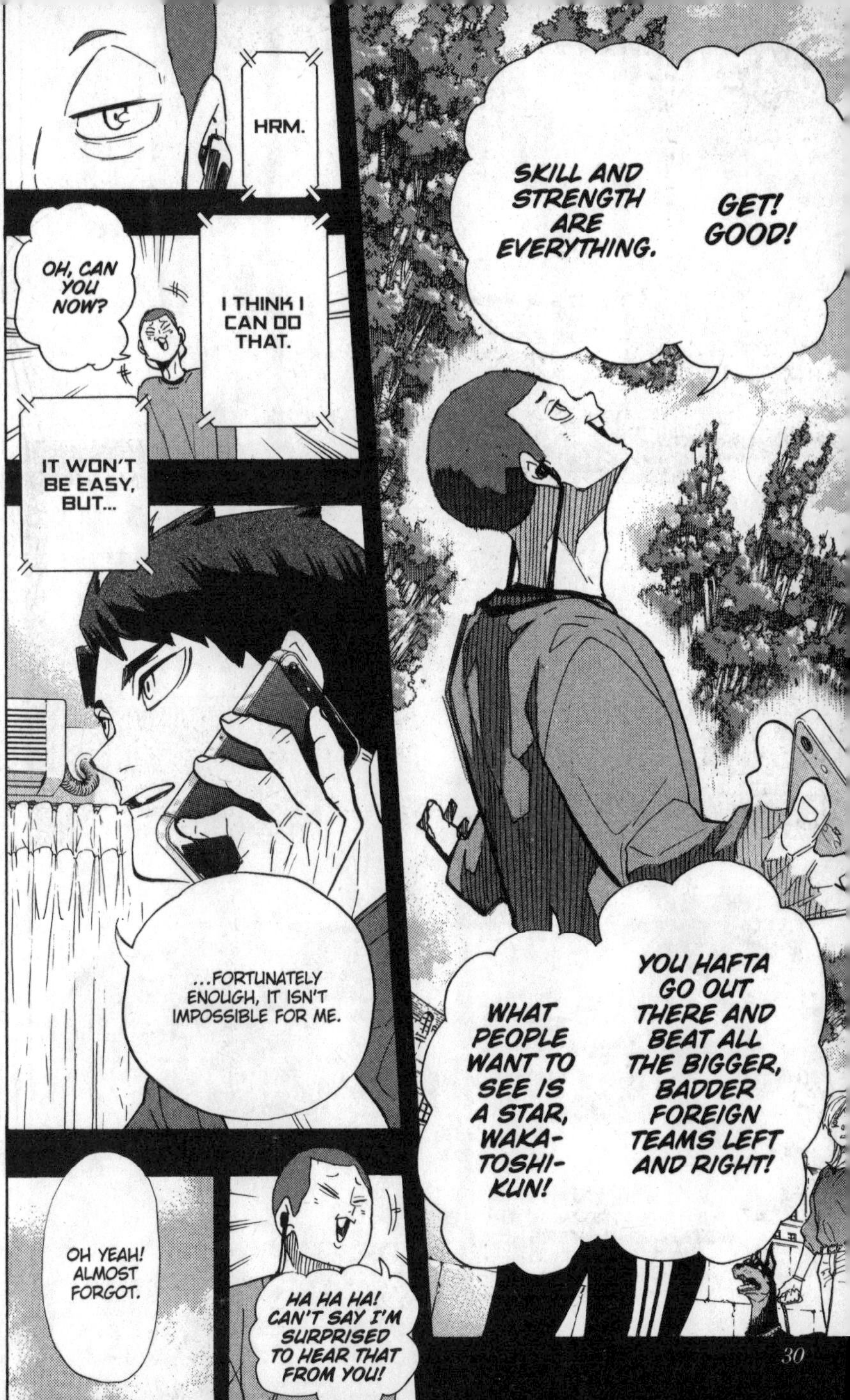
GET! GOOD!
SKILL AND STRENGTH ARE EVERYTHING.
YOU HAFTA GO OUT THERE AND BEAT ALL THE BIGGER, BADDER FOREIGN TEAMS LEFT AND RIGHT!
WHAT PEOPLE WANT TO SEE IS A STAR, WAKA-TOSHI-KUN!
HRM.
I THINK I CAN DO THAT.
OH, CAN YOU NOW?
IT WON'T BE EASY, BUT...
...FORTUNATELY ENOUGH, IT ISN'T IMPOSSIBLE FOR ME.
HA HA HA! CAN'T SAY I'M SURPRISED TO HEAR THAT FROM YOU!
OH YEAH! ALMOST FORGOT.

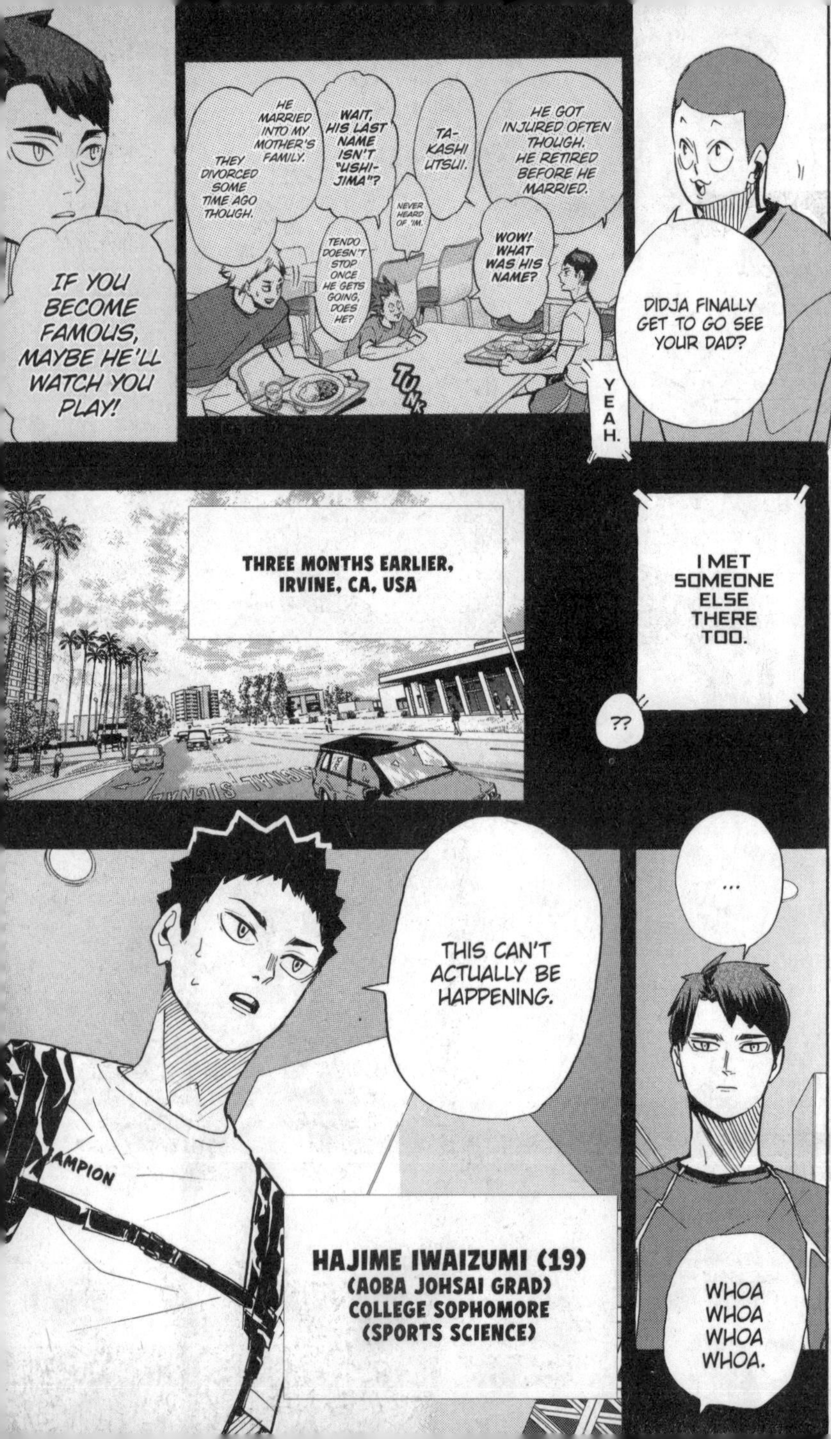
DIDJA FINALLY GET TO GO SEE YOUR DAD?
YEAH.
HE GOT INJURED OFTEN THOUGH. HE RETIRED BEFORE HE MARRIED.
WOW! WHAT WAS HIS NAME?
TA-KASHI UTSUI.
NEVER HEARD OF 'IM.
WAIT, HIS LAST NAME ISN'T "USHI-JIMA"?
HE MARRIED INTO MY MOTHER'S FAMILY.
THEY DIVORCED SOME TIME AGO THOUGH.
TENDO DOESN'T STOP ONCE HE GETS GOING, DOES HE?
TUNK
IF YOU BECOME FAMOUS, MAYBE HE'LL WATCH YOU PLAY!
I MET SOMEONE ELSE THERE TOO.
??
THREE MONTHS EARLIER, IRVINE, CA, USA
...
WHOA WHOA WHOA WHOA.
THIS CAN'T ACTUALLY BE HAPPENING.
HAJIME IWAIZUMI (19)
(AOBA JOHSAI GRAD)
COLLEGE SOPHOMORE
(SPORTS SCIENCE)

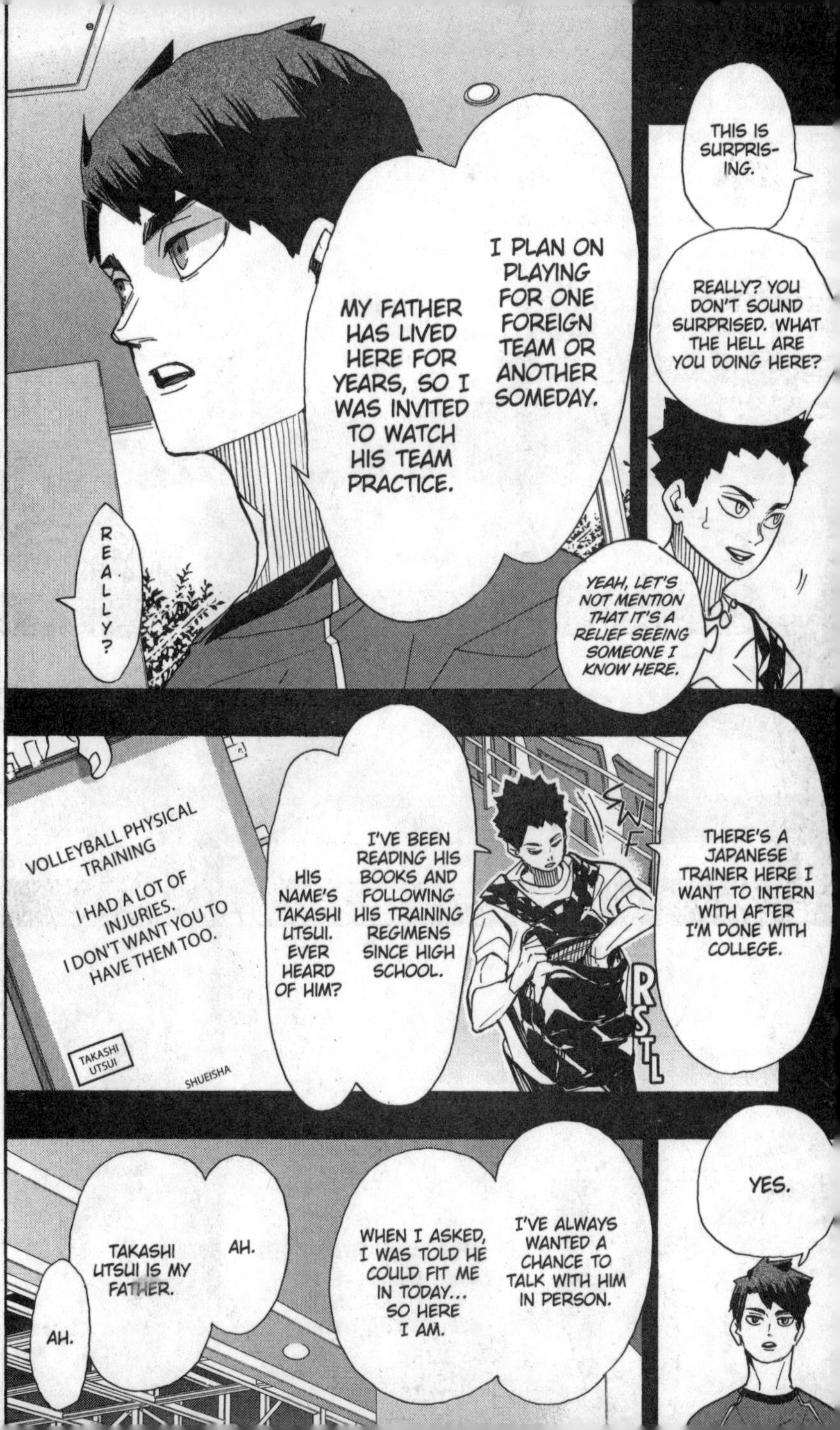

THIS IS SURPRIS-ING.
REALLY? YOU DON'T SOUND SURPRISED. WHAT THE HELL ARE YOU DOING HERE?
YEAH, LET'S NOT MENTION THAT IT'S A RELIEF SEEING SOMEONE I KNOW HERE.
I PLAN ON PLAYING FOR ONE FOREIGN TEAM OR ANOTHER SOMEDAY.
MY FATHER HAS LIVED HERE FOR YEARS, SO I WAS INVITED TO WATCH HIS TEAM PRACTICE.
REALLY?
SWF
THERE'S A JAPANESE TRAINER HERE I WANT TO INTERN WITH AFTER I'M DONE WITH COLLEGE.
RSTL
I'VE BEEN READING HIS BOOKS AND FOLLOWING HIS TRAINING REGIMENS SINCE HIGH SCHOOL.
HIS NAME'S TAKASHI UTSUI. EVER HEARD OF HIM?
VOLLEYBALL PHYSICAL TRAINING
I HAD A LOT OF INJURIES. I DON'T WANT YOU TO HAVE THEM TOO.
TAKASHI UTSUI
SHUEISHA
YES.
I'VE ALWAYS WANTED A CHANCE TO TALK WITH HIM IN PERSON.
WHEN I ASKED, I WAS TOLD HE COULD FIT ME IN TODAY... SO HERE I AM.
AH.
TAKASHI UTSUI IS MY FATHER.
AH.

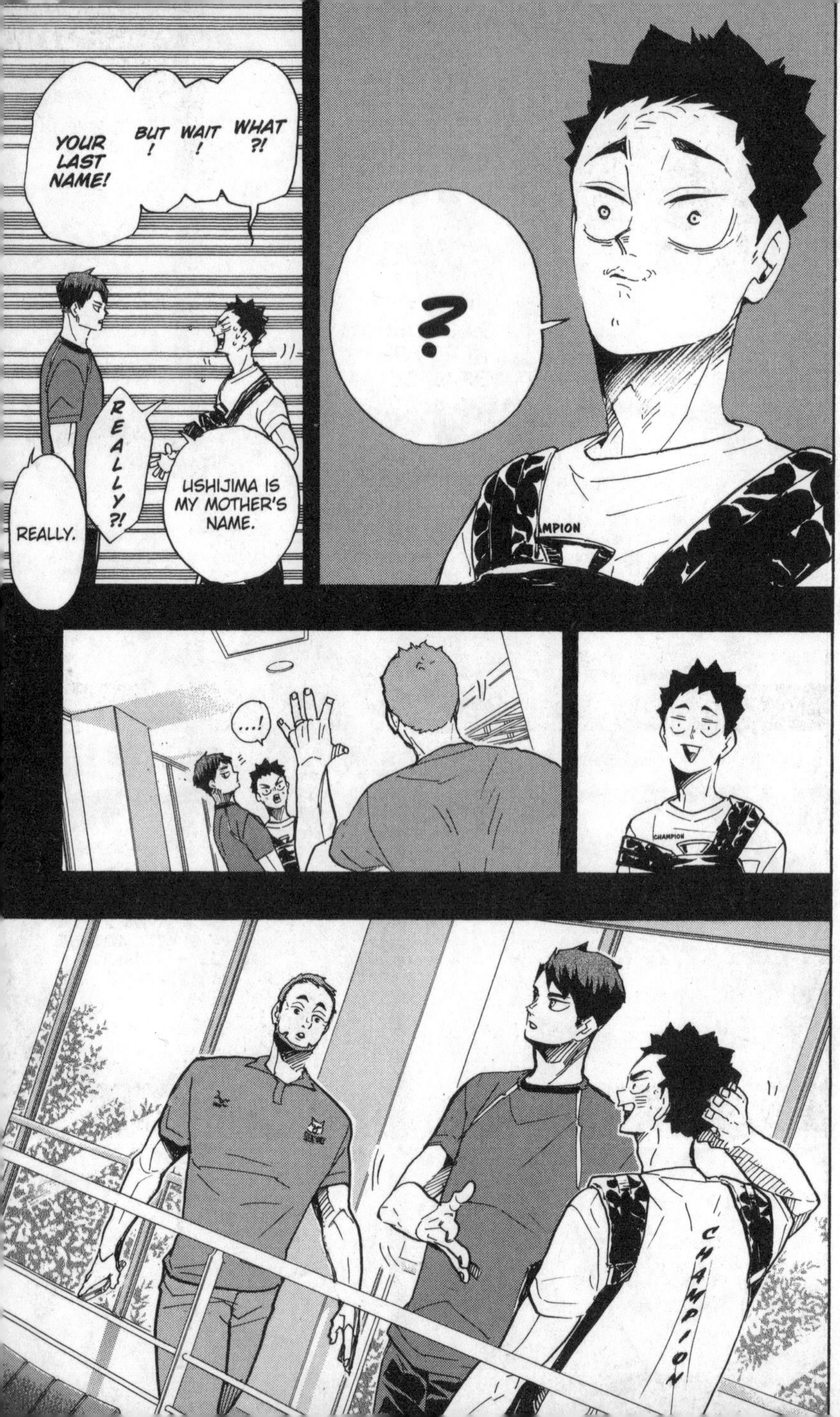
?
WHAT?! WAIT! BUT! YOUR LAST NAME!
USHIJIMA IS MY MOTHER'S NAME.
REALLY?!
REALLY.
...!
CHAMPION

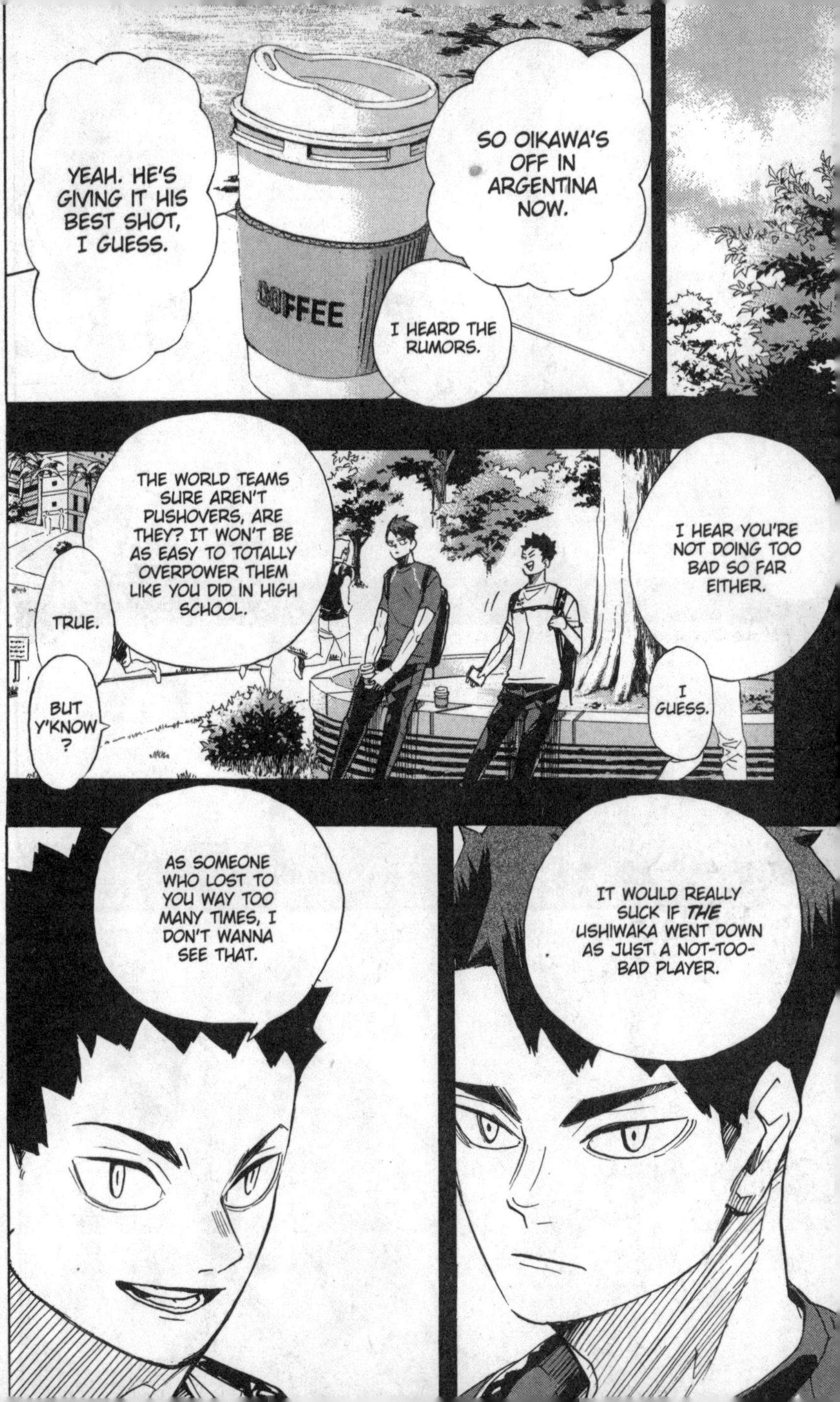
SO OIKAWA'S OFF IN ARGENTINA NOW.
I HEARD THE RUMORS.
YEAH. HE'S GIVING IT HIS BEST SHOT, I GUESS.
COFFEE
I HEAR YOU'RE NOT DOING TOO BAD SO FAR EITHER.
I GUESS.
THE WORLD TEAMS SURE AREN'T PUSHOVERS, ARE THEY? IT WON'T BE AS EASY TO TOTALLY OVERPOWER THEM LIKE YOU DID IN HIGH SCHOOL.
TRUE.
BUT Y'KNOW?
IT WOULD REALLY SUCK IF *THE* USHIWAKA WENT DOWN AS JUST A NOT-TOO-BAD PLAYER.
AS SOMEONE WHO LOST TO YOU WAY TOO MANY TIMES, I DON'T WANNA SEE THAT.

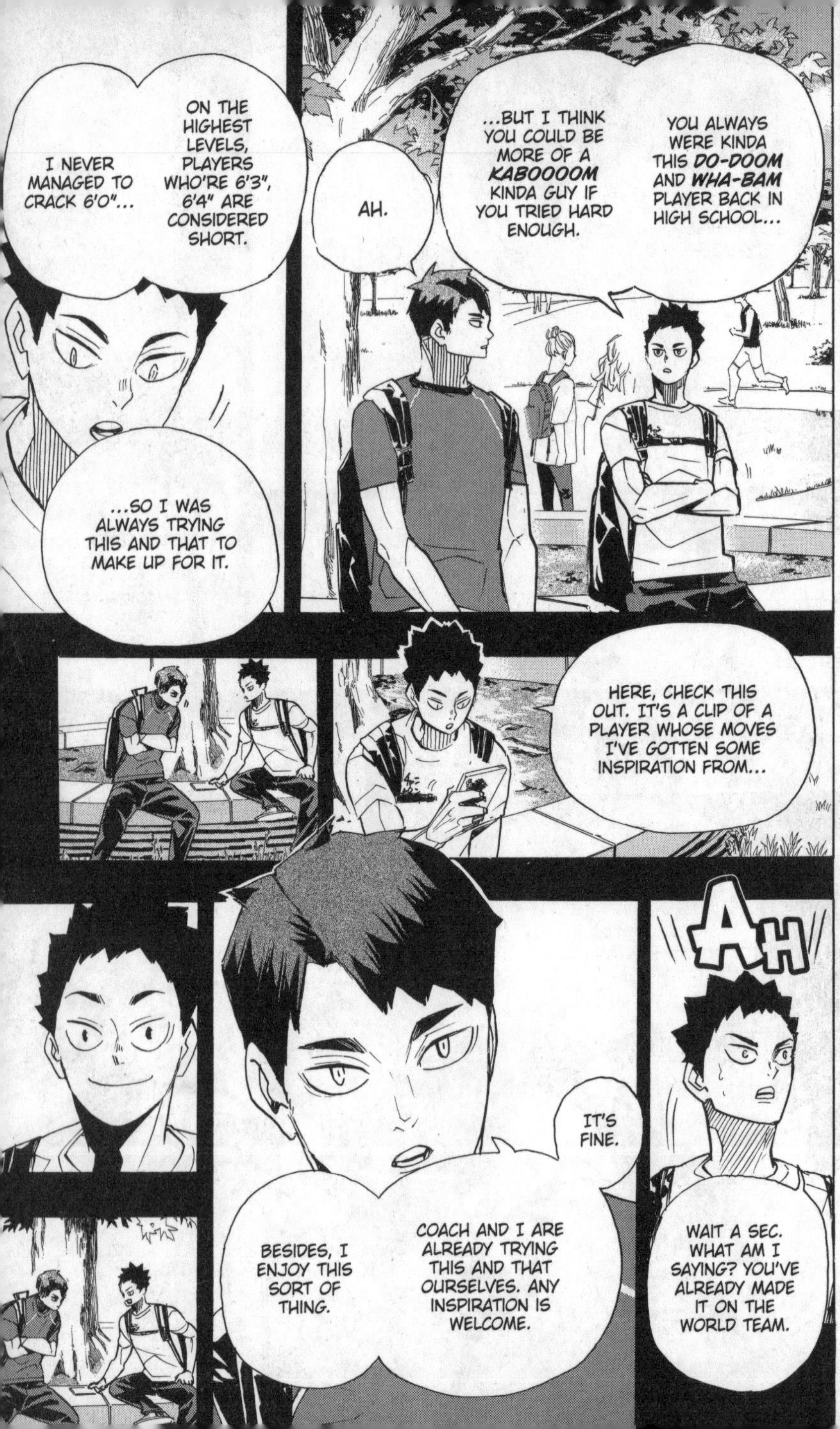
YOU ALWAYS WERE KINDA THIS DO-DOOM AND WHA-BAM PLAYER BACK IN HIGH SCHOOL...
...BUT I THINK YOU COULD BE MORE OF A KABOOOOM KINDA GUY IF YOU TRIED HARD ENOUGH.
AH.
ON THE HIGHEST LEVELS, PLAYERS WHO'RE 6'3", 6'4" ARE CONSIDERED SHORT.
I NEVER MANAGED TO CRACK 6'0"...
...SO I WAS ALWAYS TRYING THIS AND THAT TO MAKE UP FOR IT.
HERE, CHECK THIS OUT. IT'S A CLIP OF A PLAYER WHOSE MOVES I'VE GOTTEN SOME INSPIRATION FROM...
AH
WAIT A SEC. WHAT AM I SAYING? YOU'VE ALREADY MADE IT ON THE WORLD TEAM.
IT'S FINE.
COACH AND I ARE ALREADY TRYING THIS AND THAT OURSELVES. ANY INSPIRATION IS WELCOME.
BESIDES, I ENJOY THIS SORT OF THING.

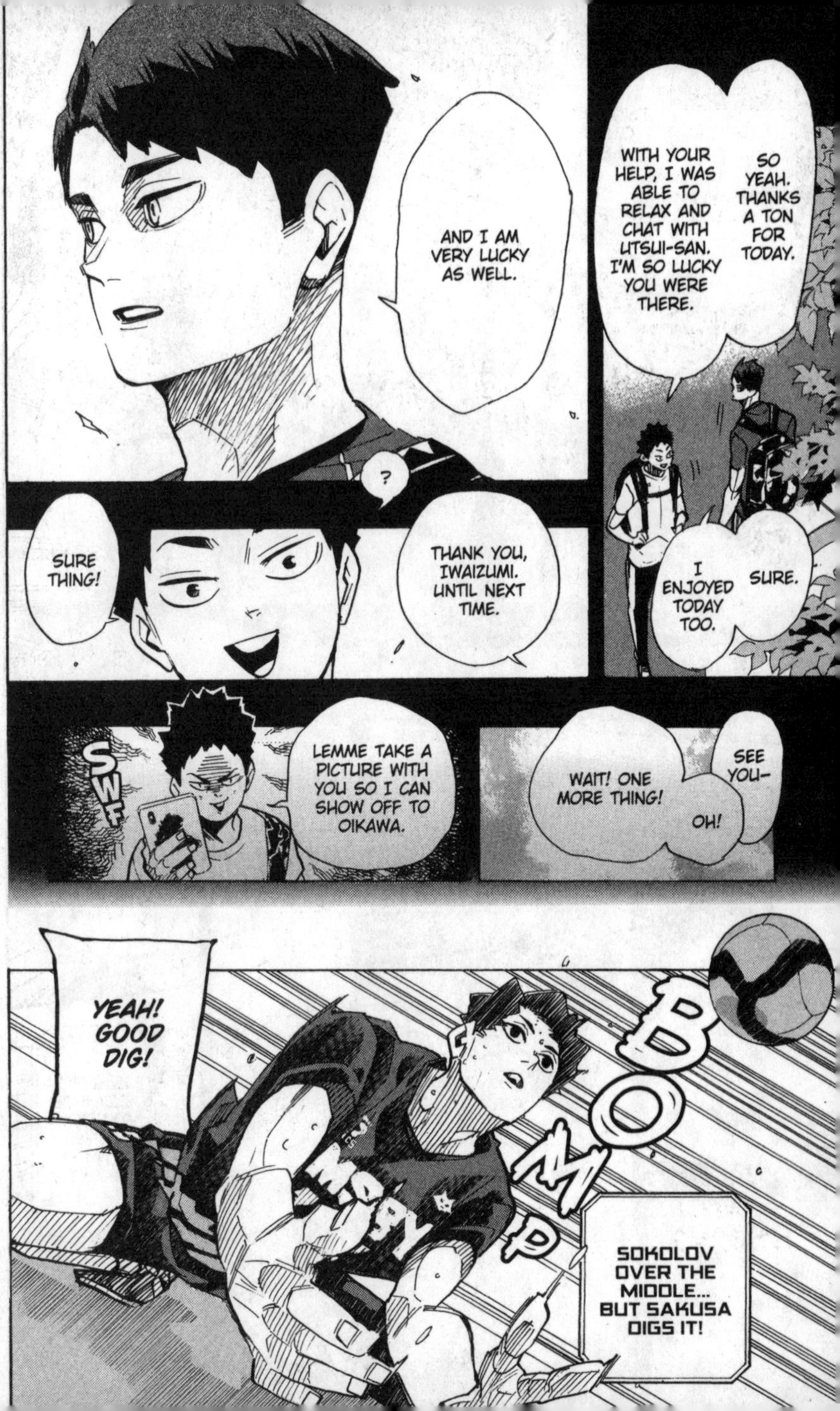
SO YEAH. THANKS A TON FOR TODAY.
WITH YOUR HELP, I WAS ABLE TO RELAX AND CHAT WITH UTSUI-SAN. I'M SO LUCKY YOU WERE THERE.
SURE.
I ENJOYED TODAY TOO.
AND I AM VERY LUCKY AS WELL.
?
THANK YOU, IWAIZUMI. UNTIL NEXT TIME.
SURE THING!
SEE YOU-
OH!
WAIT! ONE MORE THING!
LEMME TAKE A PICTURE WITH YOU SO I CAN SHOW OFF TO OIKAWA.
SWF
BOMP
YEAH! GOOD DIG!
SOKOLOV OVER THE MIDDLE... BUT SAKUSA DIGS IT!

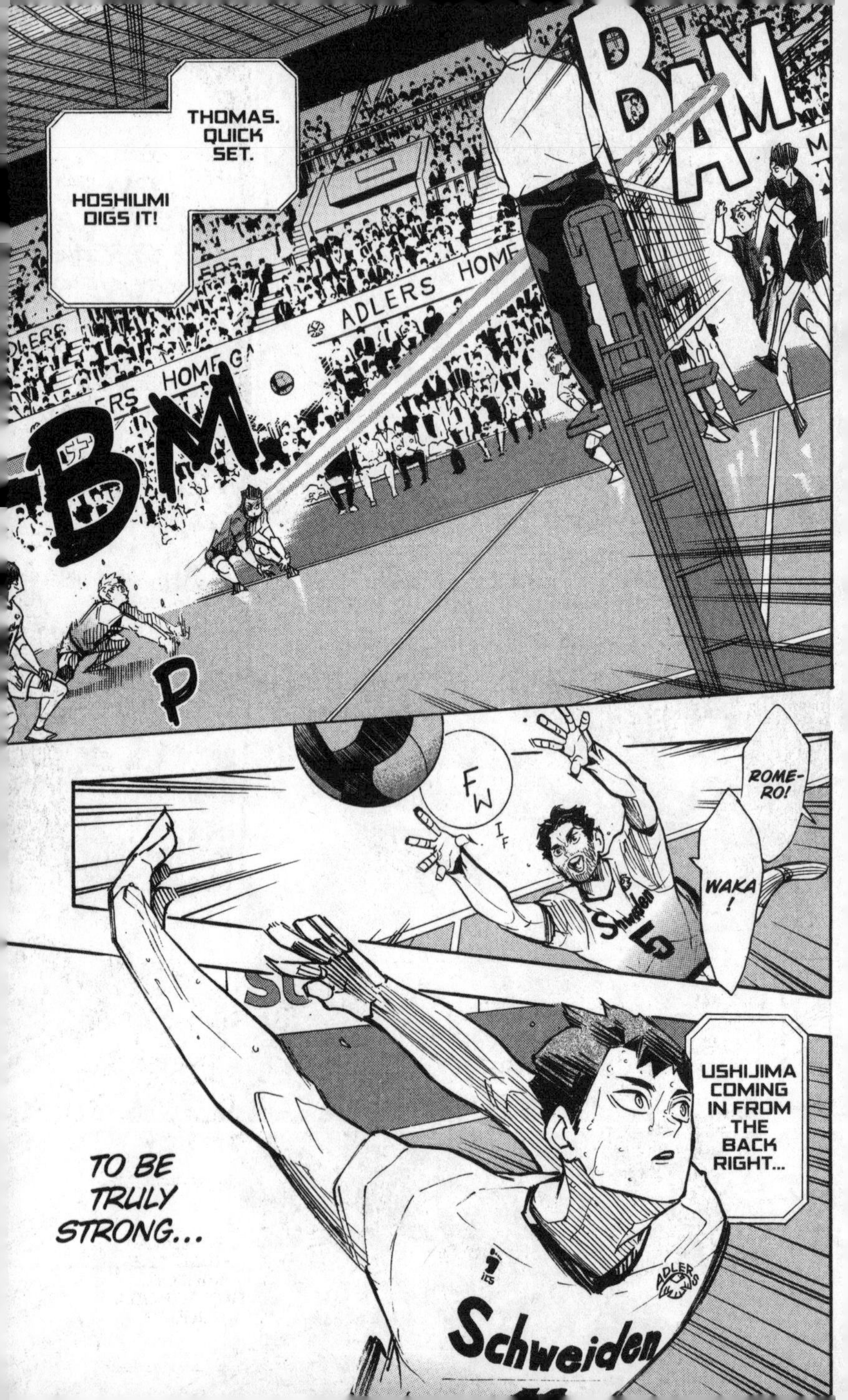
THOMAS. QUICK SET.
HOSHIUMI DIGS IT!
BAM
BAM
P
ROMERO!
WAKA!
FWIF
USHIJIMA COMING IN FROM THE BACK RIGHT...
TO BE TRULY STRONG...
Schweiden

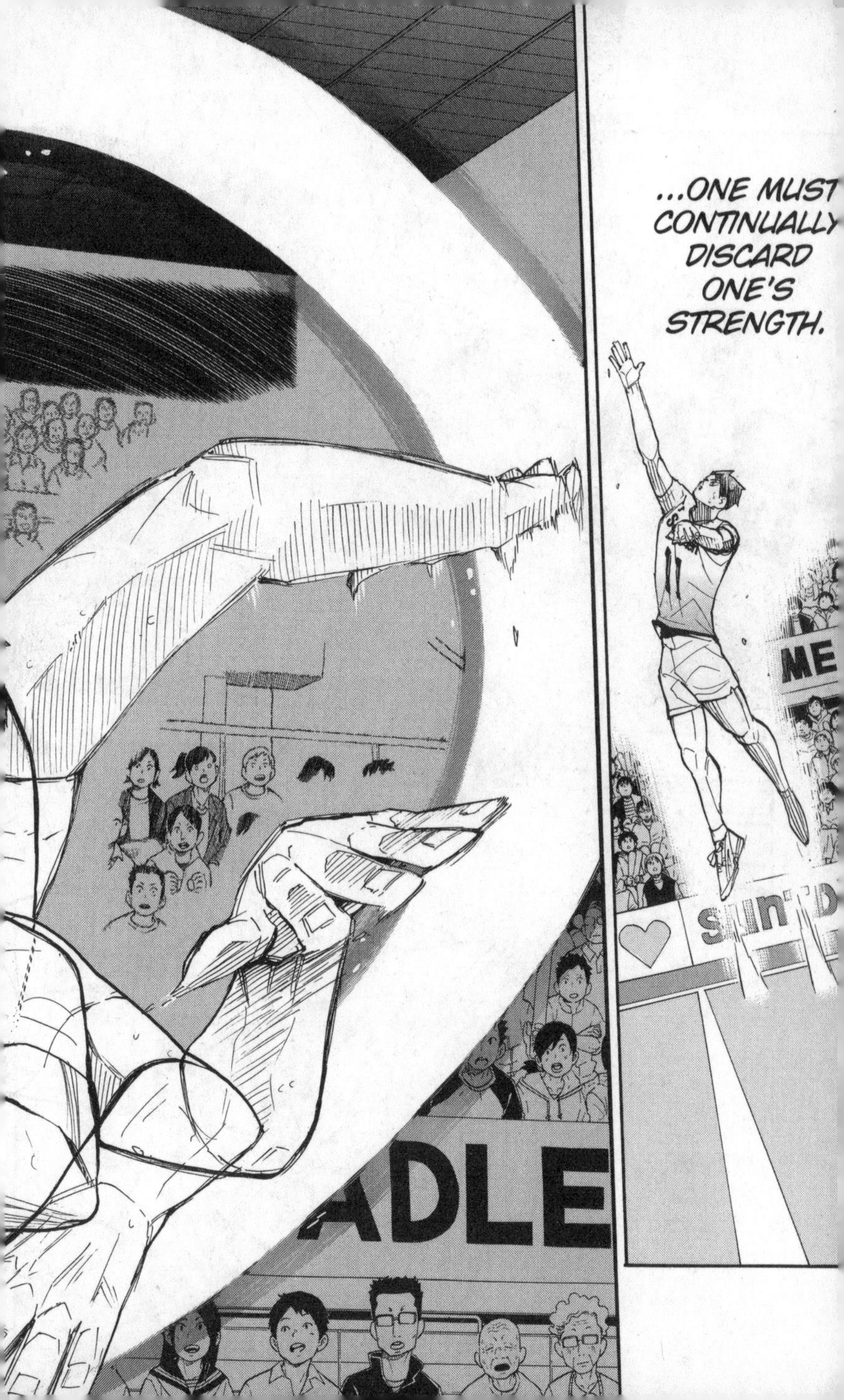
...ONE MUST CONTINUALLY DISCARD ONE'S STRENGTH.
ADLE

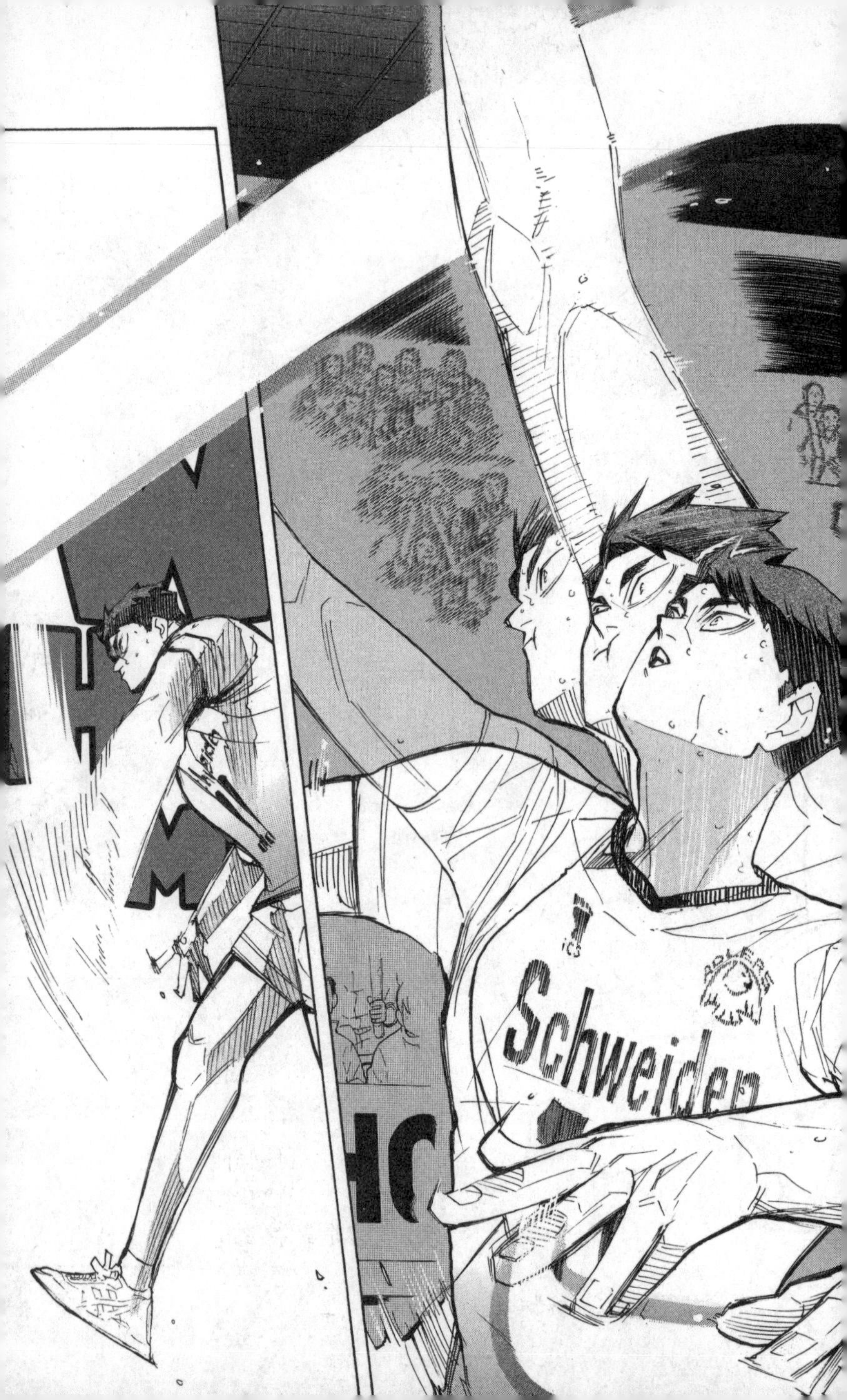
Schweiden

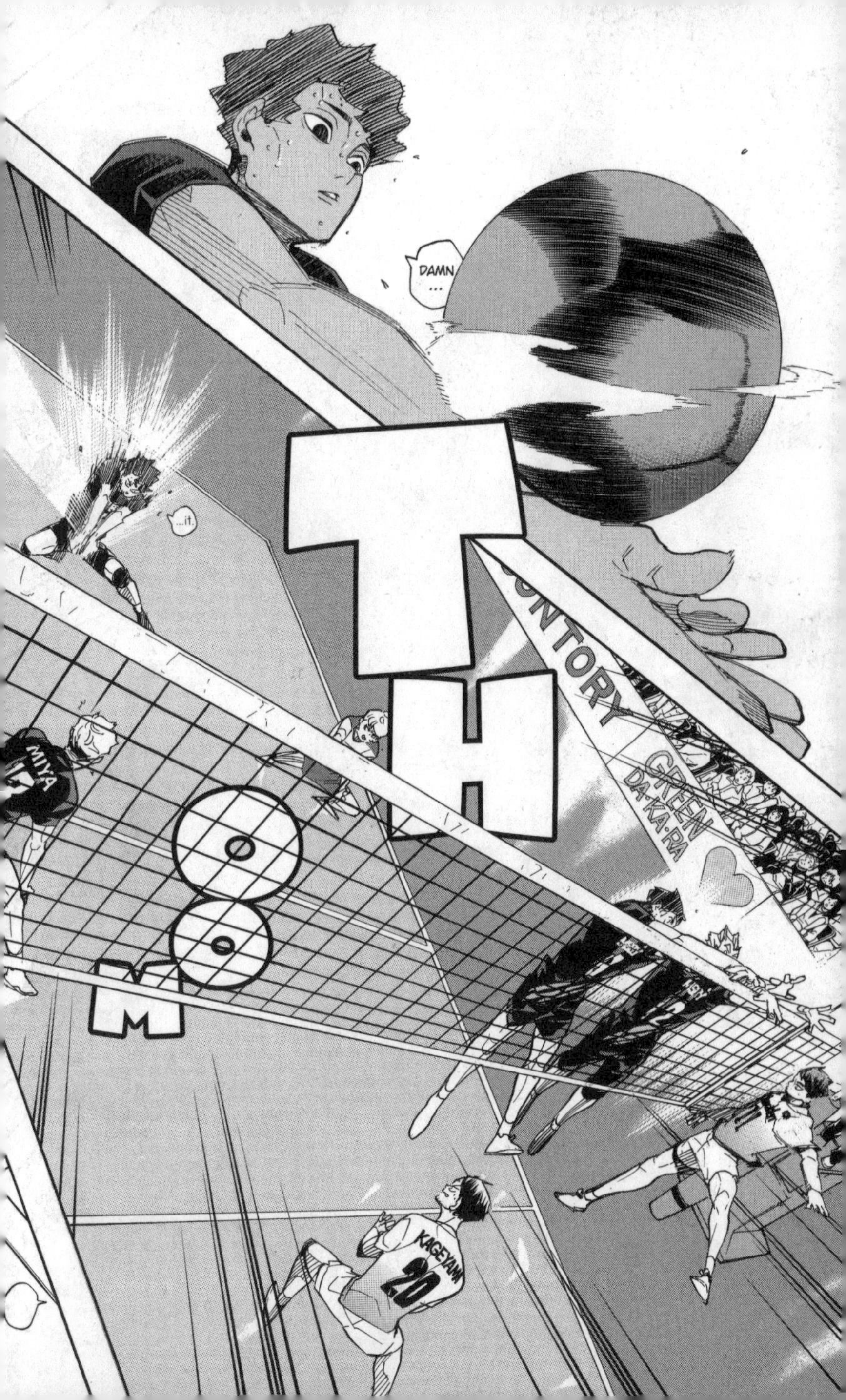
DAMN ...
...it.
THOOM
GREEN
DA·KA·RA
MIYA
20

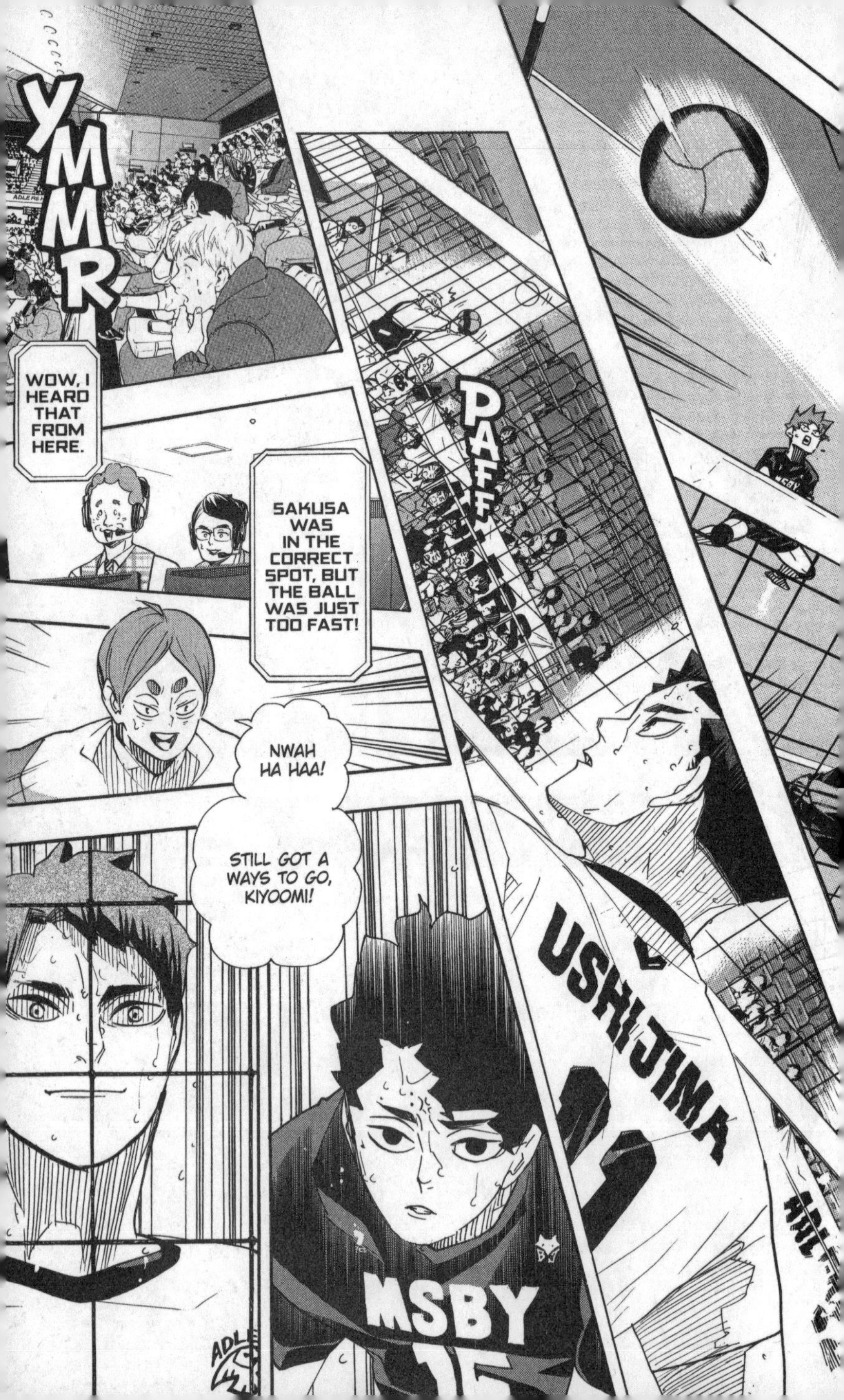
PAFF
YMMR
WOW, I HEARD THAT FROM HERE.
SAKUSA WAS IN THE CORRECT SPOT, BUT THE BALL WAS JUST TOO FAST!
NWAH HA HAA!
STILL GOT A WAYS TO GO, KIYOOMI!
USHIJIMA
MSBY

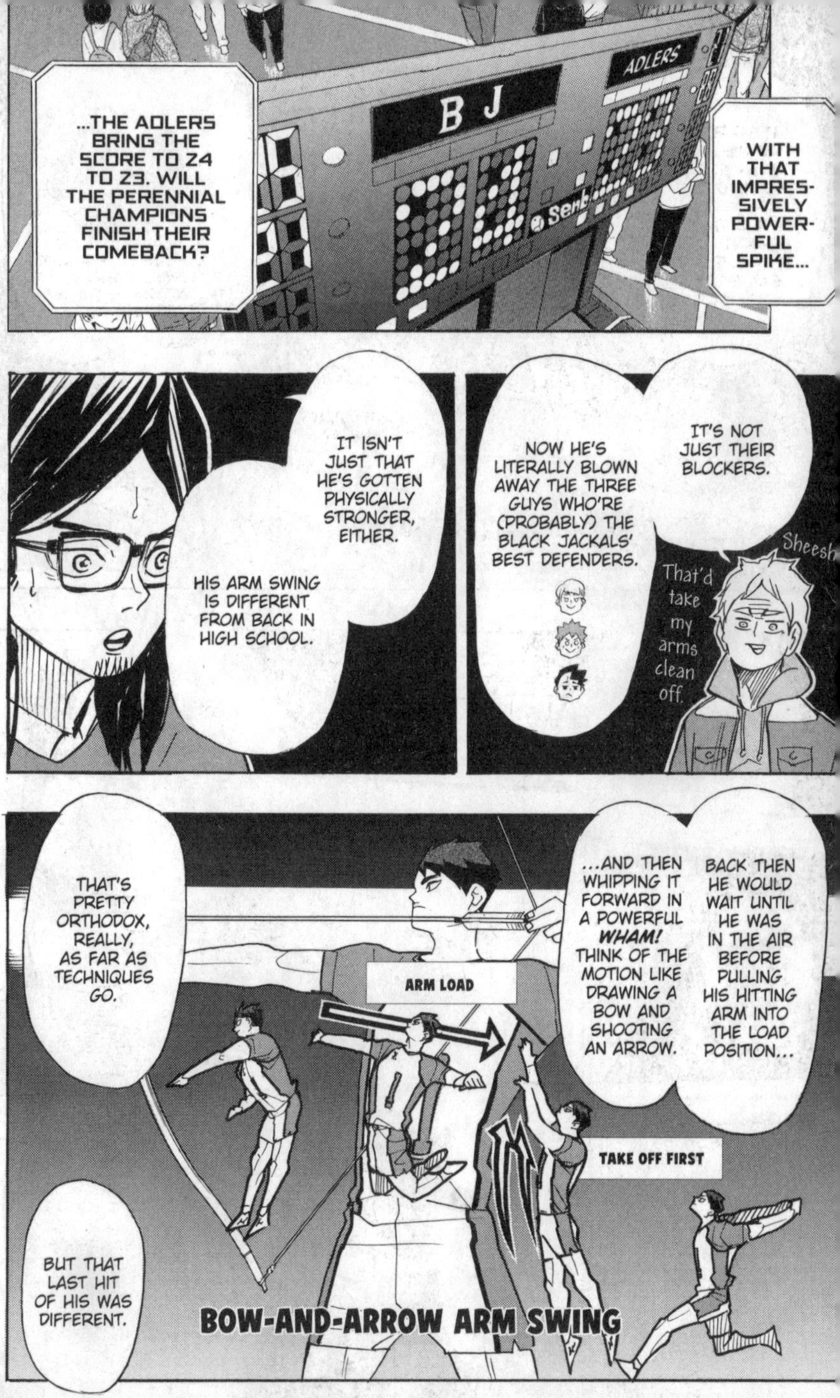
WITH THAT IMPRESSIVELY POWERFUL SPIKE...
...THE ADLERS BRING THE SCORE TO 24 TO 23. WILL THE PERENNIAL CHAMPIONS FINISH THEIR COMEBACK?
ADLERS
B J
IT'S NOT JUST THEIR BLOCKERS.
NOW HE'S LITERALLY BLOWN AWAY THE THREE GUYS WHO'RE (PROBABLY) THE BLACK JACKALS' BEST DEFENDERS.
Sheesh
That'd take my arms clean off.
IT ISN'T JUST THAT HE'S GOTTEN PHYSICALLY STRONGER, EITHER.
HIS ARM SWING IS DIFFERENT FROM BACK IN HIGH SCHOOL.
BACK THEN HE WOULD WAIT UNTIL HE WAS IN THE AIR BEFORE PULLING HIS HITTING ARM INTO THE LOAD POSITION...
...AND THEN WHIPPING IT FORWARD IN A POWERFUL WHAM! THINK OF THE MOTION LIKE DRAWING A BOW AND SHOOTING AN ARROW.
ARM LOAD
TAKE OFF FIRST
THAT'S PRETTY ORTHODOX, REALLY, AS FAR AS TECHNIQUES GO.
BUT THAT LAST HIT OF HIS WAS DIFFERENT.
BOW-AND-ARROW ARM SWING

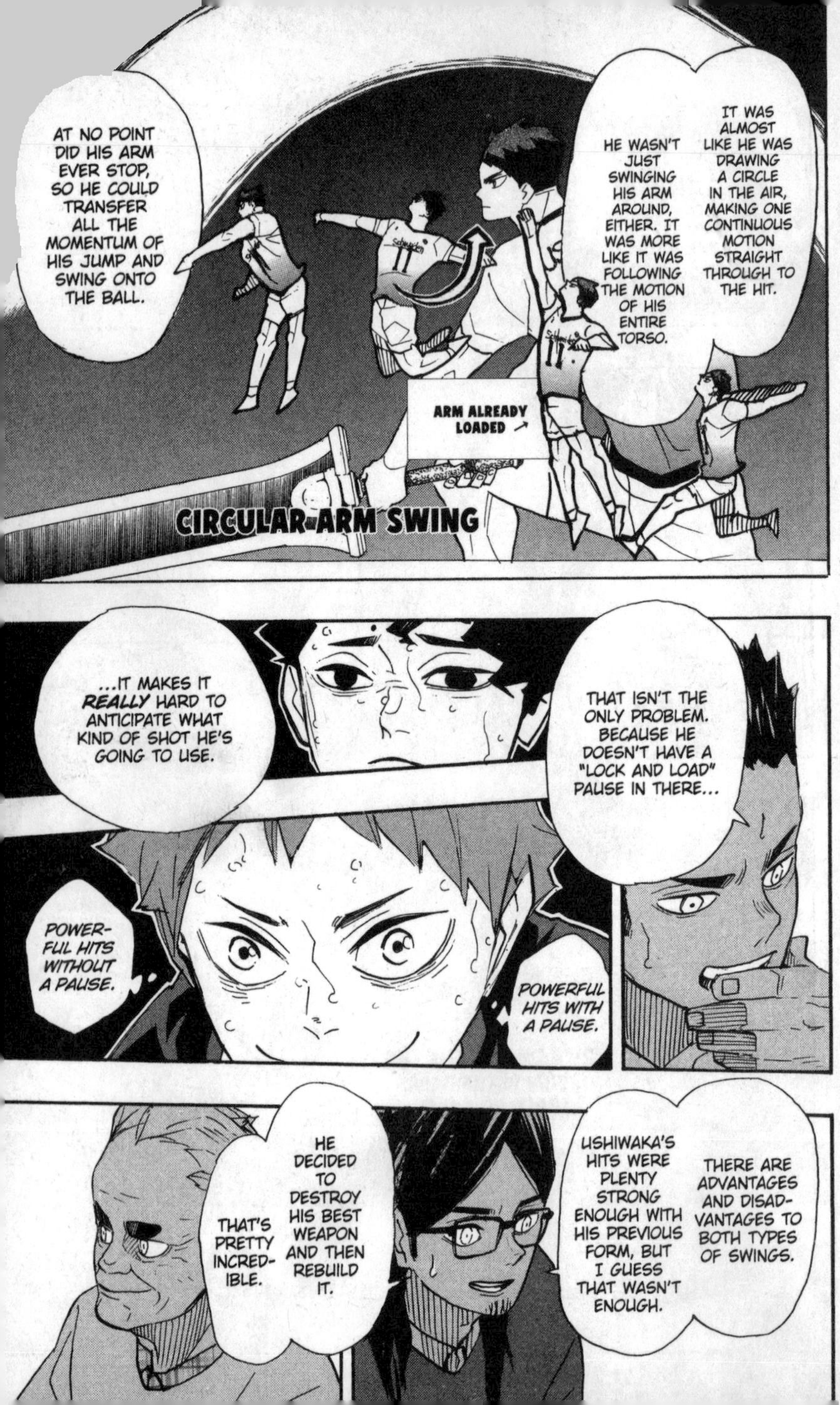

IT WAS ALMOST LIKE HE WAS DRAWING A CIRCLE IN THE AIR, MAKING ONE CONTINUOUS MOTION STRAIGHT THROUGH TO THE HIT.
HE WASN'T JUST SWINGING HIS ARM AROUND, EITHER. IT WAS MORE LIKE IT WAS FOLLOWING THE MOTION OF HIS ENTIRE TORSO.
AT NO POINT DID HIS ARM EVER STOP, SO HE COULD TRANSFER ALL THE MOMENTUM OF HIS JUMP AND SWING ONTO THE BALL.
ARM ALREADY LOADED
CIRCULAR ARM SWING
THAT ISN'T THE ONLY PROBLEM. BECAUSE HE DOESN'T HAVE A "LOCK AND LOAD" PAUSE IN THERE...
...IT MAKES IT REALLY HARD TO ANTICIPATE WHAT KIND OF SHOT HE'S GOING TO USE.
POWERFUL HITS WITH A PAUSE.
POWER-FUL HITS WITHOUT A PAUSE.
THERE ARE ADVANTAGES AND DISAD-VANTAGES TO BOTH TYPES OF SWINGS.
USHIWAKA'S HITS WERE PLENTY STRONG ENOUGH WITH HIS PREVIOUS FORM, BUT I GUESS THAT WASN'T ENOUGH.
HE DECIDED TO DESTROY HIS BEST WEAPON AND THEN REBUILD IT.
THAT'S PRETTY INCRED-IBLE.

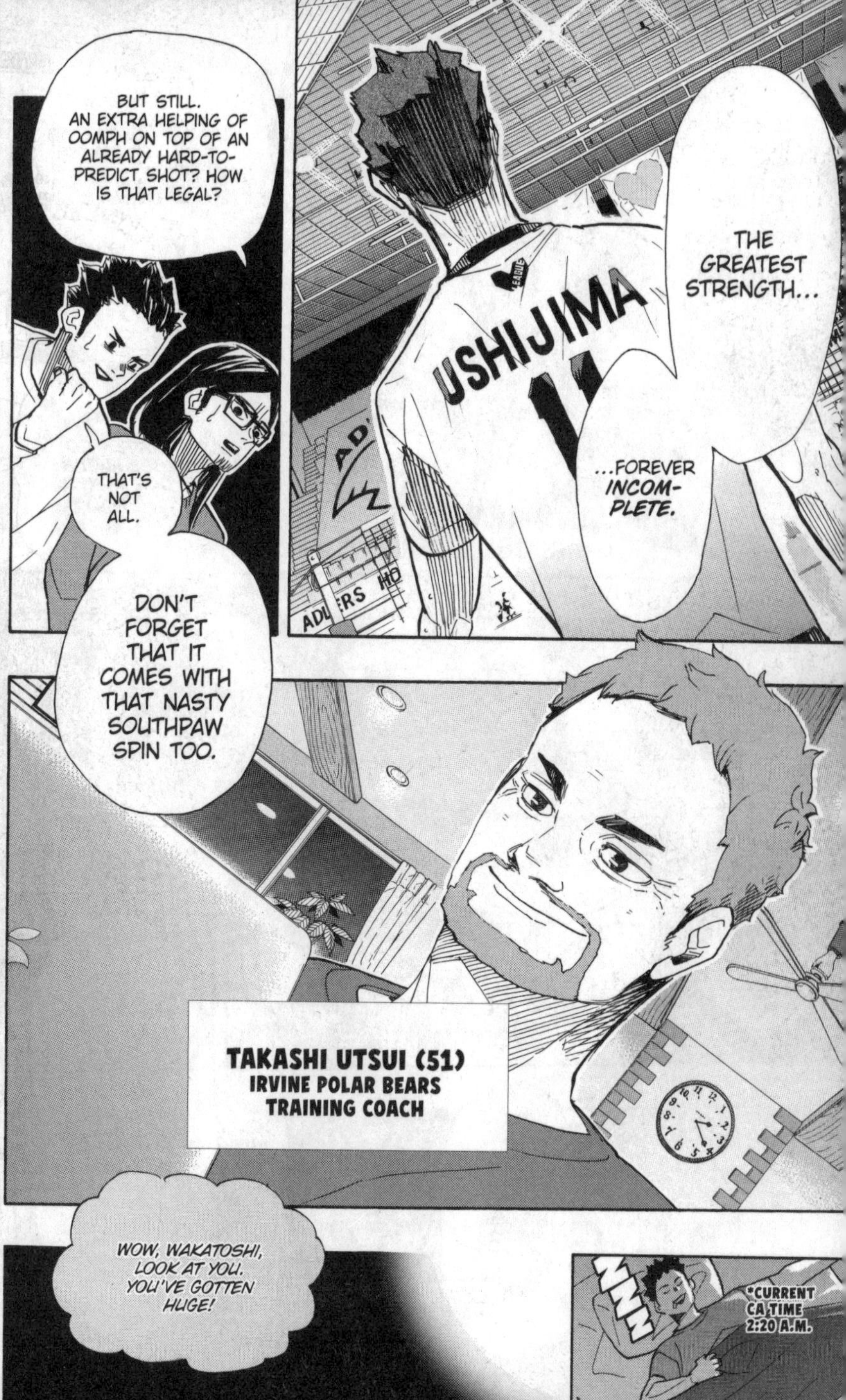
THE GREATEST STRENGTH...
USHIJIMA
...FOREVER INCOMPLETE.
BUT STILL. AN EXTRA HELPING OF OOMPH ON TOP OF AN ALREADY HARD-TO-PREDICT SHOT? HOW IS THAT LEGAL?
THAT'S NOT ALL.
DON'T FORGET THAT IT COMES WITH THAT NASTY SOUTHPAW SPIN TOO.
TAKASHI UTSUI (51)
IRVINE POLAR BEARS
TRAINING COACH
NNN
*CURRENT CA TIME 2:20 A.M.
WOW, WAKATOSHI, LOOK AT YOU. YOU'VE GOTTEN HUGE!

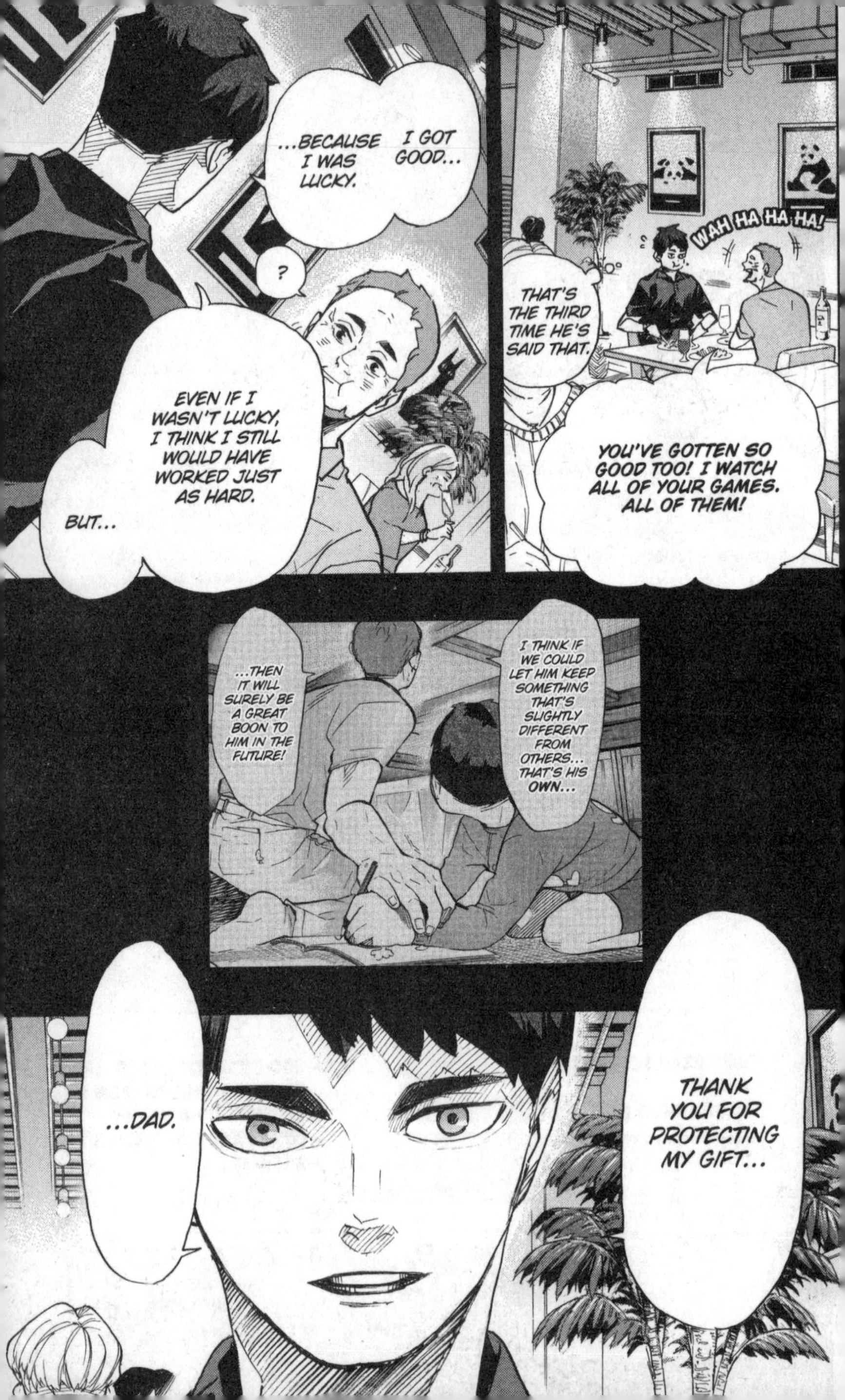
WAH HA HA HA!
THAT'S THE THIRD TIME HE'S SAID THAT.
YOU'VE GOTTEN SO GOOD TOO! I WATCH ALL OF YOUR GAMES. ALL OF THEM!
I GOT GOOD...
...BECAUSE I WAS LUCKY.
?
EVEN IF I WASN'T LUCKY, I THINK I STILL WOULD HAVE WORKED JUST AS HARD.
BUT...
I THINK IF WE COULD LET HIM KEEP SOMETHING THAT'S SLIGHTLY DIFFERENT FROM OTHERS... THAT'S HIS OWN...
...THEN IT WILL SURELY BE A GREAT BOON TO HIM IN THE FUTURE!
THANK YOU FOR PROTECTING MY GIFT...
...DAD.

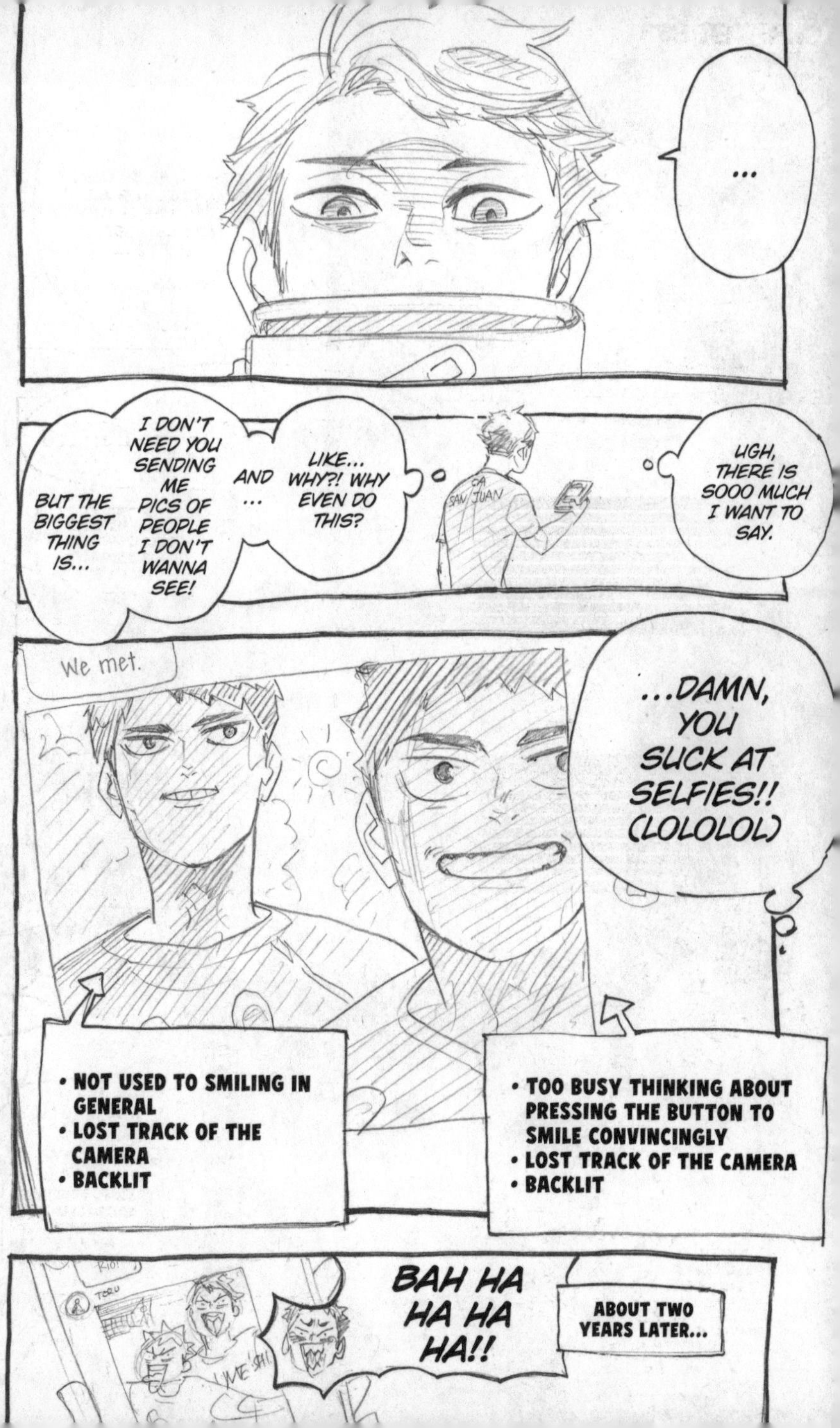
...
UGH, THERE IS SOOO MUCH I WANT TO SAY.
LIKE... WHY?! WHY EVEN DO THIS?
AND ...
I DON'T NEED YOU SENDING ME PICS OF PEOPLE I DON'T WANNA SEE!
BUT THE BIGGEST THING IS...
...DAMN, YOU SUCK AT SELFIES!! (LOLOLOL)
We met.
• TOO BUSY THINKING ABOUT PRESSING THE BUTTON TO SMILE CONVINCINGLY • LOST TRACK OF THE CAMERA • BACKLIT
• NOT USED TO SMILING IN GENERAL • LOST TRACK OF THE CAMERA • BACKLIT
ABOUT TWO YEARS LATER...
BAH HA HA HA HA!!

CHAPTER 396

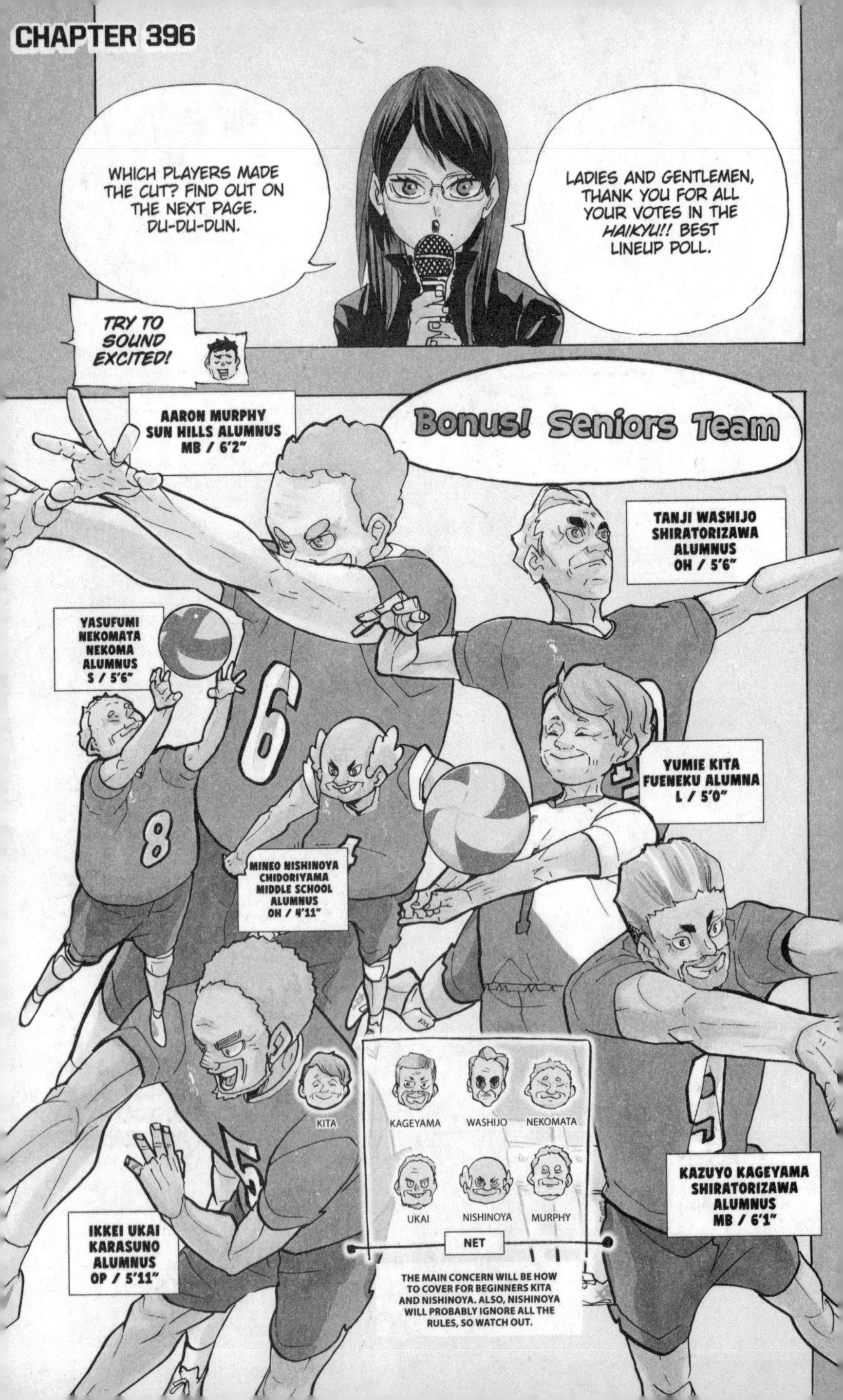
LADIES AND GENTLEMEN, THANK YOU FOR ALL YOUR VOTES IN THE *HAIKYU!!* BEST LINEUP POLL.
WHICH PLAYERS MADE THE CUT? FIND OUT ON THE NEXT PAGE. DU-DU-DUN.
TRY TO SOUND EXCITED!
Bonus! Seniors Team
TANJI WASHIJO SHIRATORIZAWA ALUMNUS OH / 5'6"
AARON MURPHY SUN HILLS ALUMNUS MB / 6'2"
YUMIE KITA FUENEKU ALUMNA L / 5'0"
YASUFUMI NEKOMATA NEKOMA ALUMNUS S / 5'6"
MINEO NISHINOYA CHIDORIYAMA MIDDLE SCHOOL ALUMNUS OH / 4'11"
KAZUYO KAGEYAMA SHIRATORIZAWA ALUMNUS MB / 6'1"
KITA
KAGEYAMA
WASHIJO
NEKOMATA
UKAI
NISHINOYA
MURPHY
NET
THE MAIN CONCERN WILL BE HOW TO COVER FOR BEGINNERS KITA AND NISHINOYA. ALSO, NISHINOYA WILL PROBABLY IGNORE ALL THE RULES, SO WATCH OUT.
IKKEI UKAI KARASUNO ALUMNUS OP / 5'11"

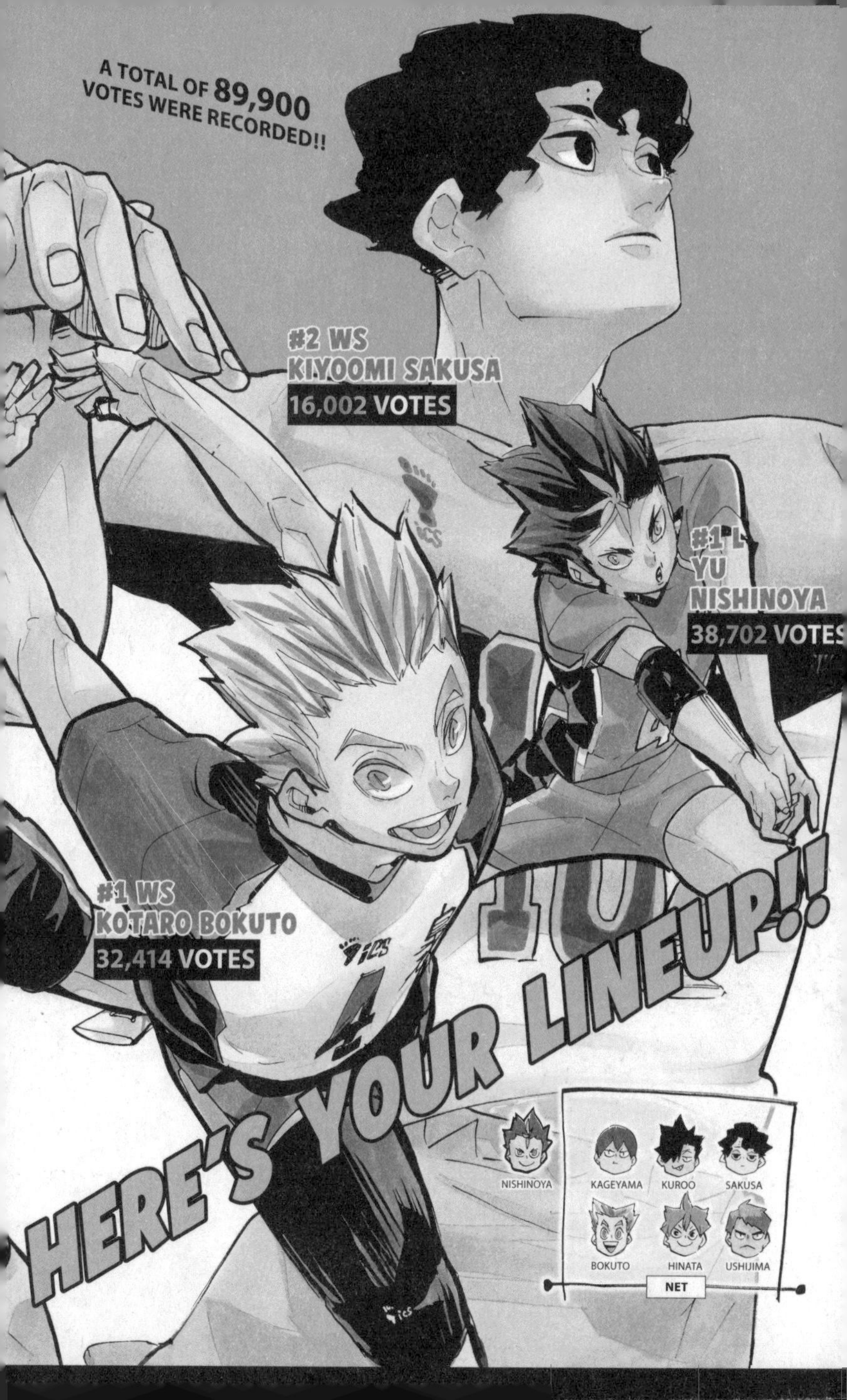
A TOTAL OF 89,900 VOTES WERE RECORDED!!
#2 WS
KIYOOMI SAKUSA
16,002 VOTES
#1 L
YU
NISHINOYA
38,702 VOTES
#1 WS
KOTARO BOKUTO
32,414 VOTES
HERE'S YOUR LINEUP!!!
NISHINOYA
KAGEYAMA
KUROO
SAKUSA
BOKUTO
HINATA
USHIJIMA
NET

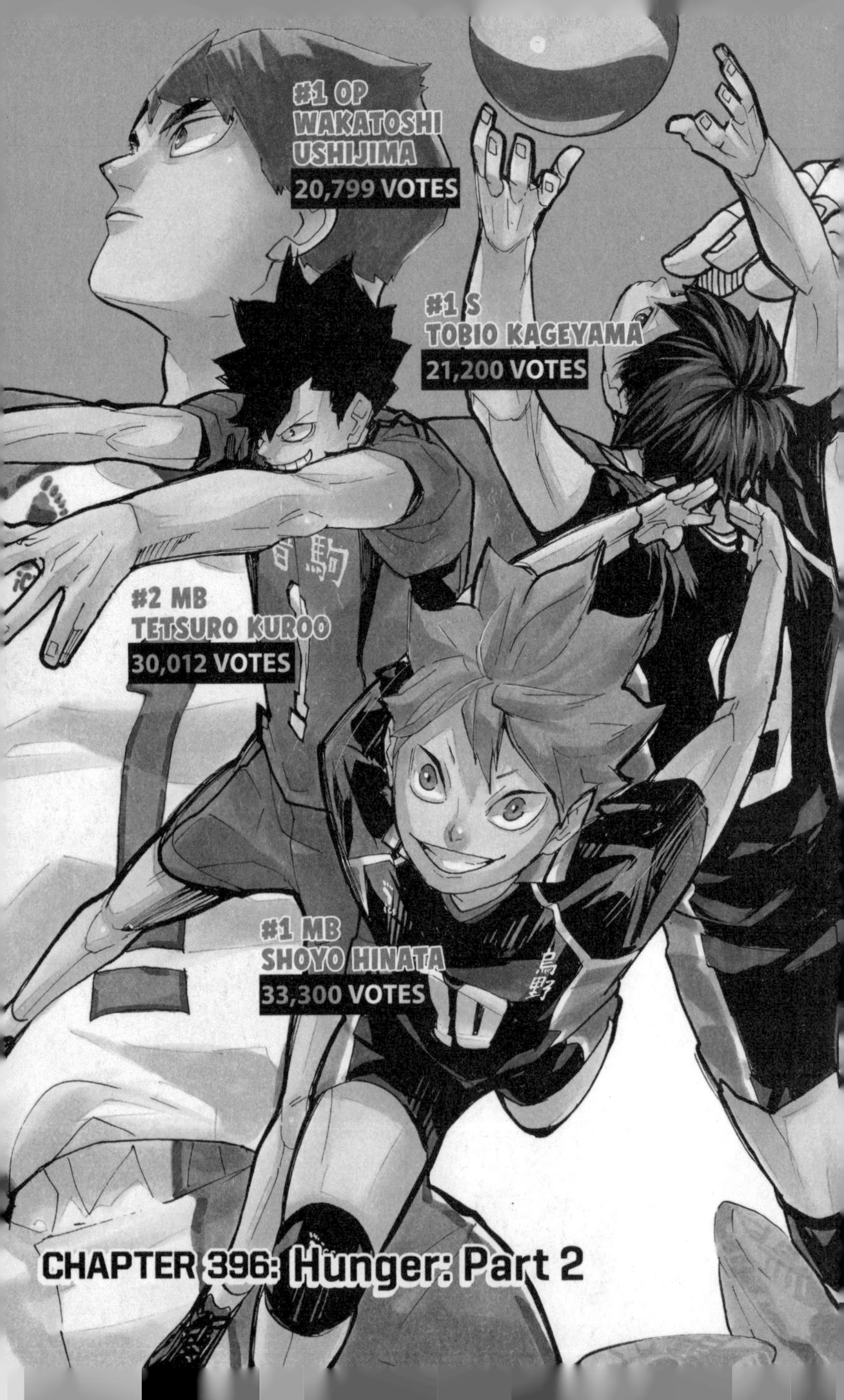
#1 OP
WAKATOSHI USHIJIMA
20,799 VOTES
#1 S
TOBIO KAGEYAMA
21,200 VOTES
#2 MB
TETSURO KUROO
30,012 VOTES
#1 MB
SHOYO HINATA
33,300 VOTES

CHAPTER 396: Hunger: Part 2

HAIKYU!!

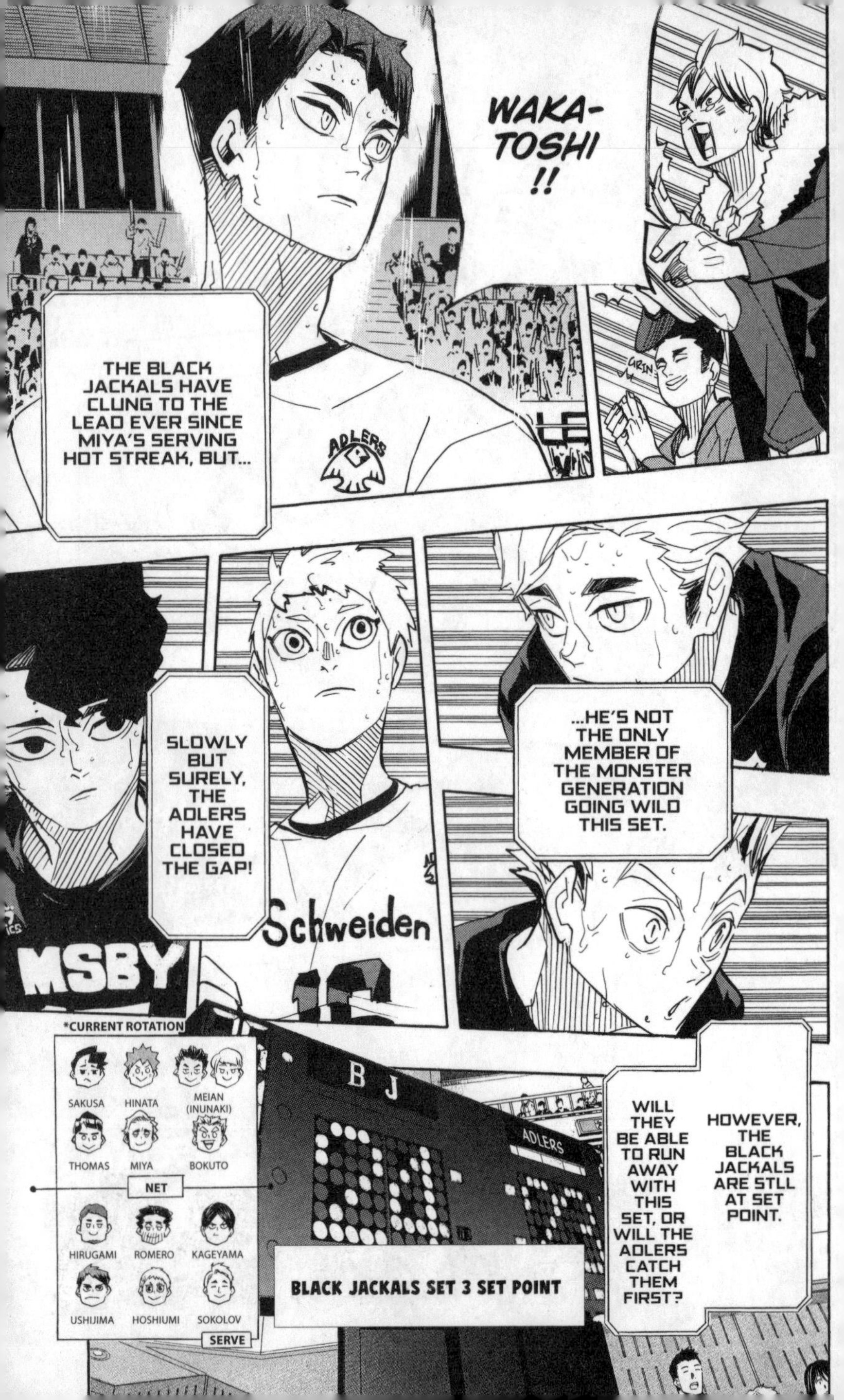
WAKA-TOSHI!!
GRIN
ADLERS
THE BLACK JACKALS HAVE CLUNG TO THE LEAD EVER SINCE MIYA'S SERVING HOT STREAK, BUT...
...HE'S NOT THE ONLY MEMBER OF THE MONSTER GENERATION GOING WILD THIS SET.
SLOWLY BUT SURELY, THE ADLERS HAVE CLOSED THE GAP!
Schweiden
MSBY
HOWEVER, THE BLACK JACKALS ARE STLL AT SET POINT.
WILL THEY BE ABLE TO RUN AWAY WITH THIS SET, OR WILL THE ADLERS CATCH THEM FIRST?
B J
ADLERS
BLACK JACKALS SET 3 SET POINT
*CURRENT ROTATION
SAKUSA
HINATA
MEIAN (INUNAKI)
THOMAS
MIYA
BOKUTO
NET
HIRUGAMI
ROMERO
KAGEYAMA
USHIJIMA
HOSHIUMI
SOKOLOV
SERVE

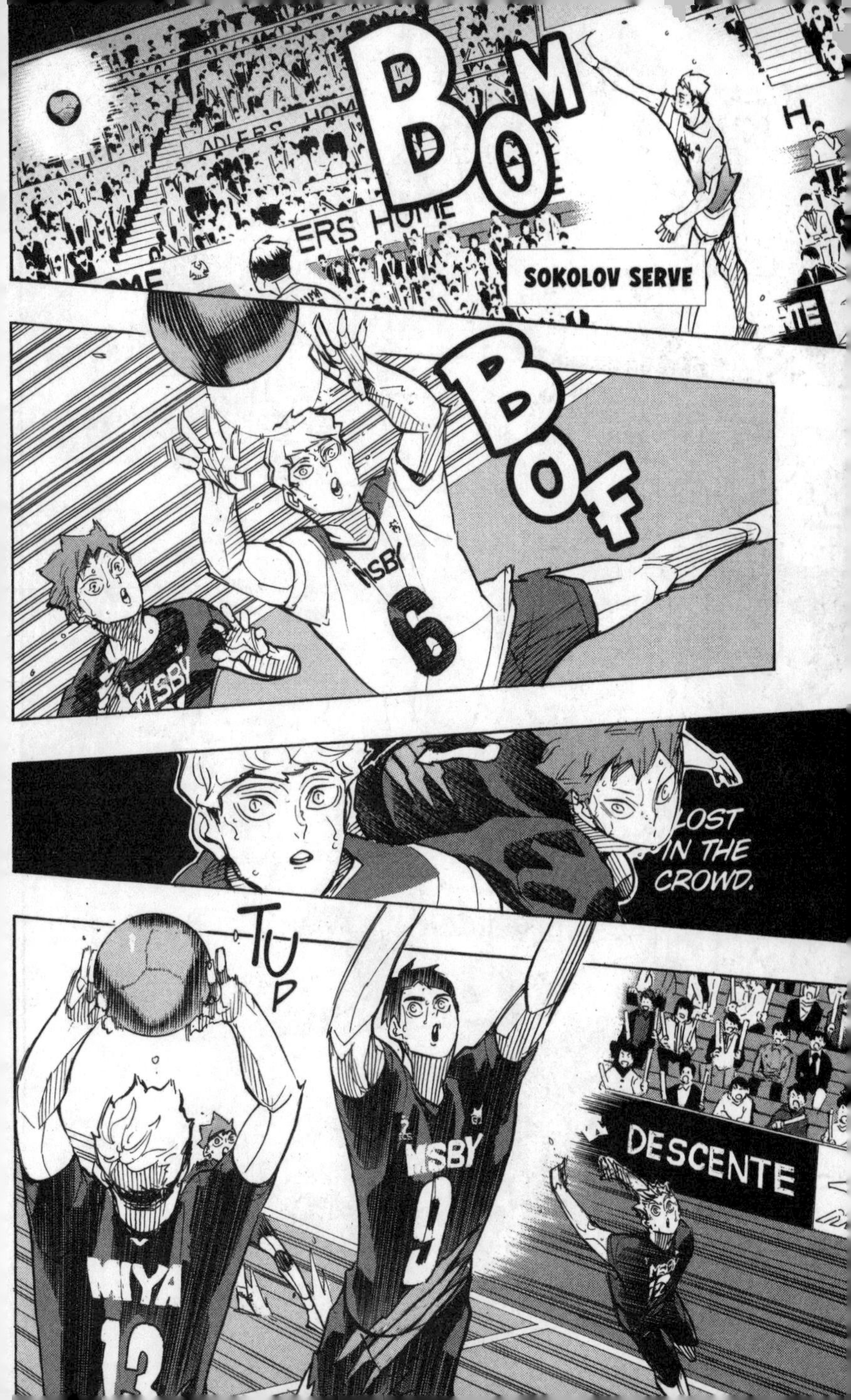
BOOM
SOKOLOV SERVE
ERS HOME
BOOF
LOST IN THE CROWD.
TUP
DESCENTE
MSBY
9
MIYA
13

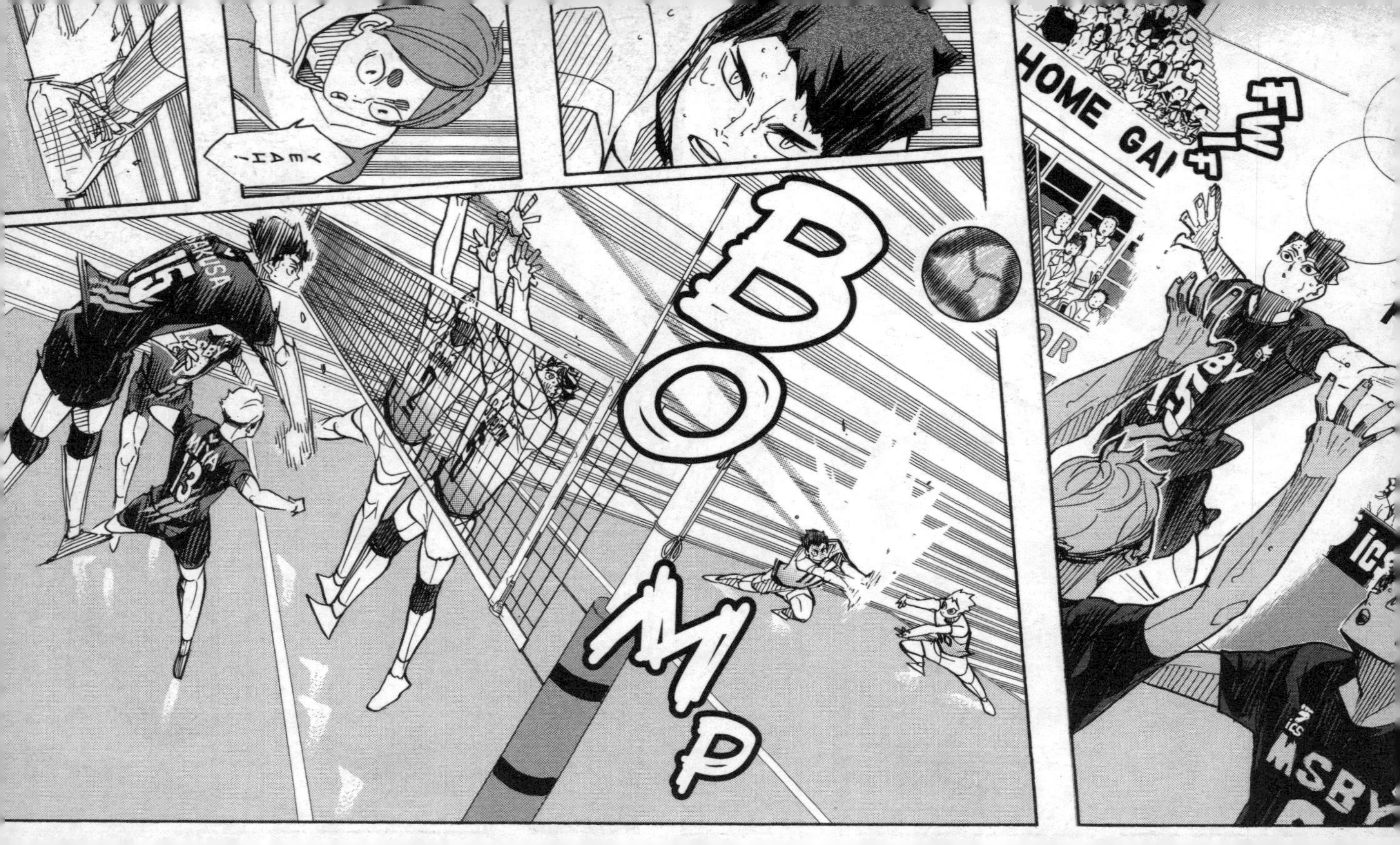

HOME GAI
FWIF
BOMP
YEAH!

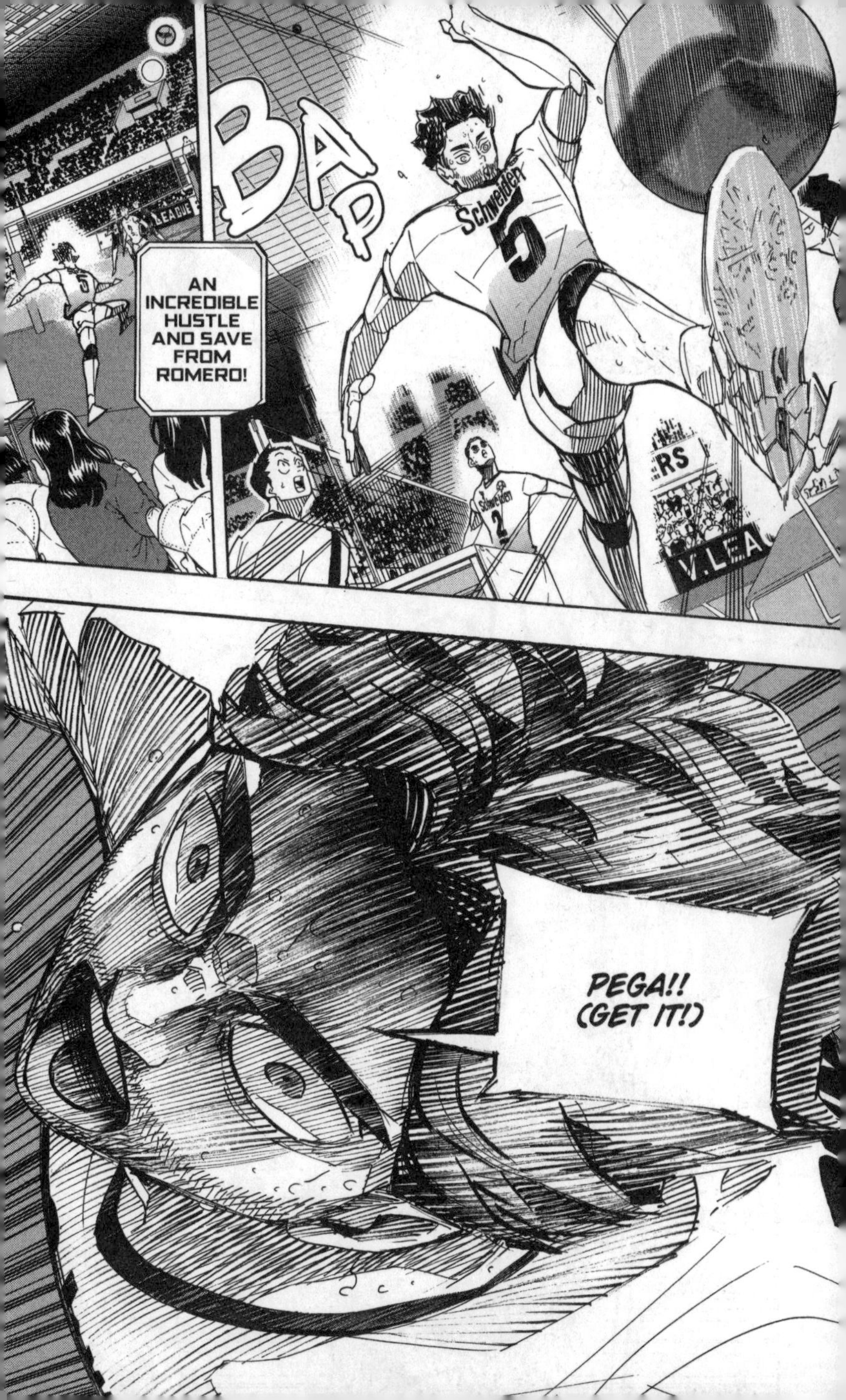
BAP
AN INCREDIBLE HUSTLE AND SAVE FROM ROMERO!
PEGA!! (GET IT!)

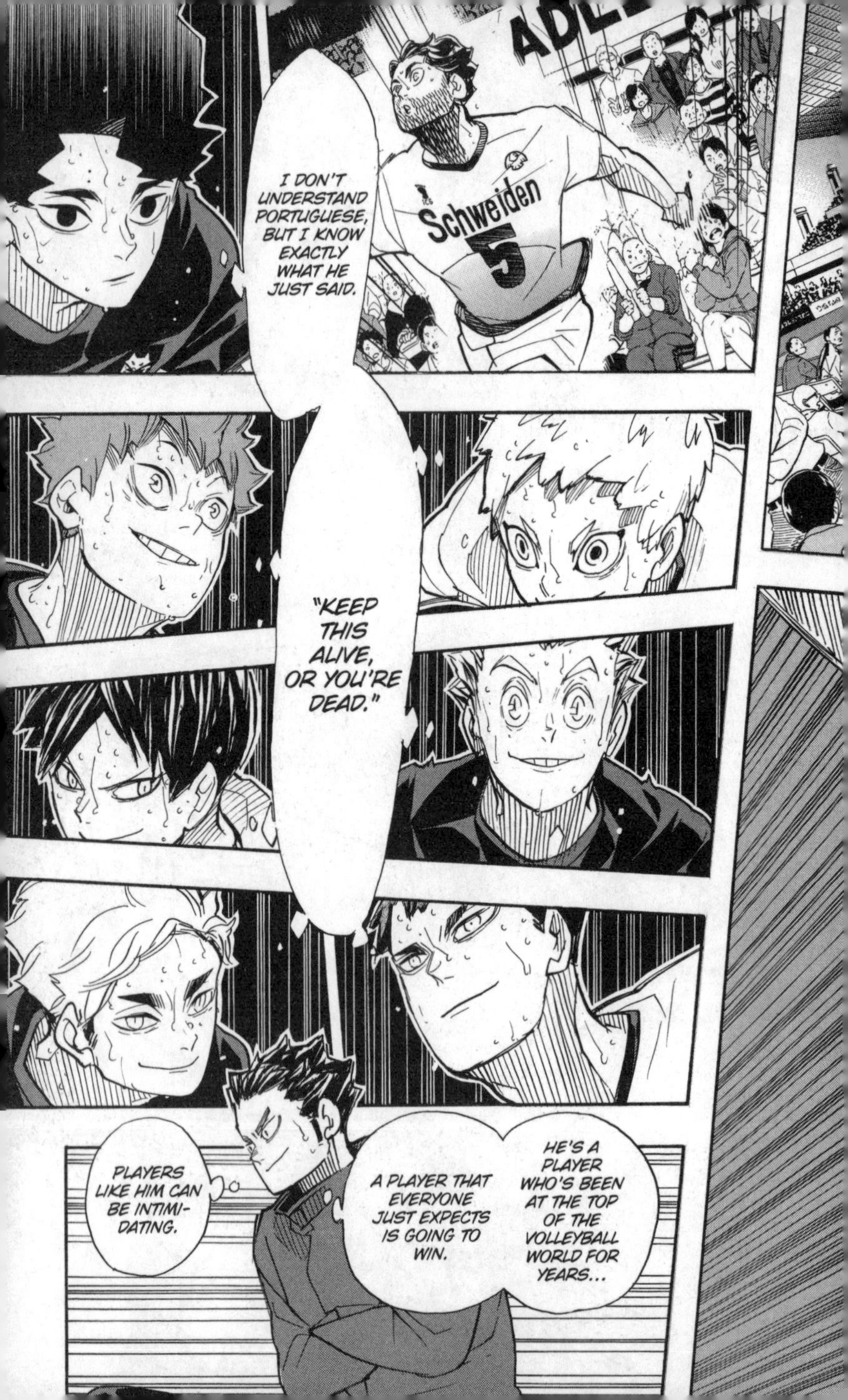

ADL
Schweiden
I DON'T UNDERSTAND PORTUGUESE, BUT I KNOW EXACTLY WHAT HE JUST SAID.
"KEEP THIS ALIVE, OR YOU'RE DEAD."
HE'S A PLAYER WHO'S BEEN AT THE TOP OF THE VOLLEYBALL WORLD FOR YEARS...
A PLAYER THAT EVERYONE JUST EXPECTS IS GOING TO WIN.
PLAYERS LIKE HIM CAN BE INTIMI-DATING.

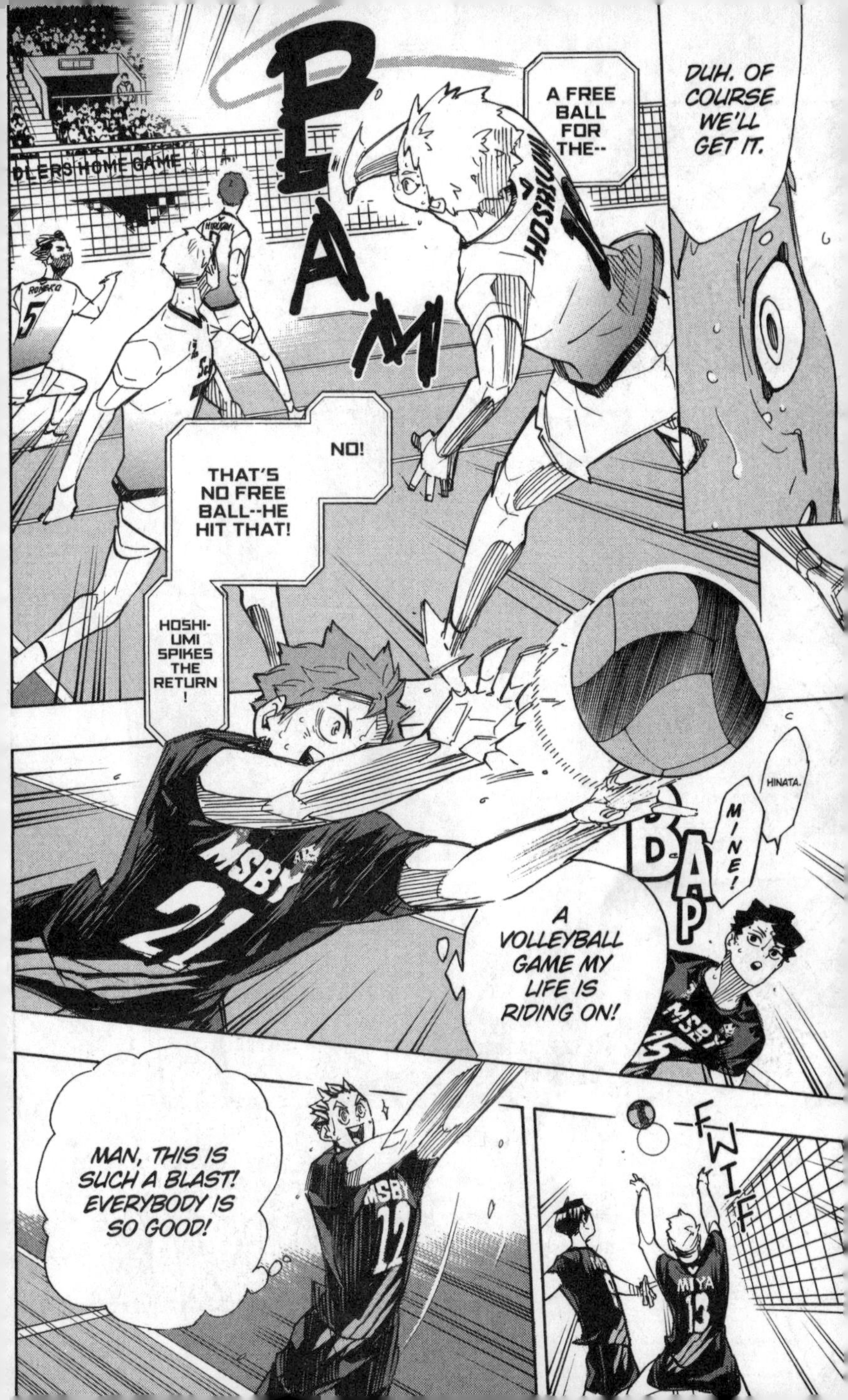
DUH. OF COURSE WE'LL GET IT.
BAM
A FREE BALL FOR THE--
DLERS HOME GAME
NO!
THAT'S NO FREE BALL--HE HIT THAT!
HOSHI-UMI SPIKES THE RETURN!
HINATA.
MINE!
BDAP
A VOLLEYBALL GAME MY LIFE IS RIDING ON!
FWIF
MAN, THIS IS SUCH A BLAST! EVERYBODY IS SO GOOD!

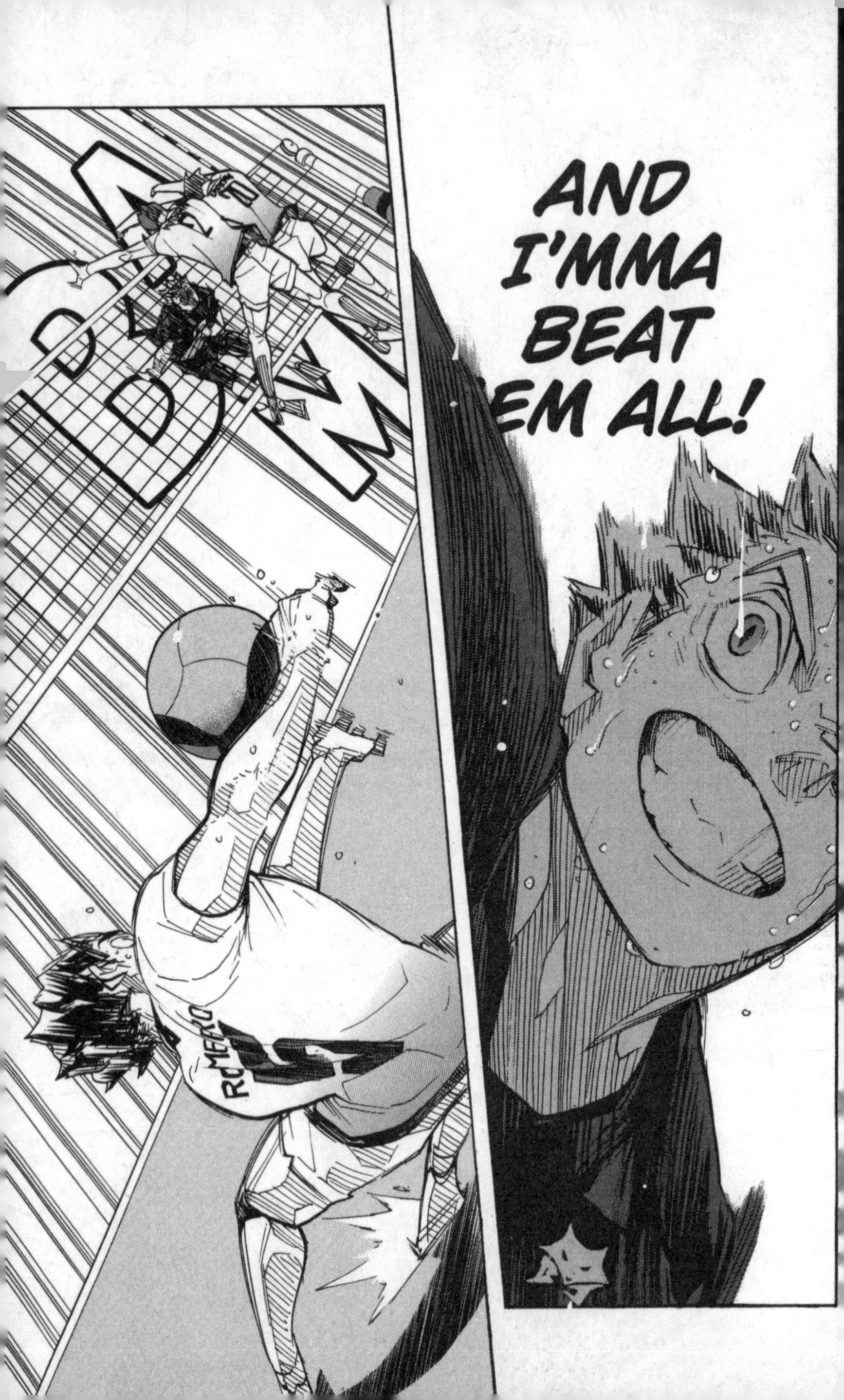
AND I'MMA BEAT 'EM ALL!

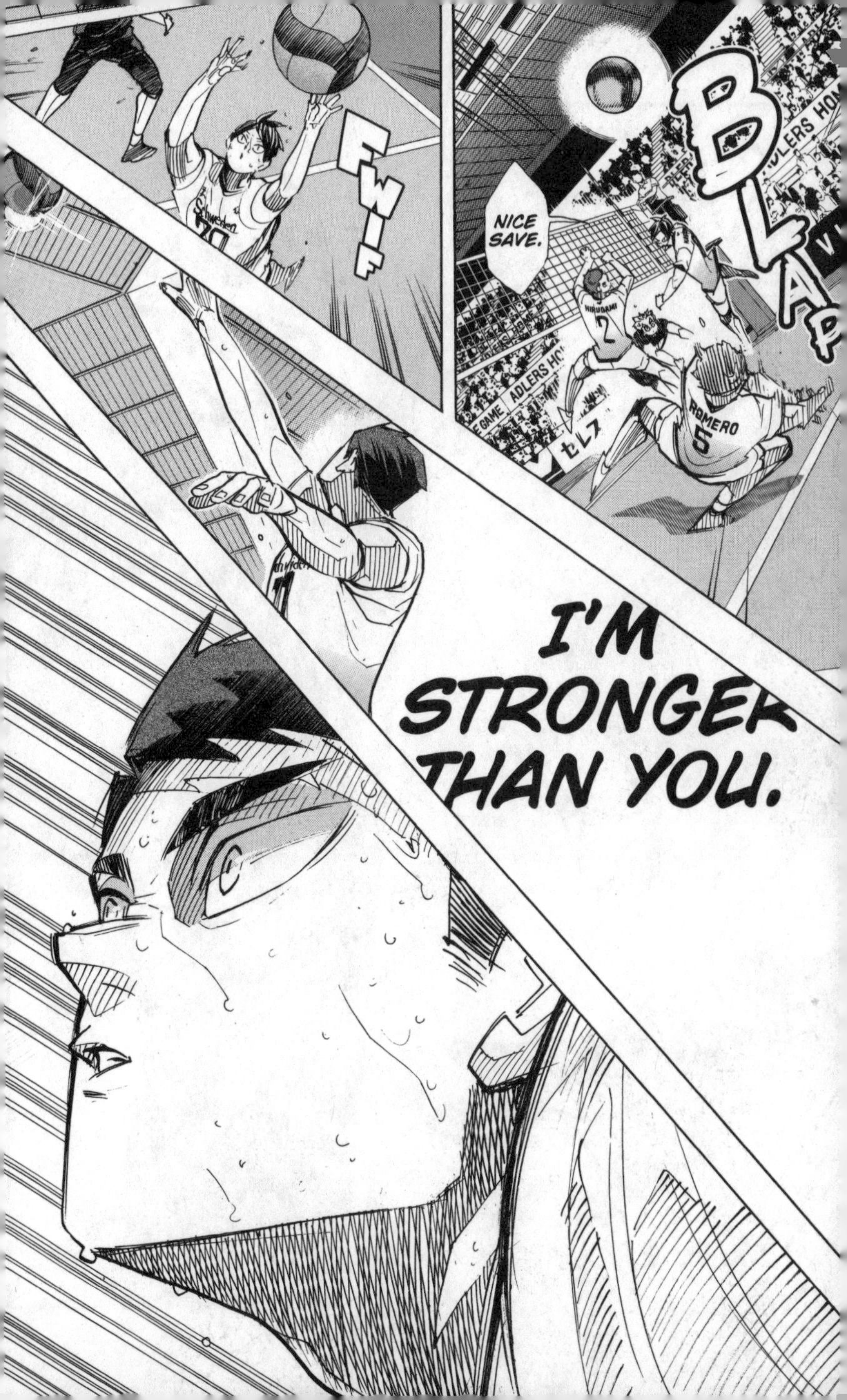
BLAP
NICE SAVE.
FWIF
I'M STRONGER THAN YOU.

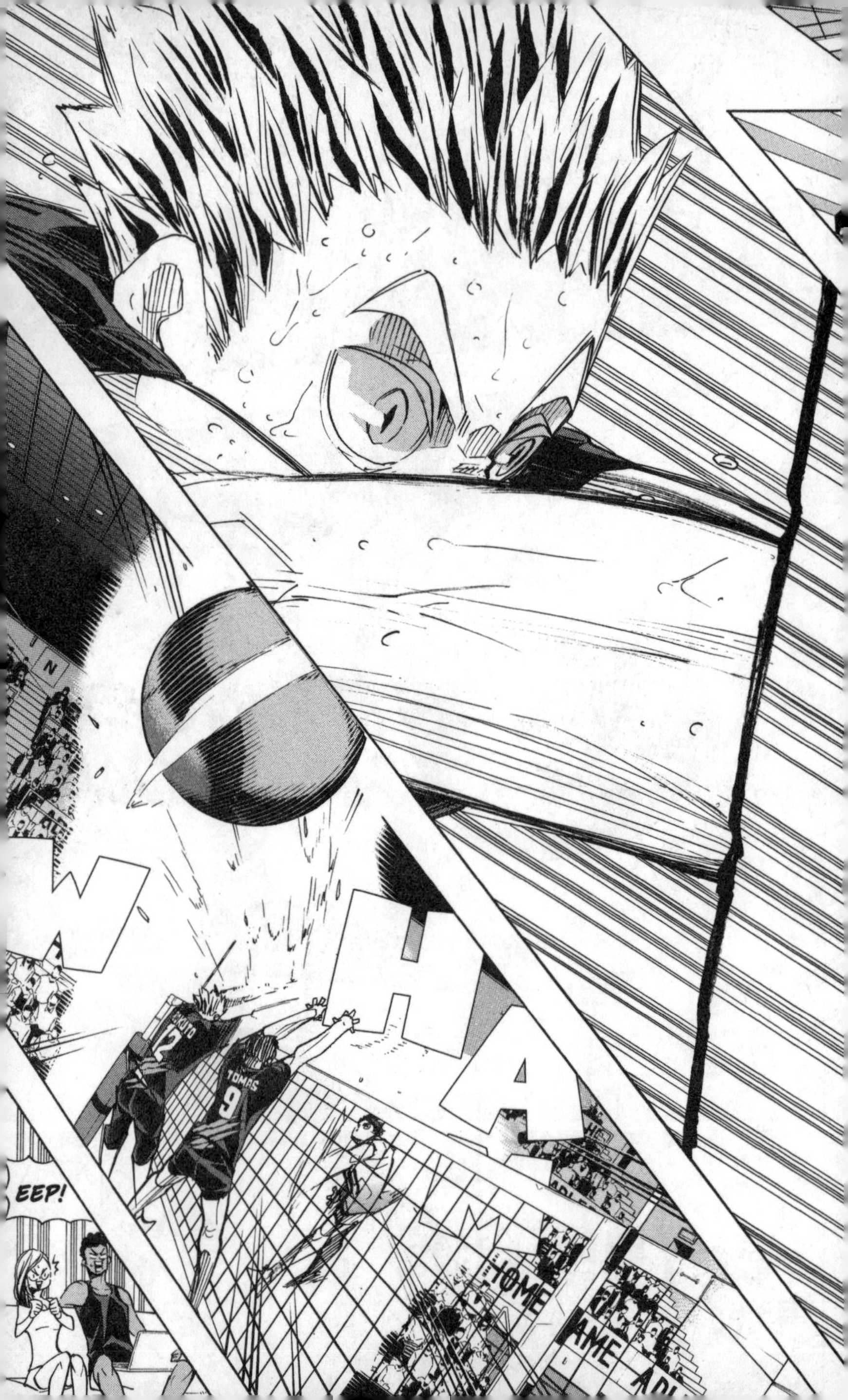
WHAM
EEP!

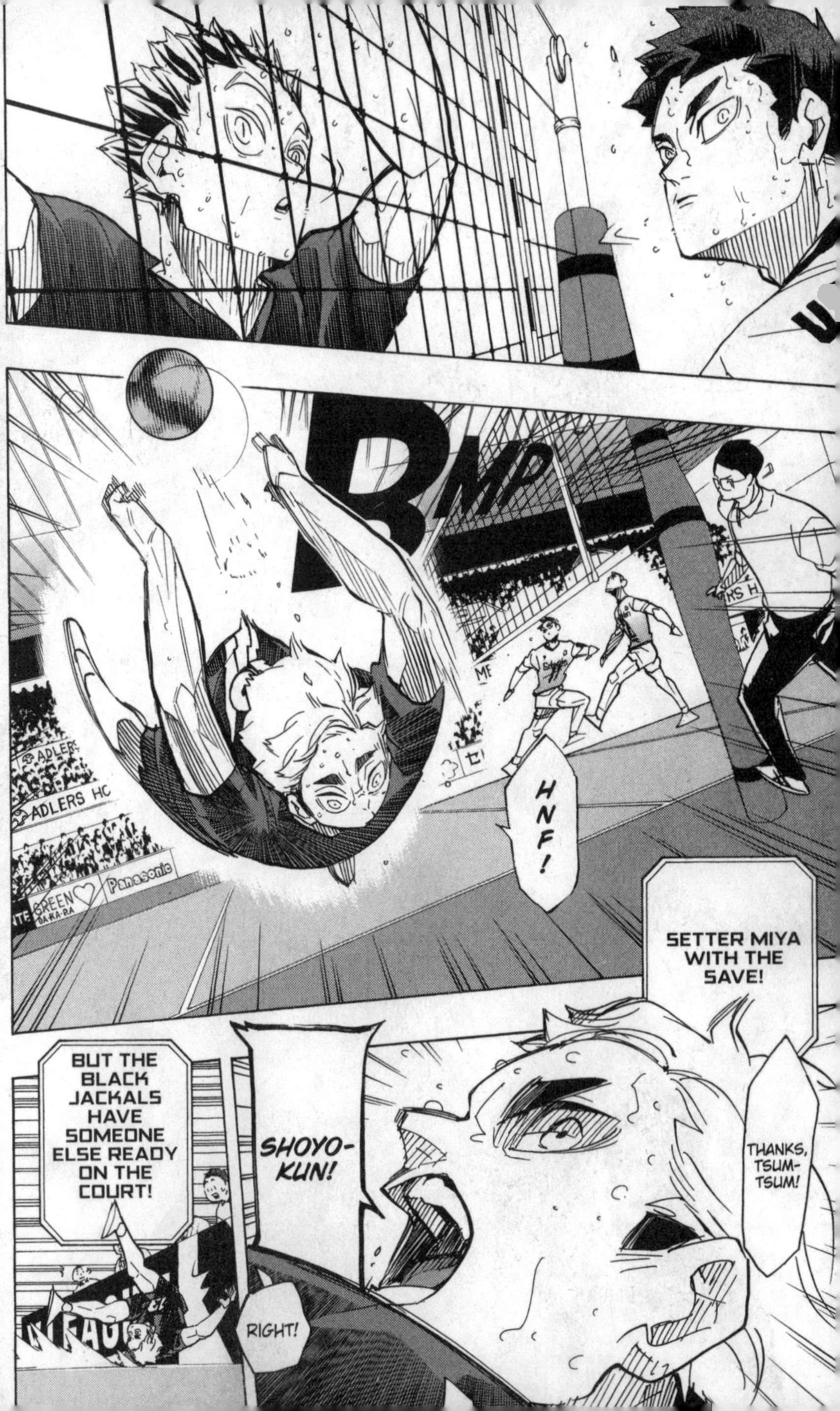
BMP
HNF!
ADLERS
ADLERS HC
GREEN DA-KA-RA
Panasonic
SETTER MIYA WITH THE SAVE!
THANKS, TSUM-TSUM!
SHOYO-KUN!
BUT THE BLACK JACKALS HAVE SOMEONE ELSE READY ON THE COURT!
RIGHT!

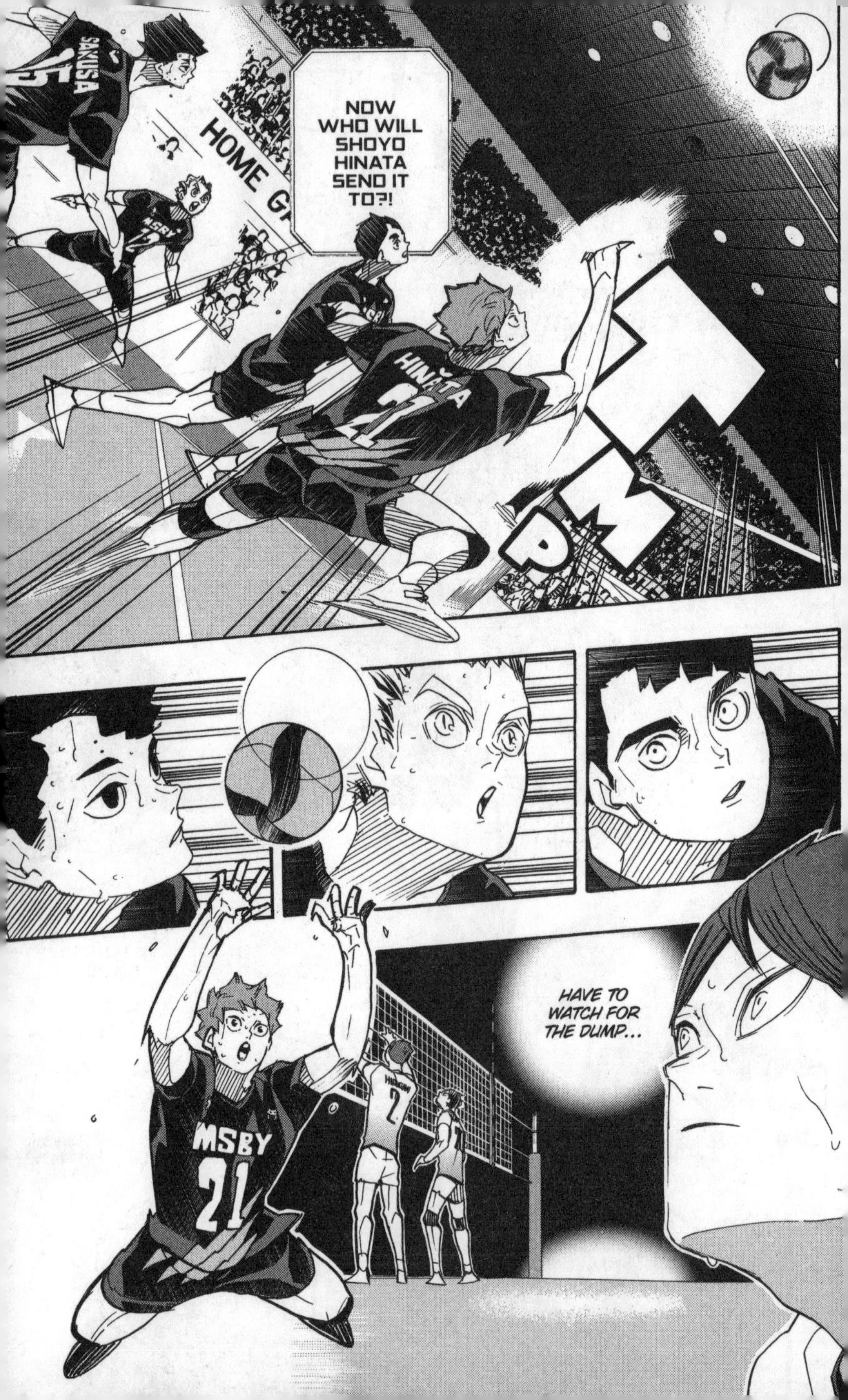

NOW WHO WILL SHOYO HINATA SEND IT TO?!
HAVE TO WATCH FOR THE DUMP...

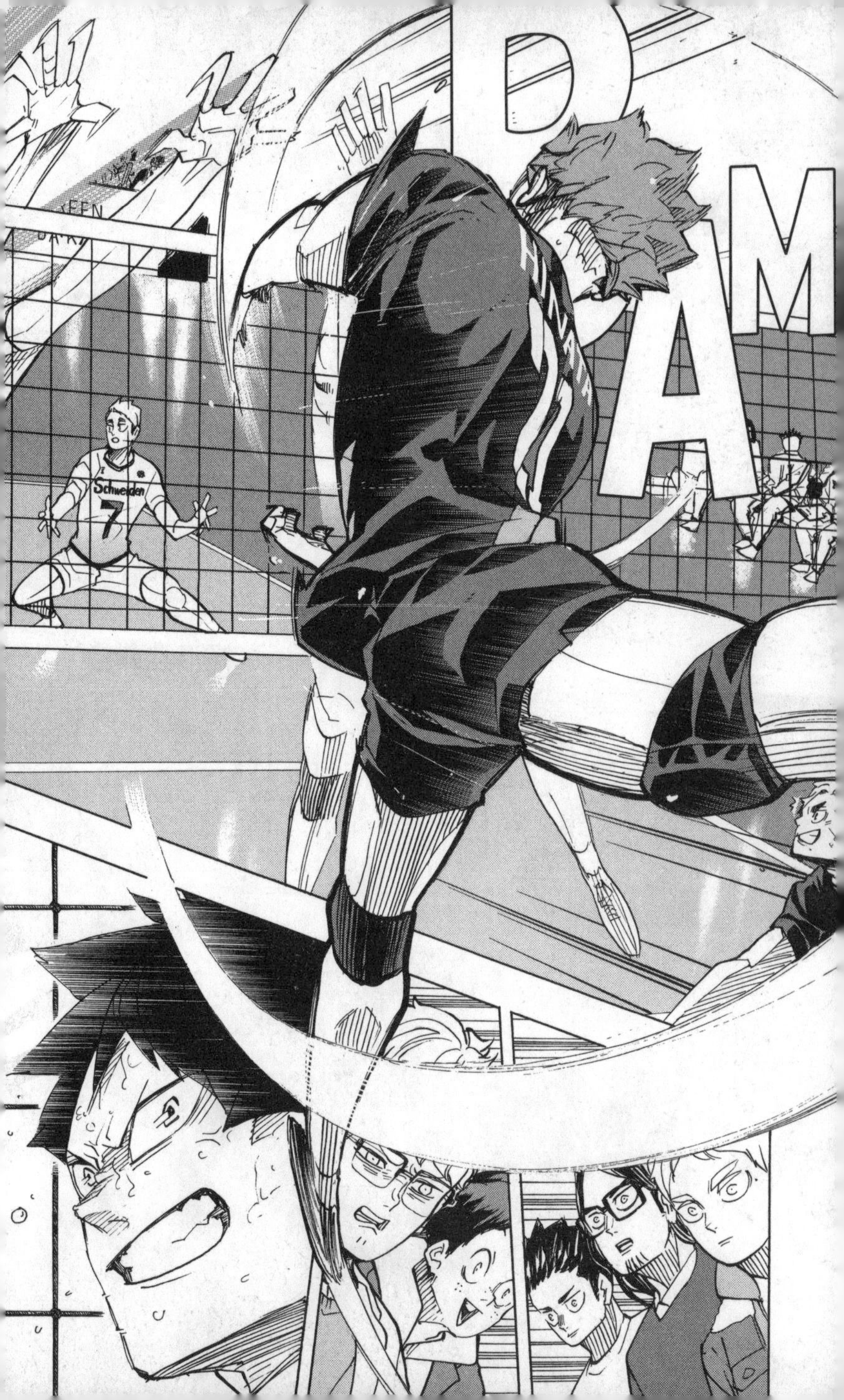
DAM
HINATA
Schweden
7

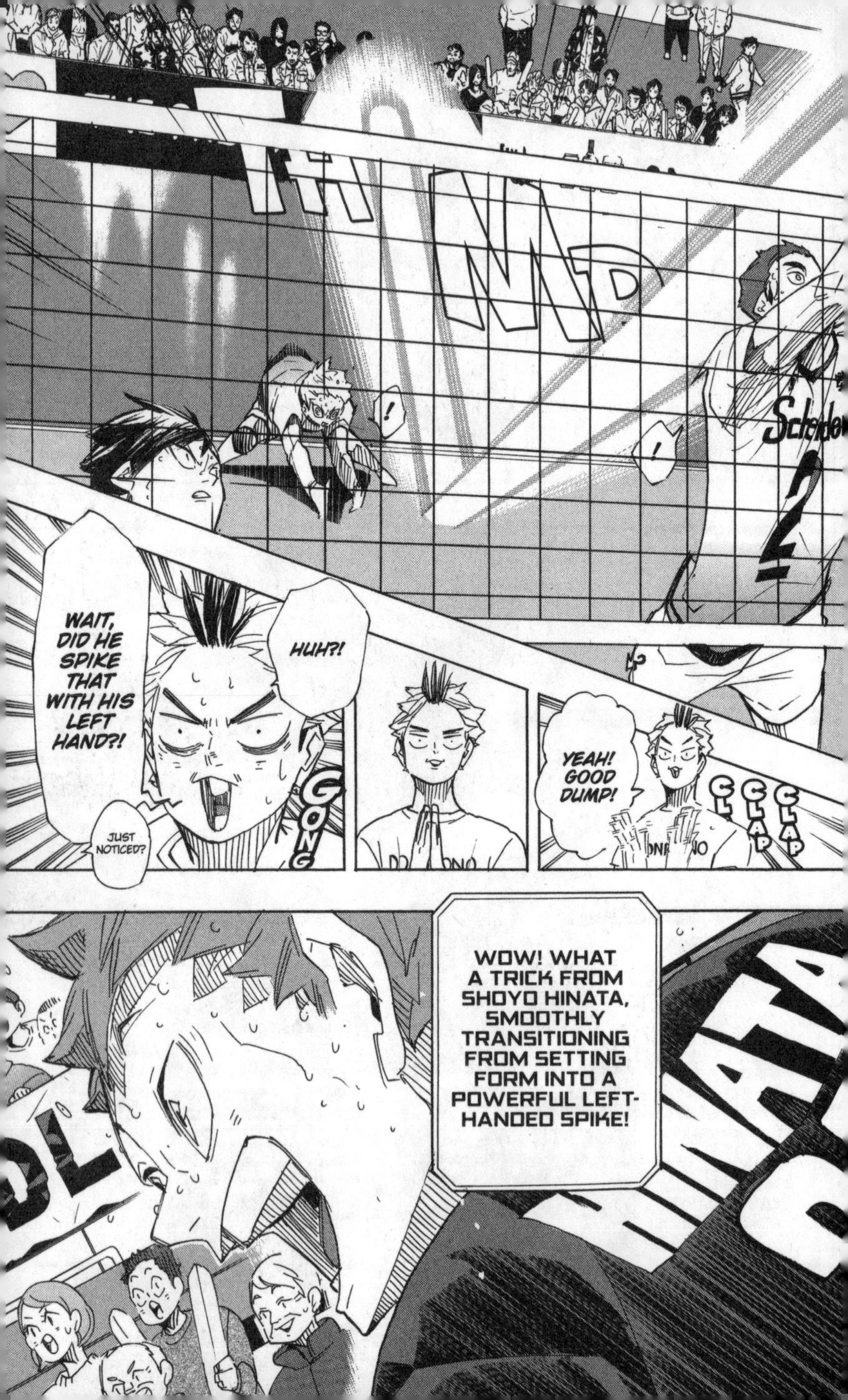
!
!
YEAH! GOOD DUMP!
CLAP
CLAP
CLAP
HUH?!
WAIT, DID HE SPIKE THAT WITH HIS LEFT HAND?!
GONG
JUST NOTICED?
WOW! WHAT A TRICK FROM SHOYO HINATA, SMOOTHLY TRANSITIONING FROM SETTING FORM INTO A POWERFUL LEFT-HANDED SPIKE!

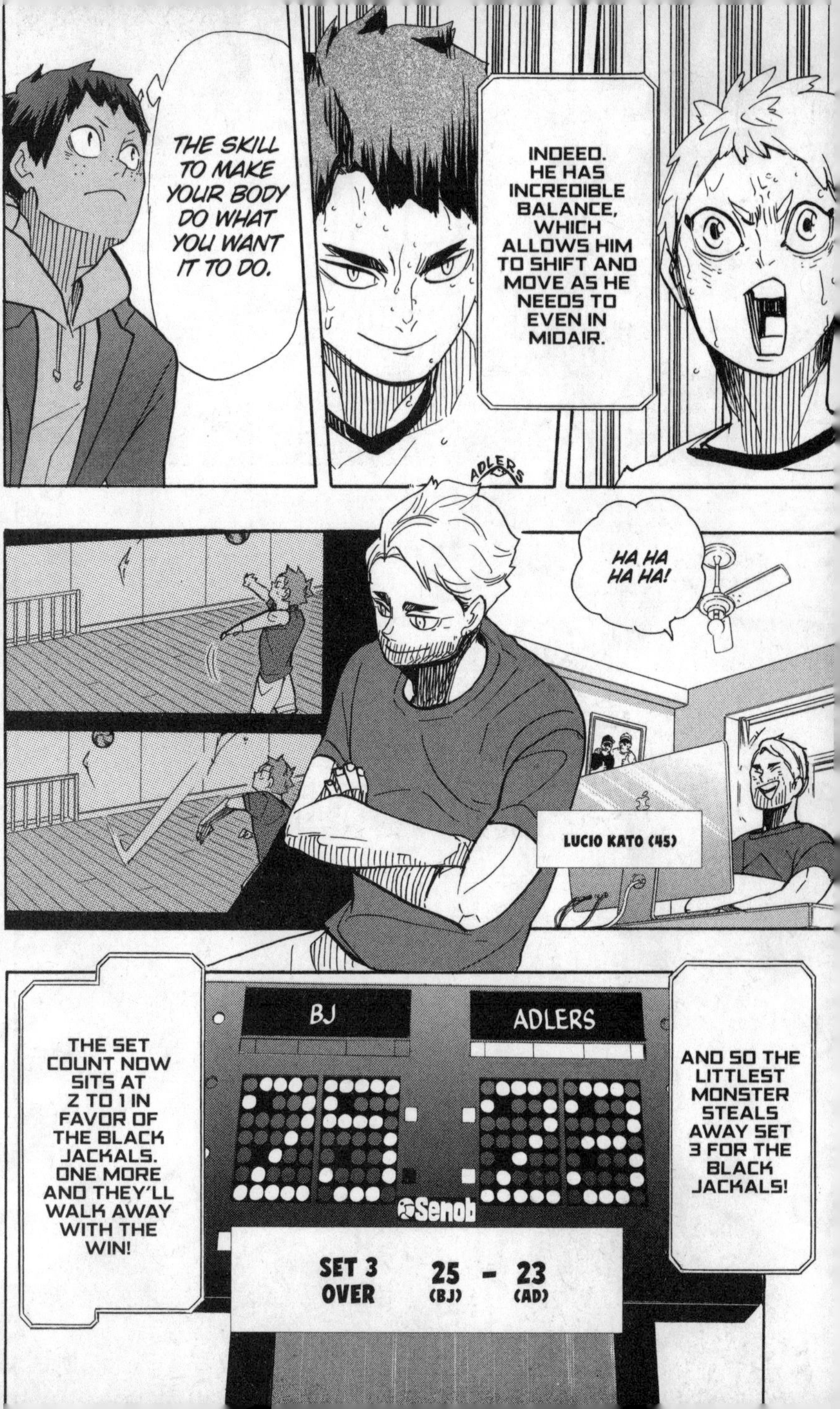
INDEED. HE HAS INCREDIBLE BALANCE, WHICH ALLOWS HIM TO SHIFT AND MOVE AS HE NEEDS TO EVEN IN MIDAIR.
THE SKILL TO MAKE YOUR BODY DO WHAT YOU WANT IT TO DO.
ADLERS
HA HA HA HA!
LUCIO KATO (45)
AND SO THE LITTLEST MONSTER STEALS AWAY SET 3 FOR THE BLACK JACKALS!
BJ
ADLERS
Senob
SET 3 OVER 25 (BJ) - 23 (AD)
THE SET COUNT NOW SITS AT 2 TO 1 IN FAVOR OF THE BLACK JACKALS. ONE MORE AND THEY'LL WALK AWAY WITH THE WIN!

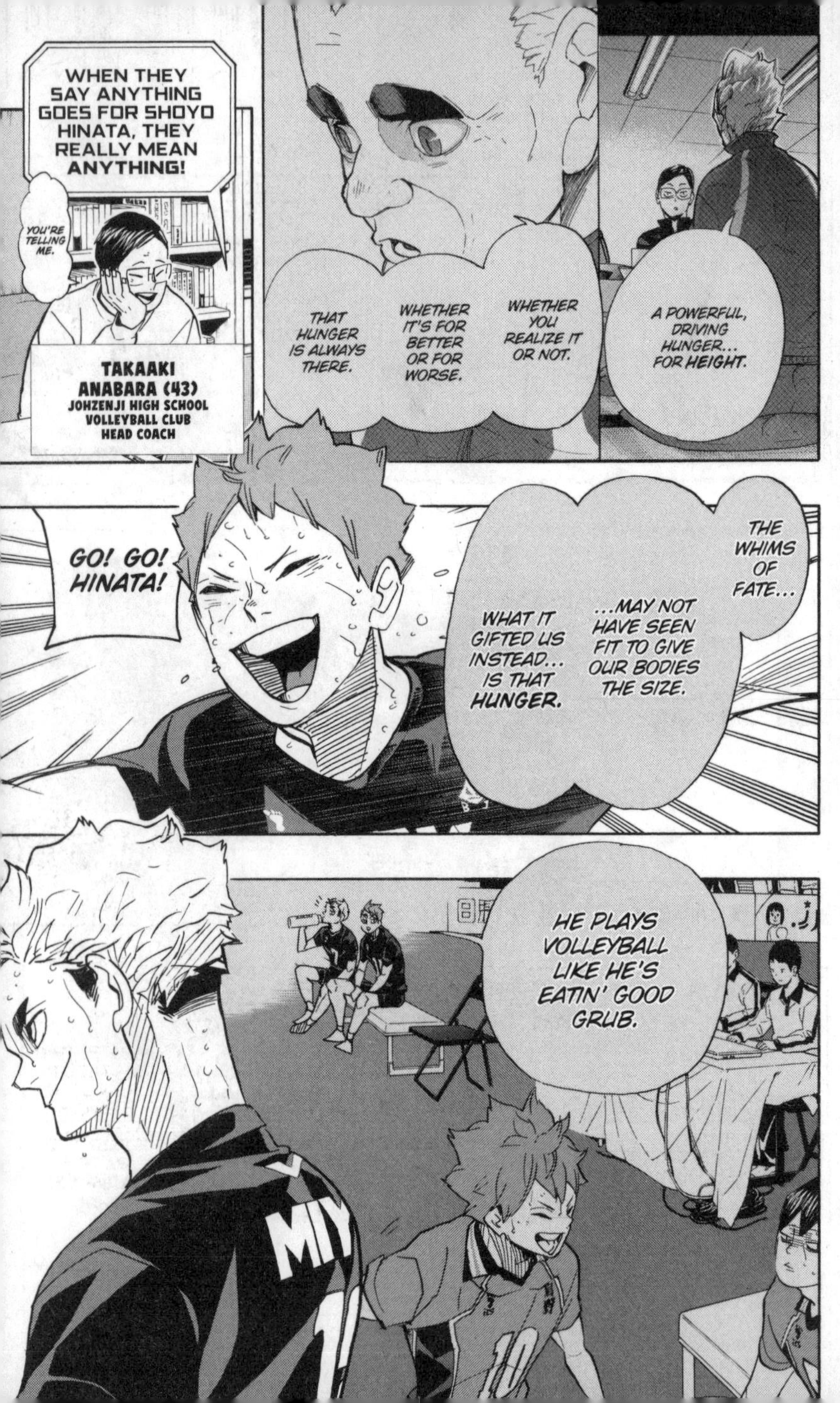
A POWERFUL, DRIVING HUNGER... FOR HEIGHT.
WHETHER YOU REALIZE IT OR NOT.
WHETHER IT'S FOR BETTER OR FOR WORSE.
THAT HUNGER IS ALWAYS THERE.
WHEN THEY SAY ANYTHING GOES FOR SHOYO HINATA, THEY REALLY MEAN ANYTHING!
YOU'RE TELLING ME.
TAKAAKI ANABARA (43)
JOHZENJI HIGH SCHOOL VOLLEYBALL CLUB HEAD COACH
THE WHIMS OF FATE...
...MAY NOT HAVE SEEN FIT TO GIVE OUR BODIES THE SIZE.
WHAT IT GIFTED US INSTEAD... IS THAT HUNGER.
GO! GO! HINATA!
HE PLAYS VOLLEYBALL LIKE HE'S EATIN' GOOD GRUB.

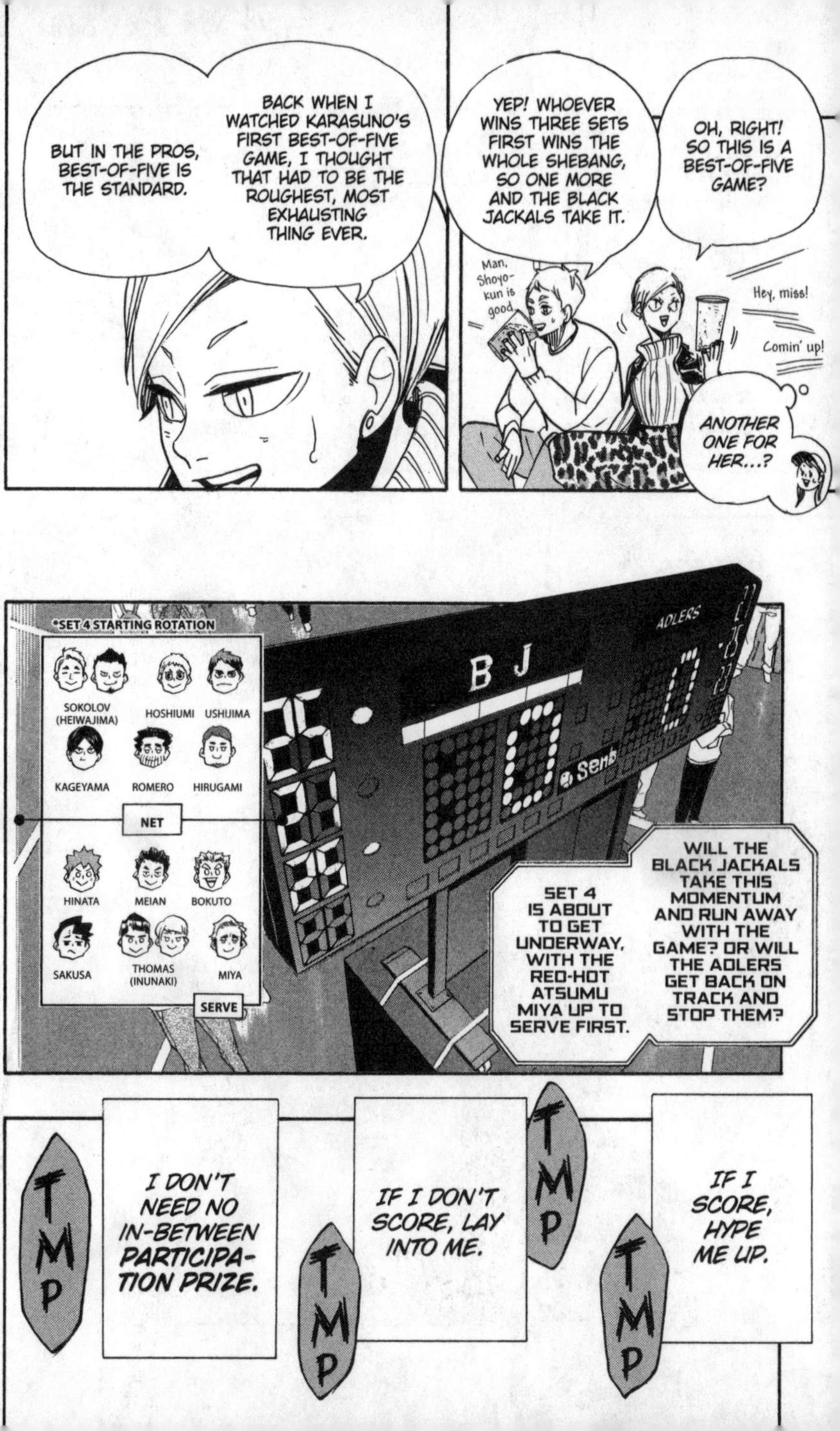
OH, RIGHT! SO THIS IS A BEST-OF-FIVE GAME?
YEP! WHOEVER WINS THREE SETS FIRST WINS THE WHOLE SHEBANG, SO ONE MORE AND THE BLACK JACKALS TAKE IT.
Hey, miss!
Comin' up!
Man, Shoyo-kun is good
ANOTHER ONE FOR HER...?
BACK WHEN I WATCHED KARASUNO'S FIRST BEST-OF-FIVE GAME, I THOUGHT THAT HAD TO BE THE ROUGHEST, MOST EXHAUSTING THING EVER.
BUT IN THE PROS, BEST-OF-FIVE IS THE STANDARD.
ADLERS
B J
*SET 4 STARTING ROTATION
SOKOLOV (HEIWAJIMA)
HOSHIUMI
USHIJIMA
KAGEYAMA
ROMERO
HIRUGAMI
NET
HINATA
MEIAN
BOKUTO
SAKUSA
THOMAS (INUNAKI)
MIYA
SERVE
WILL THE BLACK JACKALS TAKE THIS MOMENTUM AND RUN AWAY WITH THE GAME? OR WILL THE ADLERS GET BACK ON TRACK AND STOP THEM?
SET 4 IS ABOUT TO GET UNDERWAY, WITH THE RED-HOT ATSUMU MIYA UP TO SERVE FIRST.
IF I SCORE, HYPE ME UP.
TMP
TMP
IF I DON'T SCORE, LAY INTO ME.
TMP
I DON'T NEED NO IN-BETWEEN PARTICIPATION PRIZE.
TMP

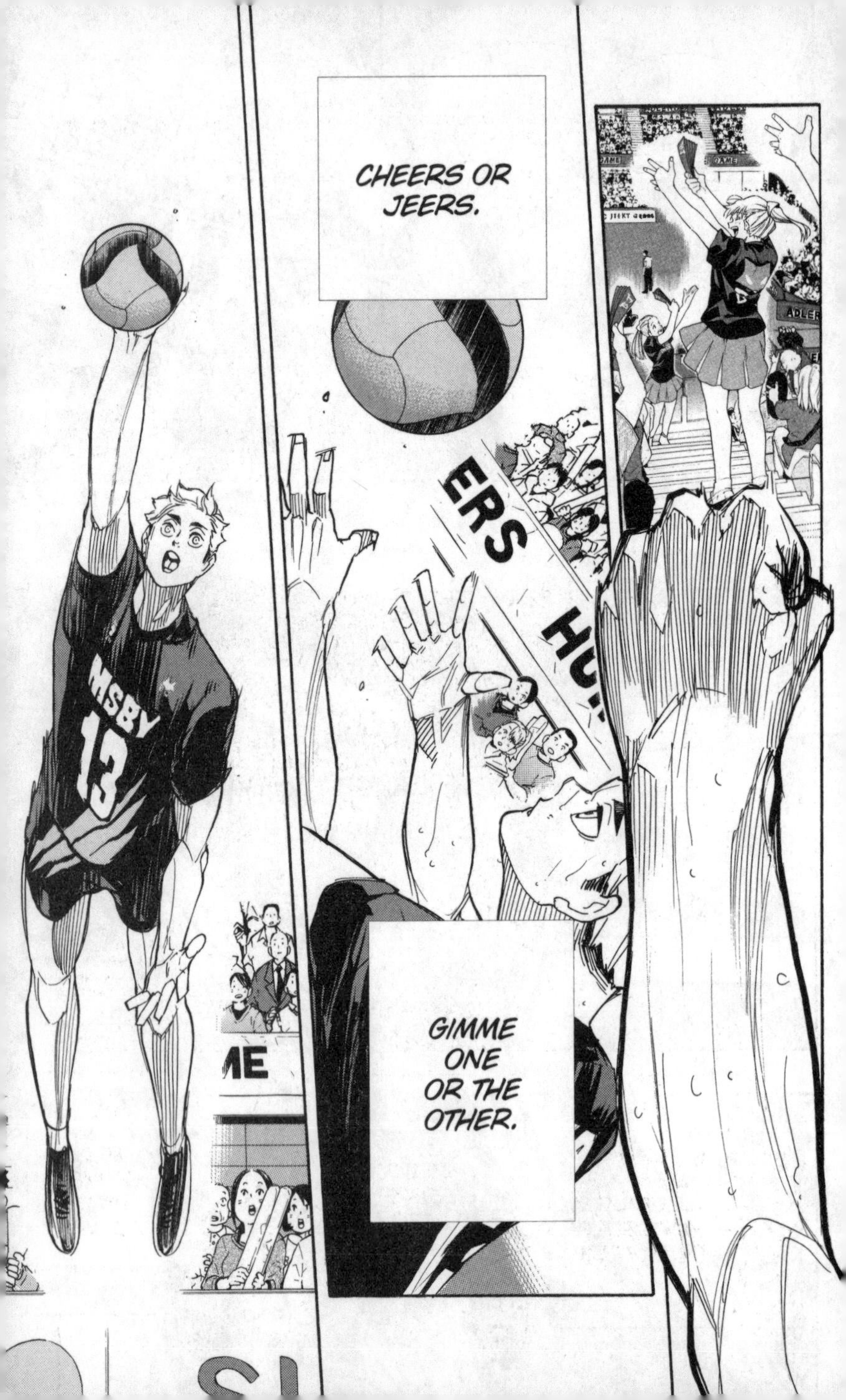
ADLER
CHEERS OR JEERS.
GIMME ONE OR THE OTHER.
MSBY
13

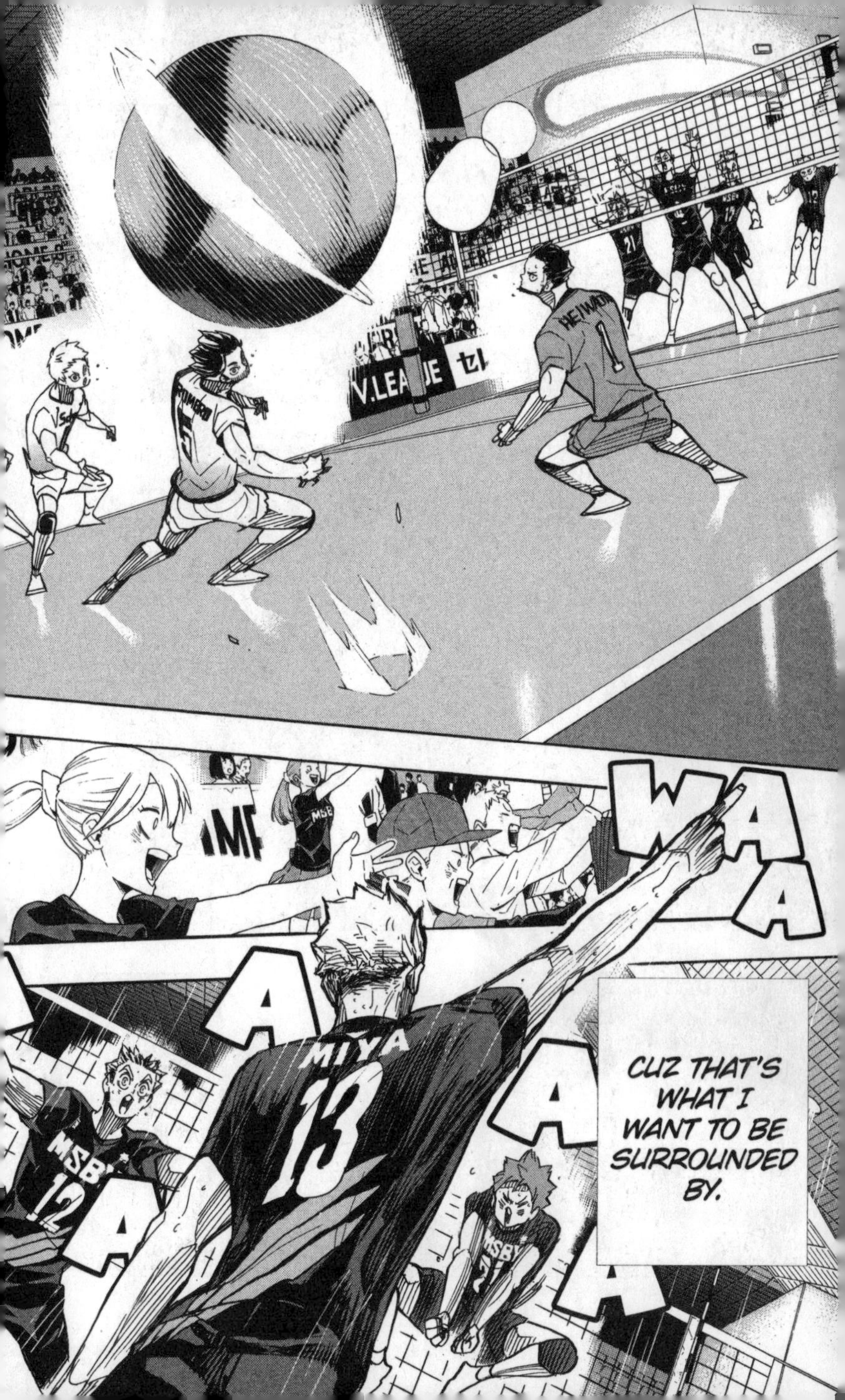
HEIWA 1
WAAAAAA
MIYA 13
MSBY 12
CUZ THAT'S WHAT I WANT TO BE SURROUNDED BY.

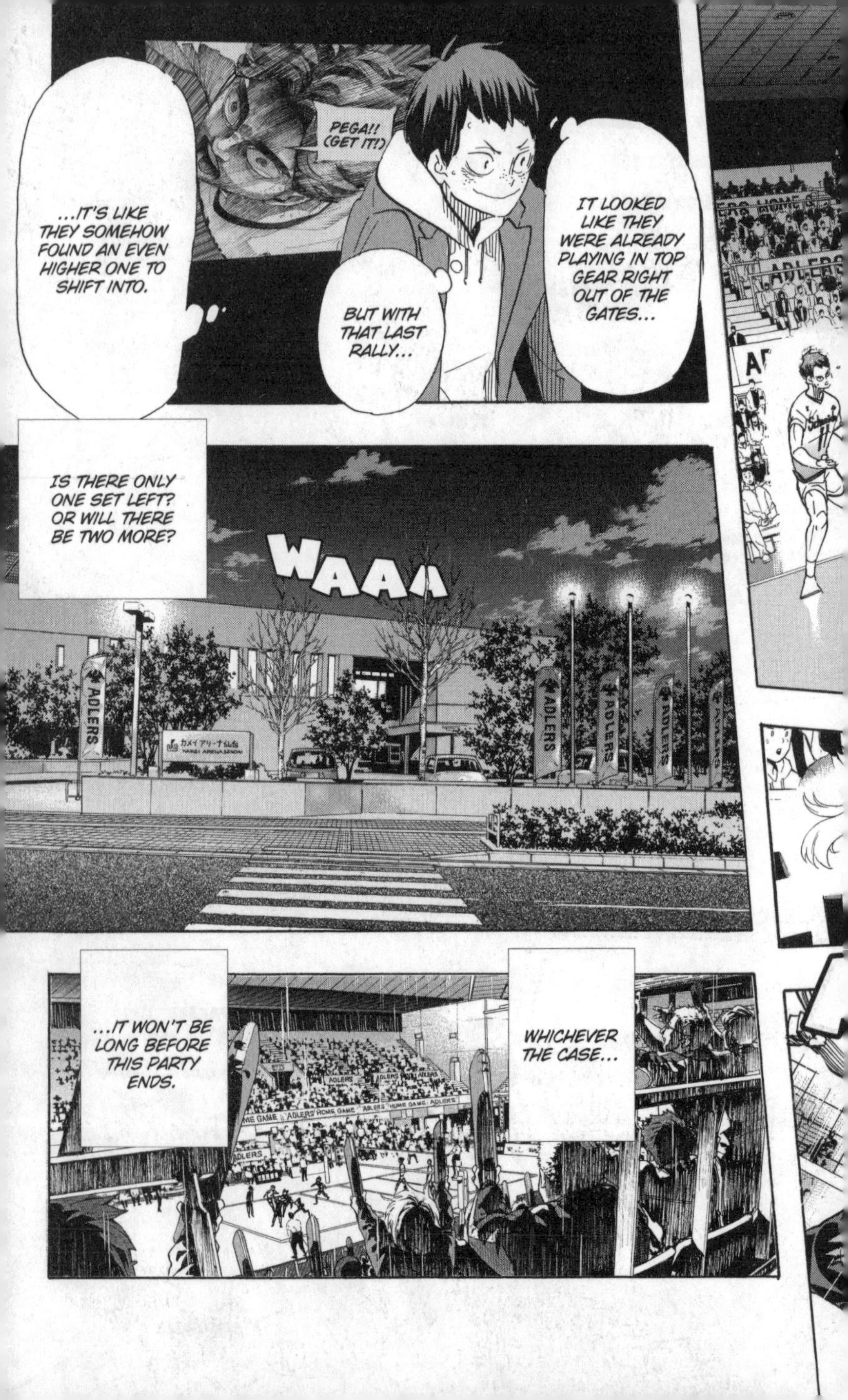

IT LOOKED LIKE THEY WERE ALREADY PLAYING IN TOP GEAR RIGHT OUT OF THE GATES...
BUT WITH THAT LAST RALLY...
PEGA!! (GET IT!)
...IT'S LIKE THEY SOMEHOW FOUND AN EVEN HIGHER ONE TO SHIFT INTO.
WAAA
IS THERE ONLY ONE SET LEFT? OR WILL THERE BE TWO MORE?
ADLERS
WHICHEVER THE CASE...
...IT WON'T BE LONG BEFORE THIS PARTY ENDS.

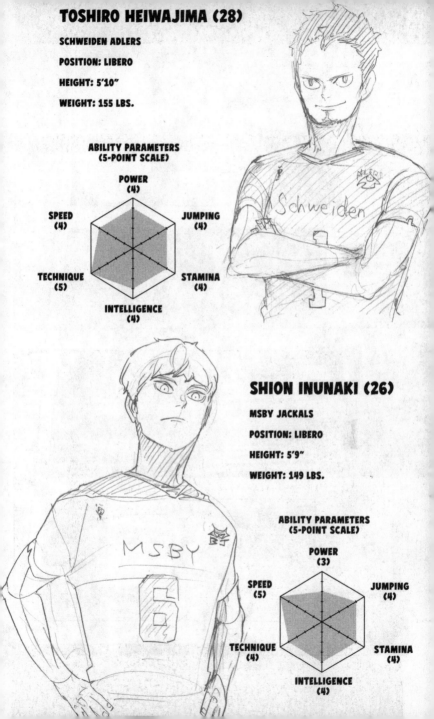

TOSHIRO HEIWAJIMA (28)

SCHWEIDEN ADLERS

POSITION: LIBERO

HEIGHT: 5'10"

WEIGHT: 155 LBS.

ABILITY PARAMETERS (5-POINT SCALE)

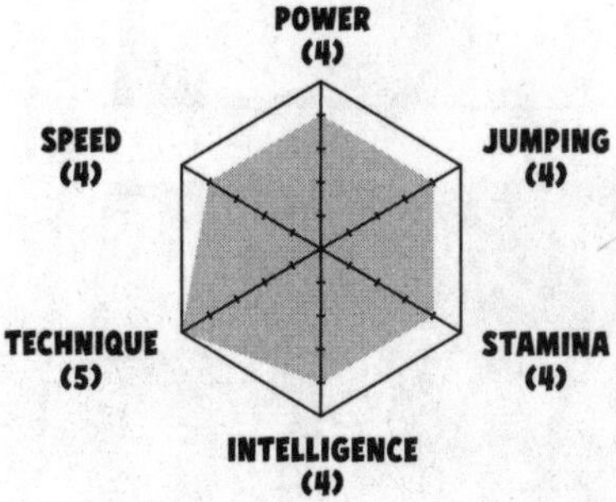
POWER (4)
JUMPING (4)
STAMINA (4)
INTELLIGENCE (4)
TECHNIQUE (5)
SPEED (4)

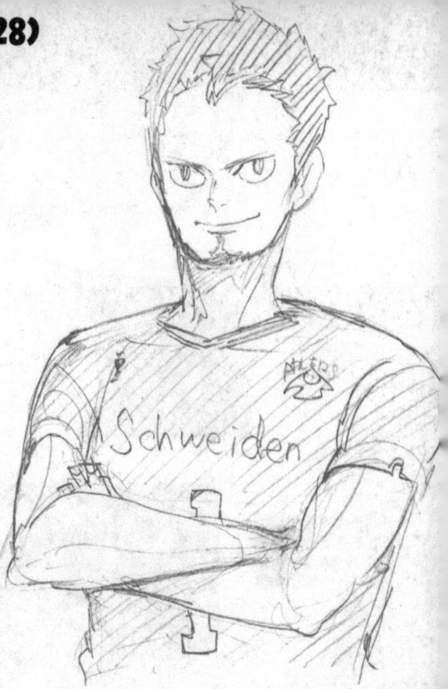
Schweiden

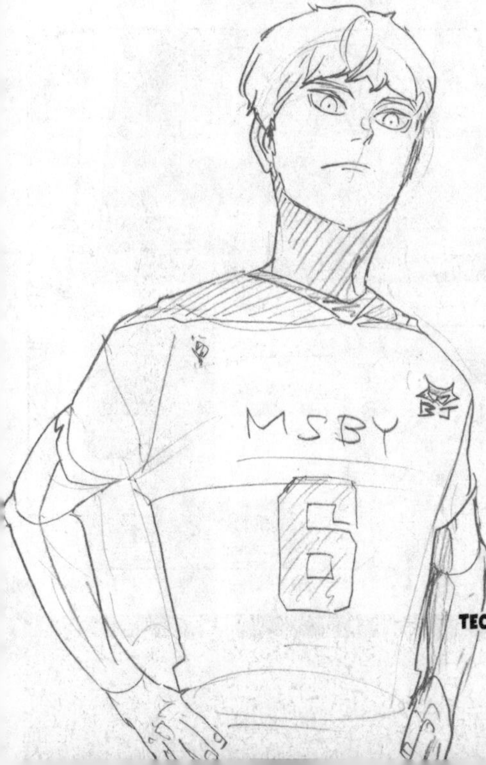
MSBY
6

SHION INUNAKI (26)

MSBY JACKALS

POSITION: LIBERO

HEIGHT: 5'9"

WEIGHT: 149 LBS.

ABILITY PARAMETERS (5-POINT SCALE)

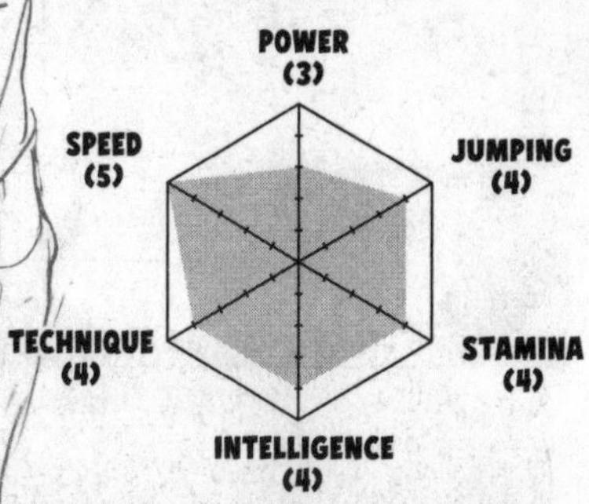
POWER (3)
JUMPING (4)
STAMINA (4)
INTELLIGENCE (4)
TECHNIQUE (4)
SPEED (5)

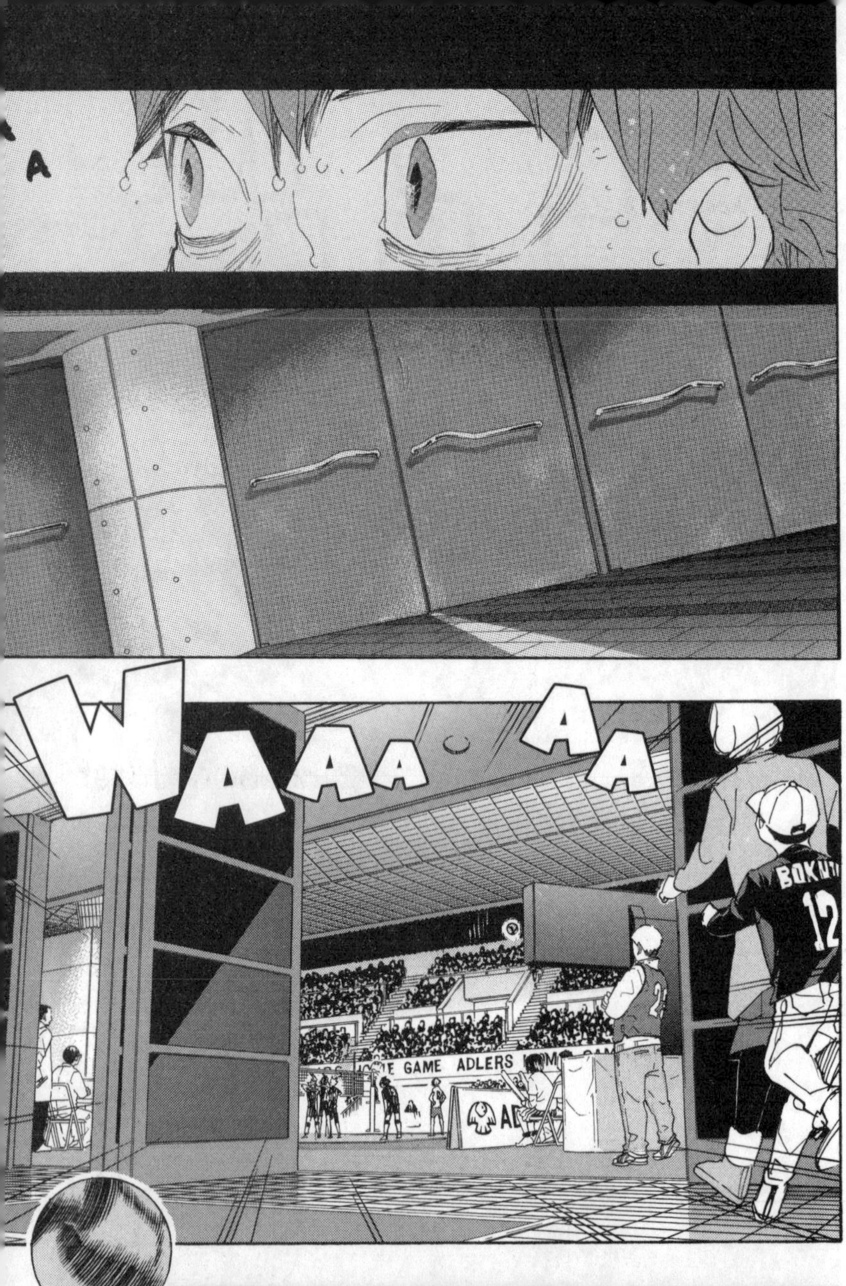
A
WAAAA
AA
GAME
ADLERS

CHAPTER 397: ▷ LOAD SAVE

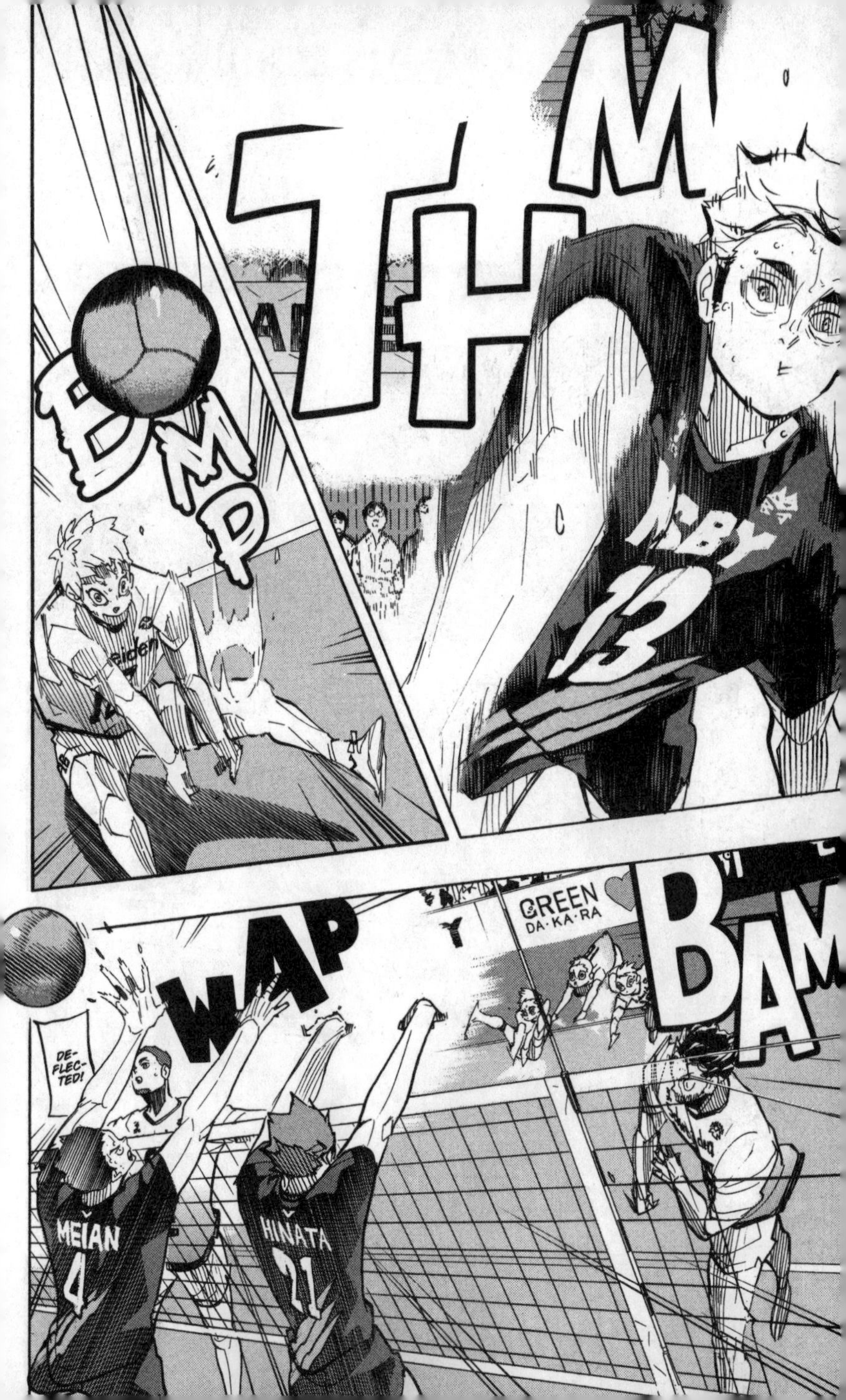
M
TH
BY
13
BMP
BAM
GREEN
DA·KA·RA
WAP
DE-FLECTED!
MEIAN
4
HINATA
21

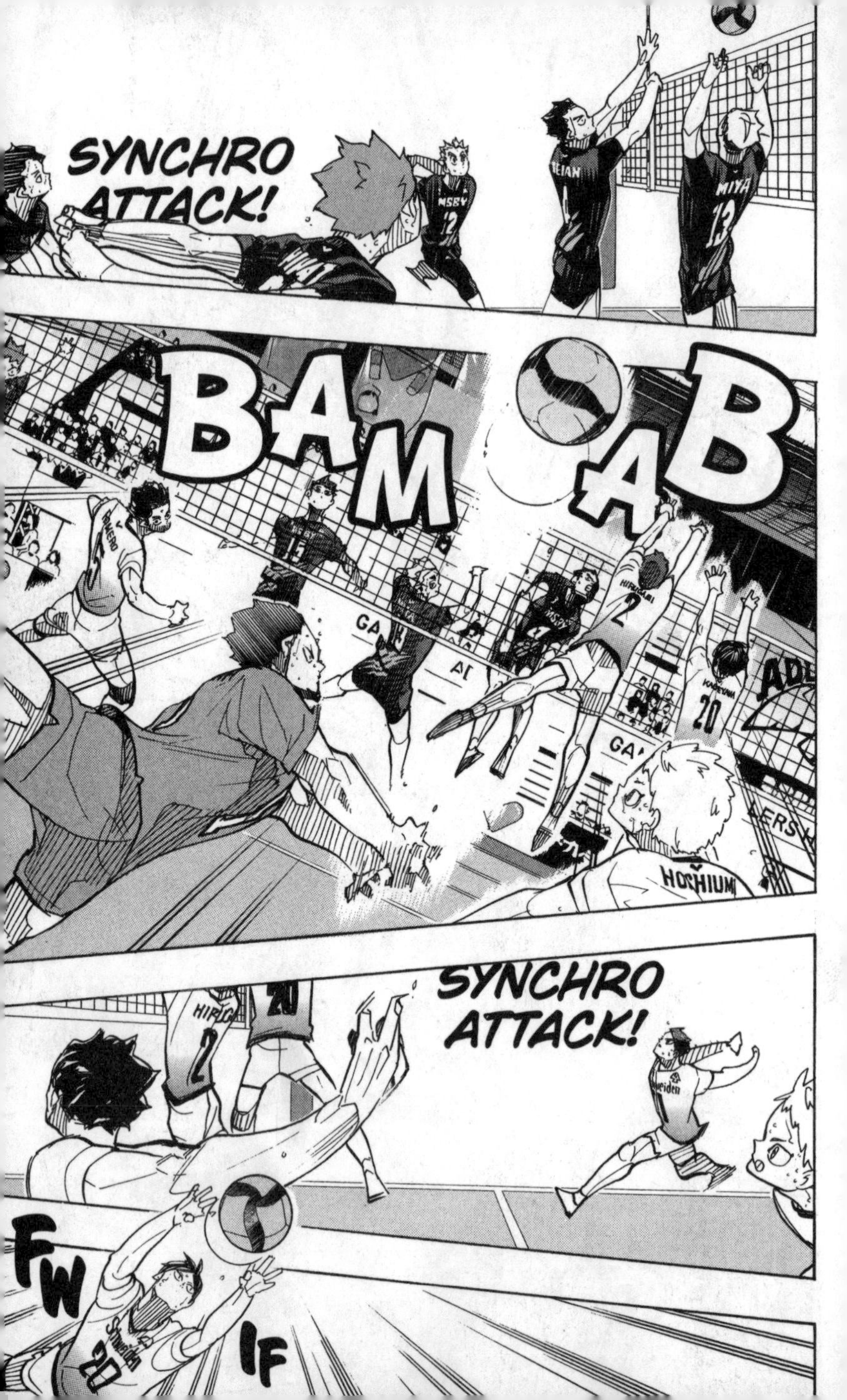
SYNCHRO ATTACK!
BAM
AB
SYNCHRO ATTACK!
FWIF

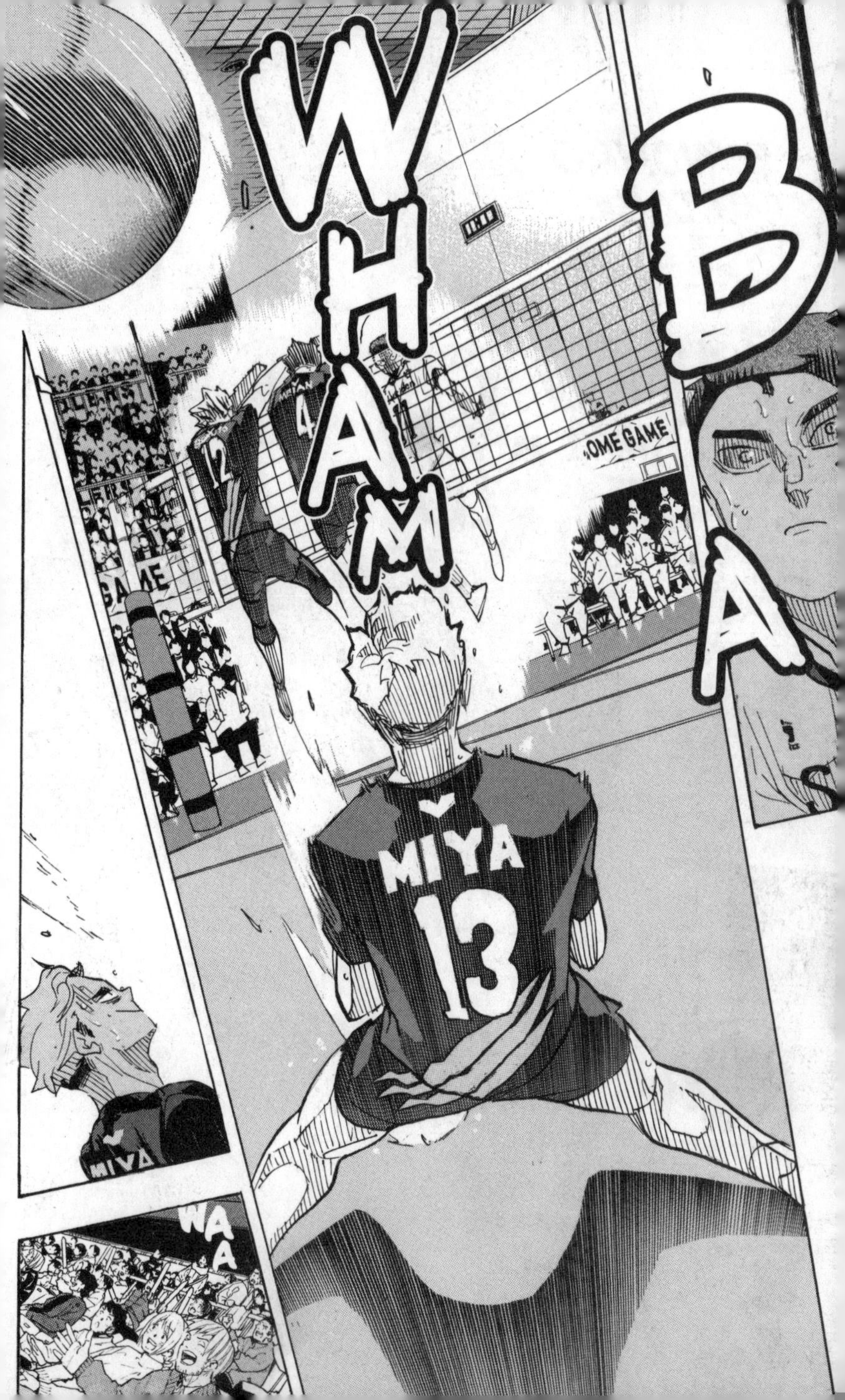
BA
WHAM
MIYA
13
WAA

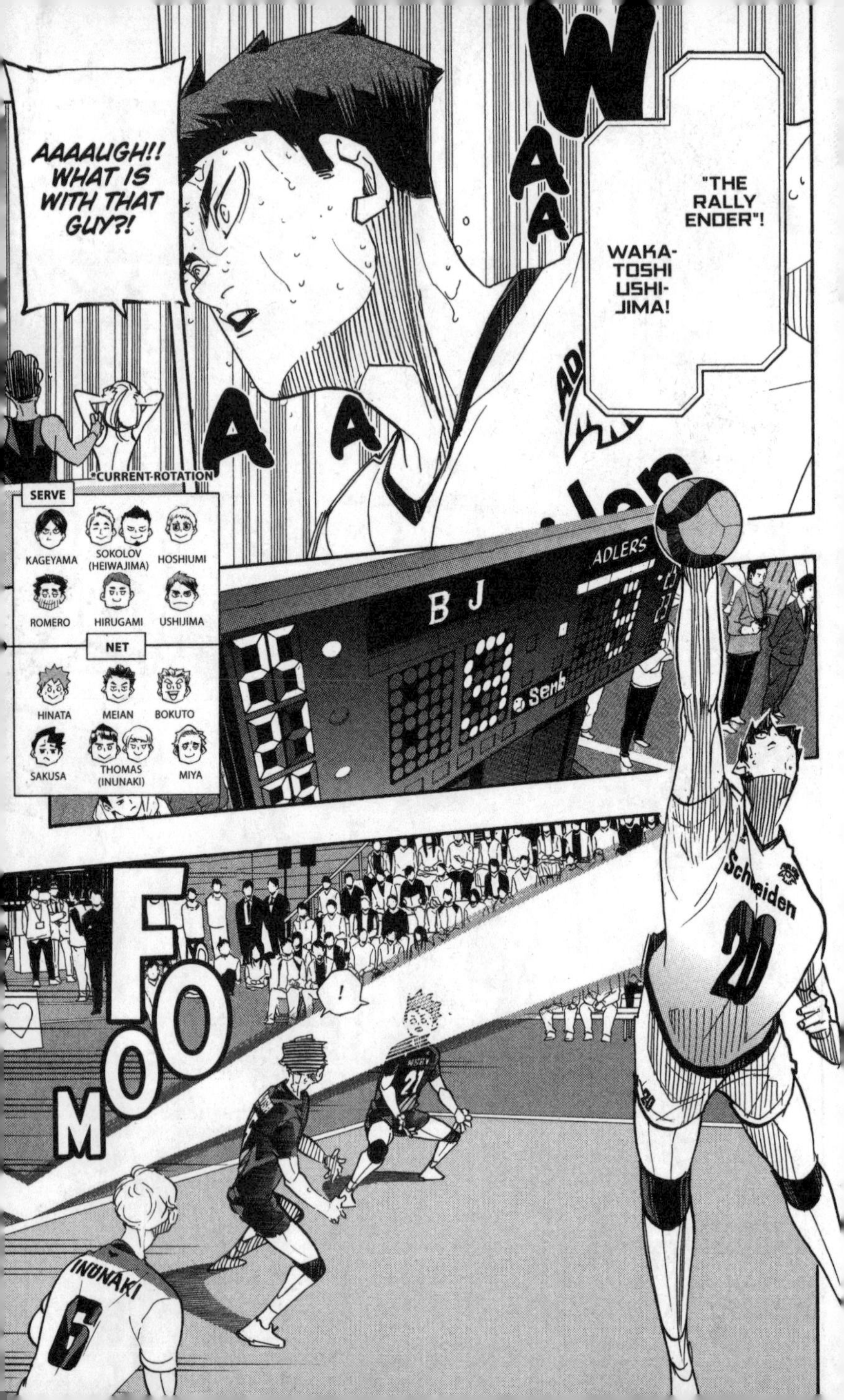
"THE RALLY ENDER"!
WAKATOSHI USHIJIMA!
WAAAA
AAAAUGH!! WHAT IS WITH THAT GUY?!
*CURRENT-ROTATION
SERVE
KAGEYAMA
SOKOLOV (HEIWAJIMA)
HOSHIUMI
ROMERO
HIRUGAMI
USHIJIMA
NET
HINATA
MEIAN
BOKUTO
SAKUSA
THOMAS (INUNAKI)
MIYA
ADLERS
BJ
Schweiden
20
FOOOM
!
21
INUNAKI
6

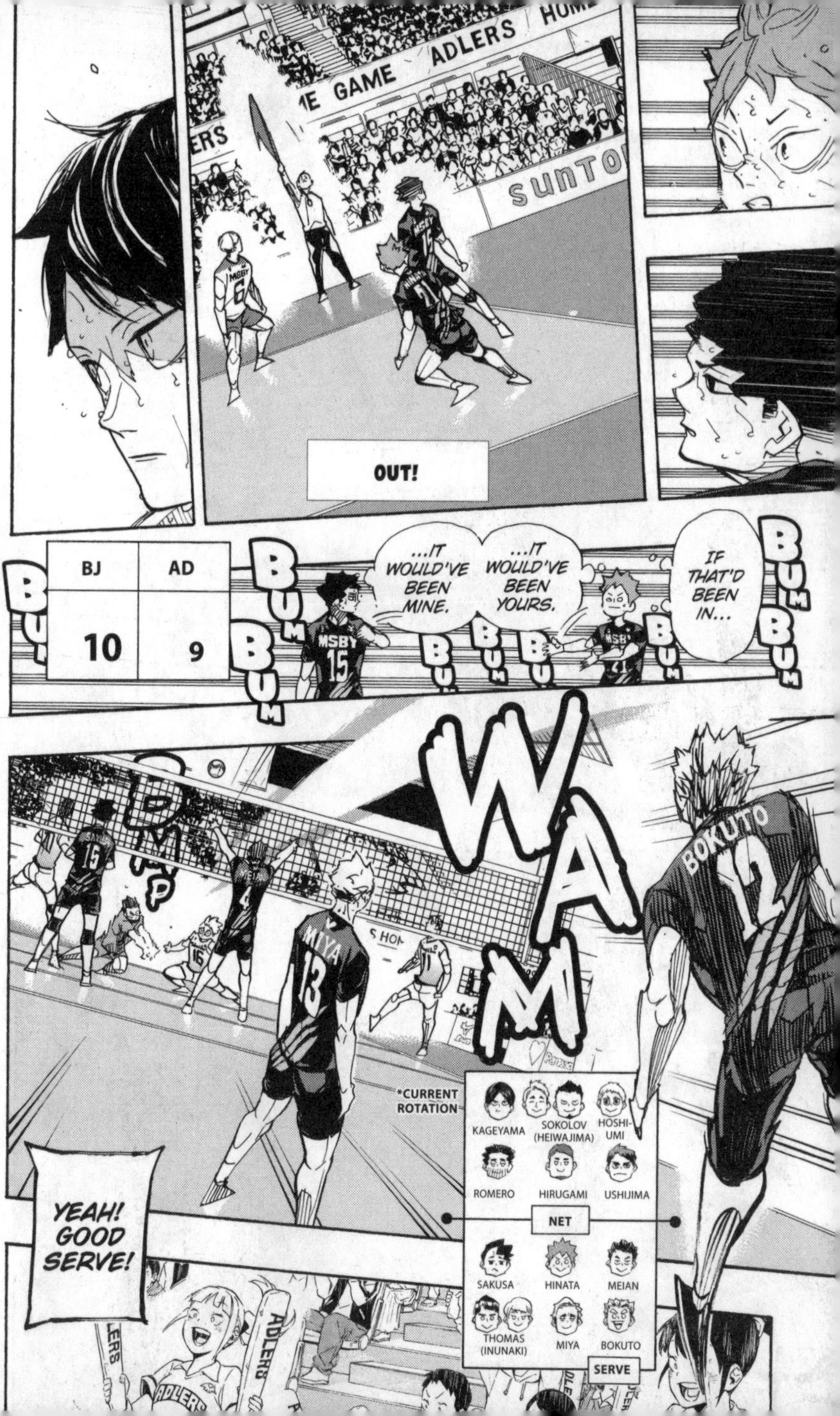

ADLERS
OUT!
BUM BUM
IF THAT'D BEEN IN...
BUM BUM
...IT WOULD'VE BEEN YOURS.
BUM BUM
...IT WOULD'VE BEEN MINE.
BUM BUM
BJ AD
10 9
BUM
WAM
BOKUTO 12
DUMP
MSBY
MIYA 13
*CURRENT ROTATION
KAGEYAMA
SOKOLOV (HEIWAJIMA)
HOSHIUMI
ROMERO
HIRUGAMI
USHIJIMA
NET
SAKUSA
HINATA
MEIAN
THOMAS (INUNAKI)
MIYA
BOKUTO
SERVE
YEAH! GOOD SERVE!
ADLERS

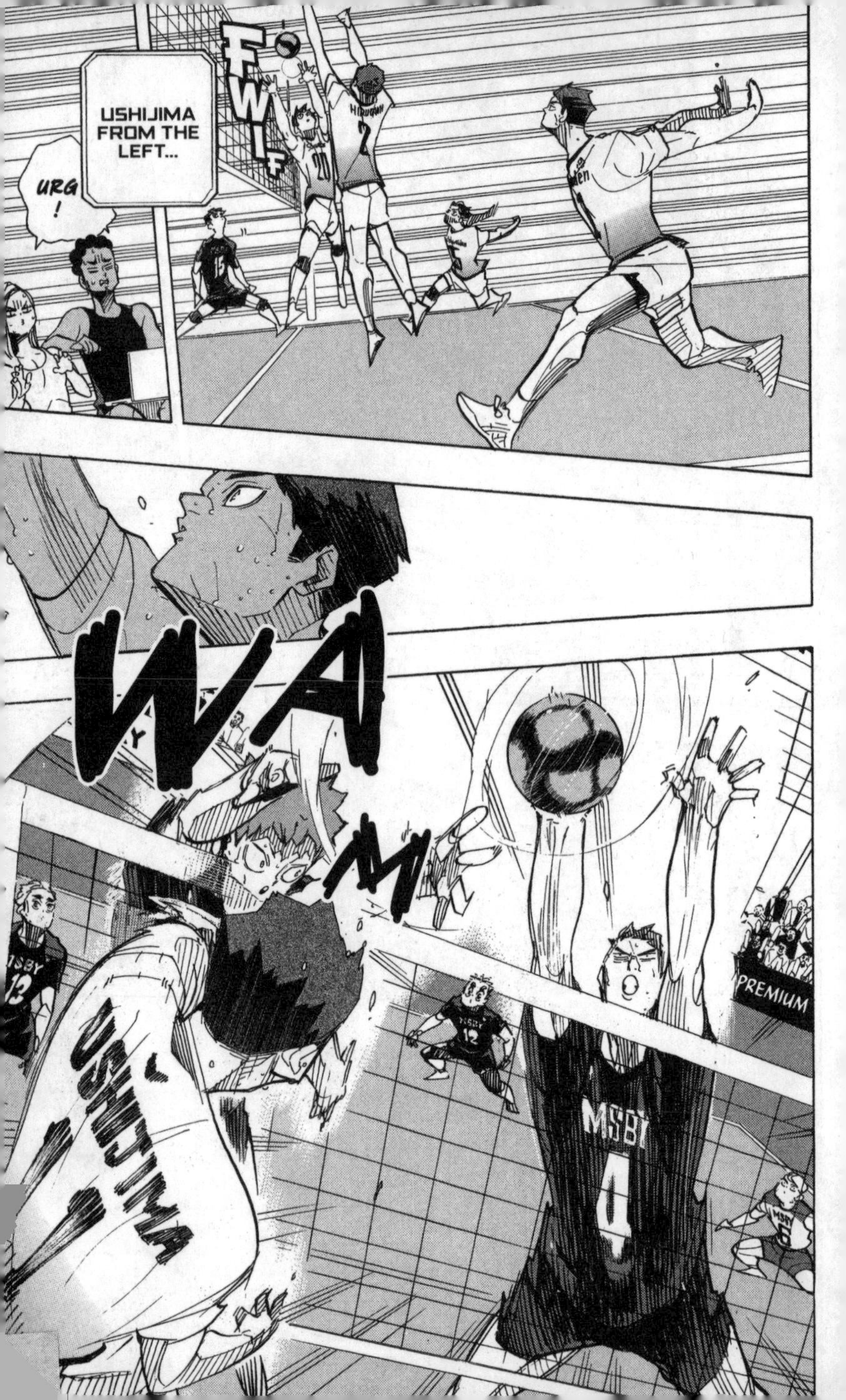
FWIF
USHIJIMA FROM THE LEFT...
URG!
WAM
USHIJIMA
MSBY
PREMIUM

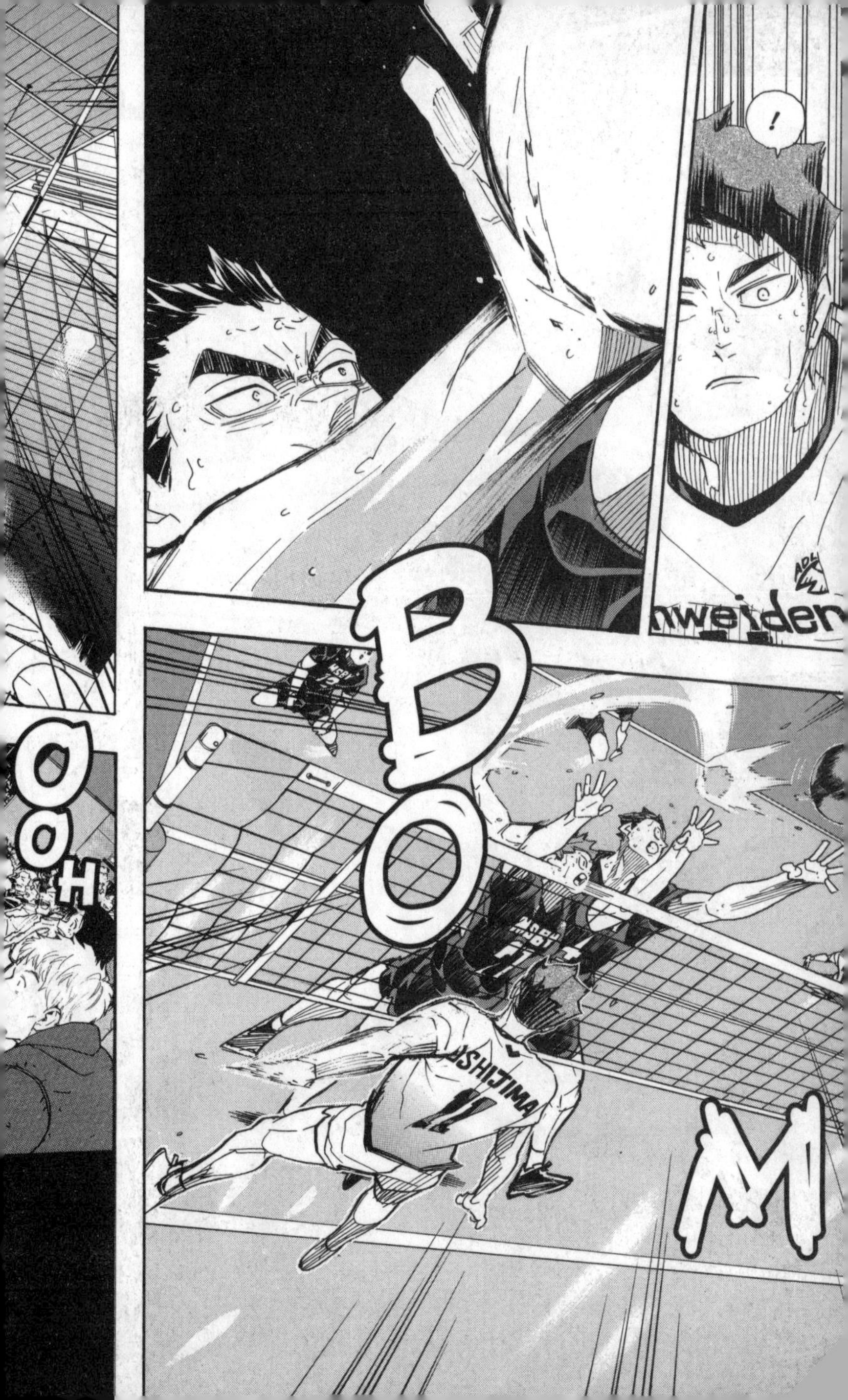
!
BOOM
OOH

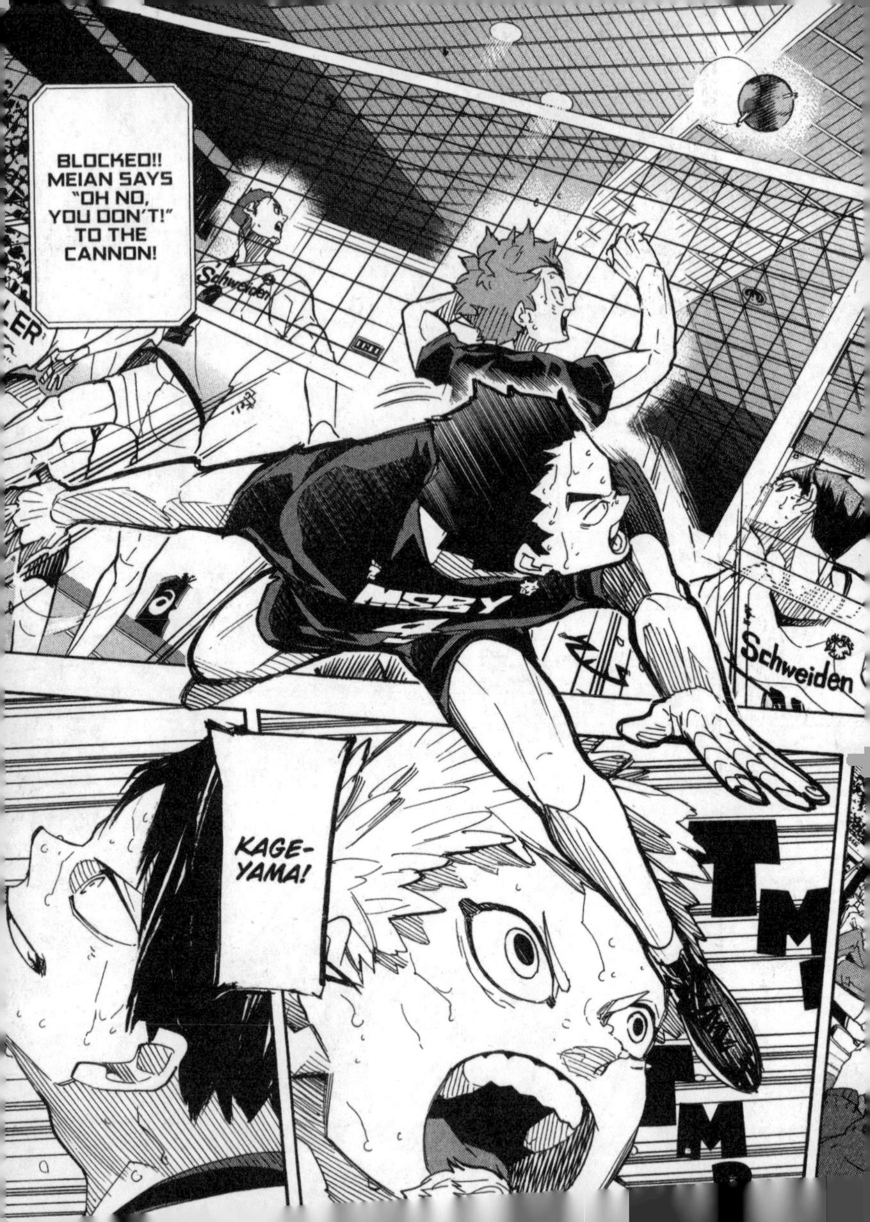

BLOCKED!! MEIAN SAYS "OH NO, YOU DON'T!" TO THE CANNON!
KAGE-YAMA!

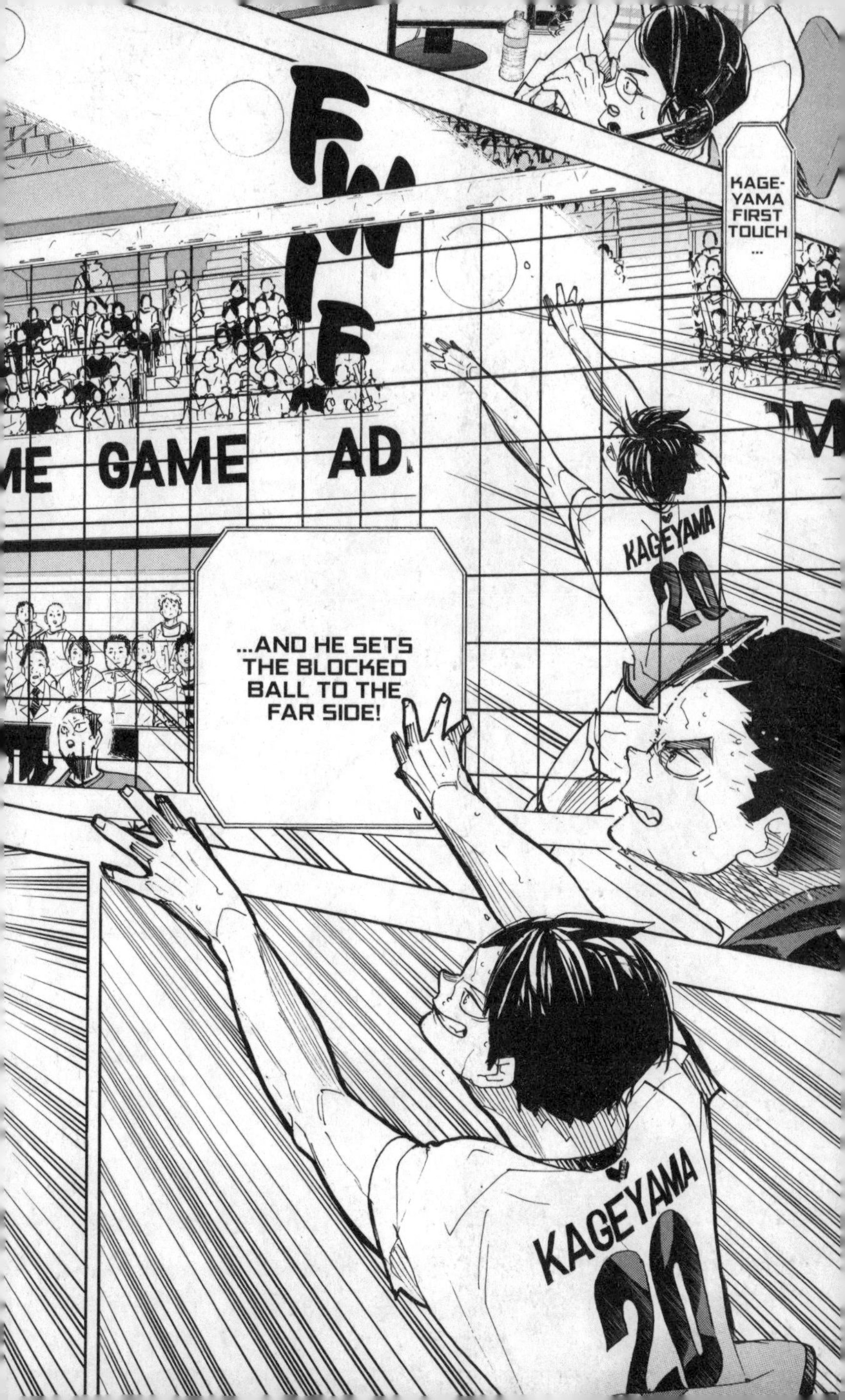
KAGE-YAMA FIRST TOUCH...
FWIF
...AND HE SETS THE BLOCKED BALL TO THE FAR SIDE!
KAGEYAMA
20
KAGEYAMA
20

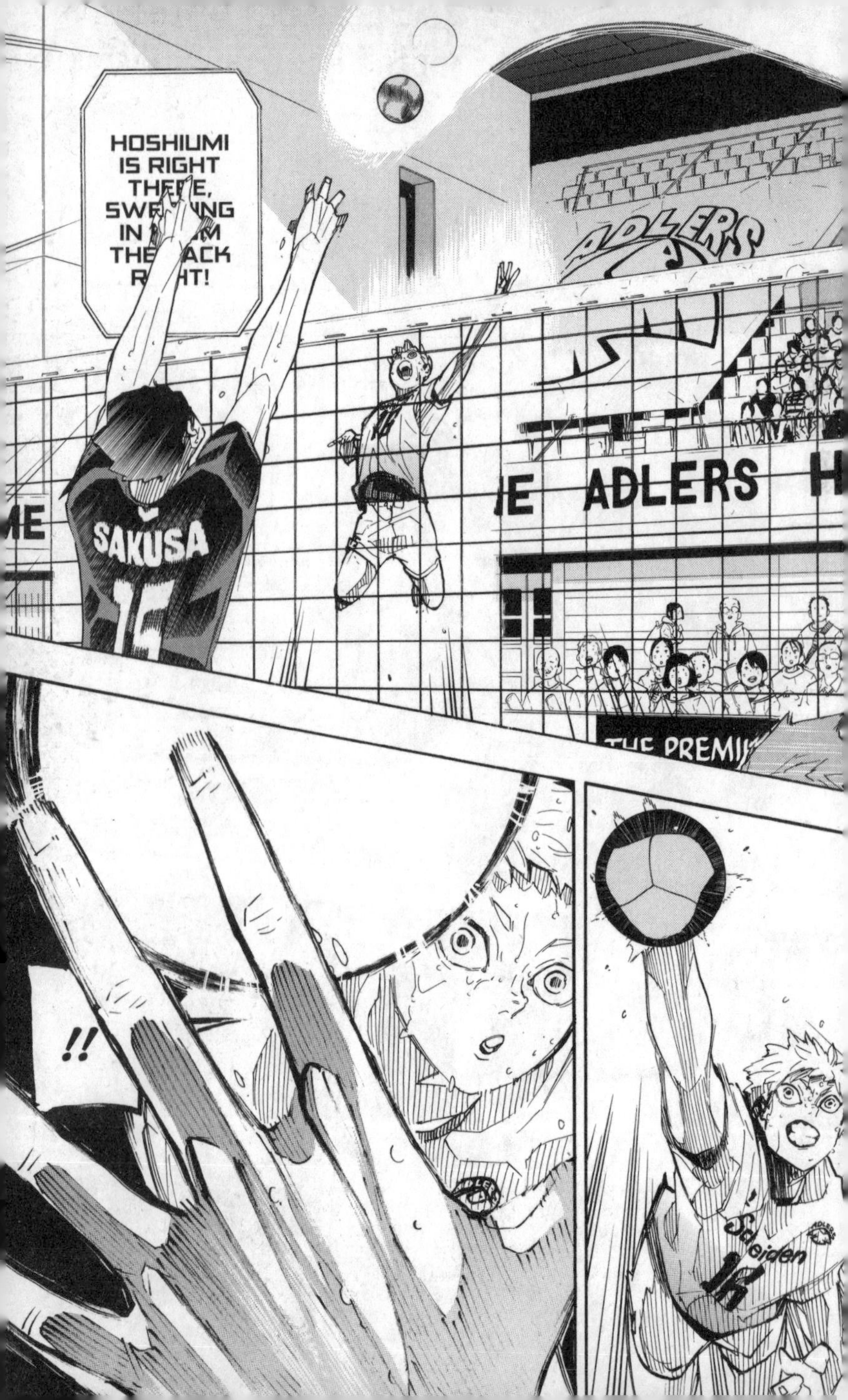
HOSHIUMI IS RIGHT THERE, SWEEPING IN FROM THE BACK RIGHT!
ADLERS
ADLERS
SAKUSA
15
THE PREMI
!!

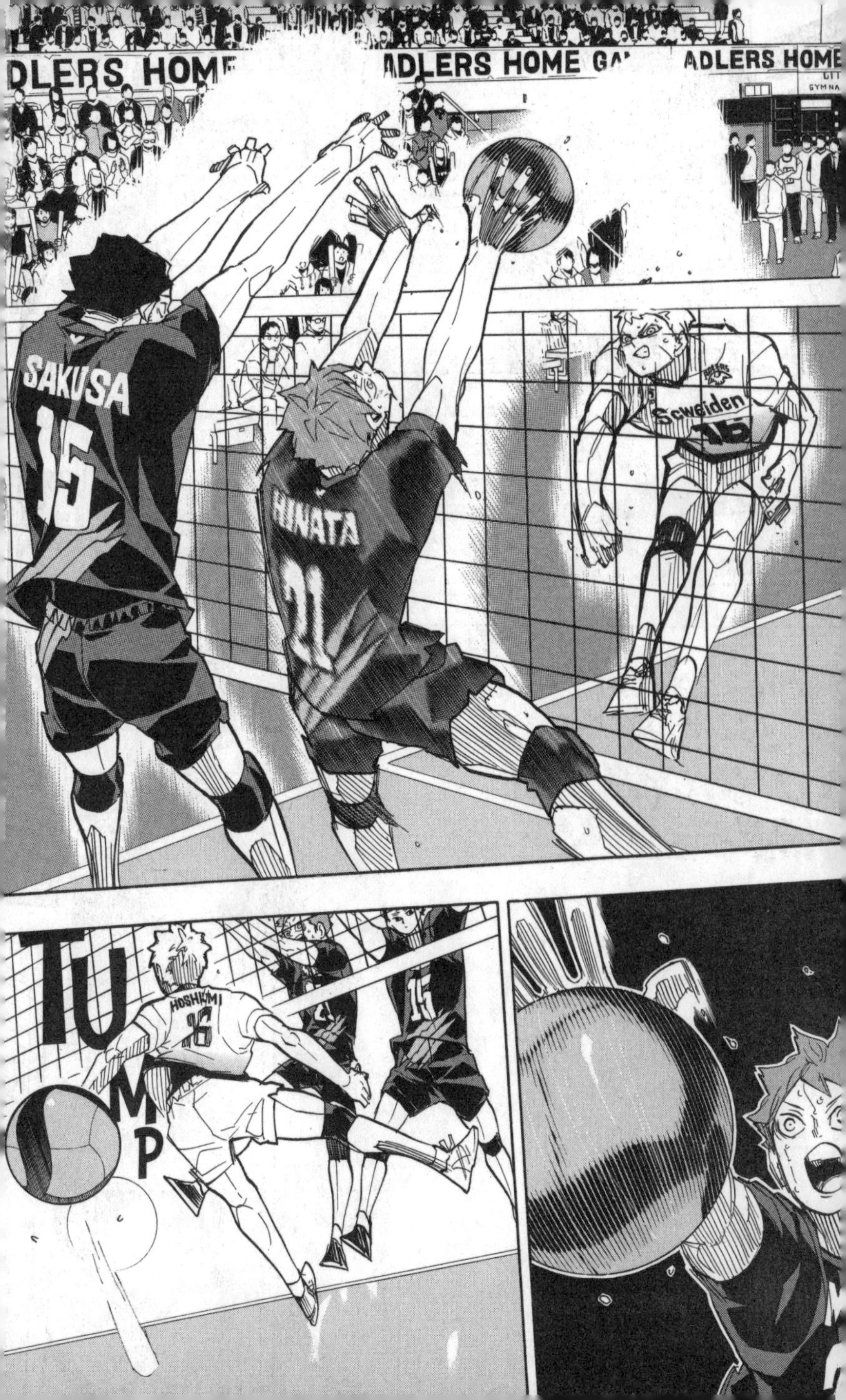

ADLERS HOME
SAKUSA
15
HINATA
21
Schweiden
TUMP

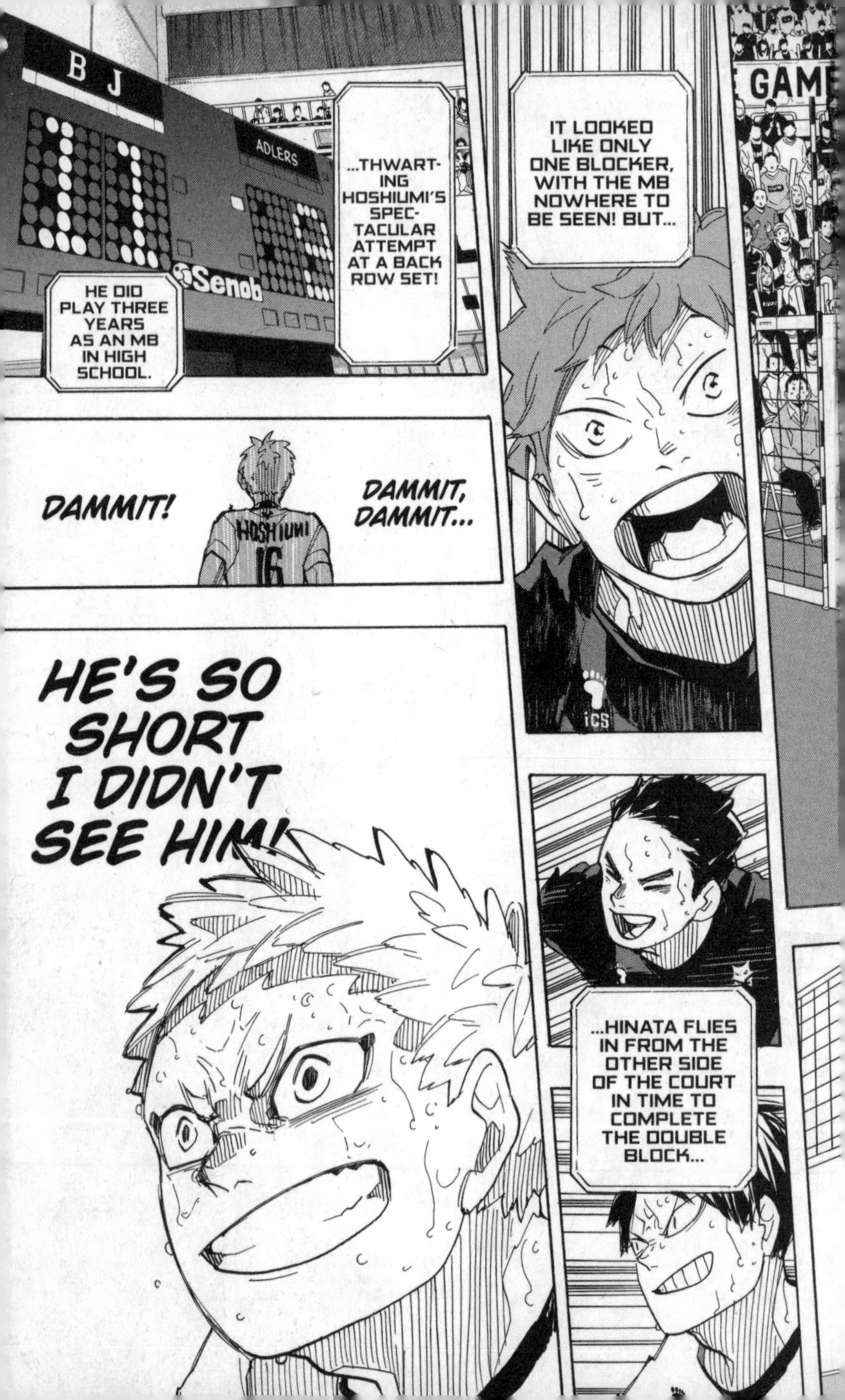
IT LOOKED LIKE ONLY ONE BLOCKER, WITH THE MB NOWHERE TO BE SEEN! BUT...
...HINATA FLIES IN FROM THE OTHER SIDE OF THE COURT IN TIME TO COMPLETE THE DOUBLE BLOCK...
...THWARTING HOSHIUMI'S SPECTACULAR ATTEMPT AT A BACK ROW SET!
HE DID PLAY THREE YEARS AS AN MB IN HIGH SCHOOL.
DAMMIT, DAMMIT...
DAMMIT!
HE'S SO SHORT I DIDN'T SEE HIM!

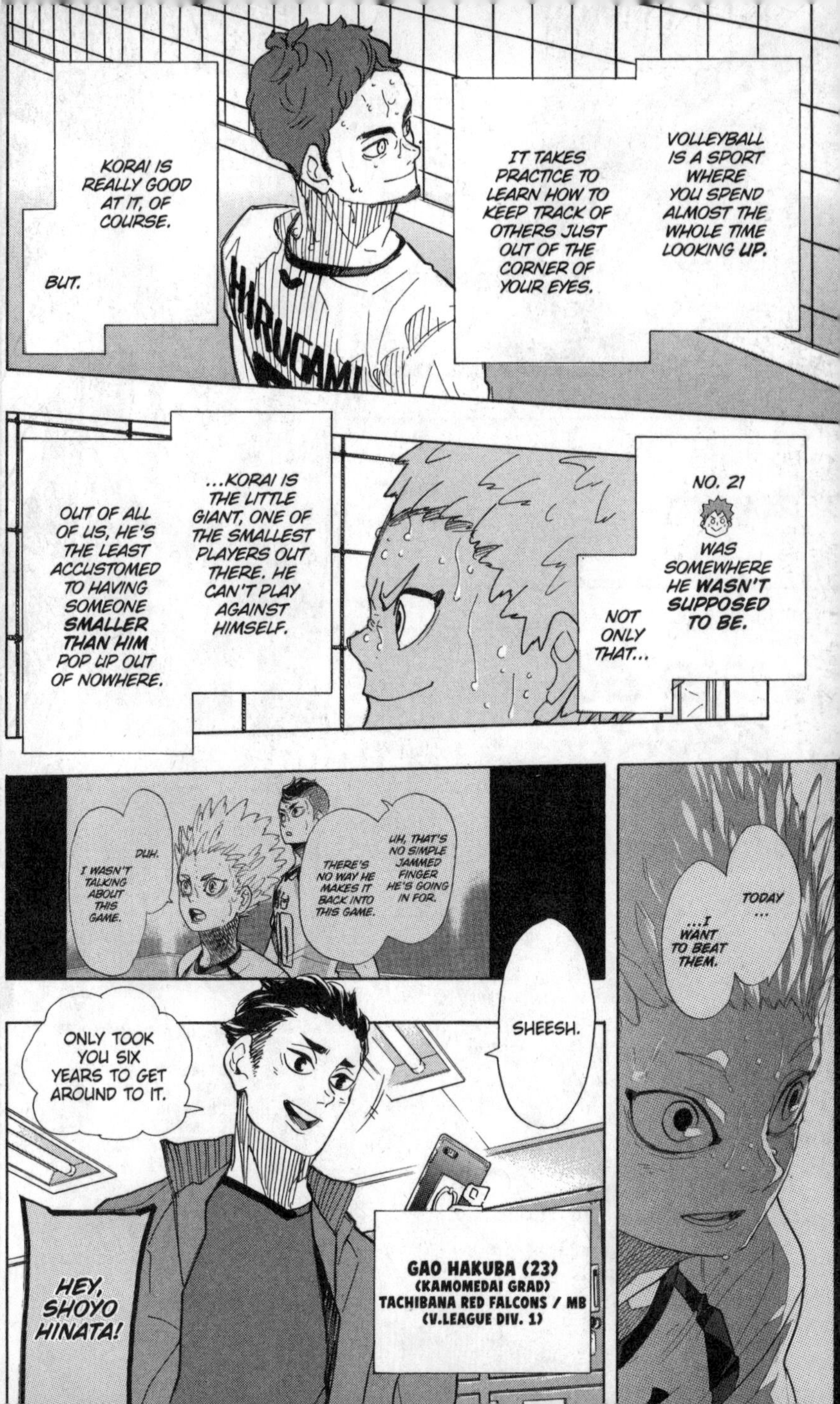
VOLLEYBALL IS A SPORT WHERE YOU SPEND ALMOST THE WHOLE TIME LOOKING **UP**.
IT TAKES PRACTICE TO LEARN HOW TO KEEP TRACK OF OTHERS JUST OUT OF THE CORNER OF YOUR EYES.
KORAI IS REALLY GOOD AT IT, OF COURSE.
BUT.
NO. 21 WAS SOMEWHERE HE **WASN'T SUPPOSED TO BE.**
NOT ONLY THAT...
...KORAI IS THE LITTLE GIANT, ONE OF THE SMALLEST PLAYERS OUT THERE. HE CAN'T PLAY AGAINST HIMSELF.
OUT OF ALL OF US, HE'S THE LEAST ACCUSTOMED TO HAVING SOMEONE **SMALLER THAN HIM** POP UP OUT OF NOWHERE.
TODAY...
...I WANT TO BEAT THEM.
UH, THAT'S NO SIMPLE JAMMED FINGER HE'S GOING IN FOR.
THERE'S NO WAY HE MAKES IT BACK INTO THIS GAME.
DUH.
I WASN'T TALKING ABOUT THIS GAME.
SHEESH.
ONLY TOOK YOU SIX YEARS TO GET AROUND TO IT.
GAO HAKUBA (23)
(KAMOMEDAI GRAD)
TACHIBANA RED FALCONS / MB
(V.LEAGUE DIV. 1)
HEY, SHOYO HINATA!

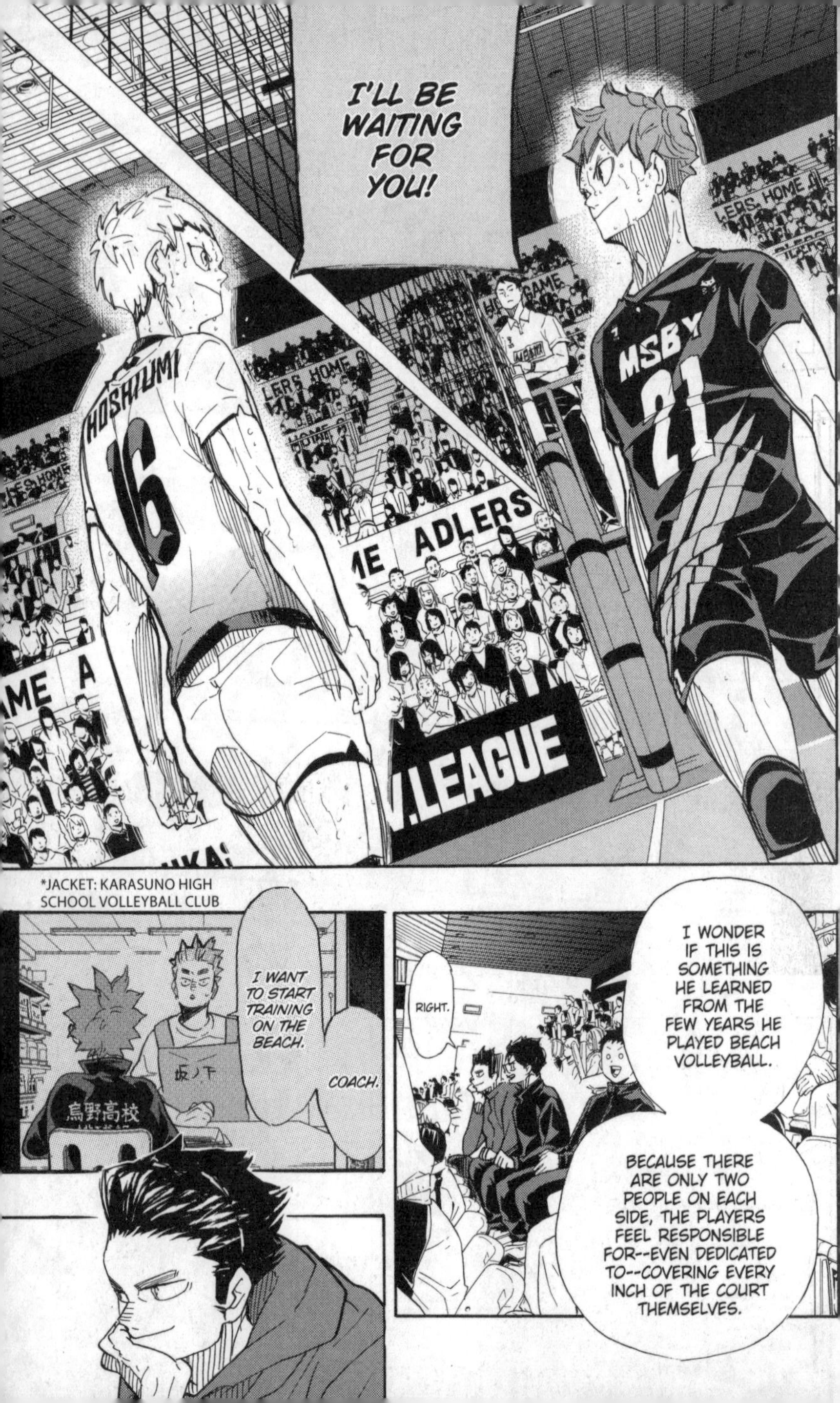
I'LL BE WAITING FOR YOU!
HOSHIUMI
16
MSBY
21
ADLERS
V.LEAGUE
*JACKET: KARASUNO HIGH SCHOOL VOLLEYBALL CLUB
I WONDER IF THIS IS SOMETHING HE LEARNED FROM THE FEW YEARS HE PLAYED BEACH VOLLEYBALL.
RIGHT.
BECAUSE THERE ARE ONLY TWO PEOPLE ON EACH SIDE, THE PLAYERS FEEL RESPONSIBLE FOR--EVEN DEDICATED TO--COVERING EVERY INCH OF THE COURT THEMSELVES.
I WANT TO START TRAINING ON THE BEACH.
COACH.
烏野高校
坂ノ下

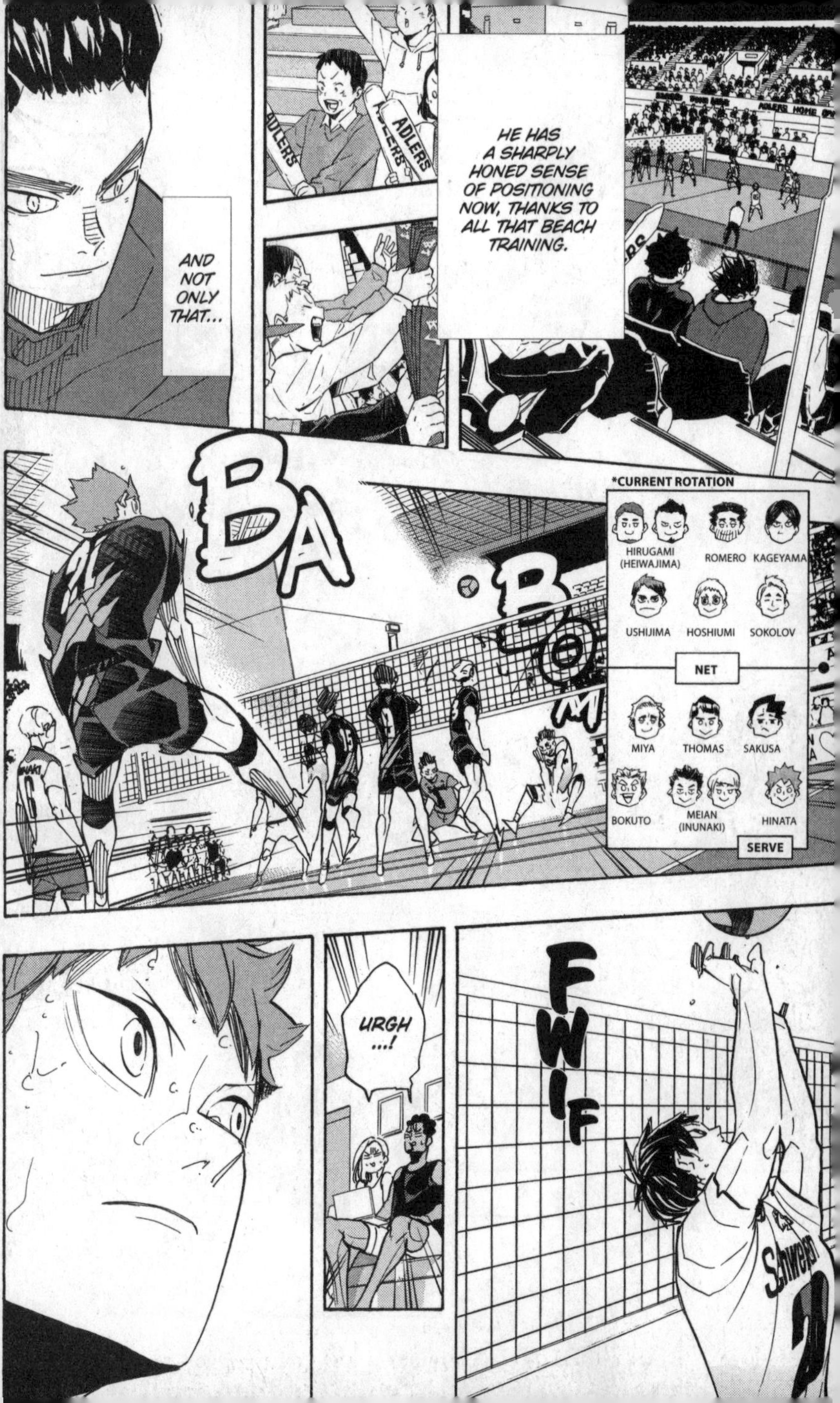

ADLERS HOME
HE HAS A SHARPLY HONED SENSE OF POSITIONING NOW, THANKS TO ALL THAT BEACH TRAINING.
ADLERS
ADLERS
ADLERS
AND NOT ONLY THAT...
BA-BOM
*CURRENT ROTATION
HIRUGAMI (HEIWAJIMA)
ROMERO
KAGEYAMA
USHIJIMA
HOSHIUMI
SOKOLOV
NET
MIYA
THOMAS
SAKUSA
BOKUTO
MEIAN (INUNAKI)
HINATA
SERVE
FWIF
URGH ...!
Schweiden

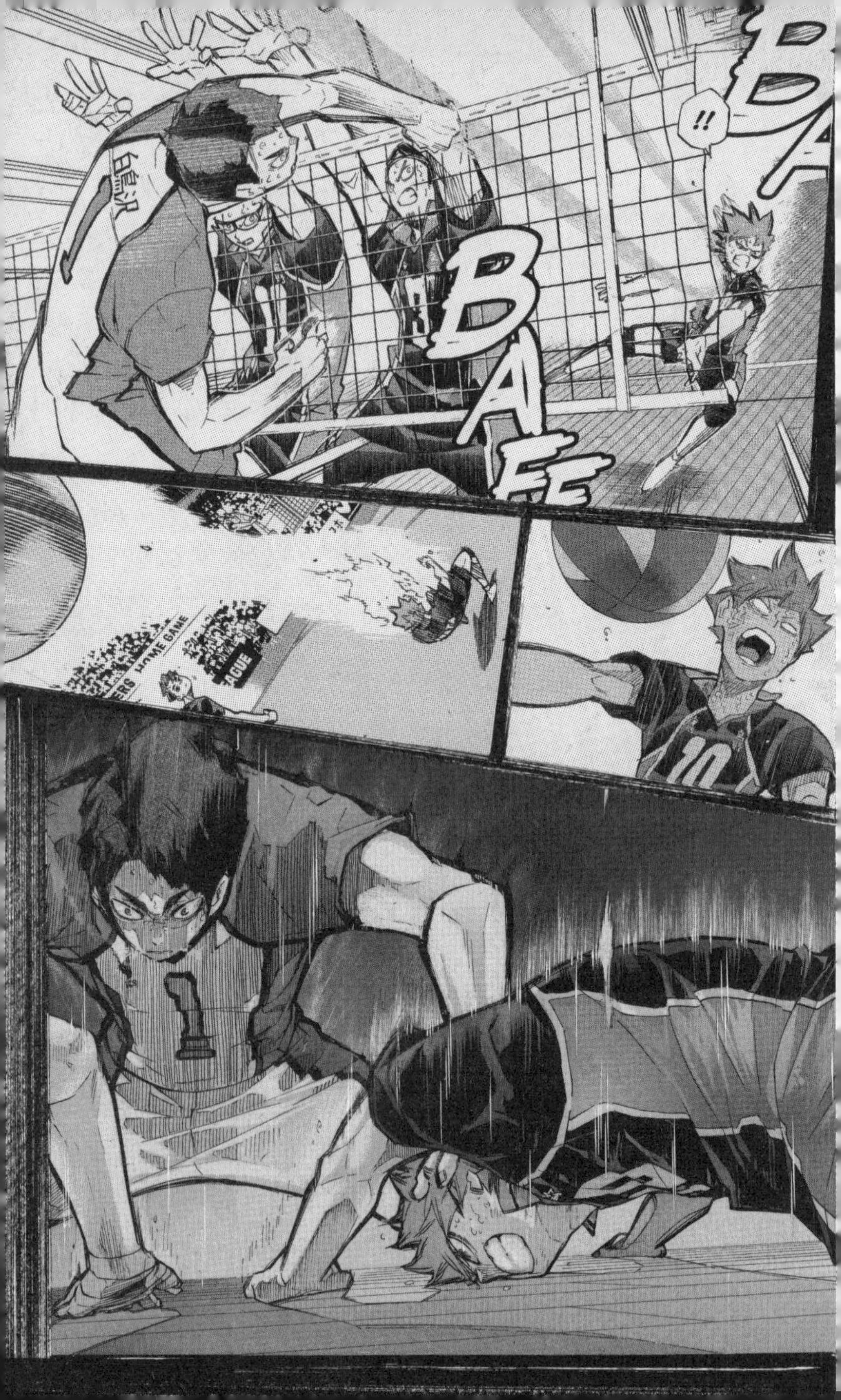

BA
!!
BAFF
HOME GAME

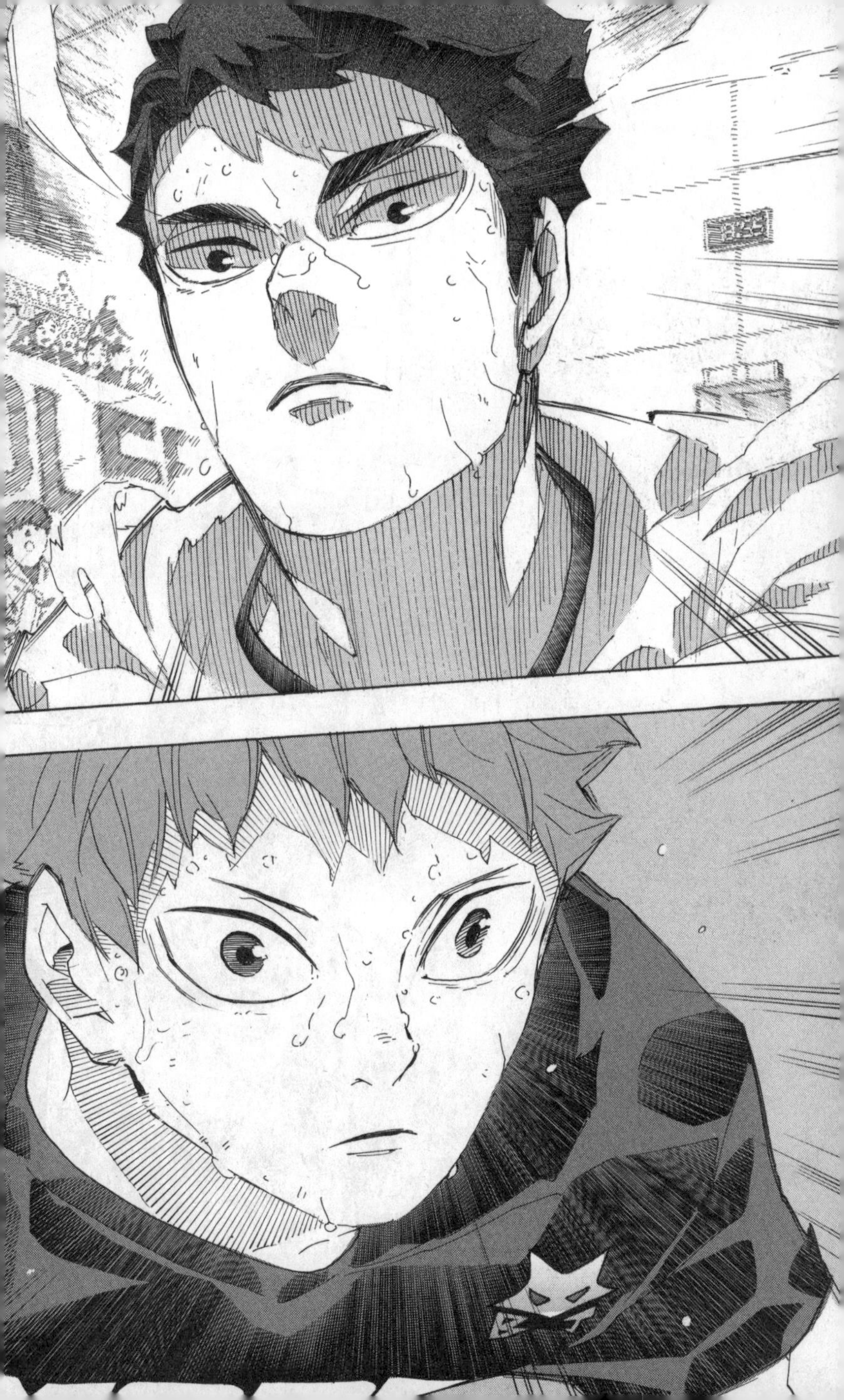

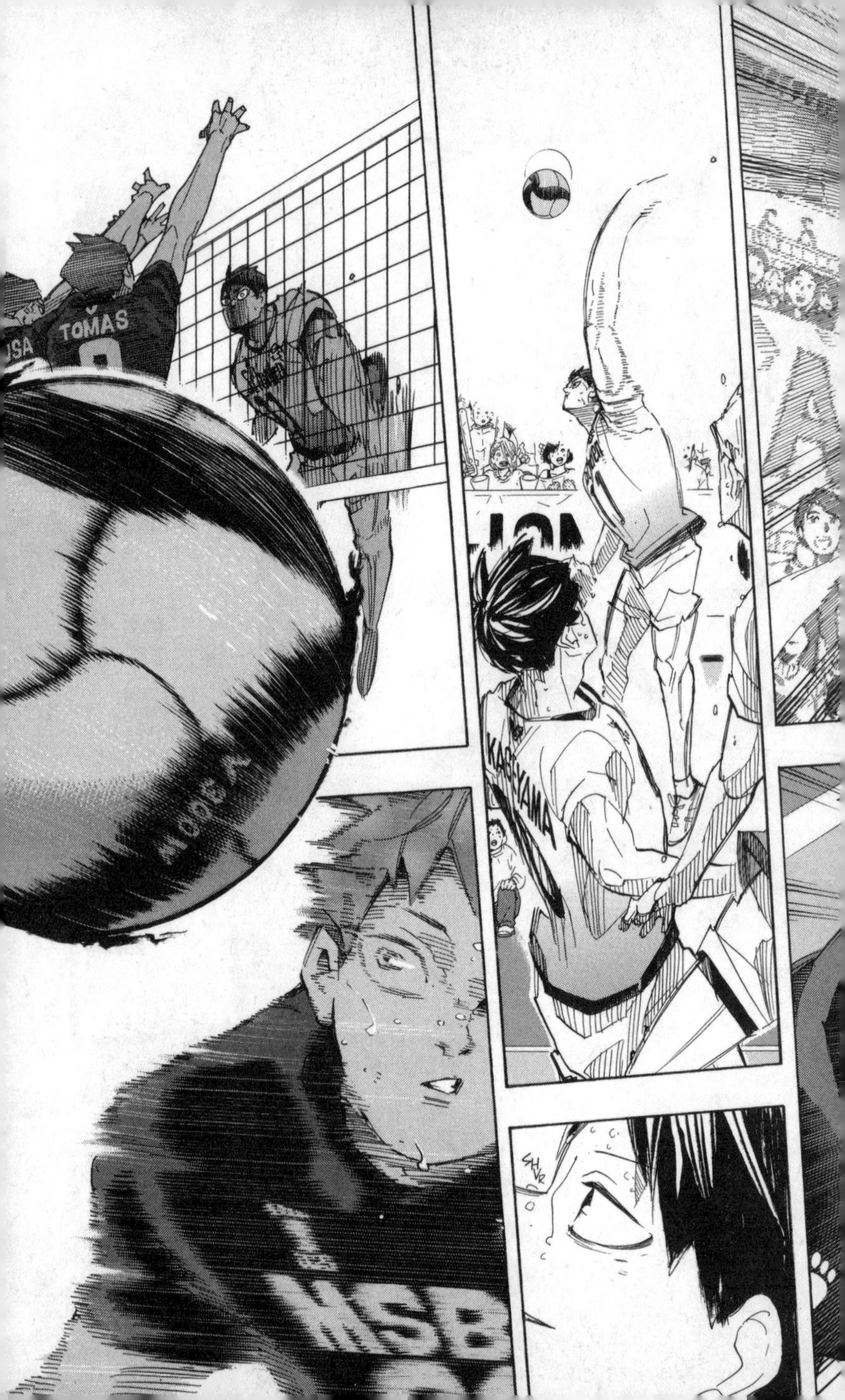
KAGEYAMA
SHVR
TOMAS
USA
MSB

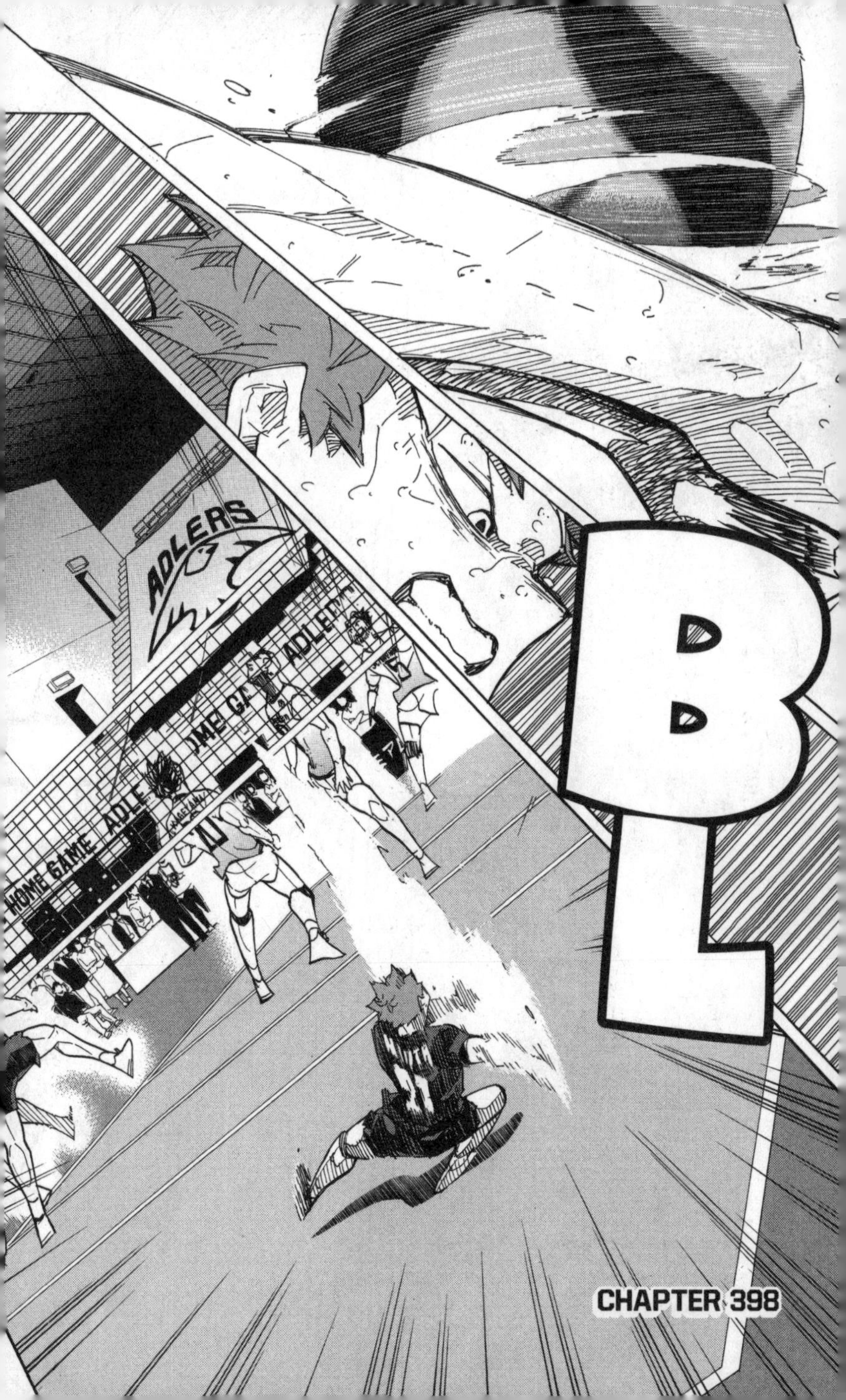
B
L
ADLERS
ADLERS
HOME GAME ADLE
CHAPTER 398

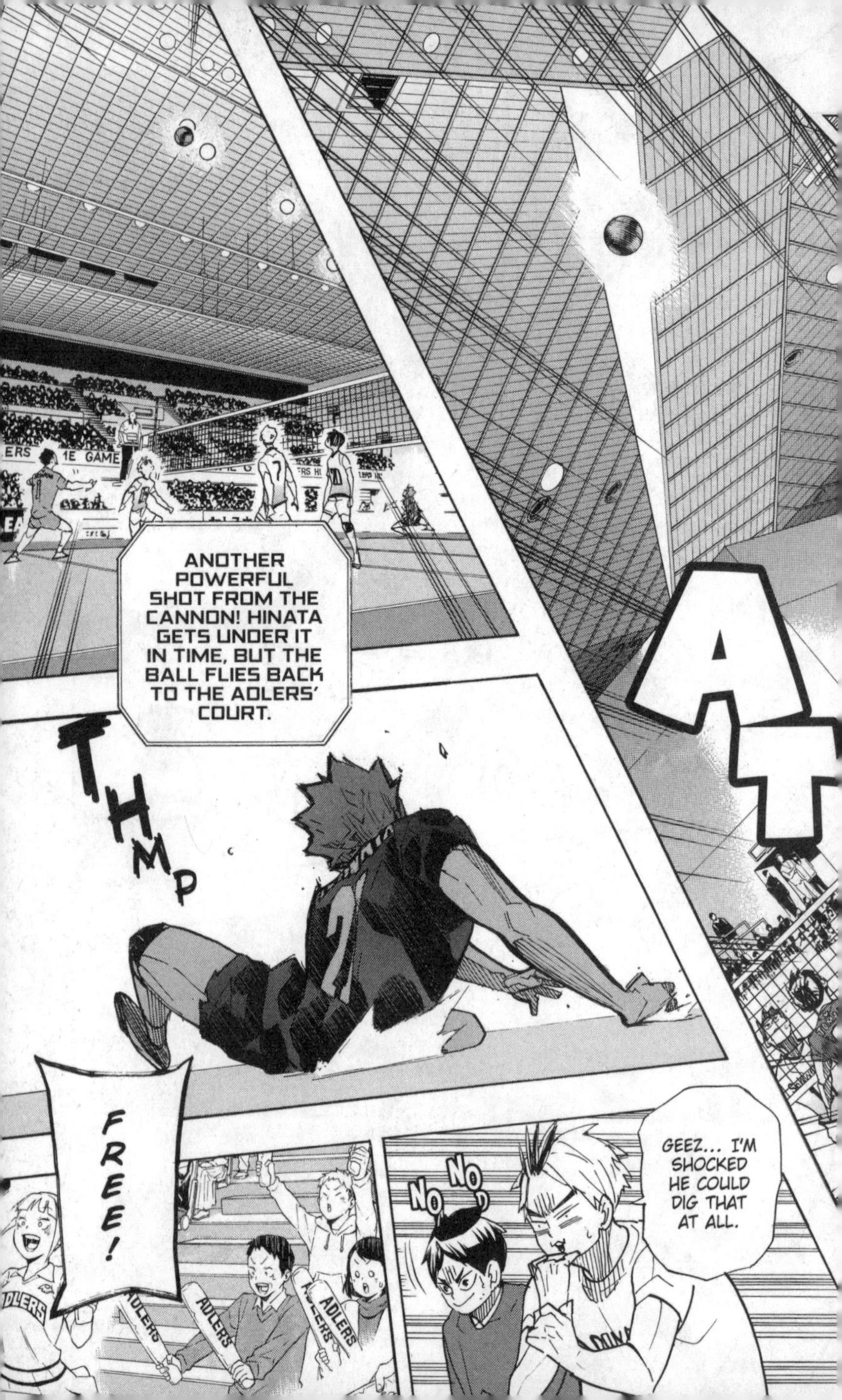
ANOTHER POWERFUL SHOT FROM THE CANNON! HINATA GETS UNDER IT IN TIME, BUT THE BALL FLIES BACK TO THE ADLERS' COURT.
A
THMP
GEEZ... I'M SHOCKED HE COULD DIG THAT AT ALL.
NOD NOD
FREE!
ADLERS
ADLERS
ADLERS
ADLERS

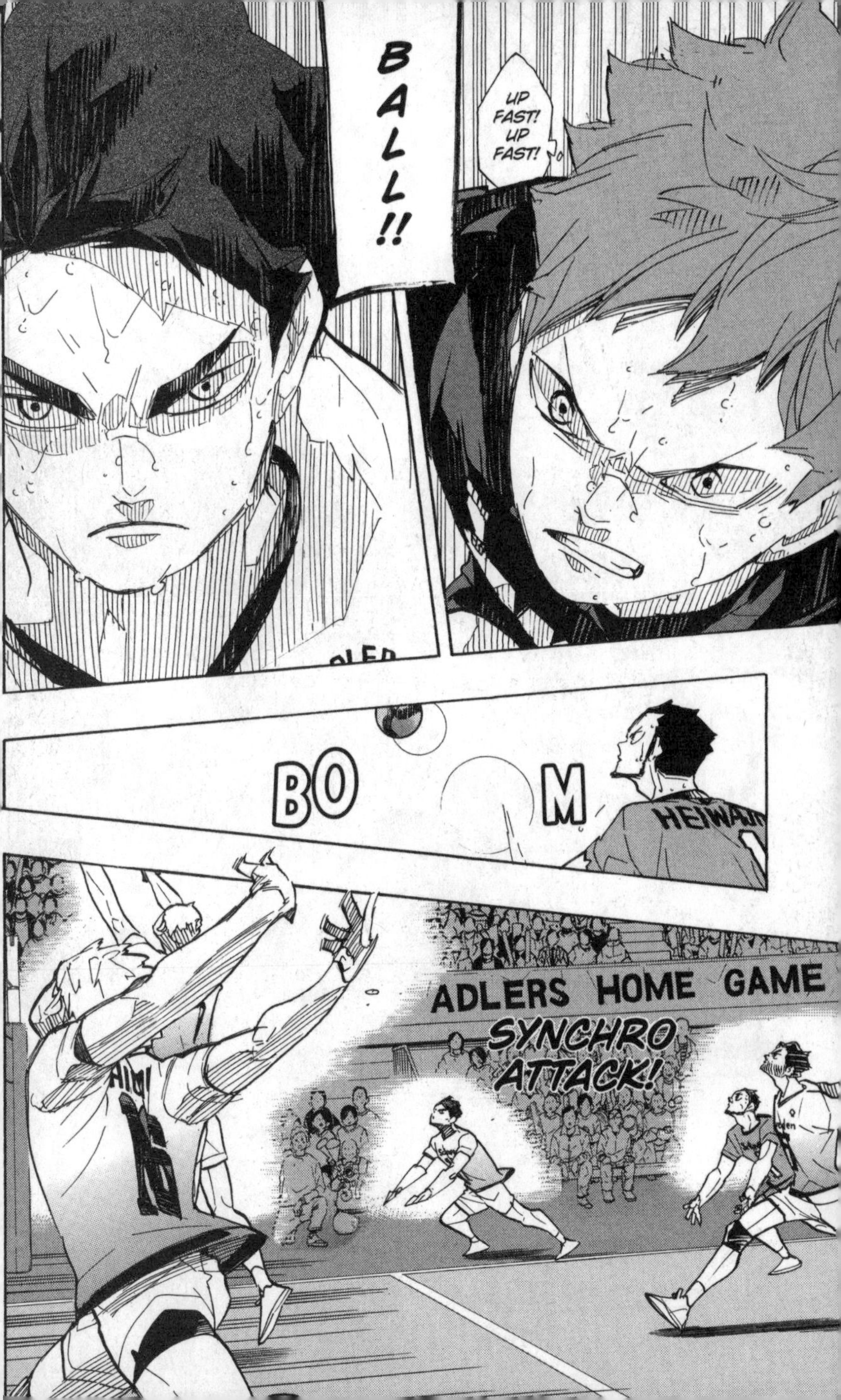
UP FAST! UP FAST!
BALL!!
BO M
ADLERS HOME GAME
SYNCHRO ATTACK!

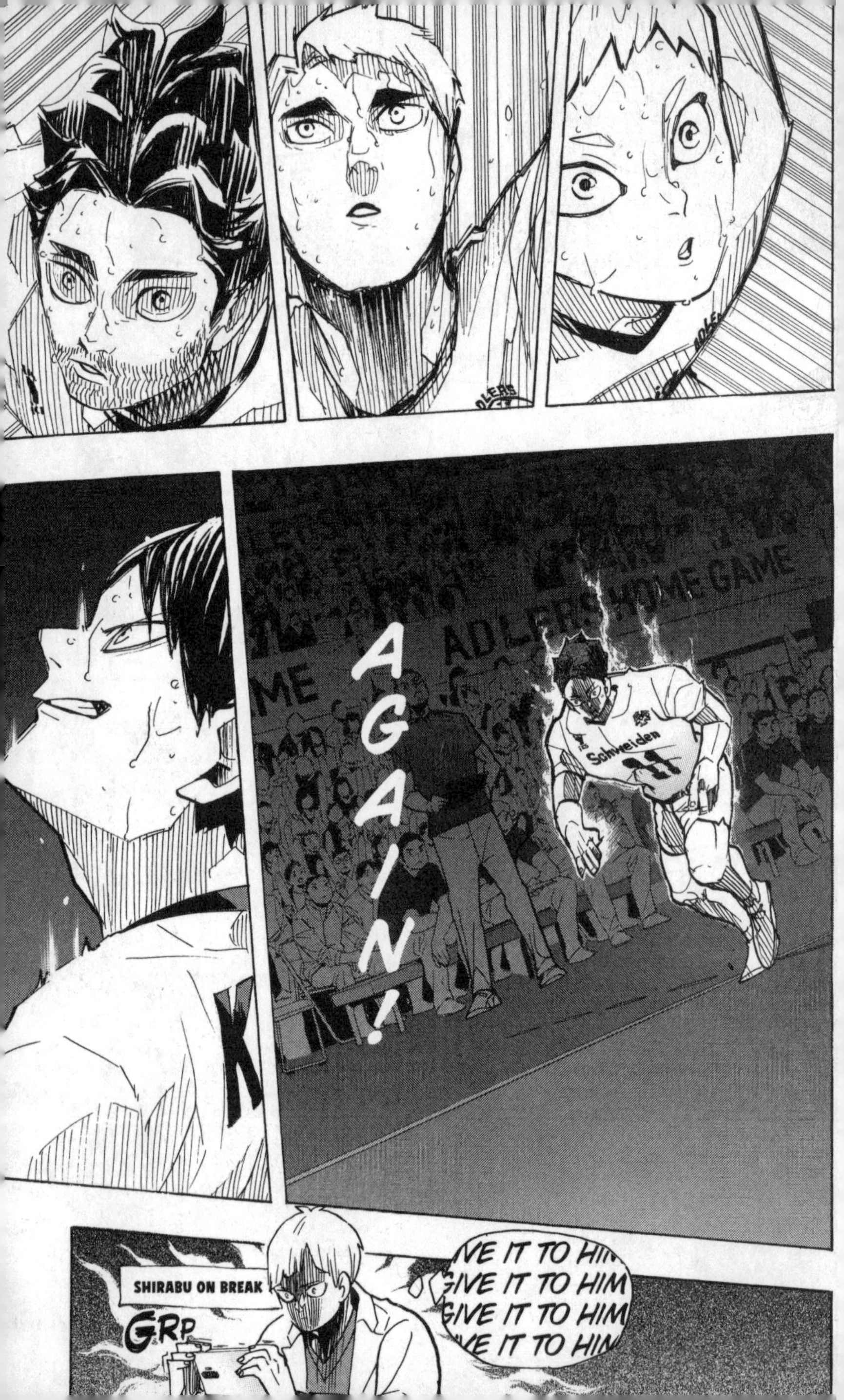
ADLERS HOME GAME
AGAIN!
Schweiden
VE IT TO HI
GIVE IT TO HIM
GIVE IT TO HIM
VE IT TO HI
SHIRABU ON BREAK
GRP

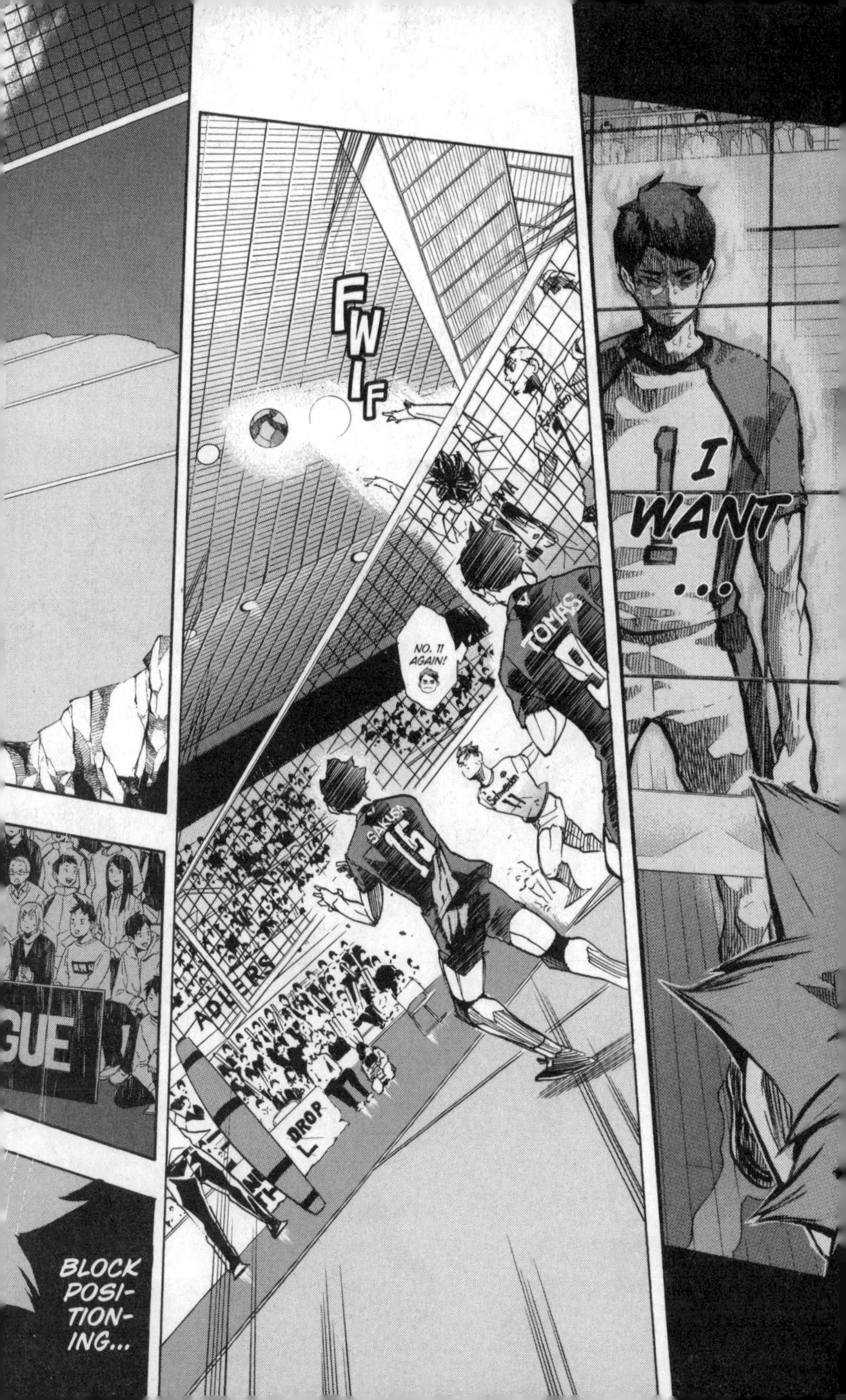

I WANT ...
FWIF
NO. 11 AGAIN!
TOMAS
SAKUSA
DROP
BLOCK POSI-TION-ING...

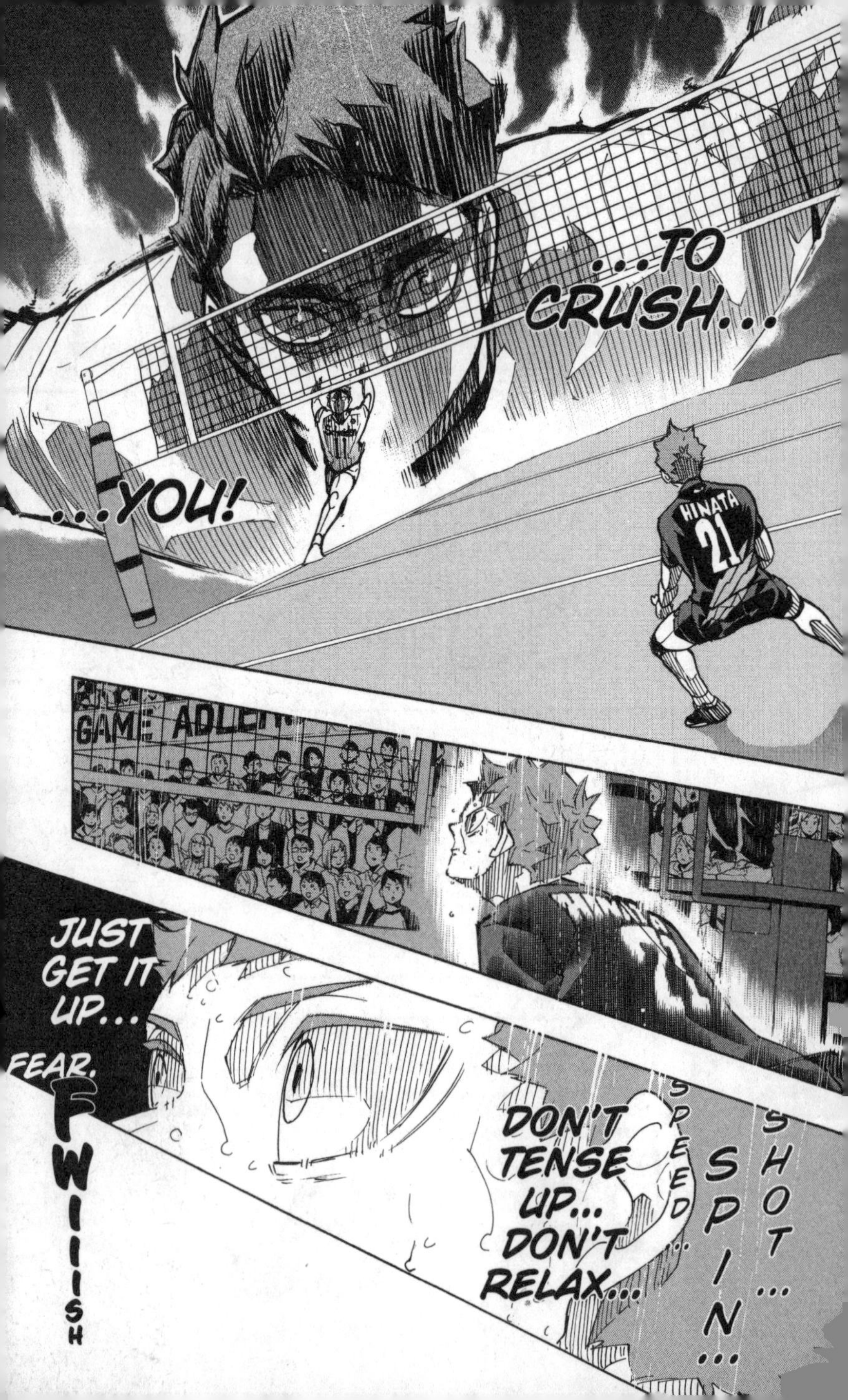
...TO CRUSH...
...YOU!
SHOT...
SPIN...
SPEED...
DON'T TENSE UP... DON'T RELAX...
JUST GET IT UP...
FEAR.
FWIIISH

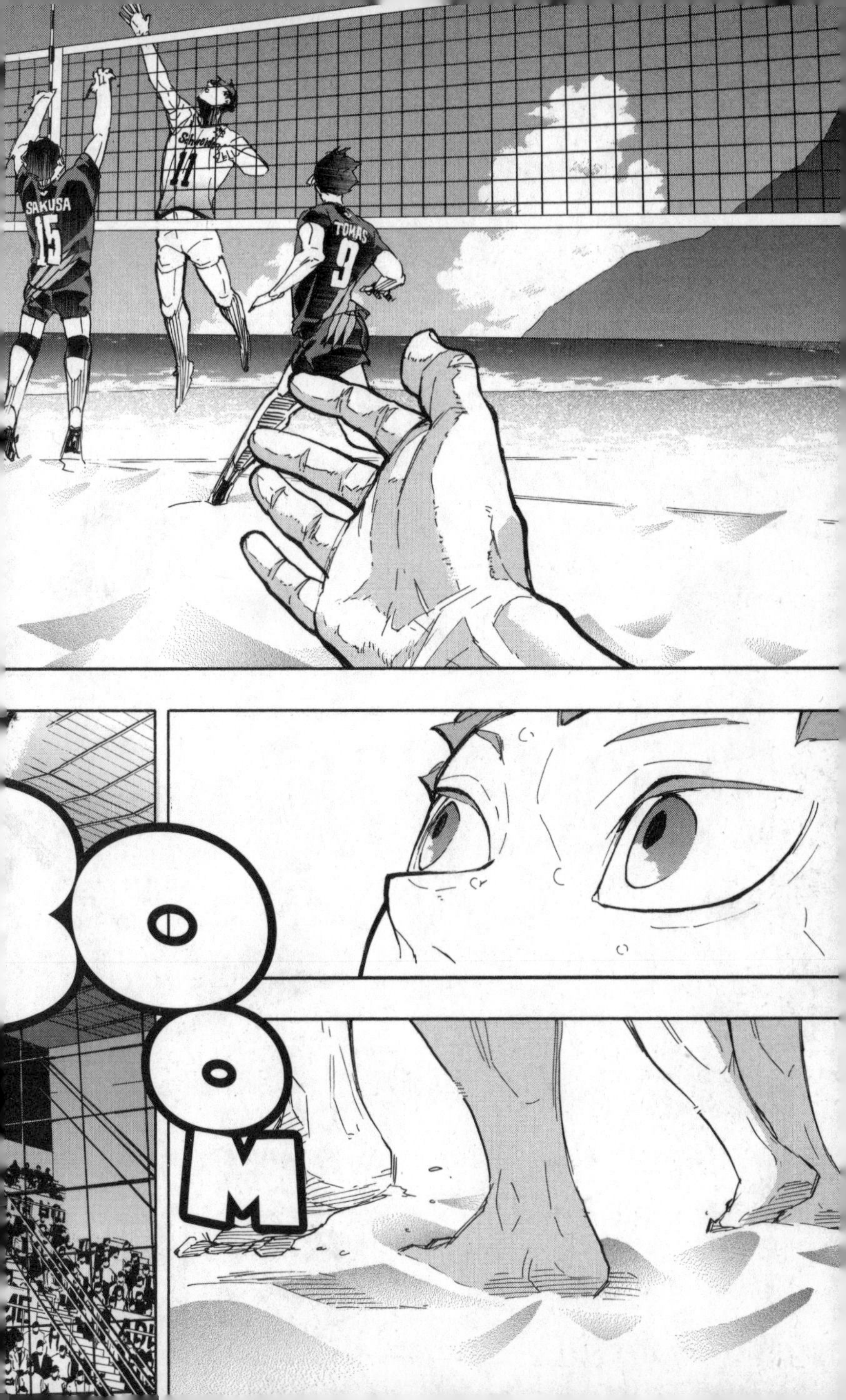
SAKUSA
15
11
TOMAS
9
BOOM

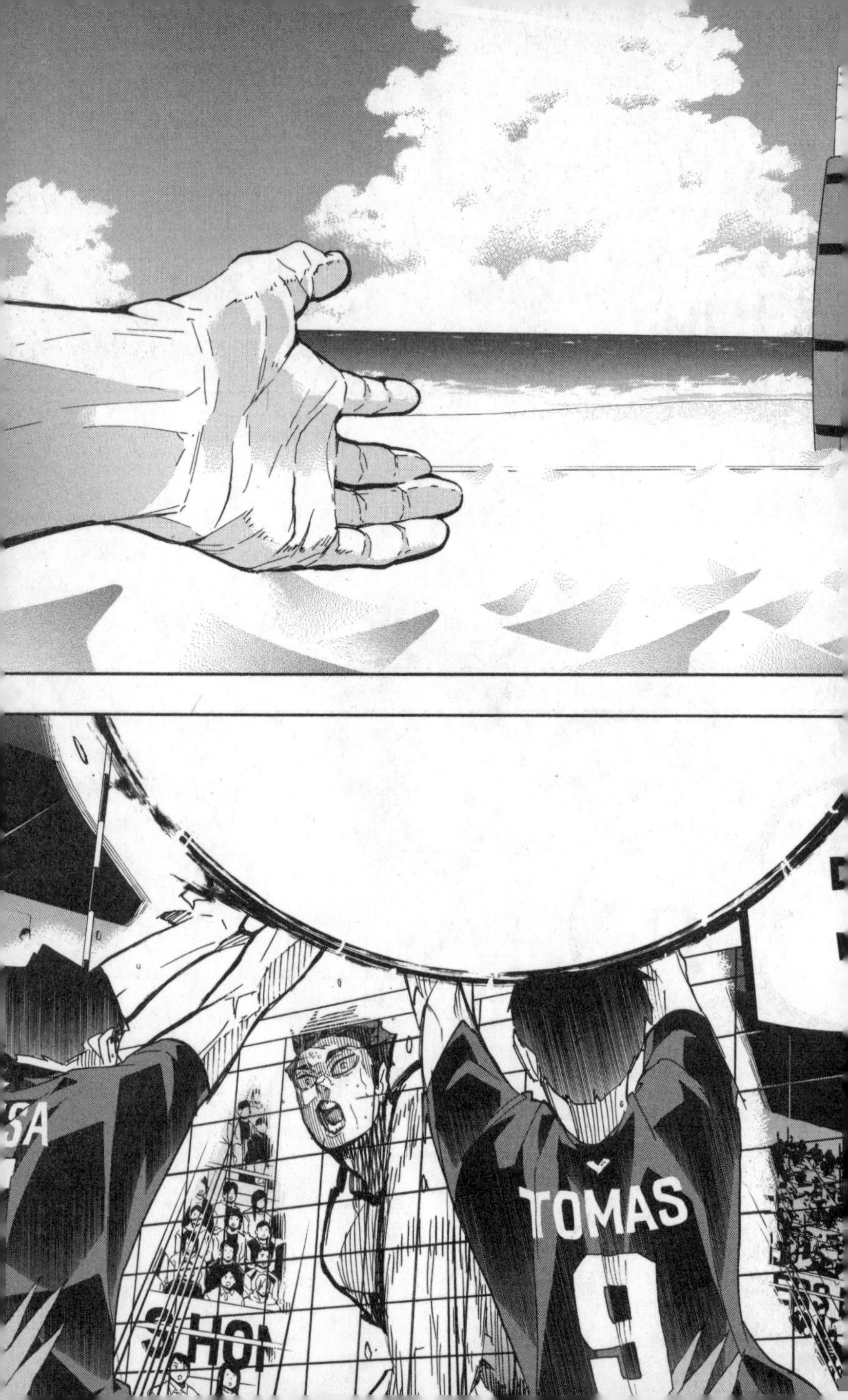
TOMAS

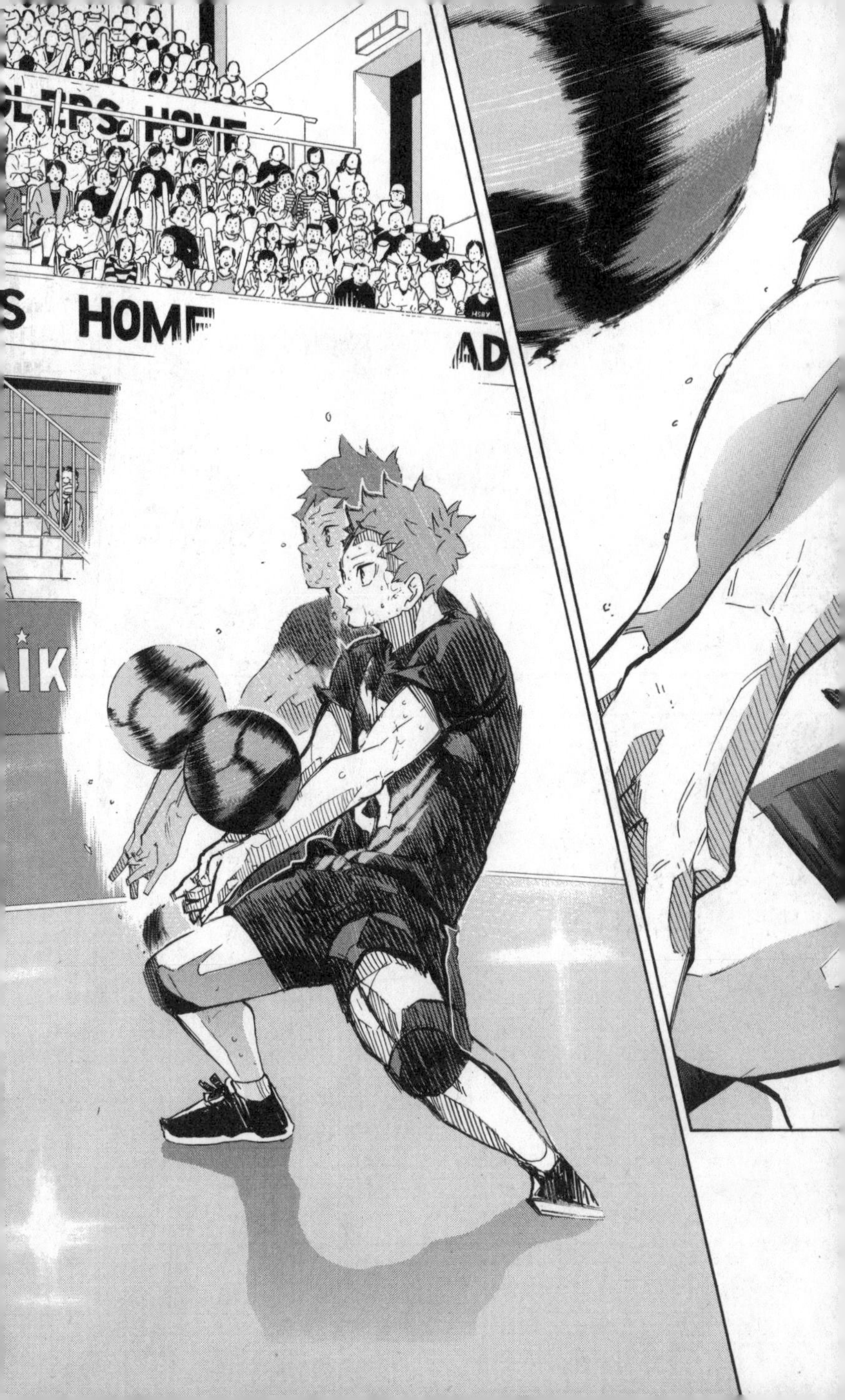
S HOME
AD

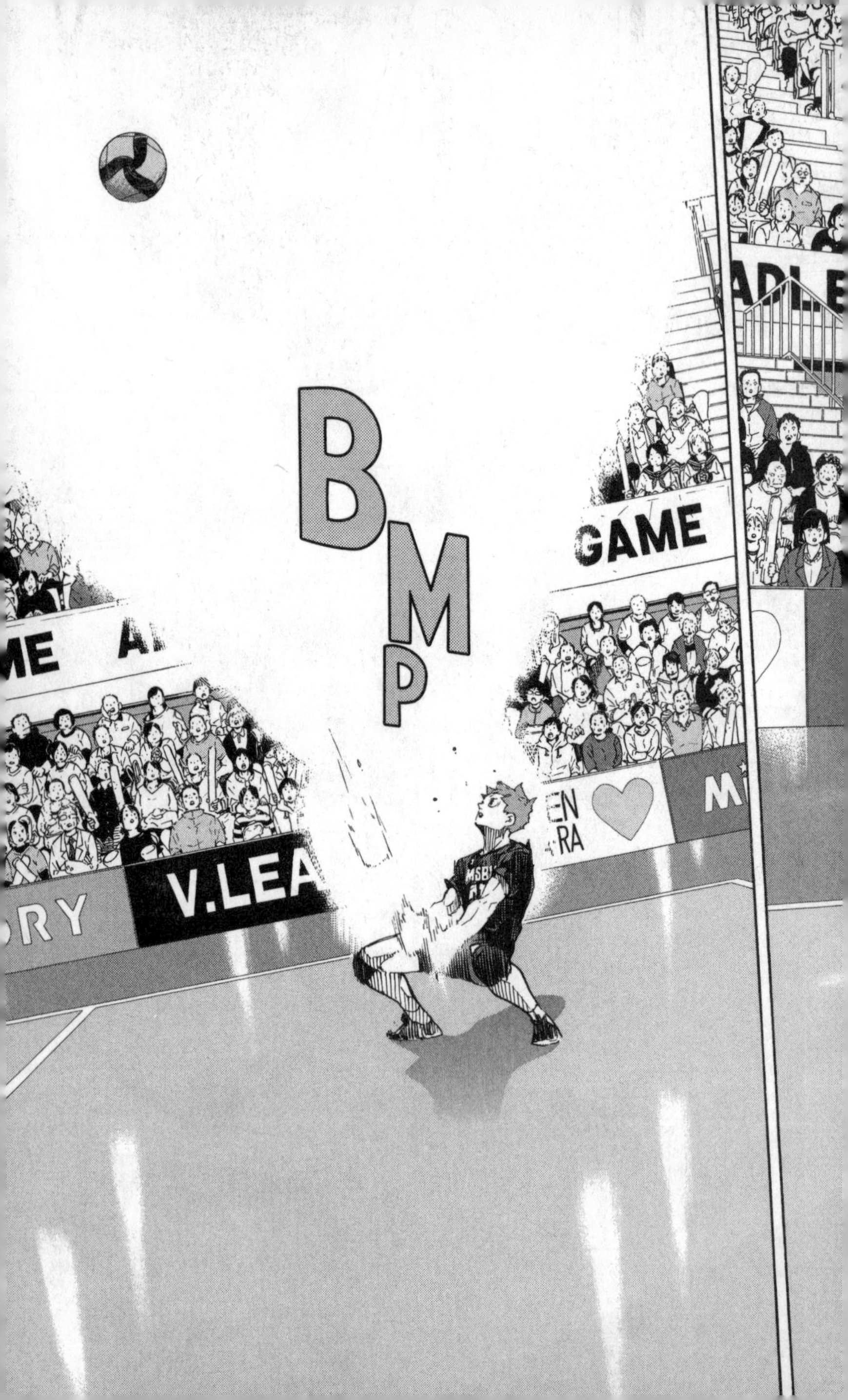

ADL.E
GAME
BMP
ME
V.LEA
RY

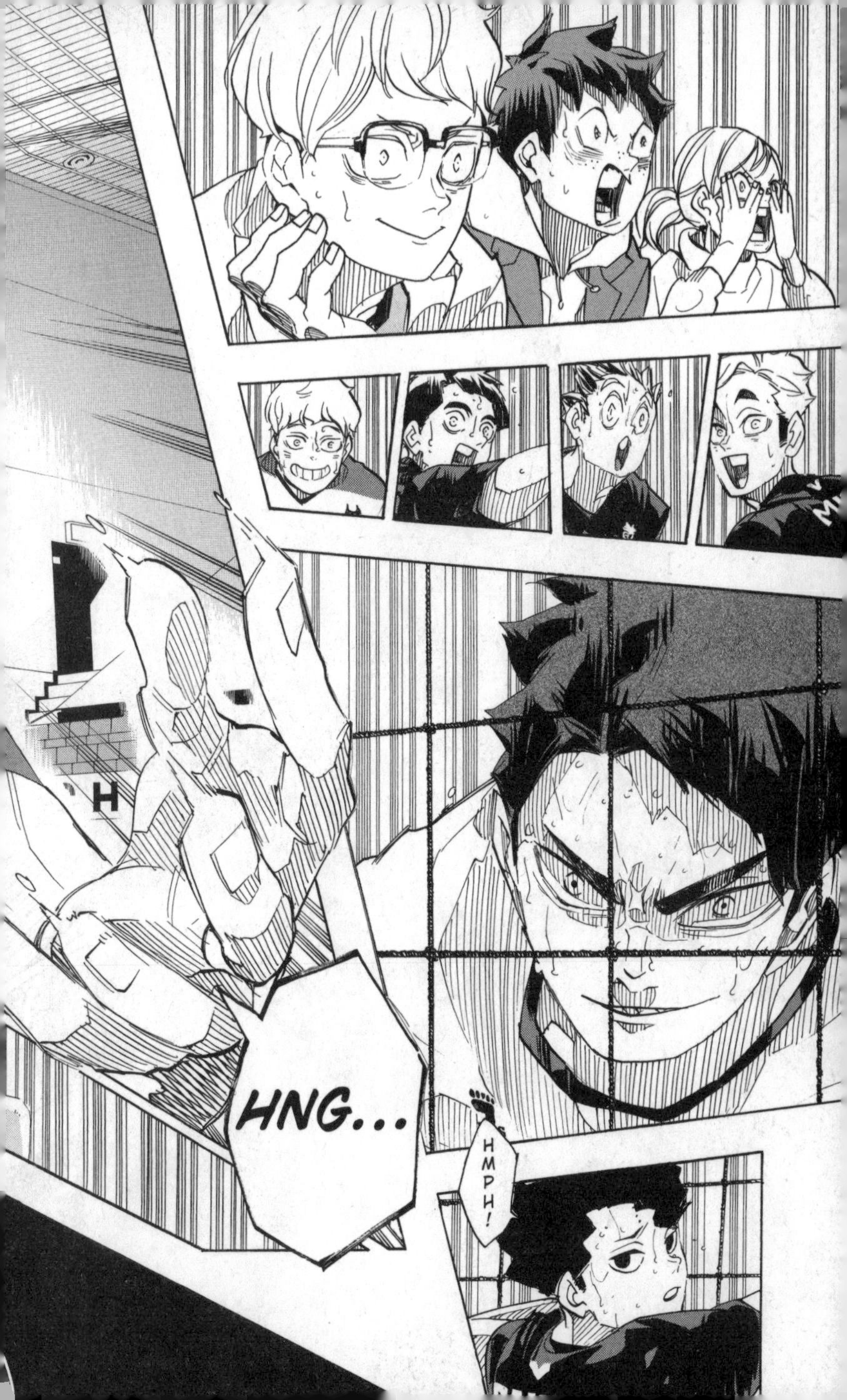
HNG...
HMPH!

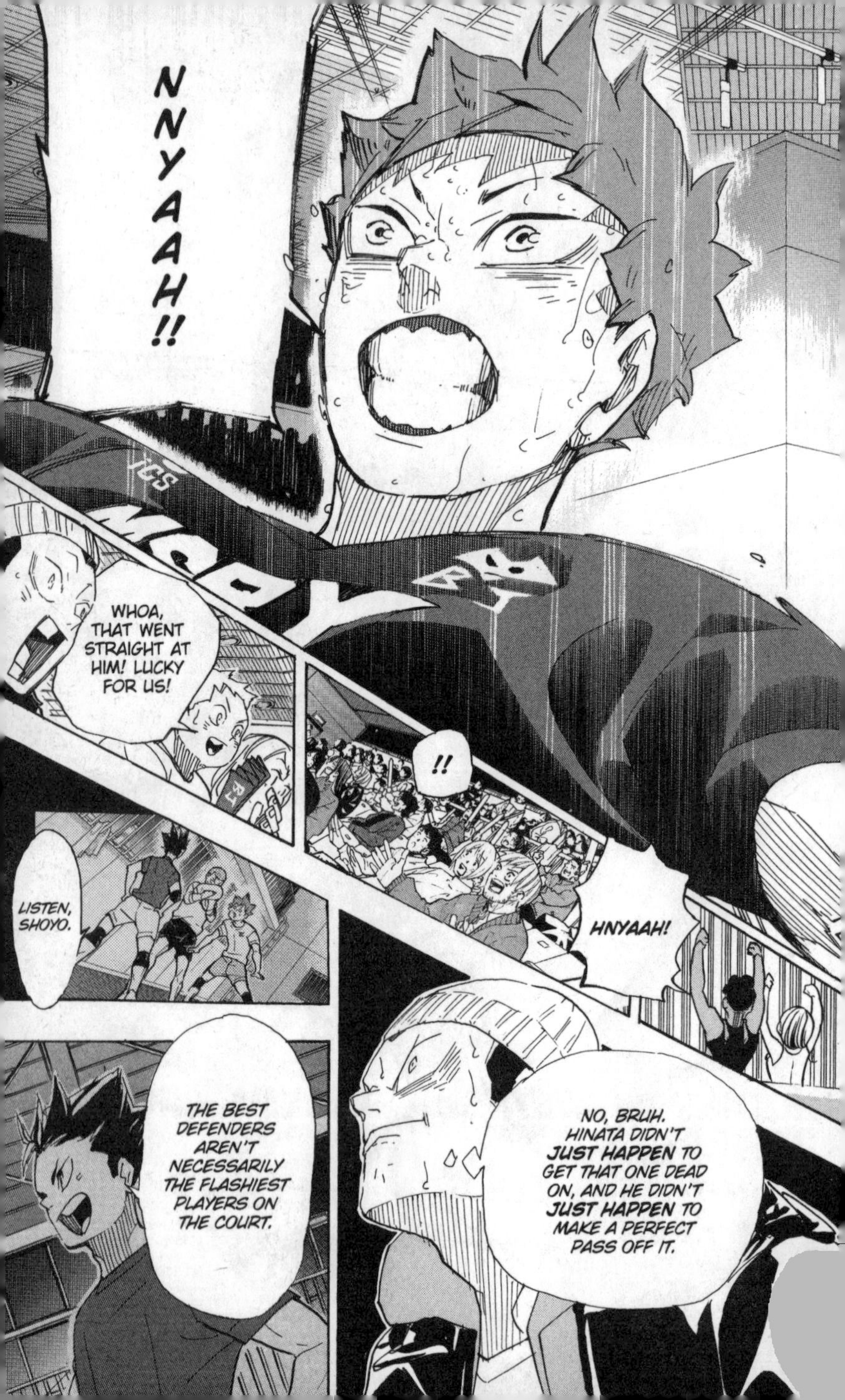
NNYAAAH!!
!!
WHOA, THAT WENT STRAIGHT AT HIM! LUCKY FOR US!
HNYAAH!
LISTEN, SHOYO.
NO, BRUH. HINATA DIDN'T **JUST HAPPEN** TO GET THAT ONE DEAD ON, AND HE DIDN'T **JUST HAPPEN** TO MAKE A PERFECT PASS OFF IT.
THE BEST DEFENDERS AREN'T NECESSARILY THE FLASHIEST PLAYERS ON THE COURT.

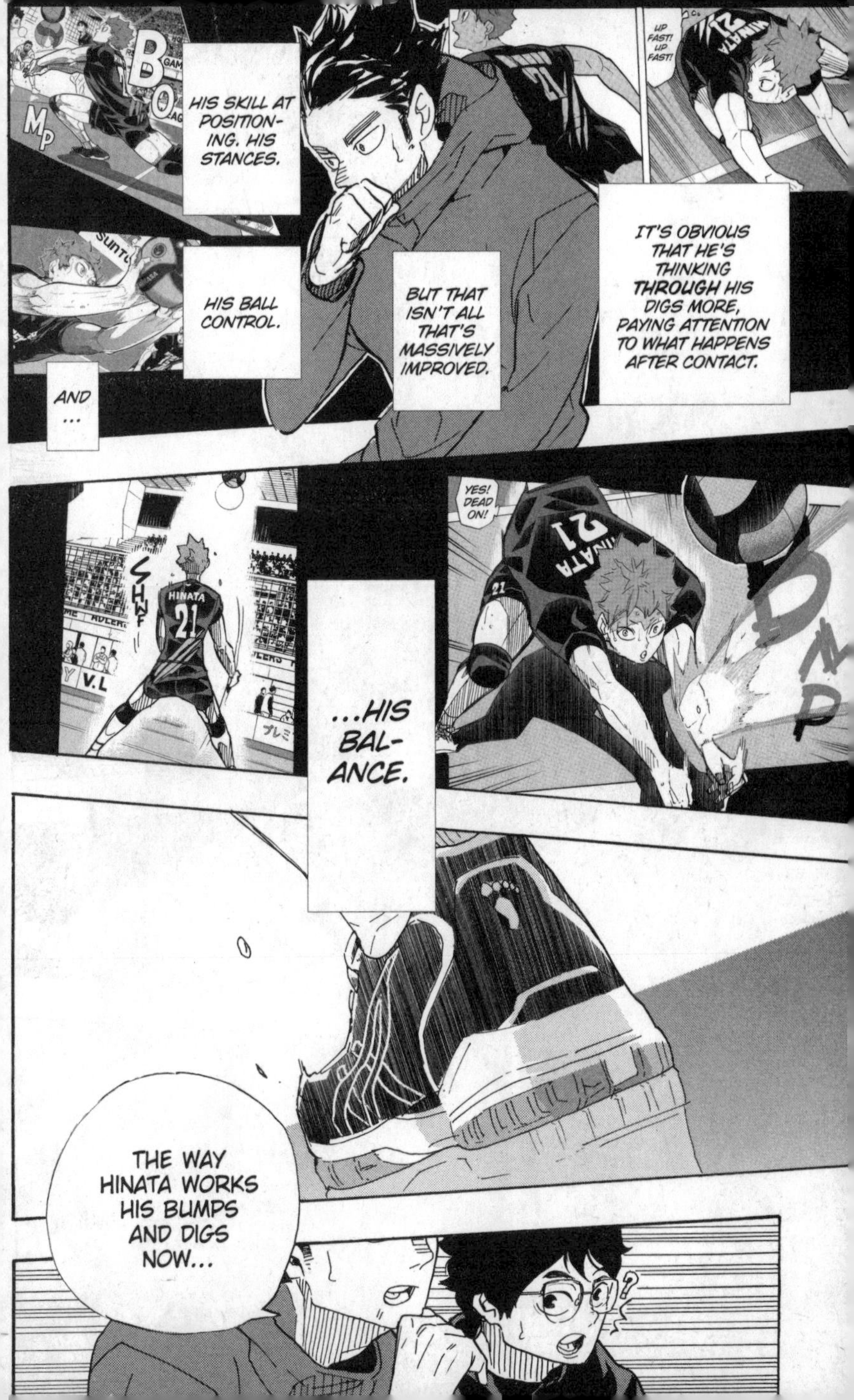
UP FAST! UP FAST!
IT'S OBVIOUS THAT HE'S THINKING **THROUGH** HIS DIGS MORE, PAYING ATTENTION TO WHAT HAPPENS AFTER CONTACT.
BUT THAT ISN'T ALL THAT'S MASSIVELY IMPROVED.
BOMP
HIS SKILL AT POSITIONING. HIS STANCES.
HIS BALL CONTROL.
AND ...
YES! DEAD ON!
SHWF
...HIS BALANCE.
THE WAY HINATA WORKS HIS BUMPS AND DIGS NOW...

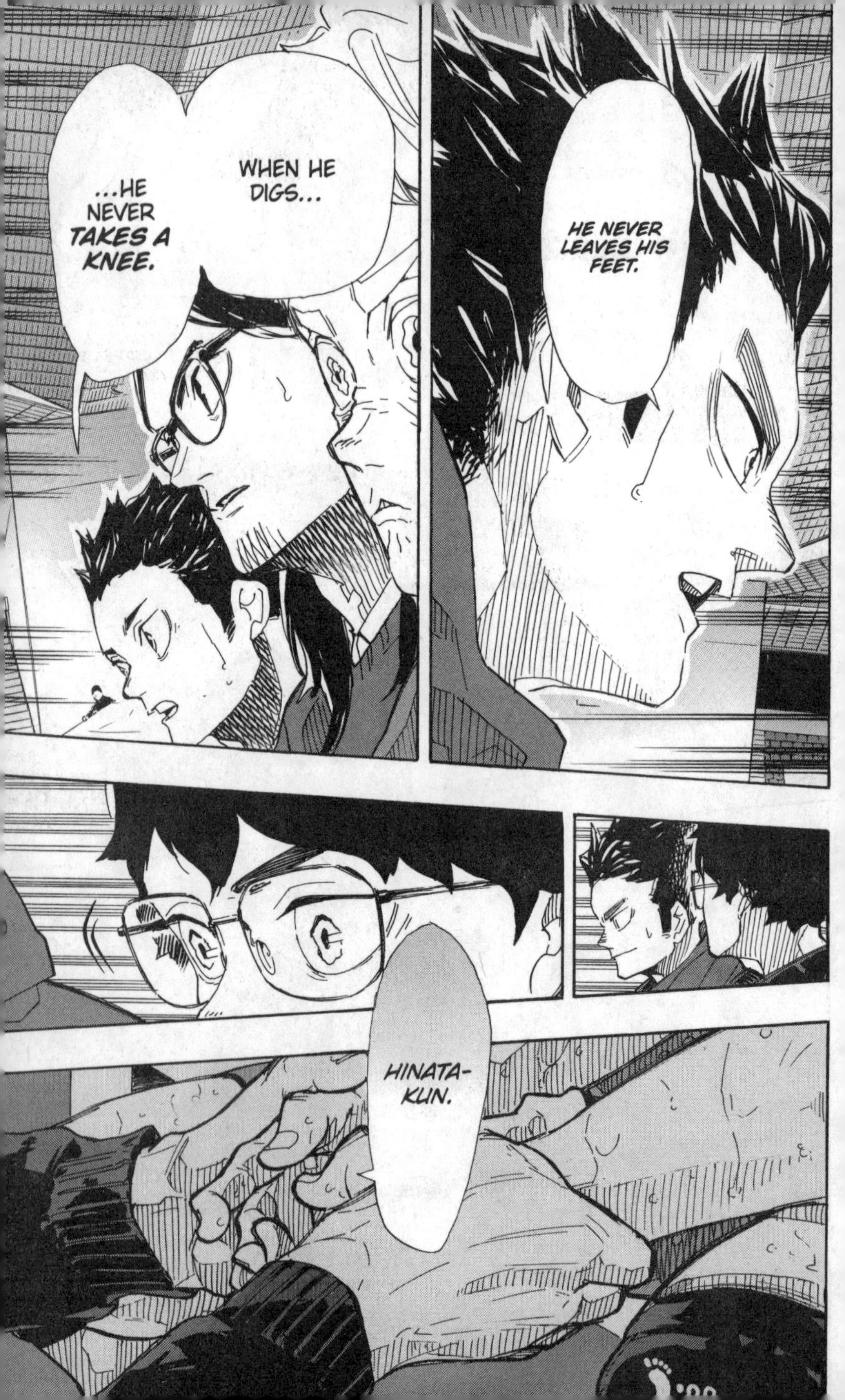
HE NEVER LEAVES HIS FEET.
WHEN HE DIGS...
...HE NEVER TAKES A KNEE.
HINATA-KUN.

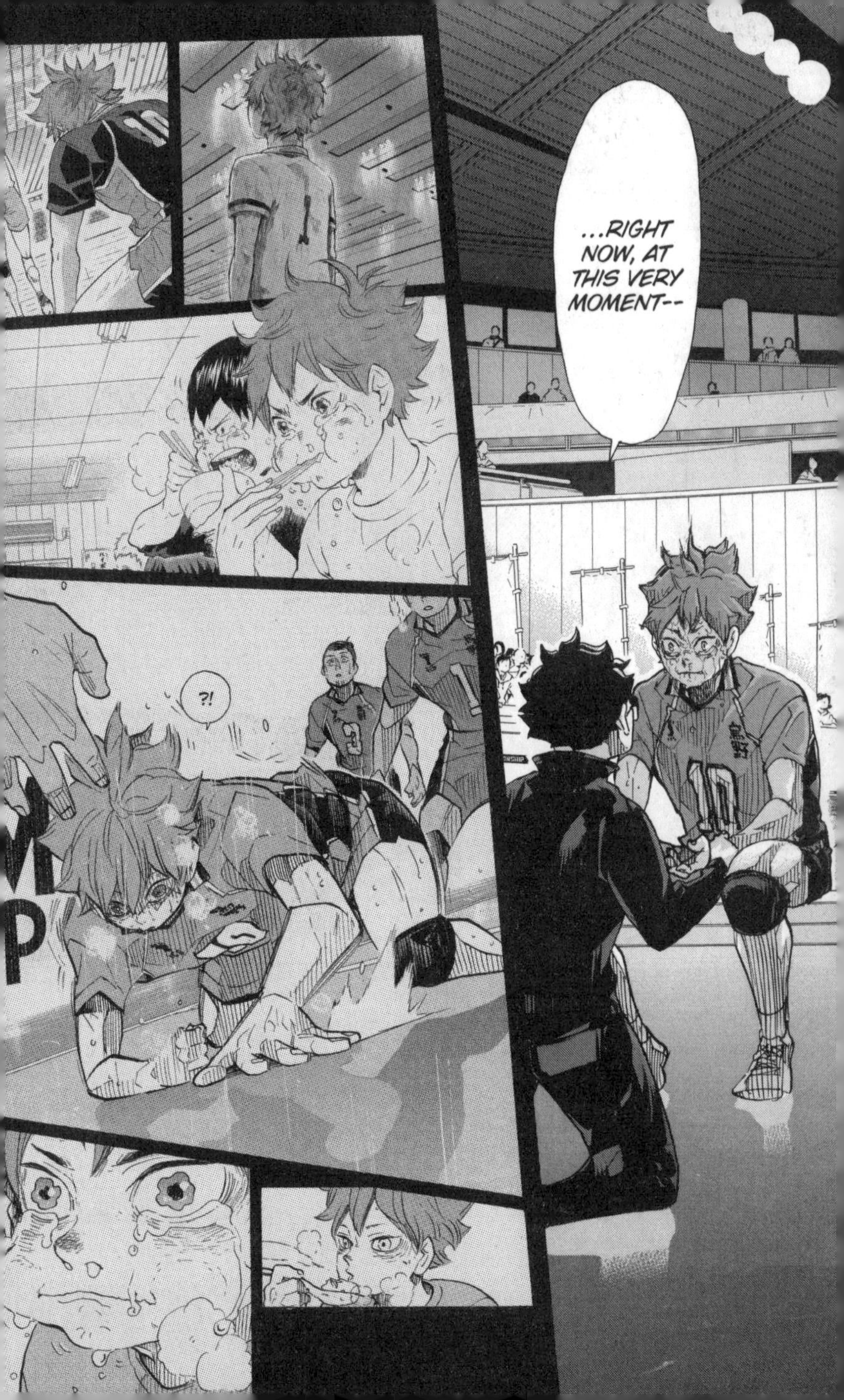

...RIGHT NOW, AT THIS VERY MOMENT--
?!

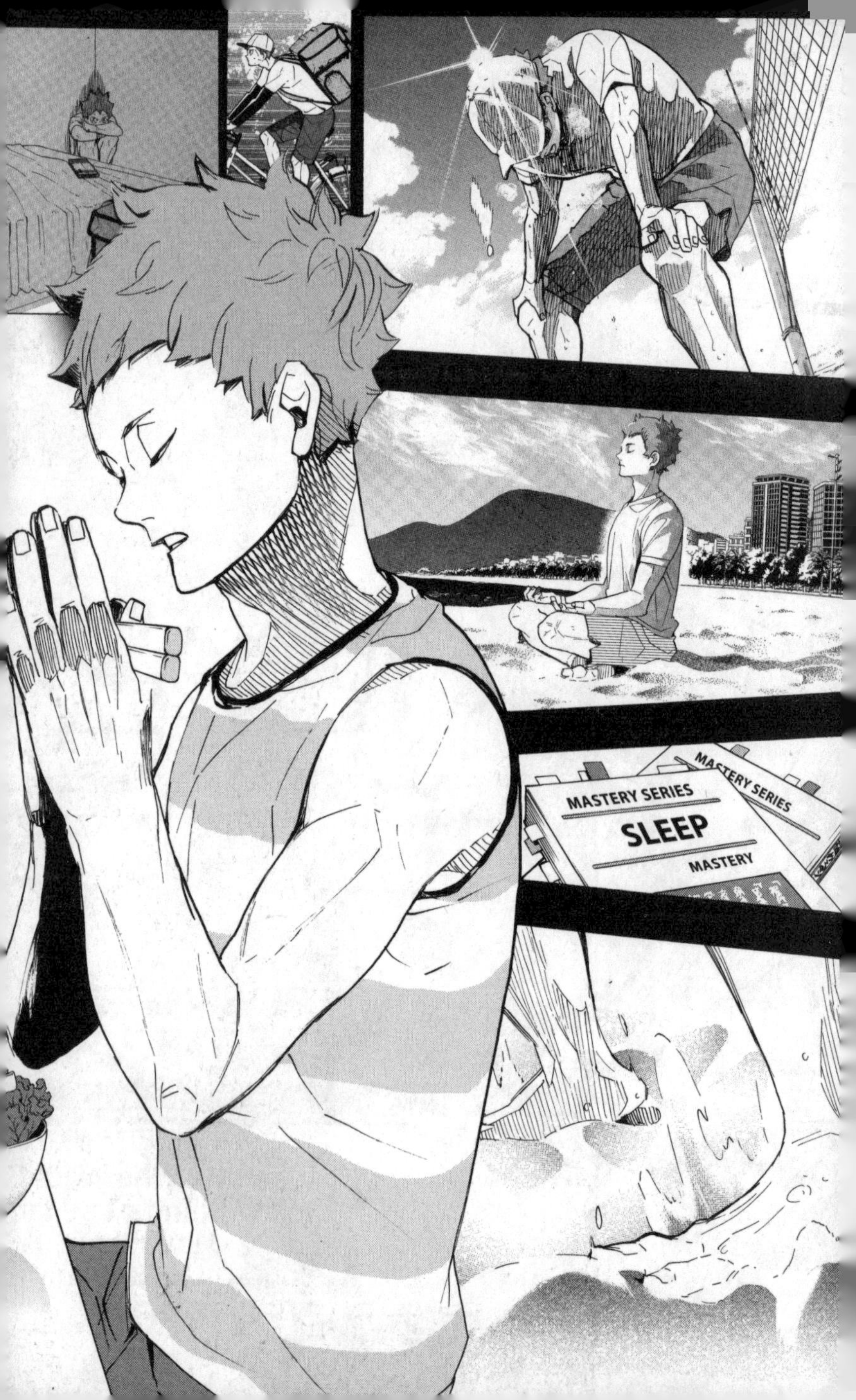
MASTERY SERIES
SLEEP
MASTERY
MASTERY SERIES

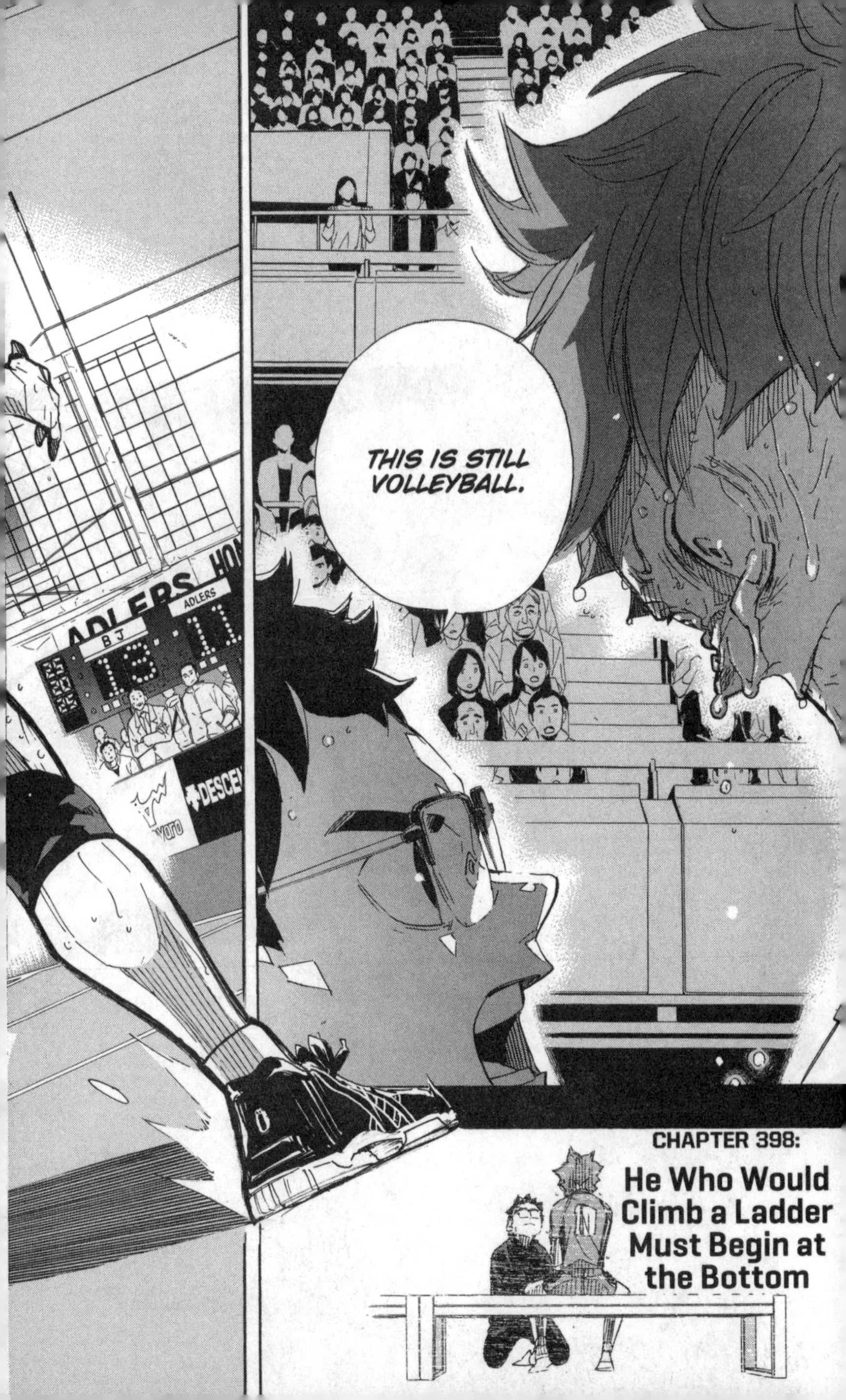
THIS IS STILL VOLLEYBALL.
ADLERS
BJ

CHAPTER 398:

He Who Would Climb a Ladder Must Begin at the Bottom

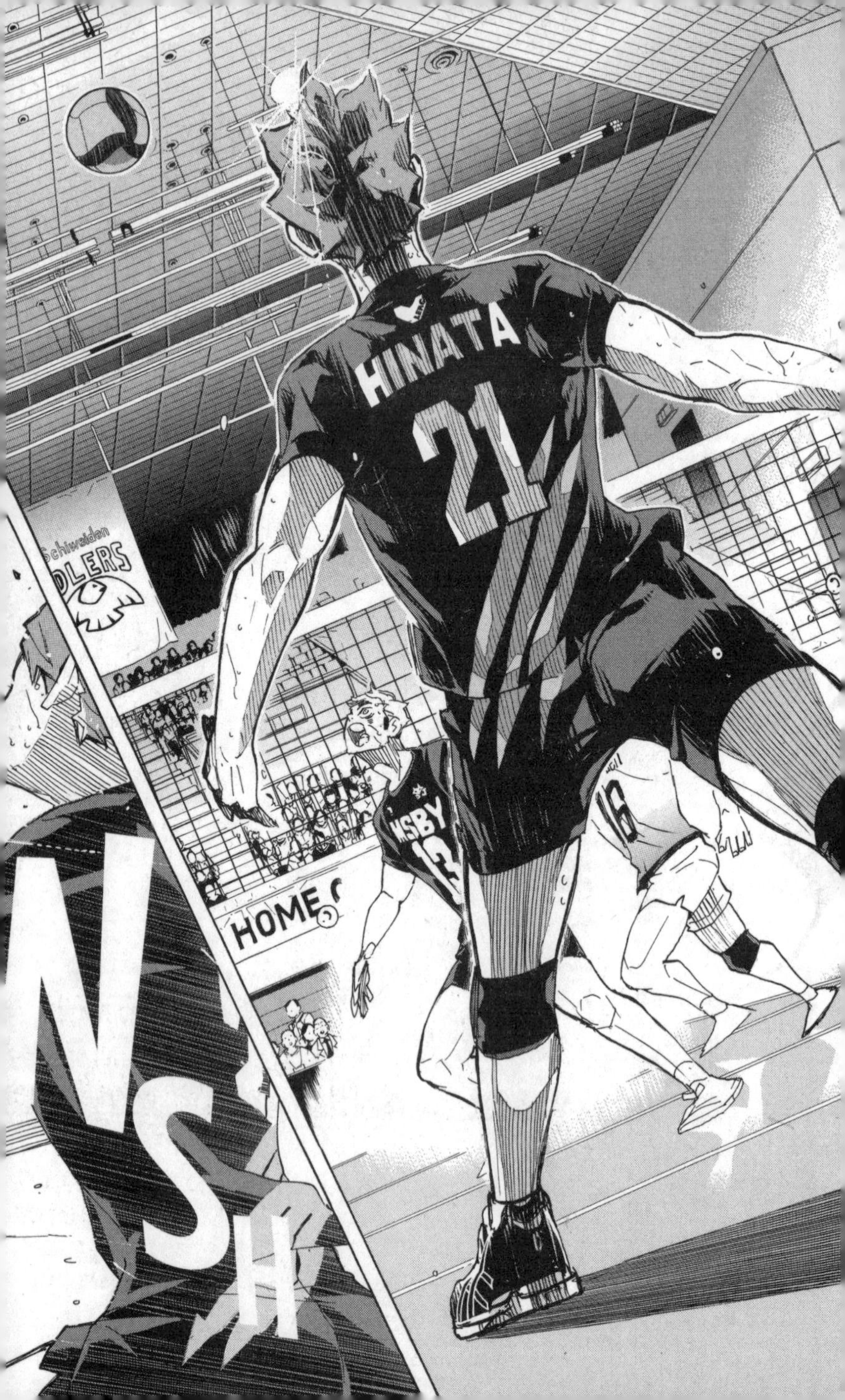

Schweiden
DLERS
HINATA
21
MSBY
13
16
HOME
N
S
H

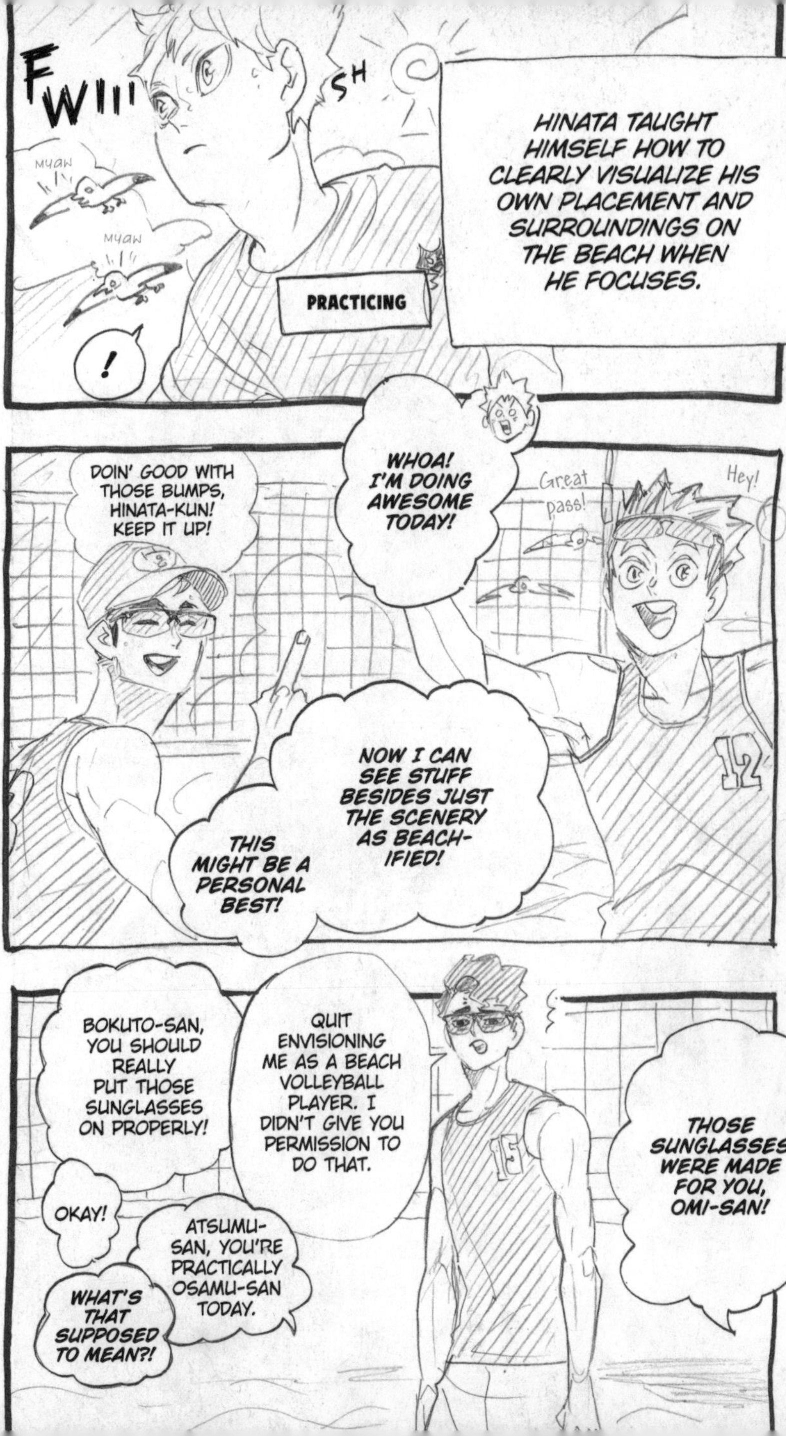
HINATA TAUGHT HIMSELF HOW TO CLEARLY VISUALIZE HIS OWN PLACEMENT AND SURROUNDINGS ON THE BEACH WHEN HE FOCUSES.
FWIII'SH
PRACTICING
myaw
myaw
!
Hey!
Great pass!
WHOA! I'M DOING AWESOME TODAY!
DOIN' GOOD WITH THOSE BUMPS, HINATA-KUN! KEEP IT UP!
NOW I CAN SEE STUFF BESIDES JUST THE SCENERY AS BEACH-IFIED!
THIS MIGHT BE A PERSONAL BEST!
THOSE SUNGLASSES WERE MADE FOR YOU, OMI-SAN!
QUIT ENVISIONING ME AS A BEACH VOLLEYBALL PLAYER. I DIDN'T GIVE YOU PERMISSION TO DO THAT.
BOKUTO-SAN, YOU SHOULD REALLY PUT THOSE SUNGLASSES ON PROPERLY!
OKAY!
ATSUMU-SAN, YOU'RE PRACTICALLY OSAMU-SAN TODAY.
WHAT'S THAT SUPPOSED TO MEAN?!

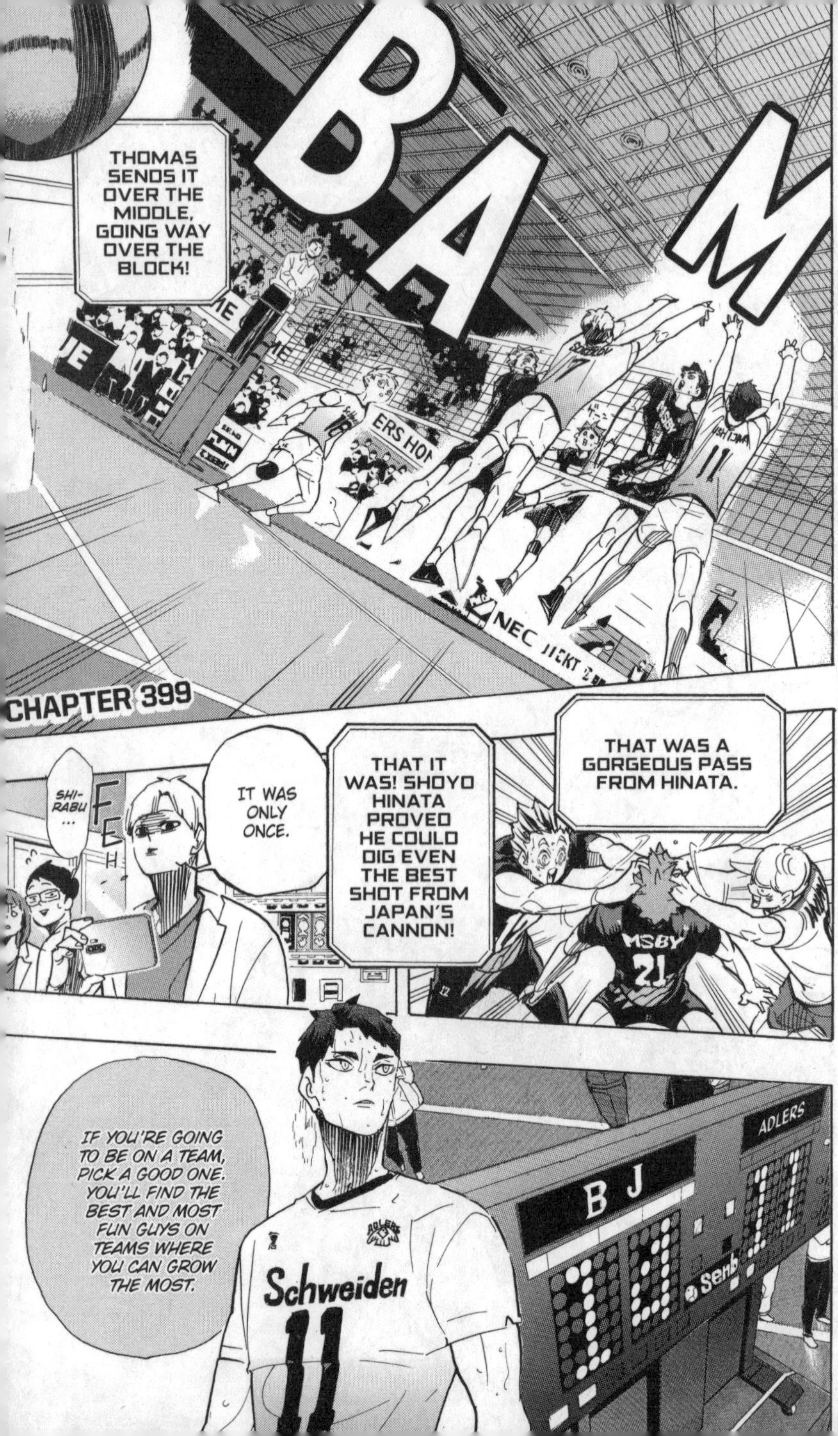
BAM
THOMAS SENDS IT OVER THE MIDDLE, GOING WAY OVER THE BLOCK!
CHAPTER 399
THAT WAS A GORGEOUS PASS FROM HINATA.
THAT IT WAS! SHOYO HINATA PROVED HE COULD DIG EVEN THE BEST SHOT FROM JAPAN'S CANNON!
MSBY
21
IT WAS ONLY ONCE.
SHI-RABU...
FEH
IF YOU'RE GOING TO BE ON A TEAM, PICK A GOOD ONE. YOU'LL FIND THE BEST AND MOST FUN GUYS ON TEAMS WHERE YOU CAN GROW THE MOST.
ADLERS
B J
Schweiden
11

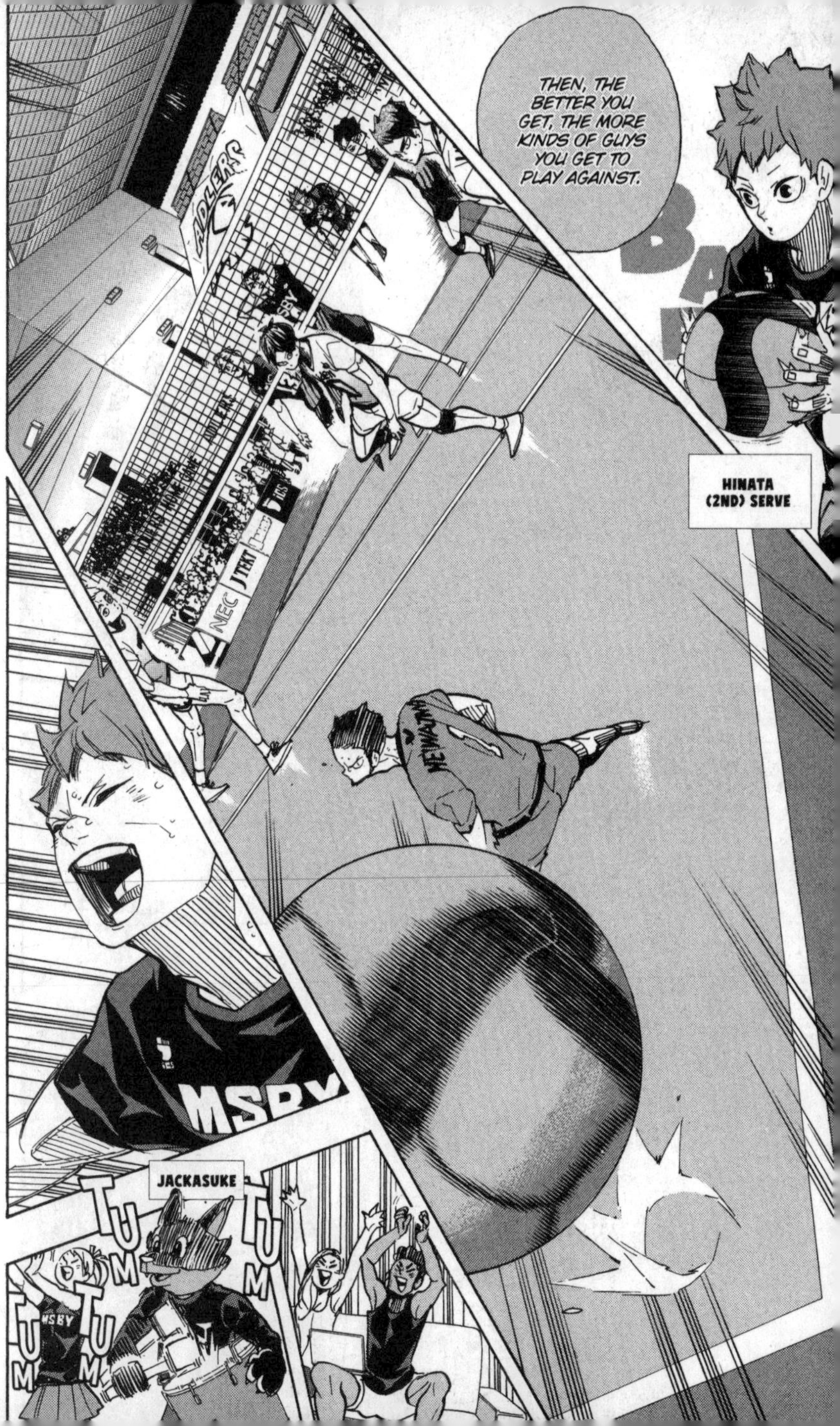
THEN, THE BETTER YOU GET, THE MORE KINDS OF GUYS YOU GET TO PLAY AGAINST.
HINATA (2ND) SERVE
MSBY
JACKASUKE
TUM TUM
TUM TUM

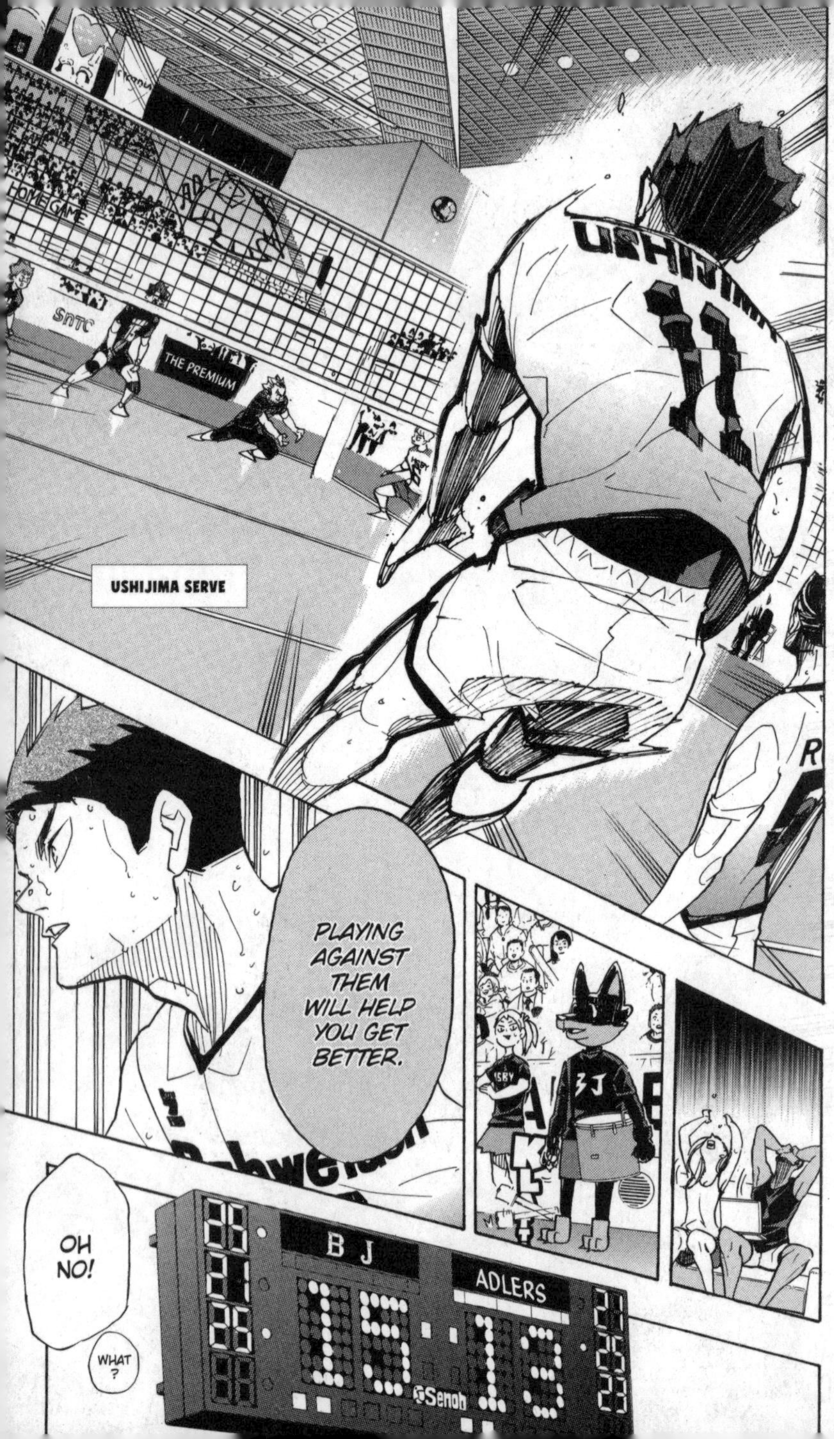
HOME GAME
THE PREMIUM
USHIJIMA
11
USHIJIMA SERVE
PLAYING AGAINST THEM WILL HELP YOU GET BETTER.
OH NO!
WHAT?
B J
ADLERS
Senoh

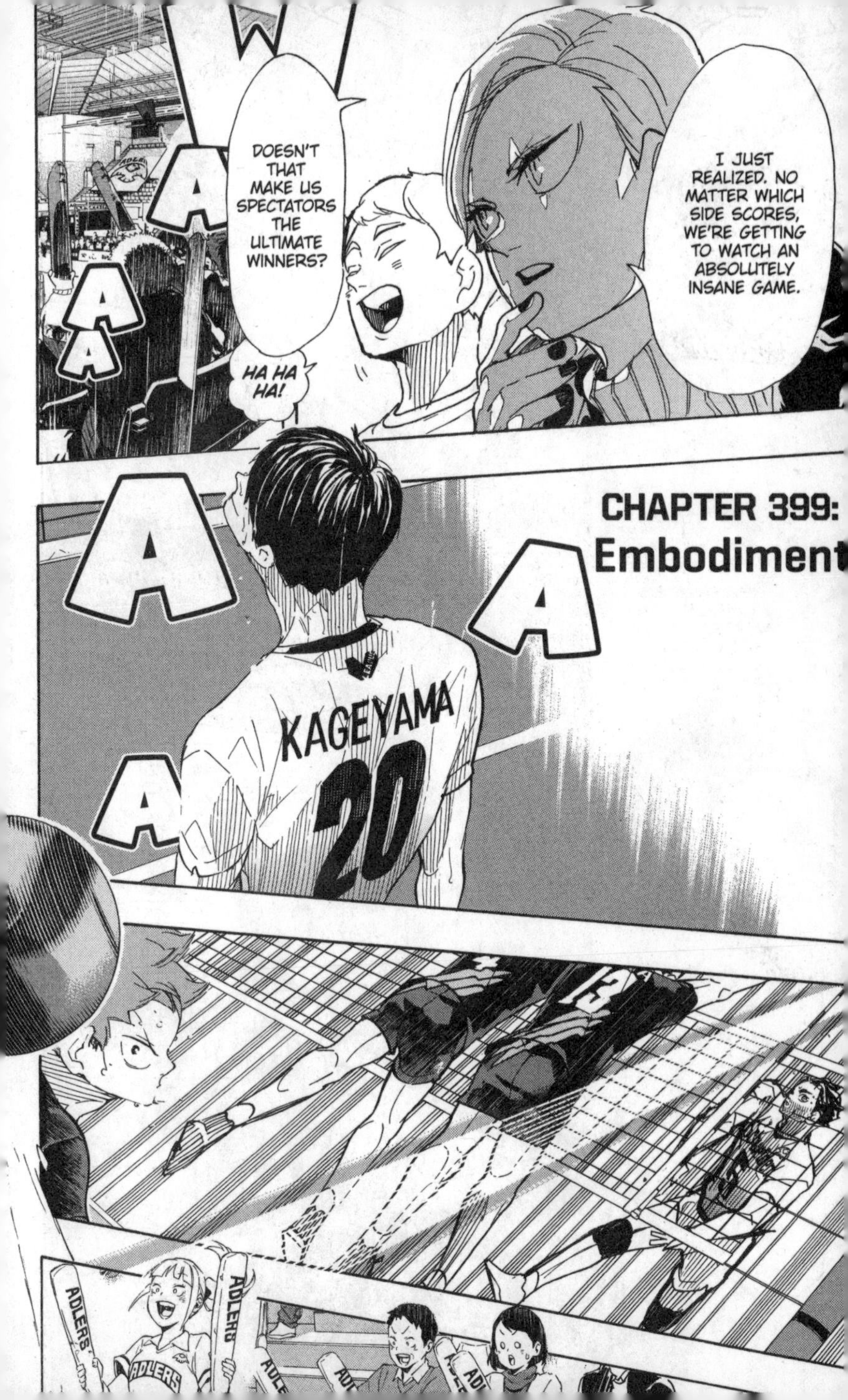

I JUST REALIZED. NO MATTER WHICH SIDE SCORES, WE'RE GETTING TO WATCH AN ABSOLUTELY INSANE GAME.
DOESN'T THAT MAKE US SPECTATORS THE ULTIMATE WINNERS?
HA HA HA!
WAAAA
CHAPTER 399:
Embodiment
AAA
KAGEYAMA
20
13
ADLERS
ADLERS
ADLERS

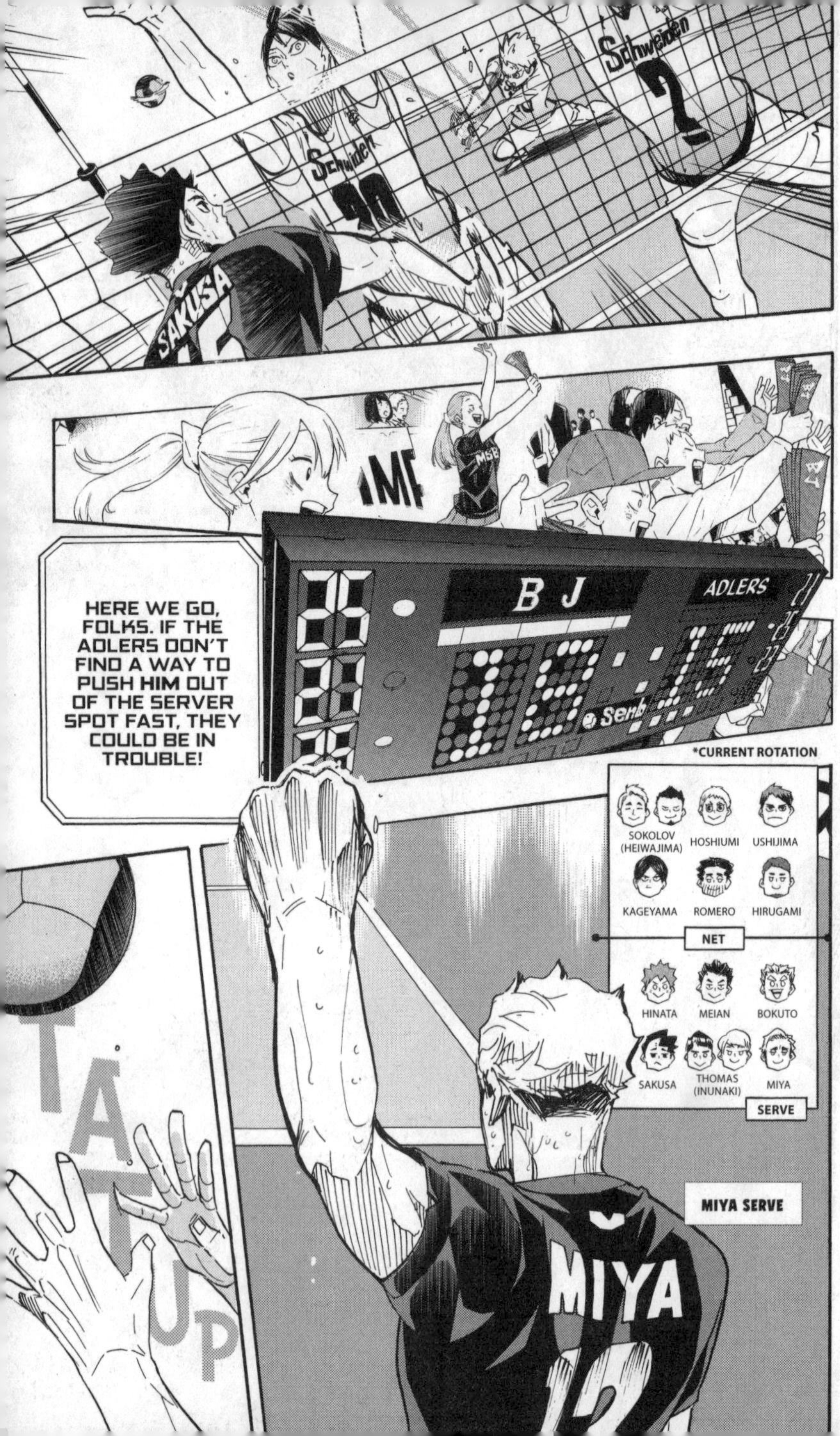
Schweiden
SAKUSA
B J
ADLERS
HERE WE GO, FOLKS. IF THE ADLERS DON'T FIND A WAY TO PUSH HIM OUT OF THE SERVER SPOT FAST, THEY COULD BE IN TROUBLE!
*CURRENT ROTATION
SOKOLOV (HEIWAJIMA)
HOSHIUMI
USHIJIMA
KAGEYAMA
ROMERO
HIRUGAMI
NET
HINATA
MEIAN
BOKUTO
SAKUSA
THOMAS (INUNAKI)
MIYA
SERVE
MIYA SERVE
TAT
UP
MIYA

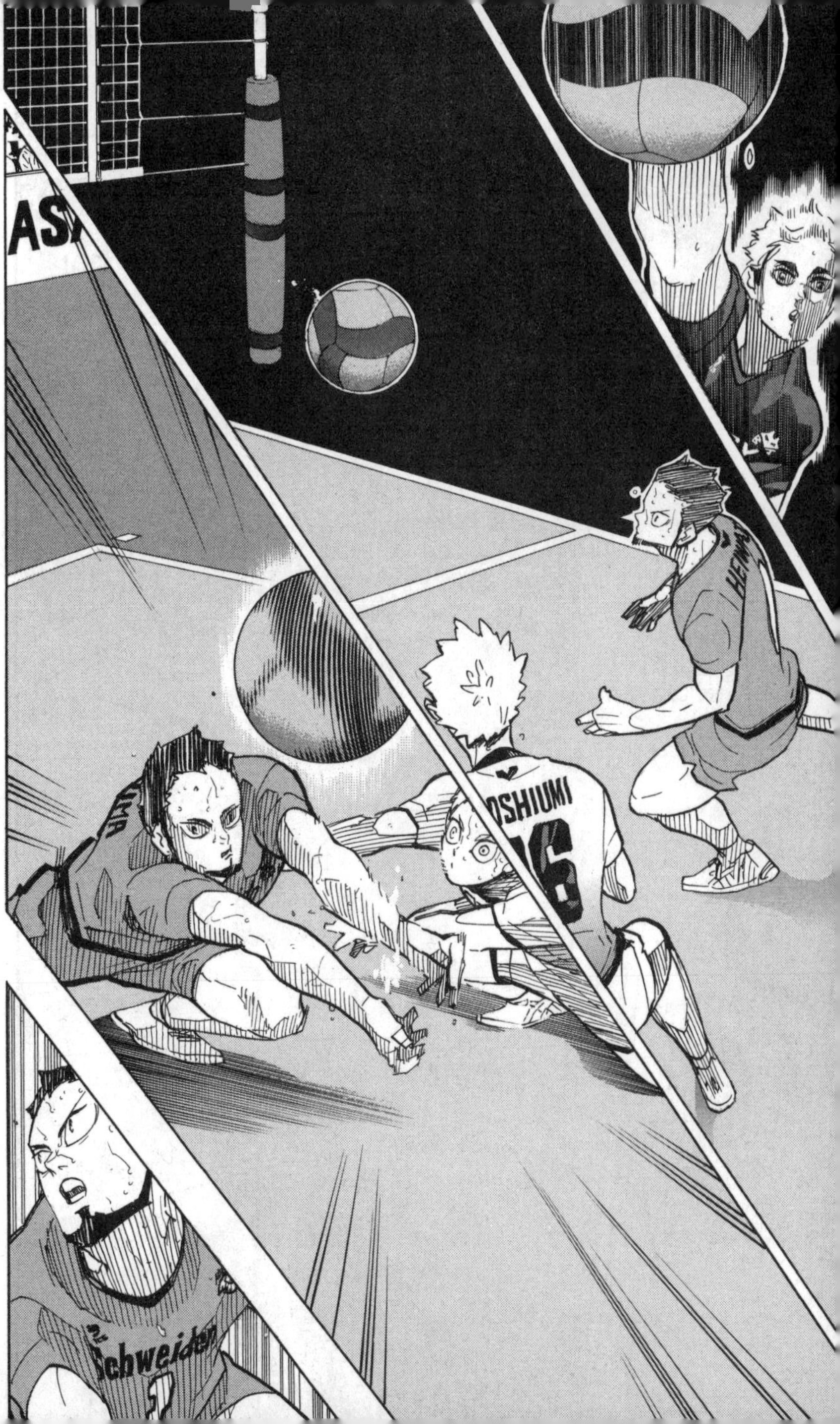
Schweiden

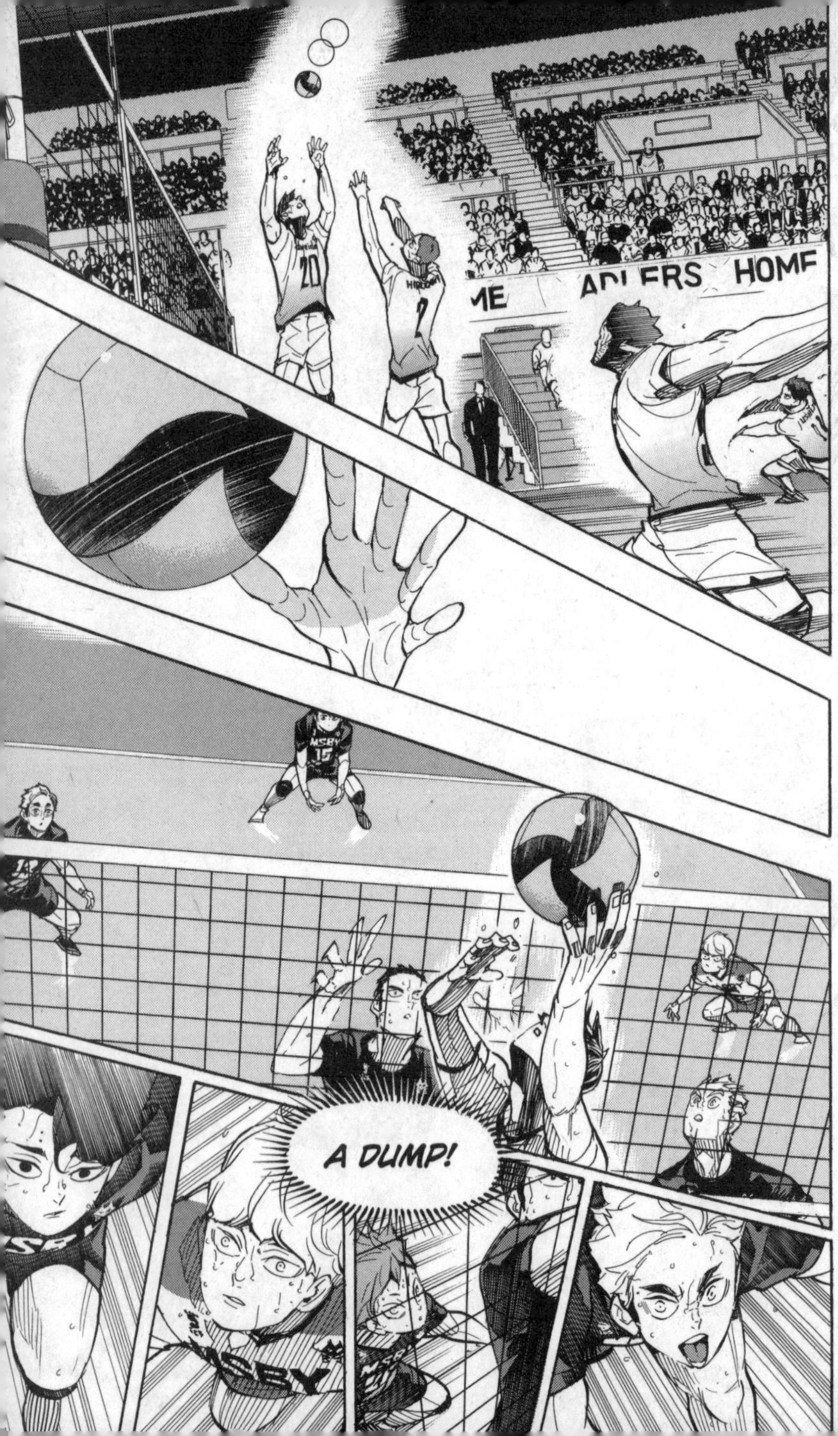
ME ADLERS HOME
A DUMP!

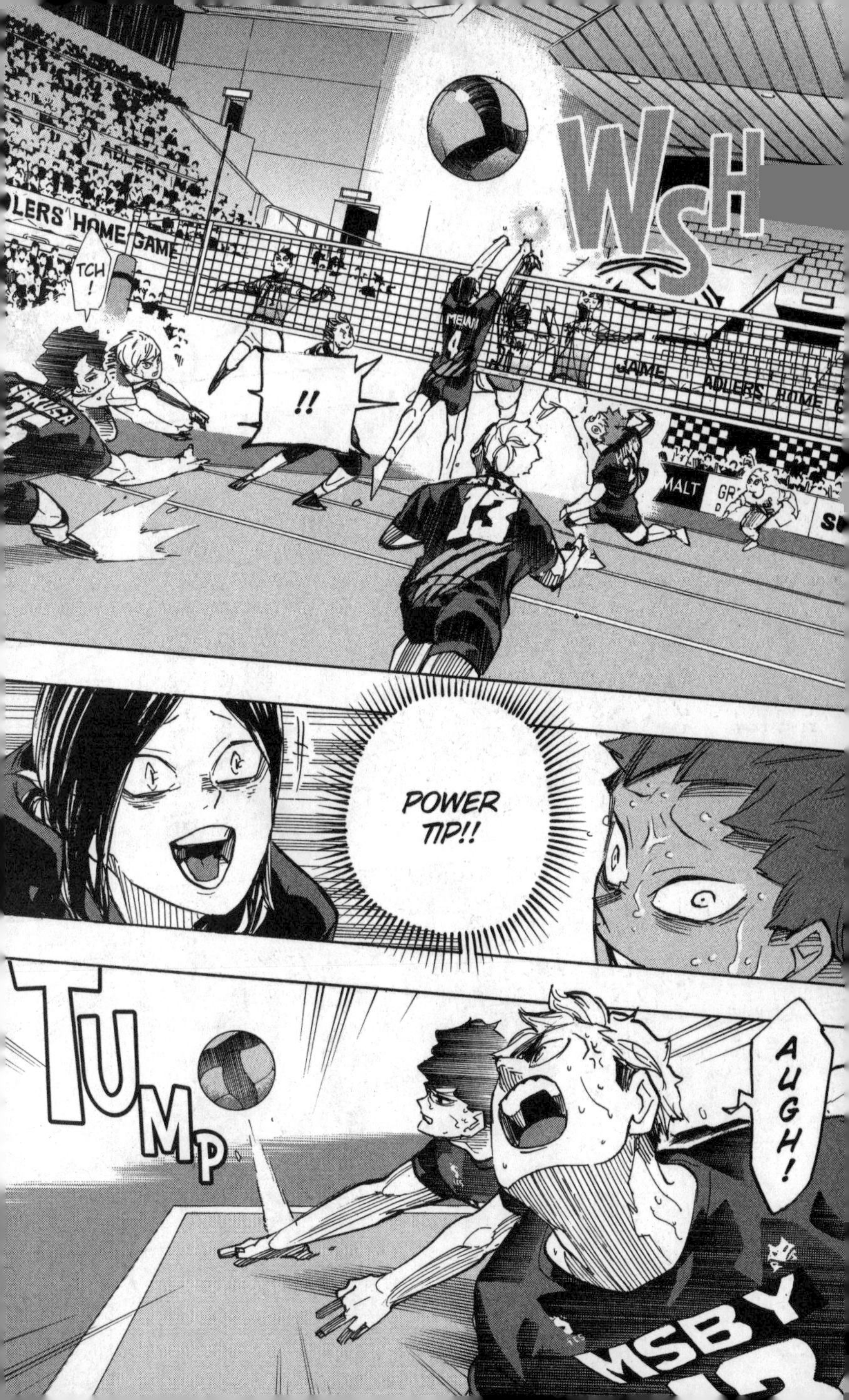

WSH
TCH!
!!
ADLERS HOME GAME
POWER TIP!!
AUGH!
TUMP
MSBY

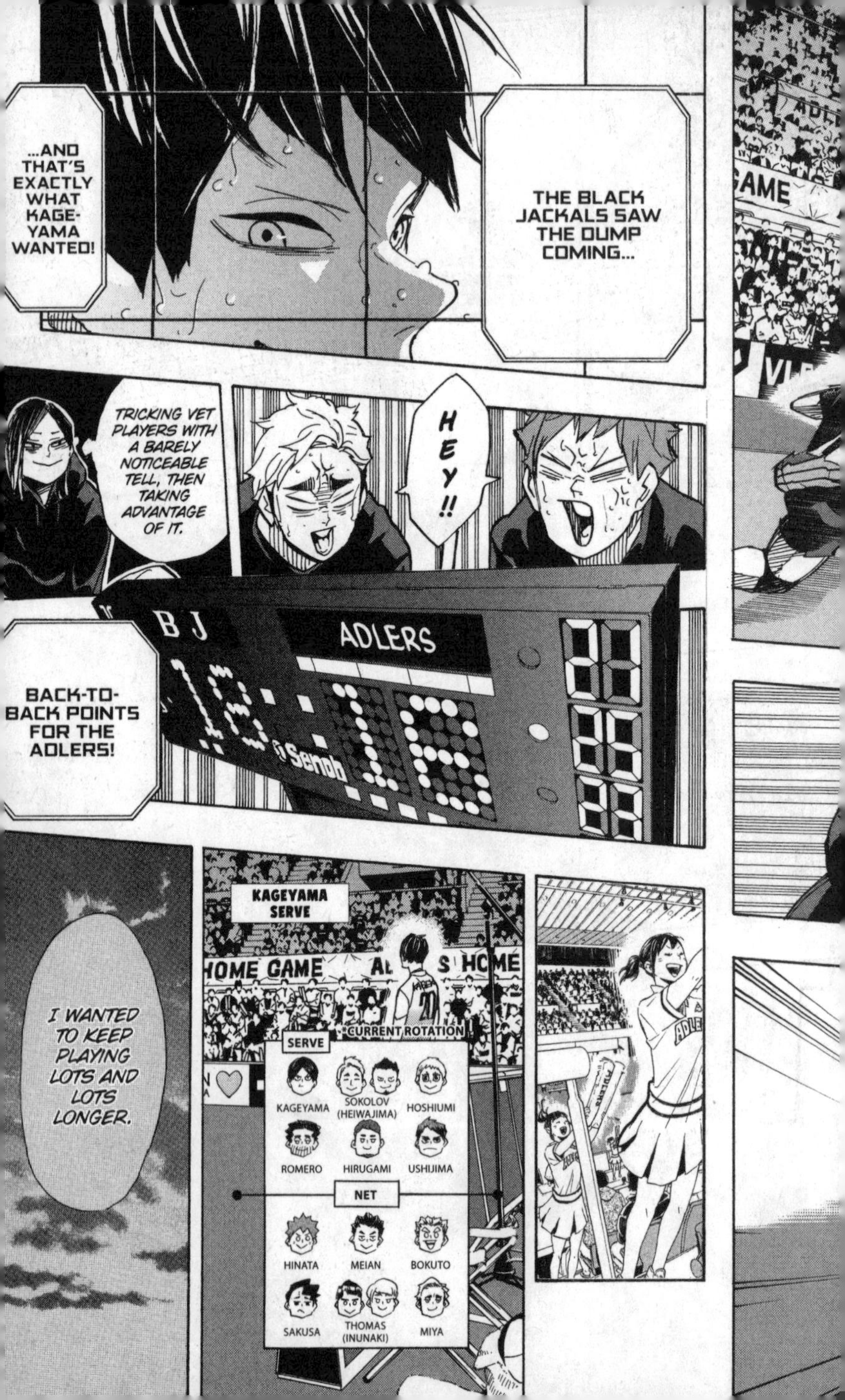
THE BLACK JACKALS SAW THE DUMP COMING...
...AND THAT'S EXACTLY WHAT KAGE-YAMA WANTED!
HEY!!
TRICKING VET PLAYERS WITH A BARELY NOTICEABLE TELL, THEN TAKING ADVANTAGE OF IT.
ADLERS
B J
BACK-TO-BACK POINTS FOR THE ADLERS!
KAGEYAMA SERVE
HOME GAME
CURRENT ROTATION
SERVE
KAGEYAMA
SOKOLOV (HEIWAJIMA)
HOSHIUMI
ROMERO
HIRUGAMI
USHIJIMA
NET
HINATA
MEIAN
BOKUTO
SAKUSA
THOMAS (INUNAKI)
MIYA
I WANTED TO KEEP PLAYING LOTS AND LOTS LONGER.

SWRRR

Tp

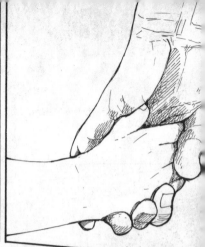

"IF YOU GET REALLY, REEEALLY GOOD, YOU'LL GET TO PLAY LOTS MORE GAMES."

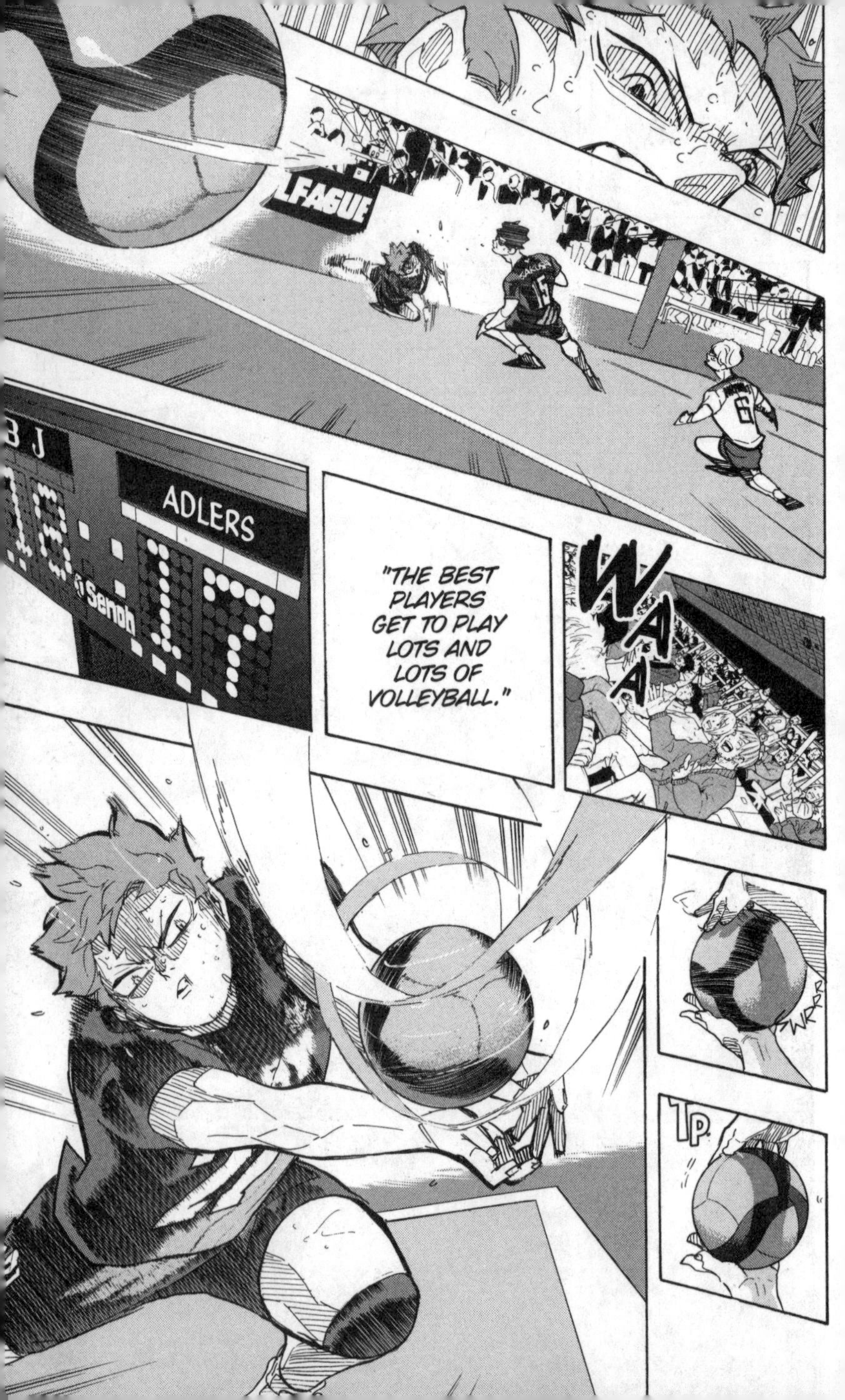
LEAGUE
SAKUSA
ADLERS
"THE BEST PLAYERS GET TO PLAY LOTS AND LOTS OF VOLLEYBALL."
WAA
WRRR
TP

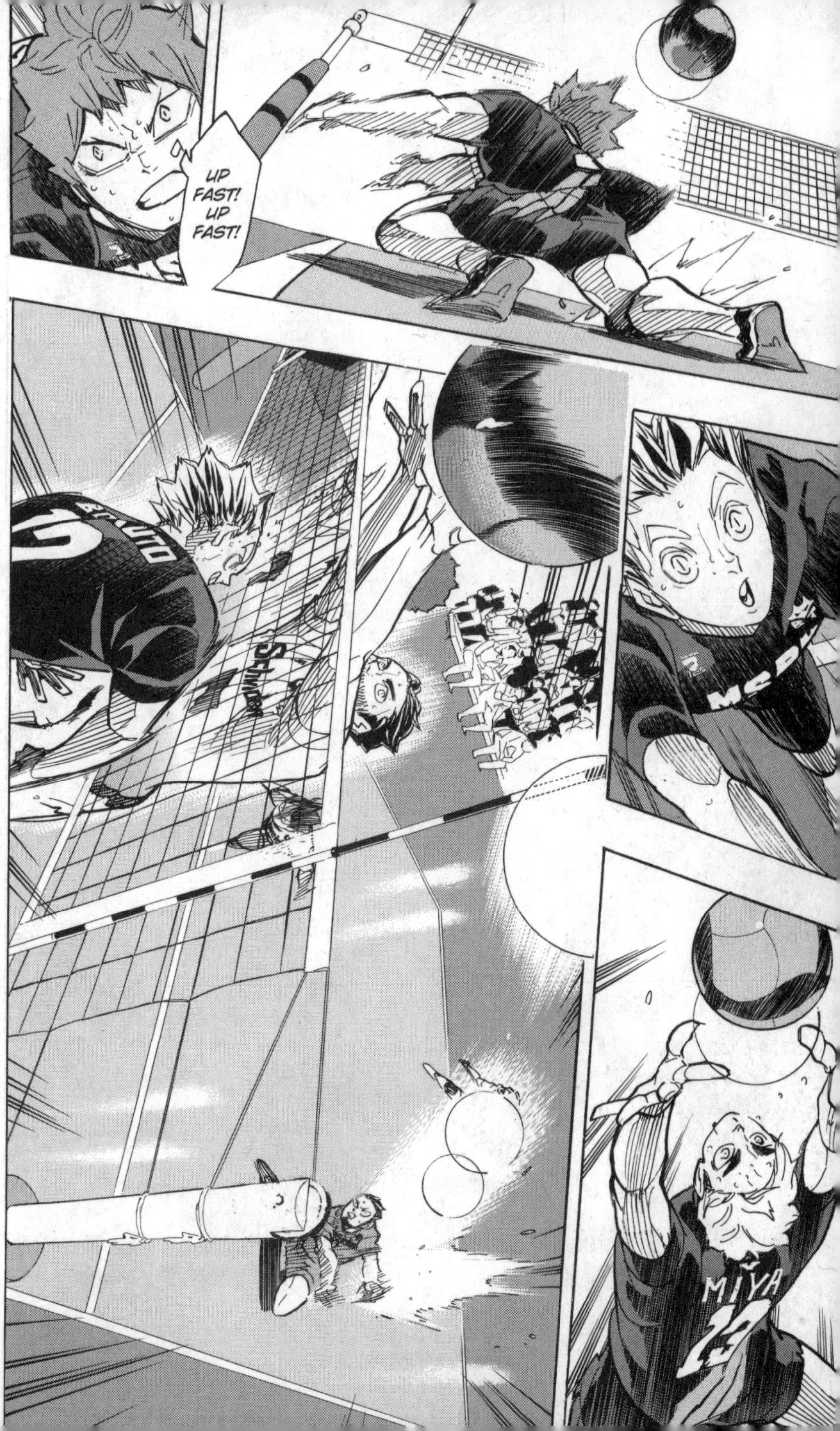
UP FAST! UP FAST!
BOKUTO
SHIMIZU
MSBY
MIYA

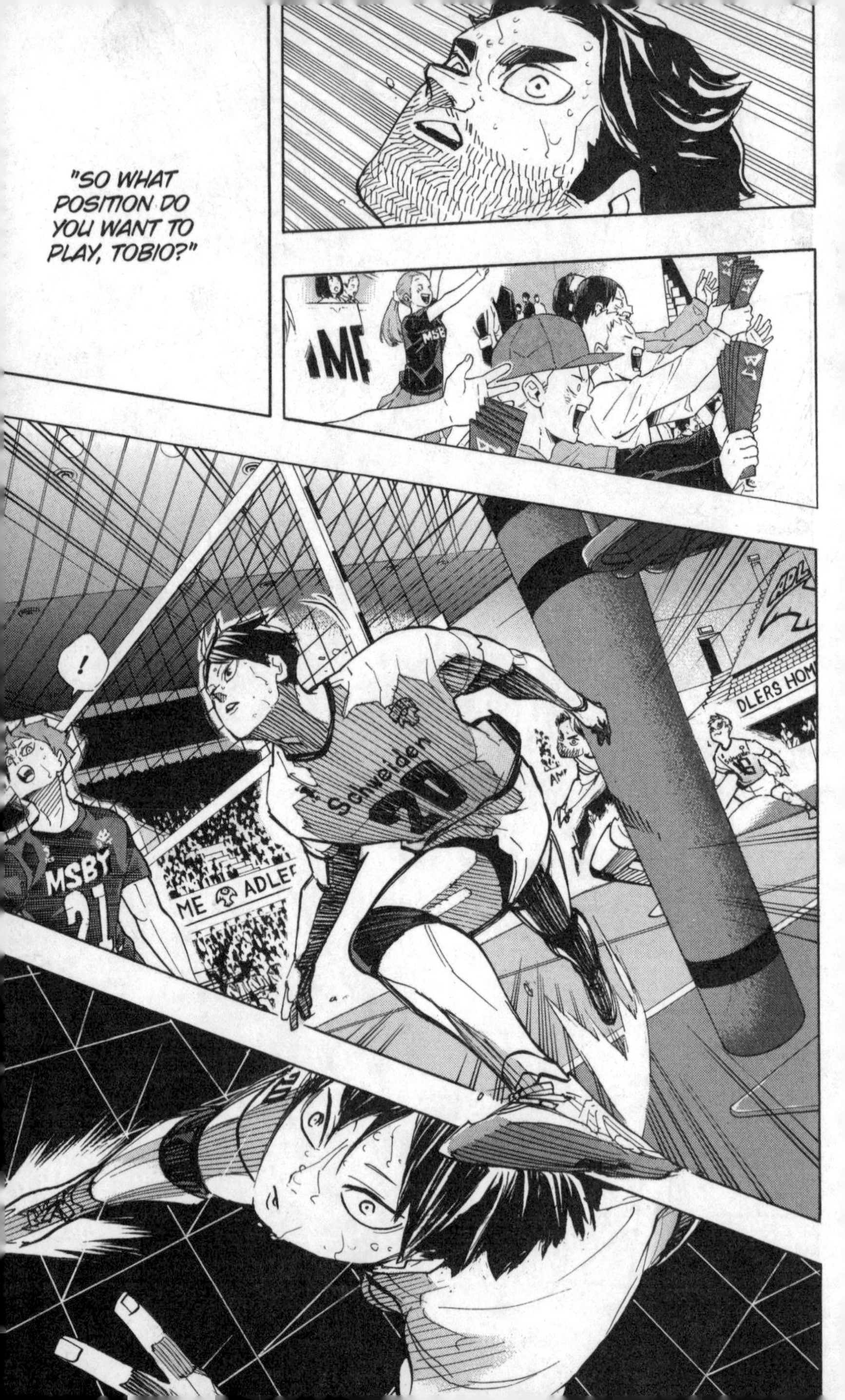
"SO WHAT POSITION DO YOU WANT TO PLAY, TOBIO?"
!

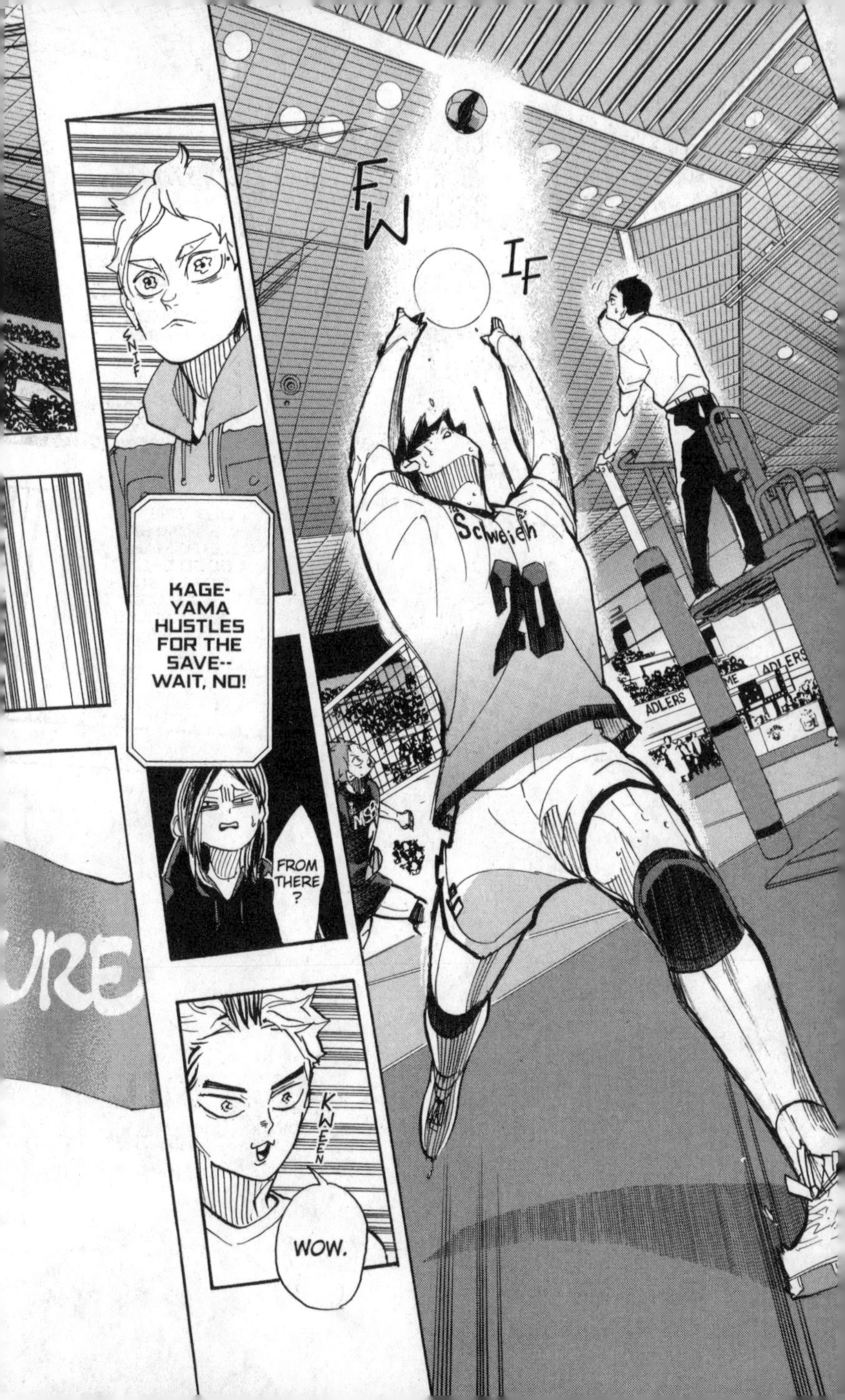
FWIF
SNIF
KAGE-YAMA HUSTLES FOR THE SAVE-- WAIT, NO!
FROM THERE?
KWEEN
WOW.

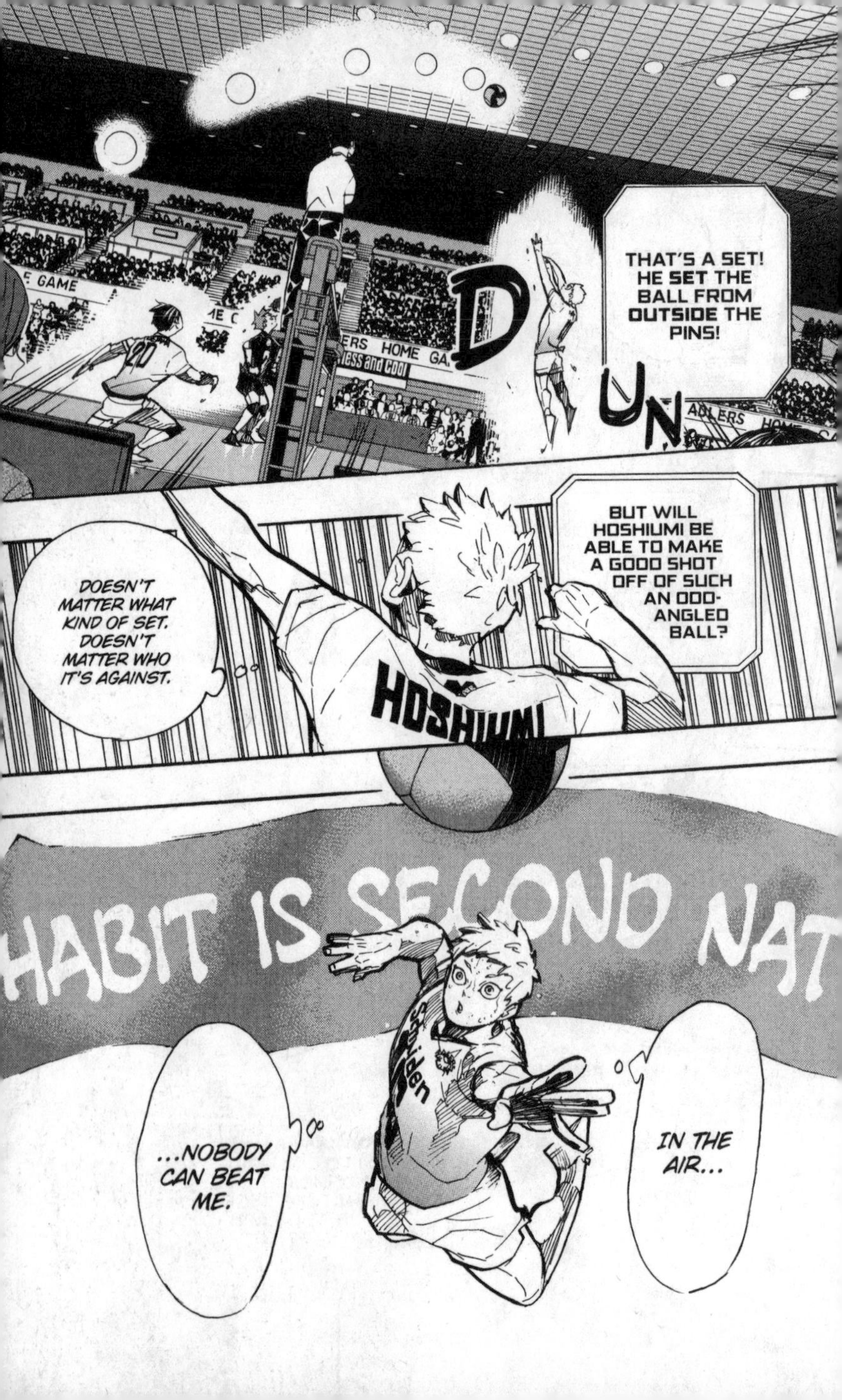
THAT'S A SET! HE SET THE BALL FROM OUTSIDE THE PINS!
DUN
ADLERS
BUT WILL HOSHIUMI BE ABLE TO MAKE A GOOD SHOT OFF OF SUCH AN ODD-ANGLED BALL?
DOESN'T MATTER WHAT KIND OF SET. DOESN'T MATTER WHO IT'S AGAINST.
HOSHIUMI
HABIT IS SECOND NAT
IN THE AIR...
...NOBODY CAN BEAT ME.

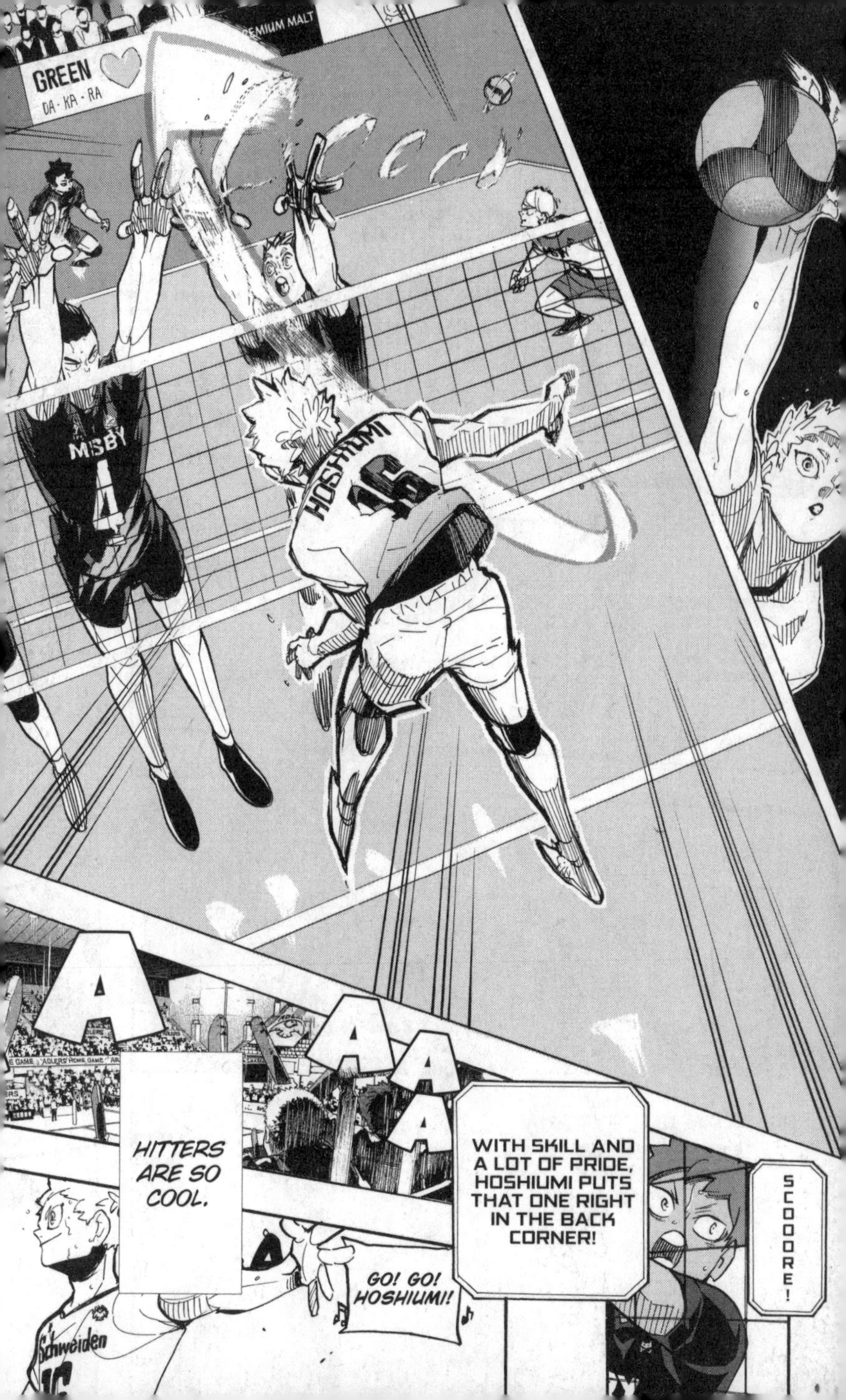
PREMIUM MALT
GREEN
DA-KA-RA
MSBY
HOSHIUMI
SCOOORE!
WITH SKILL AND A LOT OF PRIDE, HOSHIUMI PUTS THAT ONE RIGHT IN THE BACK CORNER!
AAAA
GO! GO! HOSHIUMI!
HITTERS ARE SO COOL.
Schweiden

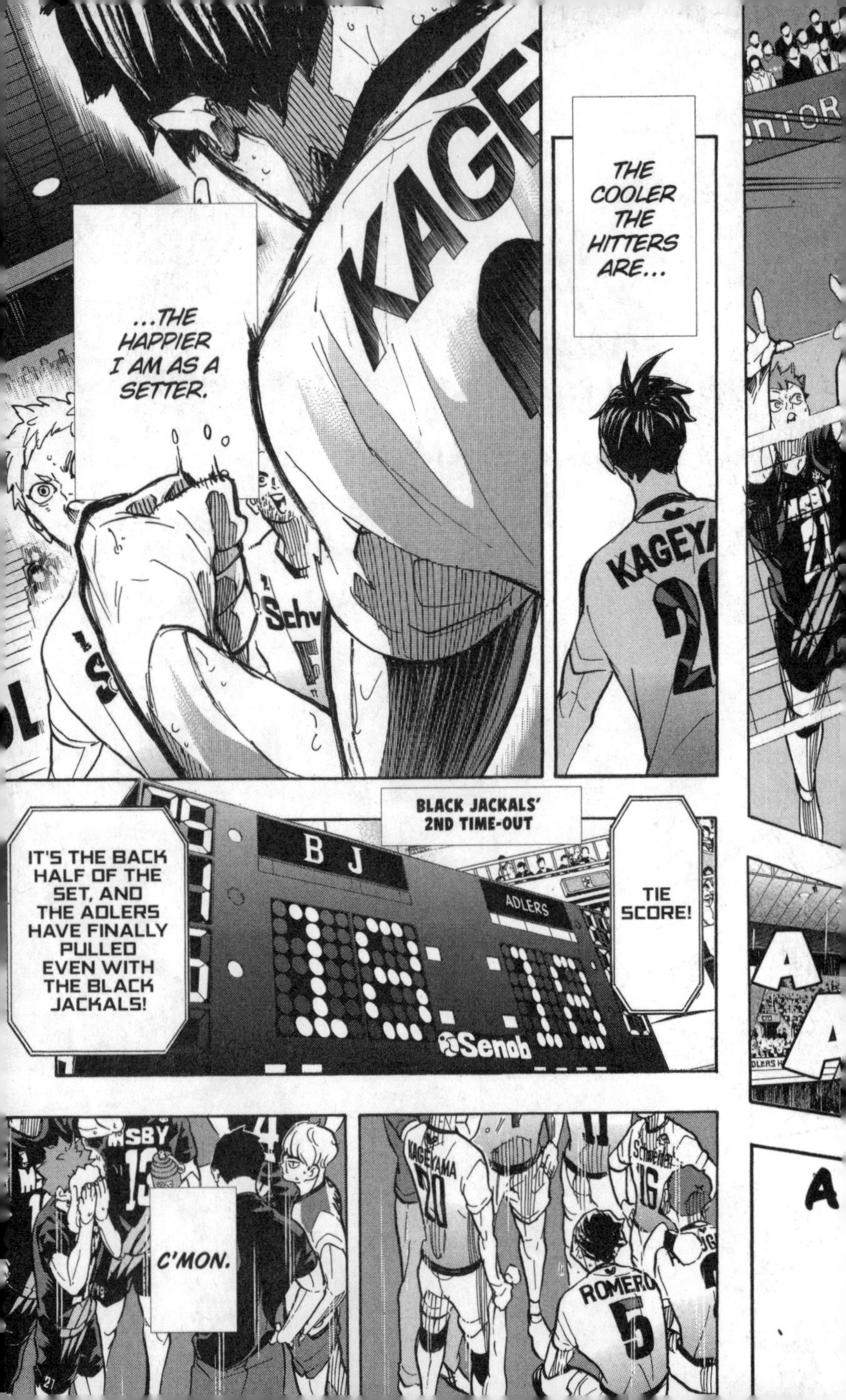
THE COOLER THE HITTERS ARE...
...THE HAPPIER I AM AS A SETTER.
BLACK JACKALS' 2ND TIME-OUT
TIE SCORE!
IT'S THE BACK HALF OF THE SET, AND THE ADLERS HAVE FINALLY PULLED EVEN WITH THE BLACK JACKALS!
C'MON.

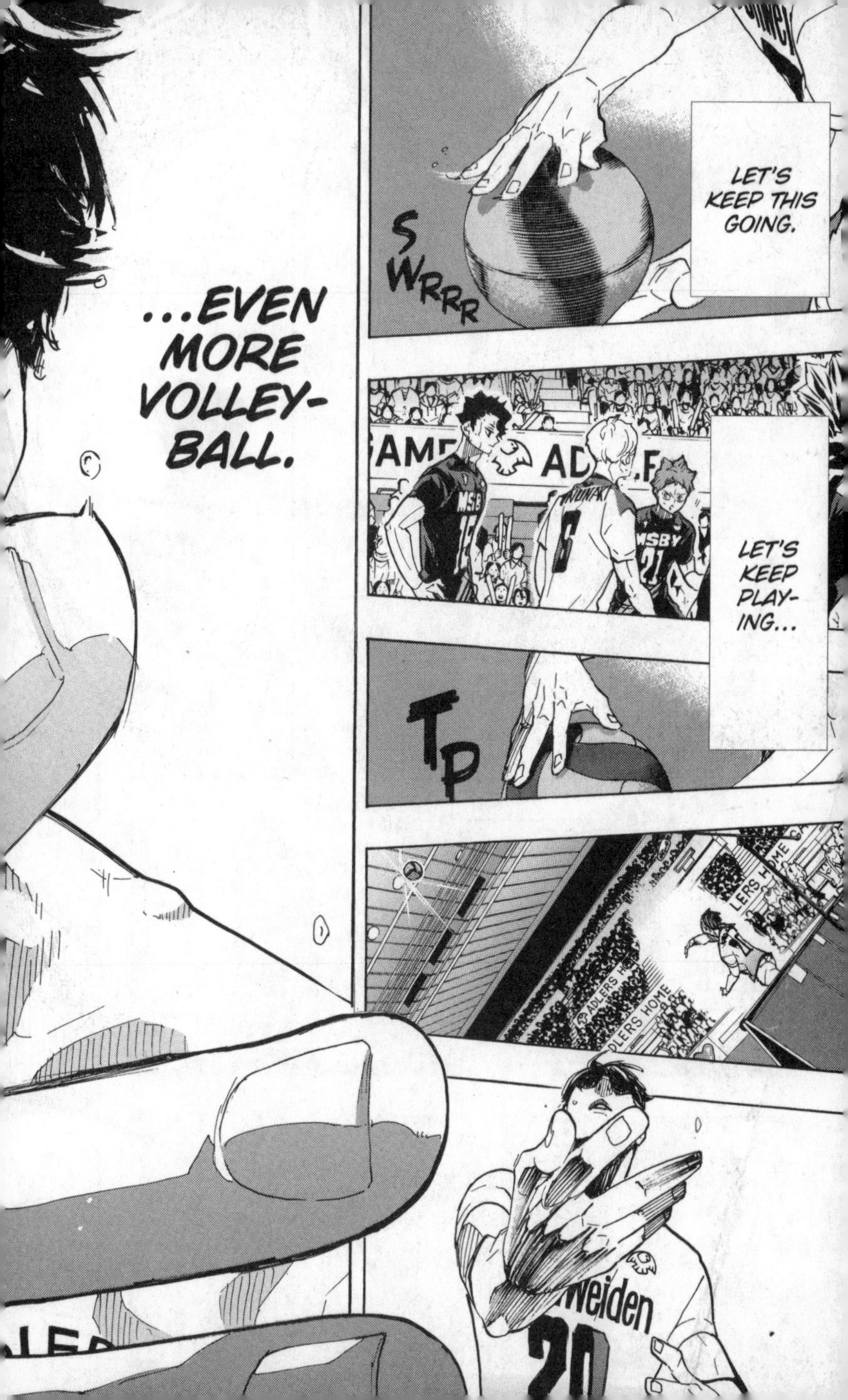
LET'S KEEP THIS GOING.
SWRRR
LET'S KEEP PLAYING...
TP
...EVEN MORE VOLLEYBALL.

HAiKYU!!

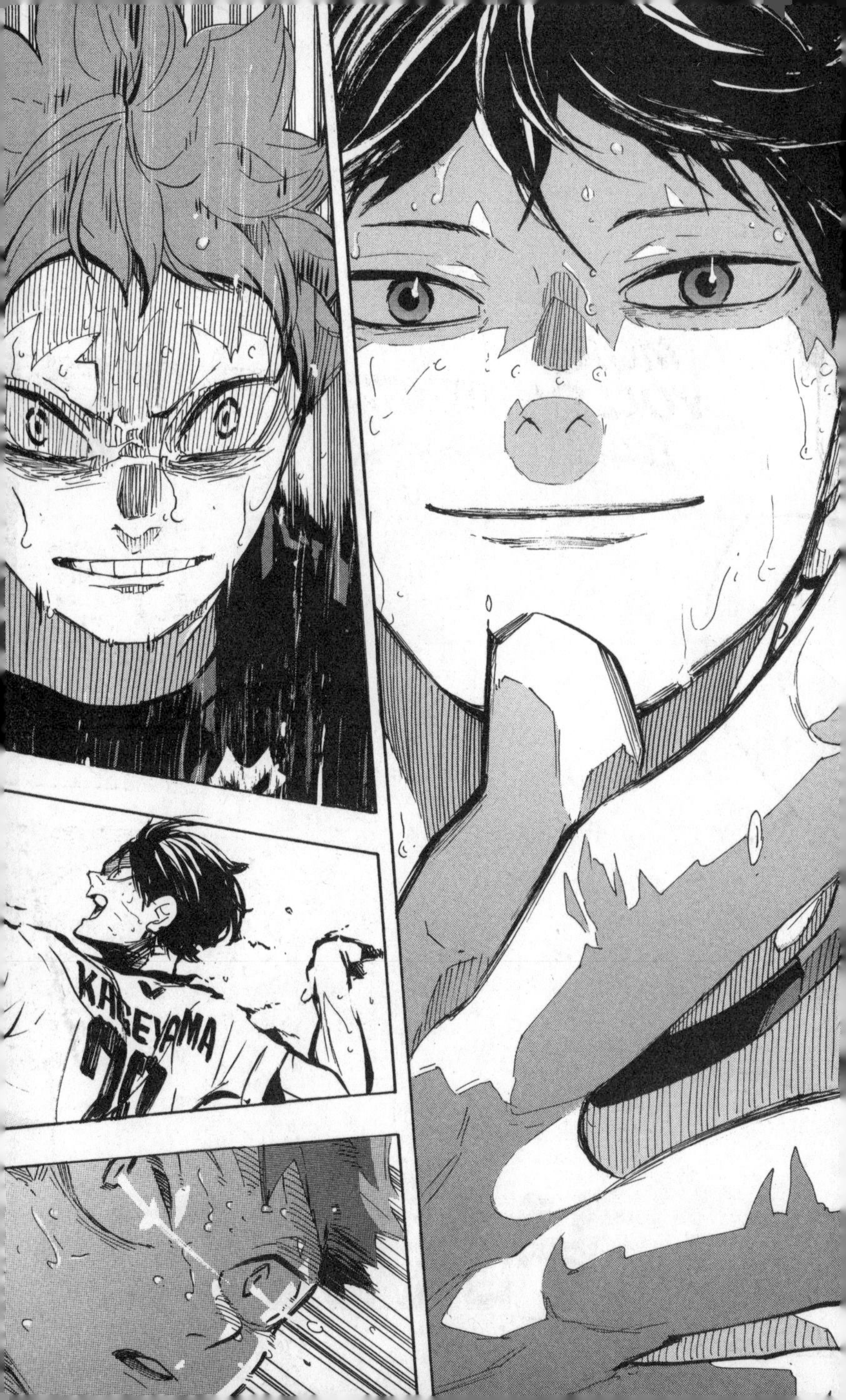
KAGEYAMA

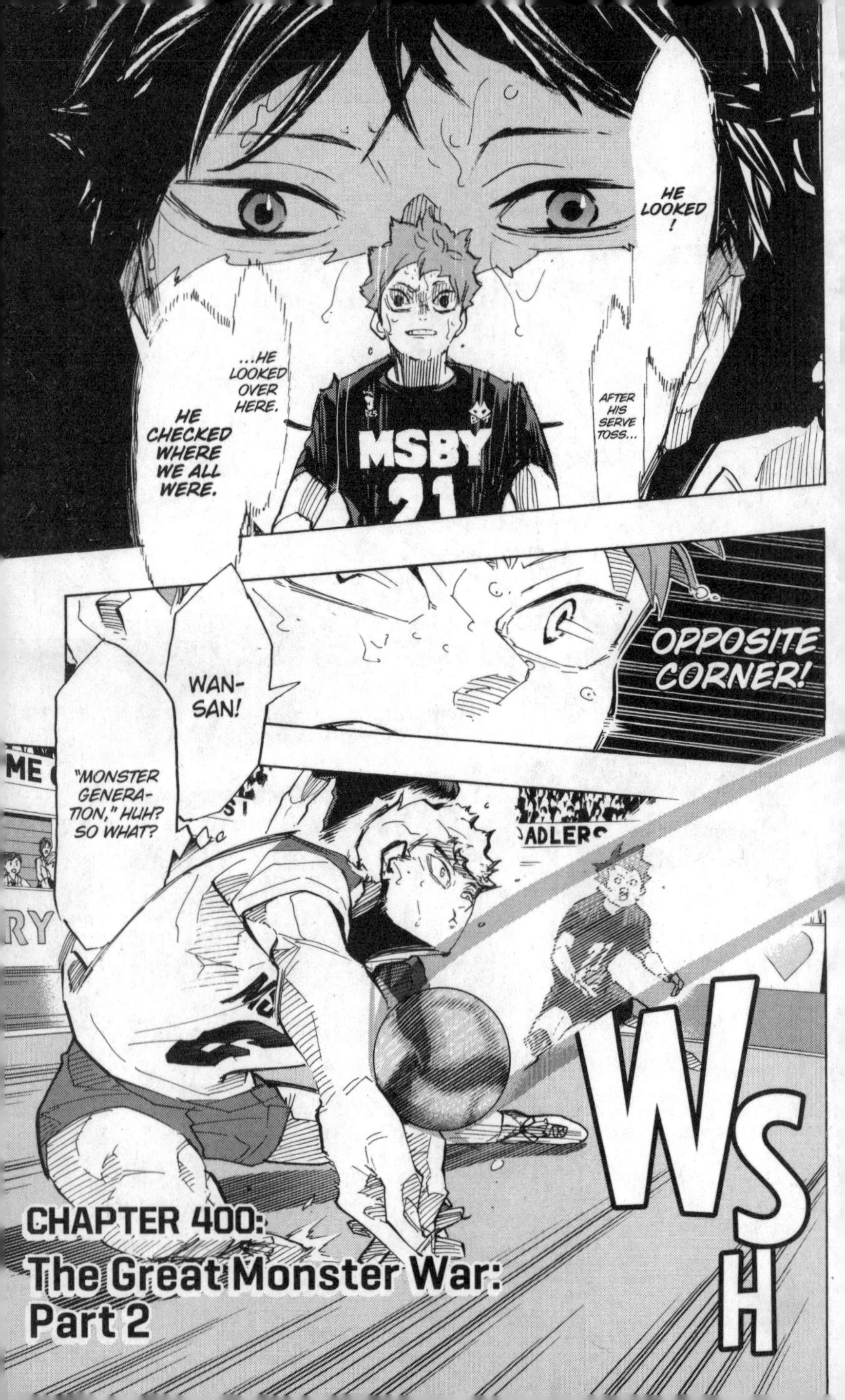
HE LOOKED!
AFTER HIS SERVE TOSS...
...HE LOOKED OVER HERE.
HE CHECKED WHERE WE ALL WERE.
MSBY 21
OPPOSITE CORNER!
WAN-SAN!
"MONSTER GENERATION," HUH? SO WHAT?
WSH
CHAPTER 400:
The Great Monster War: Part 2

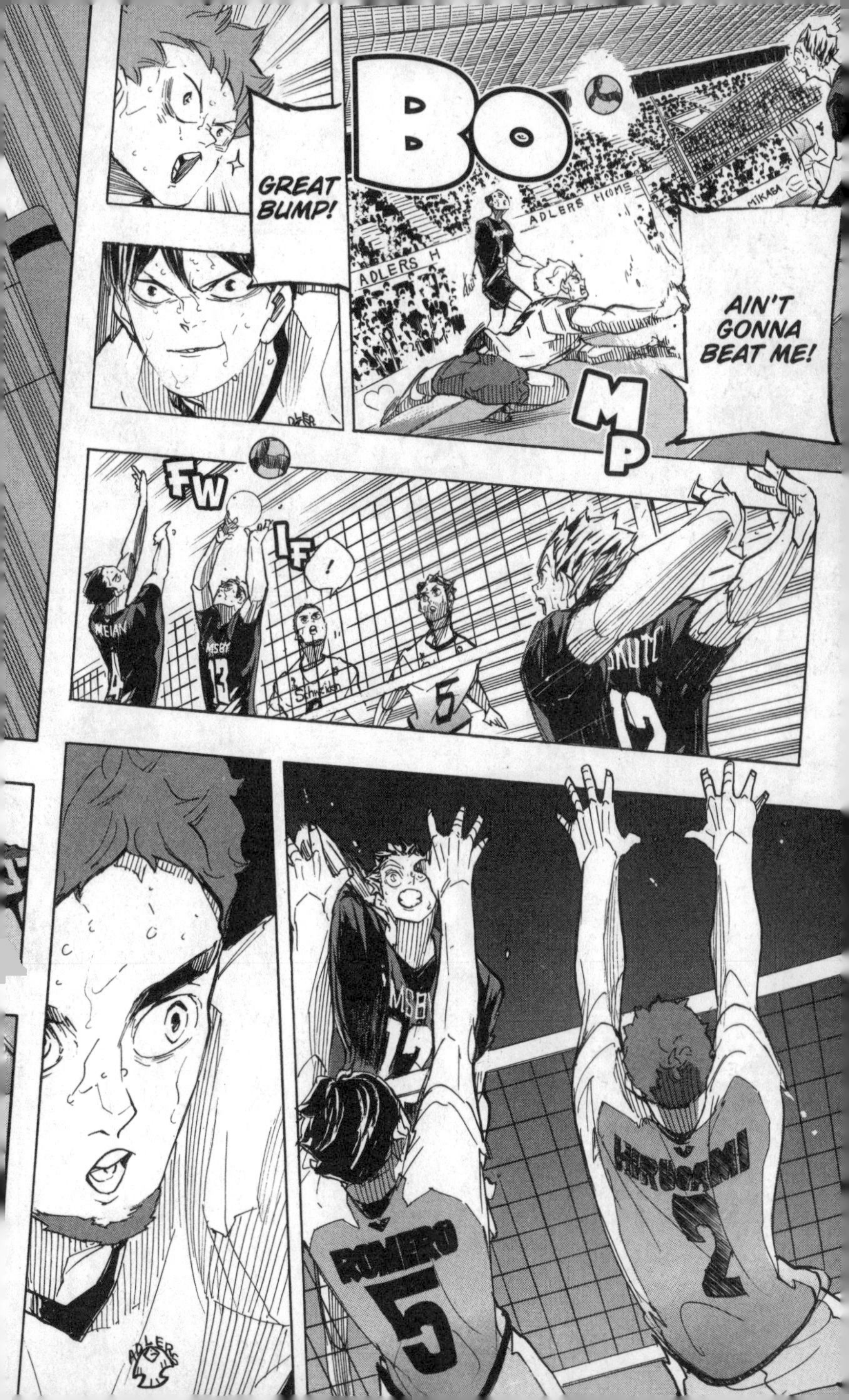
BOMP
AIN'T GONNA BEAT ME!
GREAT BUMP!
FWIF
!
ROMERO
5

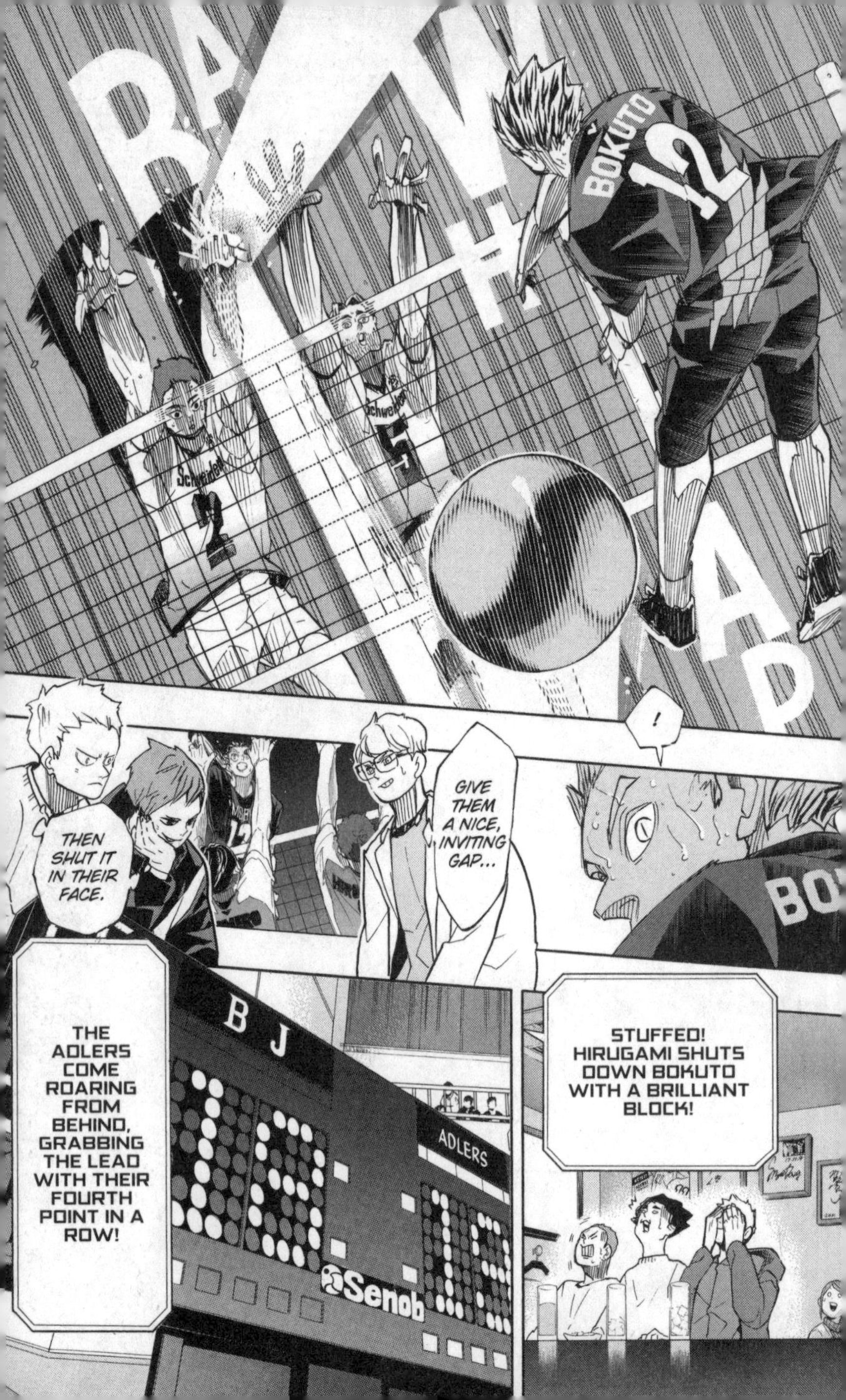
!
GIVE THEM A NICE, INVITING GAP...
THEN SHUT IT IN THEIR FACE.
STUFFED! HIRUGAMI SHUTS DOWN BOKUTO WITH A BRILLIANT BLOCK!
THE ADLERS COME ROARING FROM BEHIND, GRABBING THE LEAD WITH THEIR FOURTH POINT IN A ROW!
ADLERS

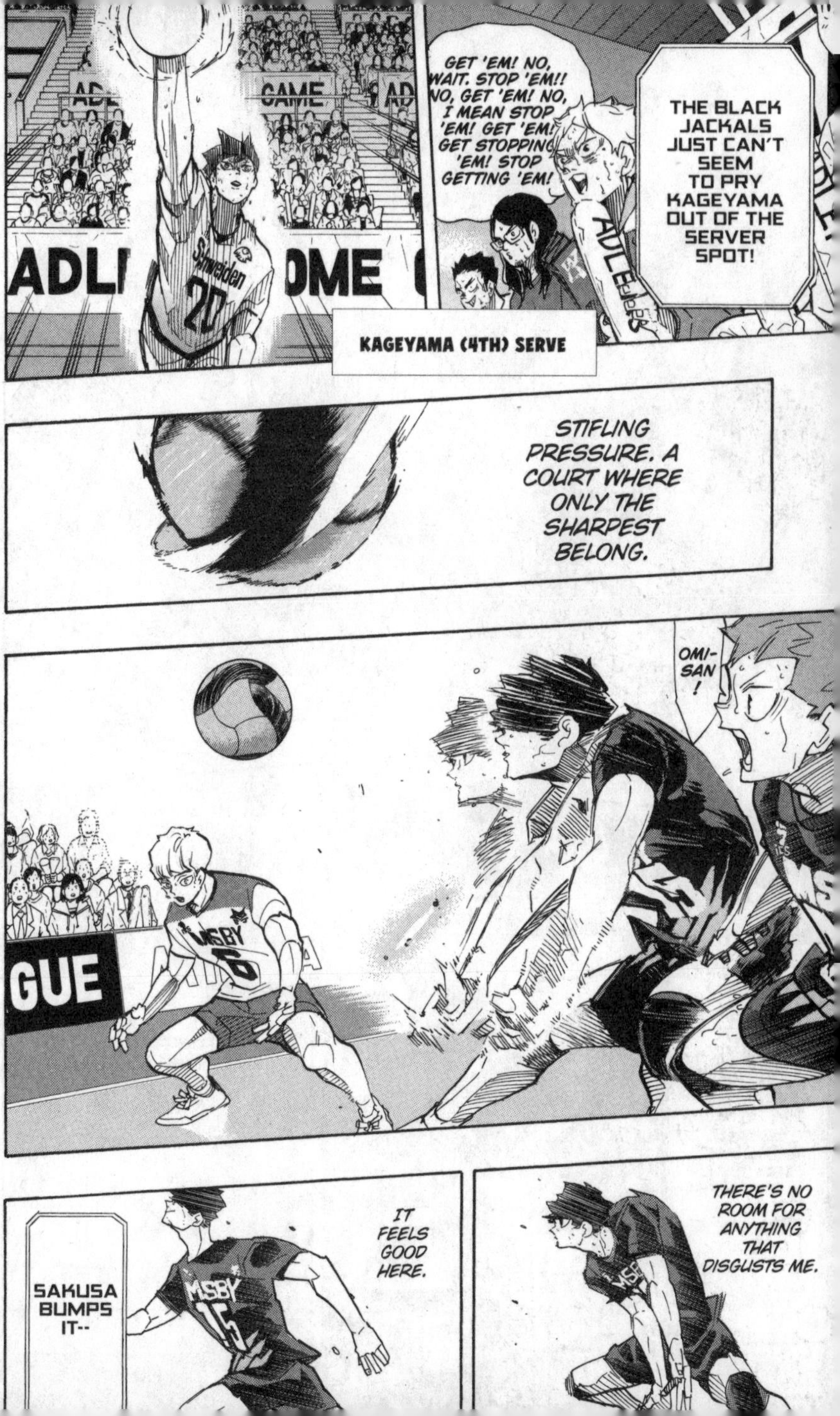
THE BLACK JACKALS JUST CAN'T SEEM TO PRY KAGEYAMA OUT OF THE SERVER SPOT!
GET 'EM! NO, WAIT. STOP 'EM!! NO, GET 'EM! NO, I MEAN STOP 'EM! GET 'EM! GET STOPPING 'EM! STOP GETTING 'EM!
GAME
KAGEYAMA (4TH) SERVE
STIFLING PRESSURE. A COURT WHERE ONLY THE SHARPEST BELONG.
OMI-SAN!
GUE
THERE'S NO ROOM FOR ANYTHING THAT DISGUSTS ME.
IT FEELS GOOD HERE.
SAKUSA BUMPS IT--

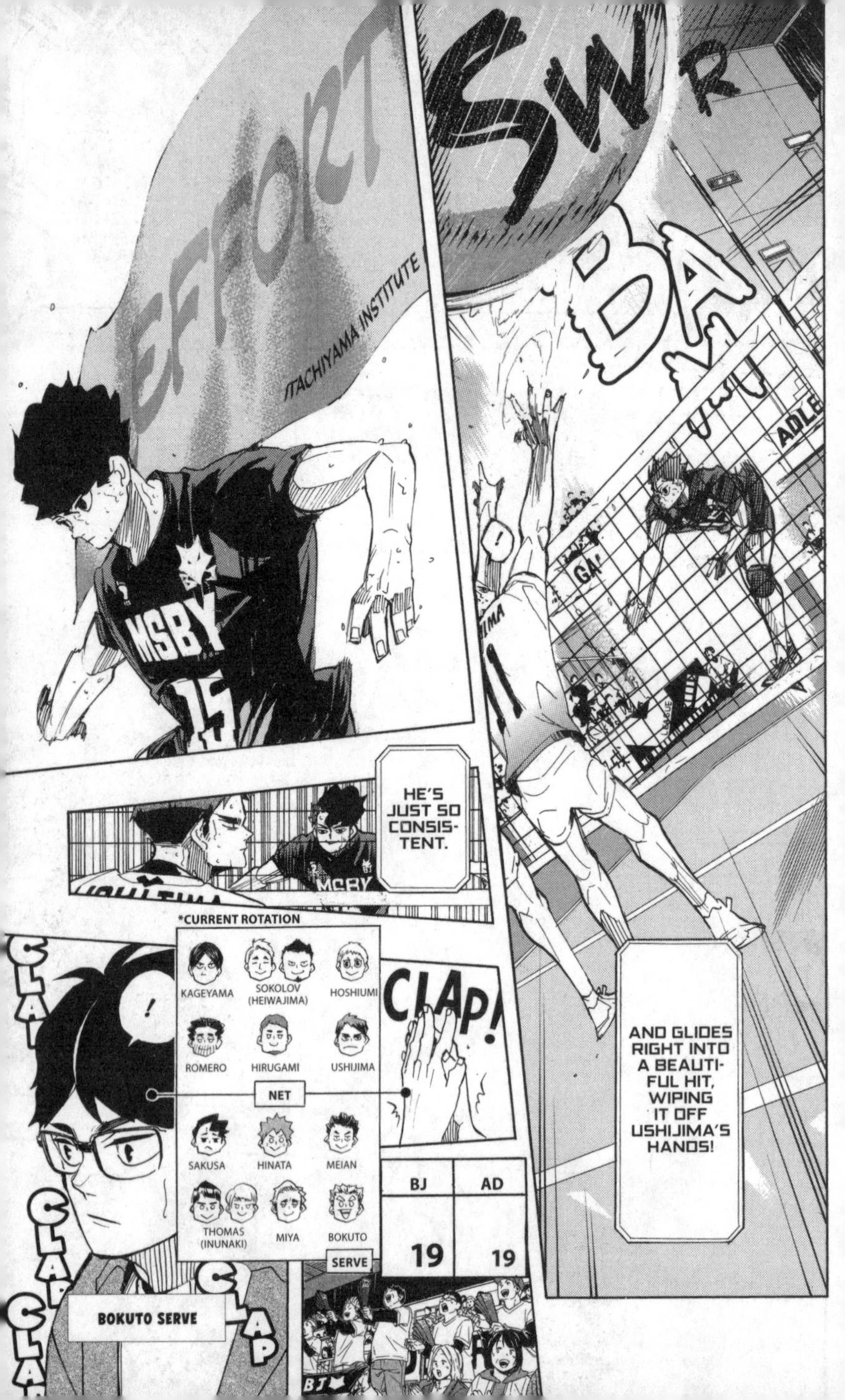
SWR
BA
ADLE
GA
AND GLIDES RIGHT INTO A BEAUTIFUL HIT, WIPING IT OFF USHIJIMA'S HANDS!
EFFORT
ITACHIYAMA INSTITUTE
MSBY
15
HE'S JUST SO CONSISTENT.
MSBY
CLAP!
*CURRENT ROTATION
KAGEYAMA
SOKOLOV (HEIWAJIMA)
HOSHIUMI
ROMERO
HIRUGAMI
USHIJIMA
NET
SAKUSA
HINATA
MEIAN
THOMAS (INUNAKI)
MIYA
BOKUTO
SERVE
BJ
AD
19
19
CLAP
CLAP
CLAP
CLAP
CLAP
BOKUTO SERVE
BJ

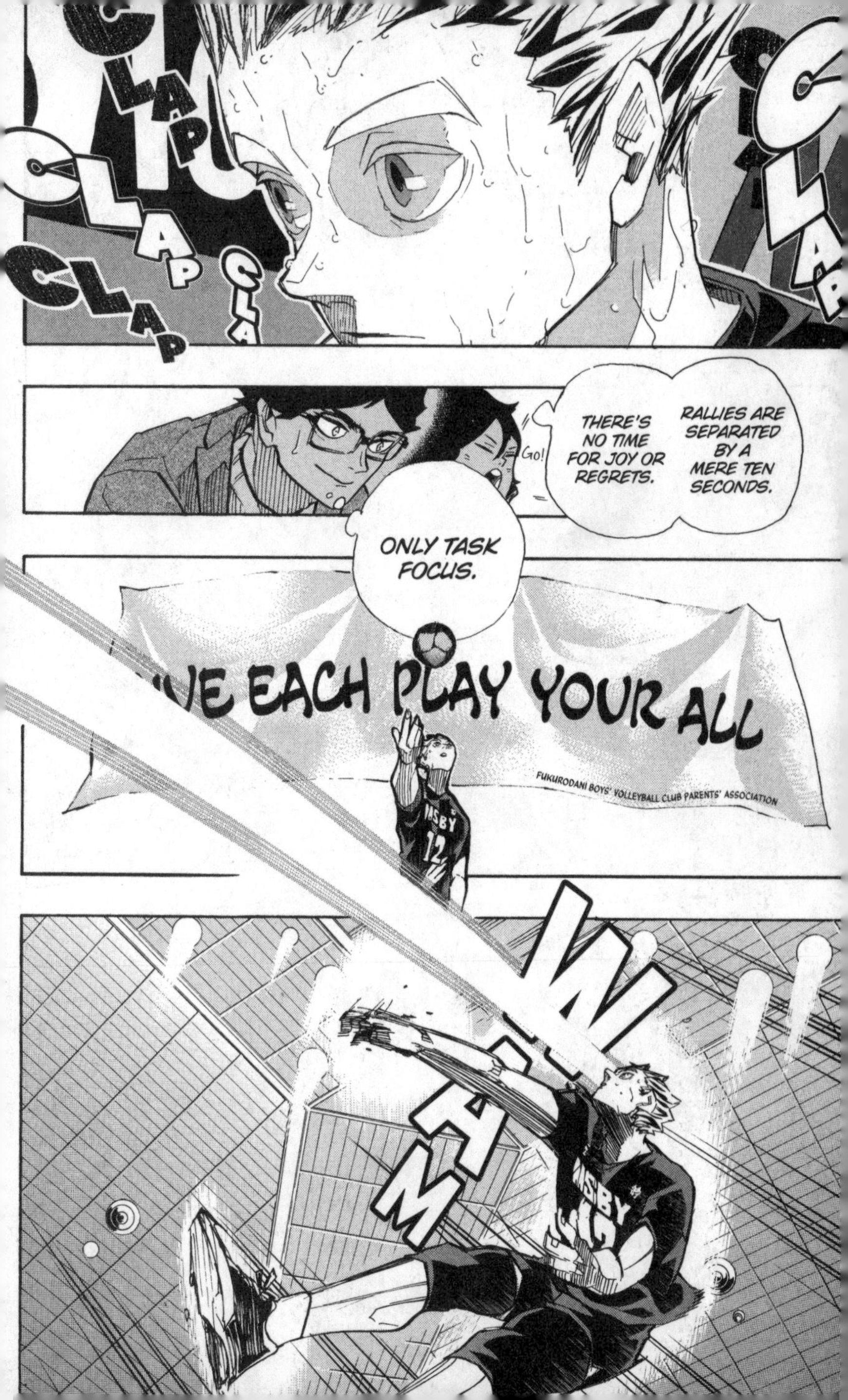
CLAP CLAP
CLAP CLAP
CLAP CLAP
RALLIES ARE SEPARATED BY A MERE TEN SECONDS.
THERE'S NO TIME FOR JOY OR REGRETS.
Go!
ONLY TASK FOCUS.
WE EACH PLAY YOUR ALL
FUKURODANI BOYS' VOLLEYBALL CLUB PARENTS' ASSOCIATION

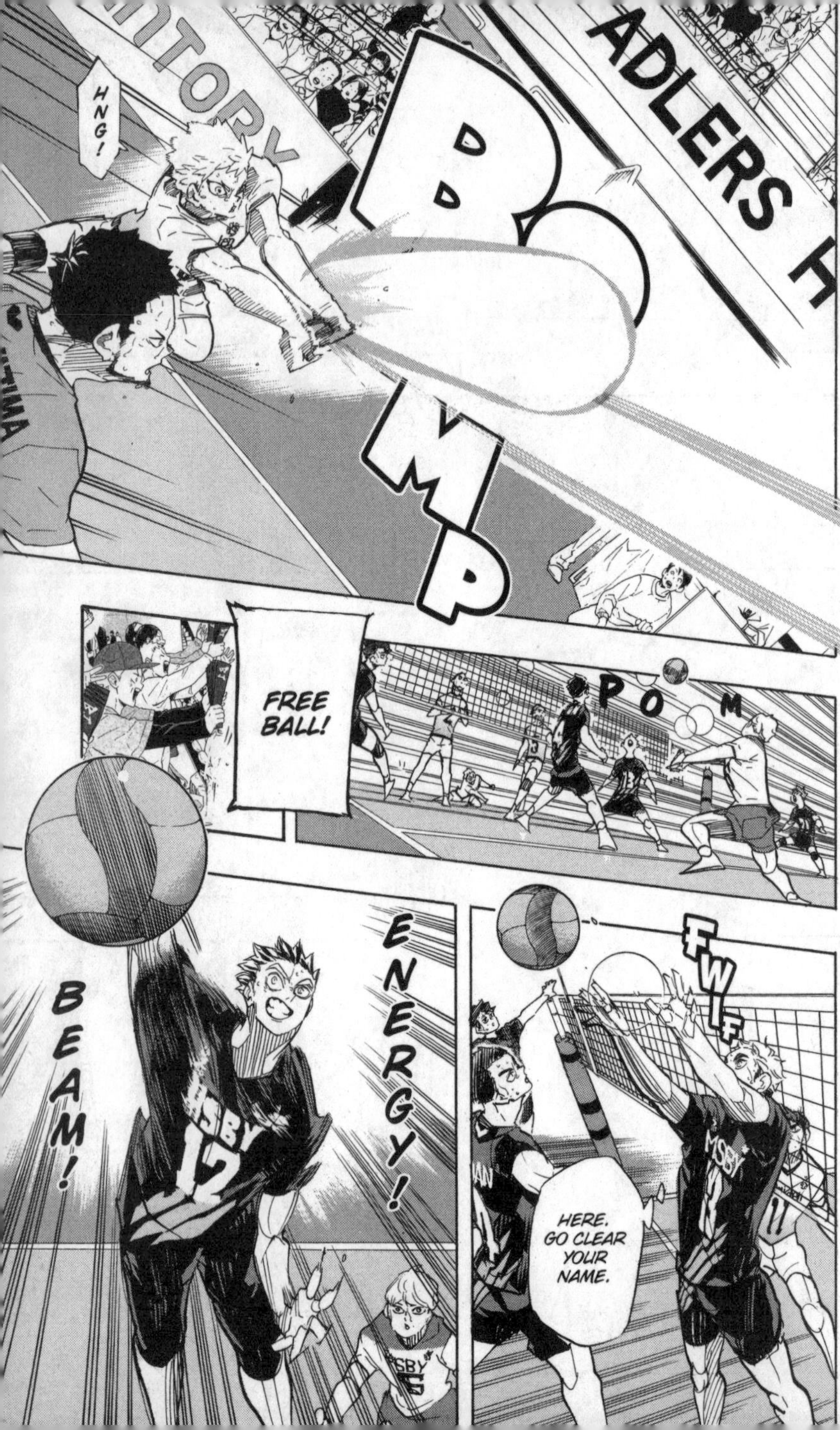
ADLERS
HNG!
BOMP
FREE BALL!
POM
ENERGY!
BEAM!
FWIP
HERE. GO CLEAR YOUR NAME.

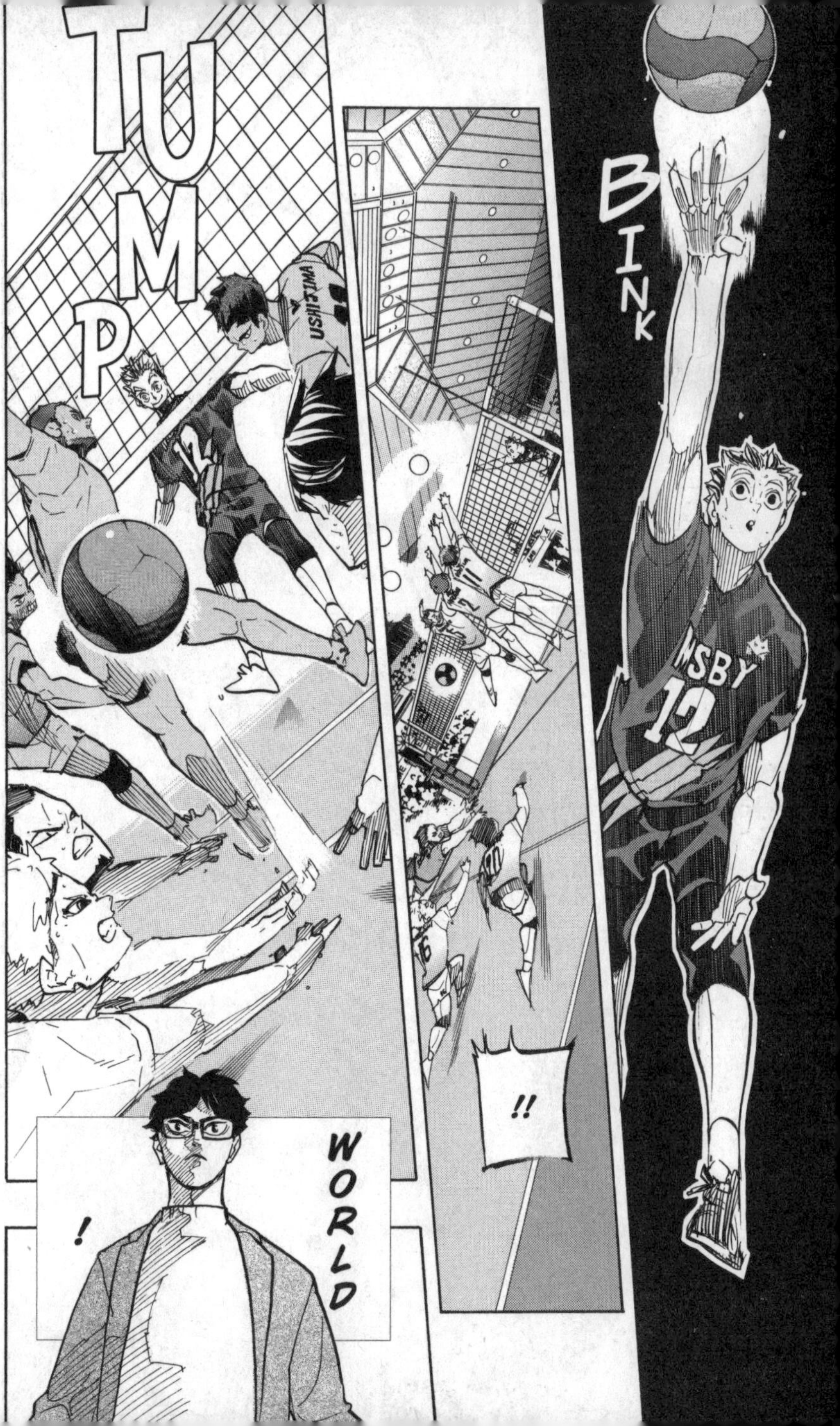
BINK
!!
TUMP
WORLD
!

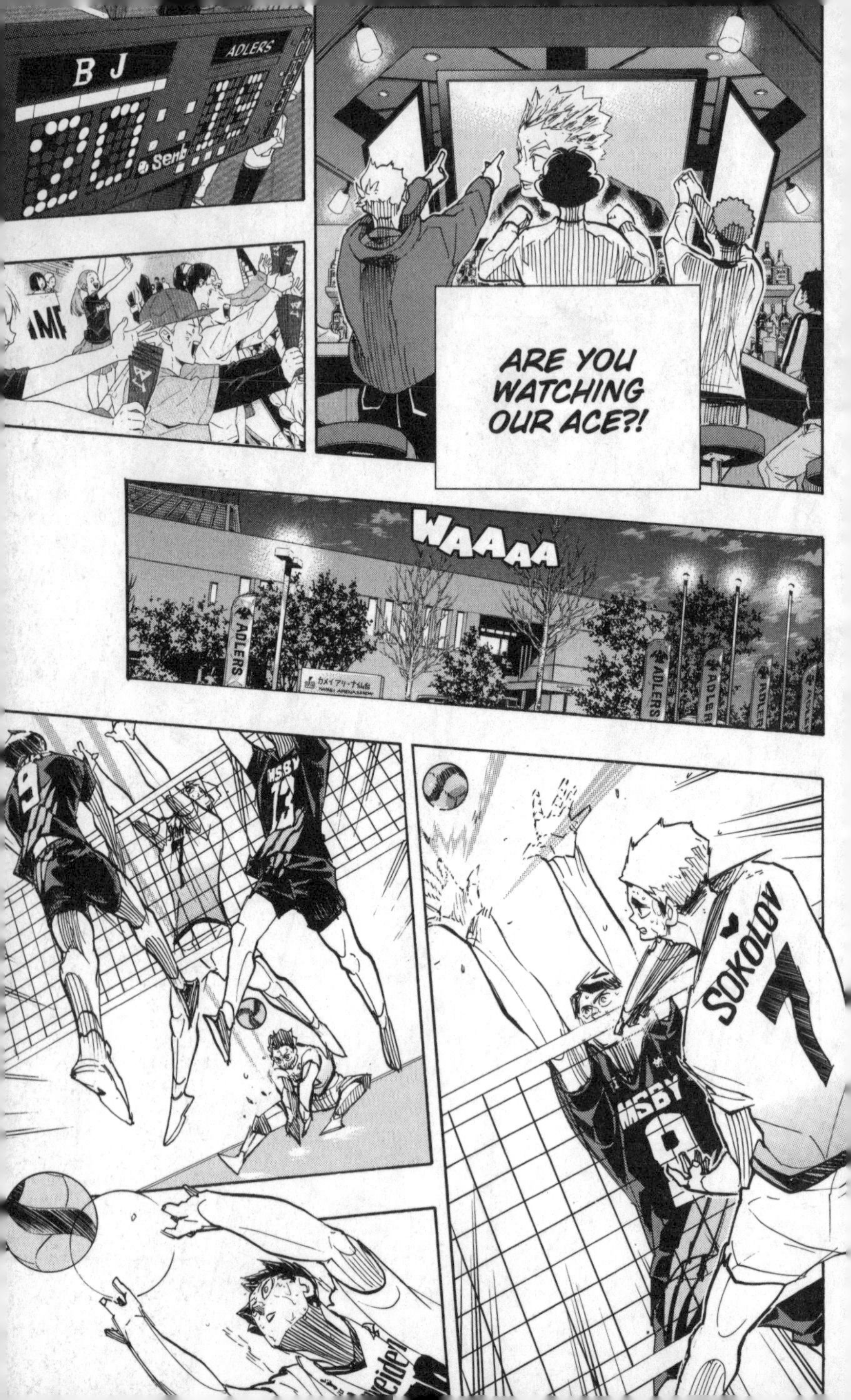
ARE YOU WATCHING OUR ACE?!
ADLERS
B J
WAAAA
ADLERS
ADLERS
ADLERS
MSBY
SOKOLOV
MSBY

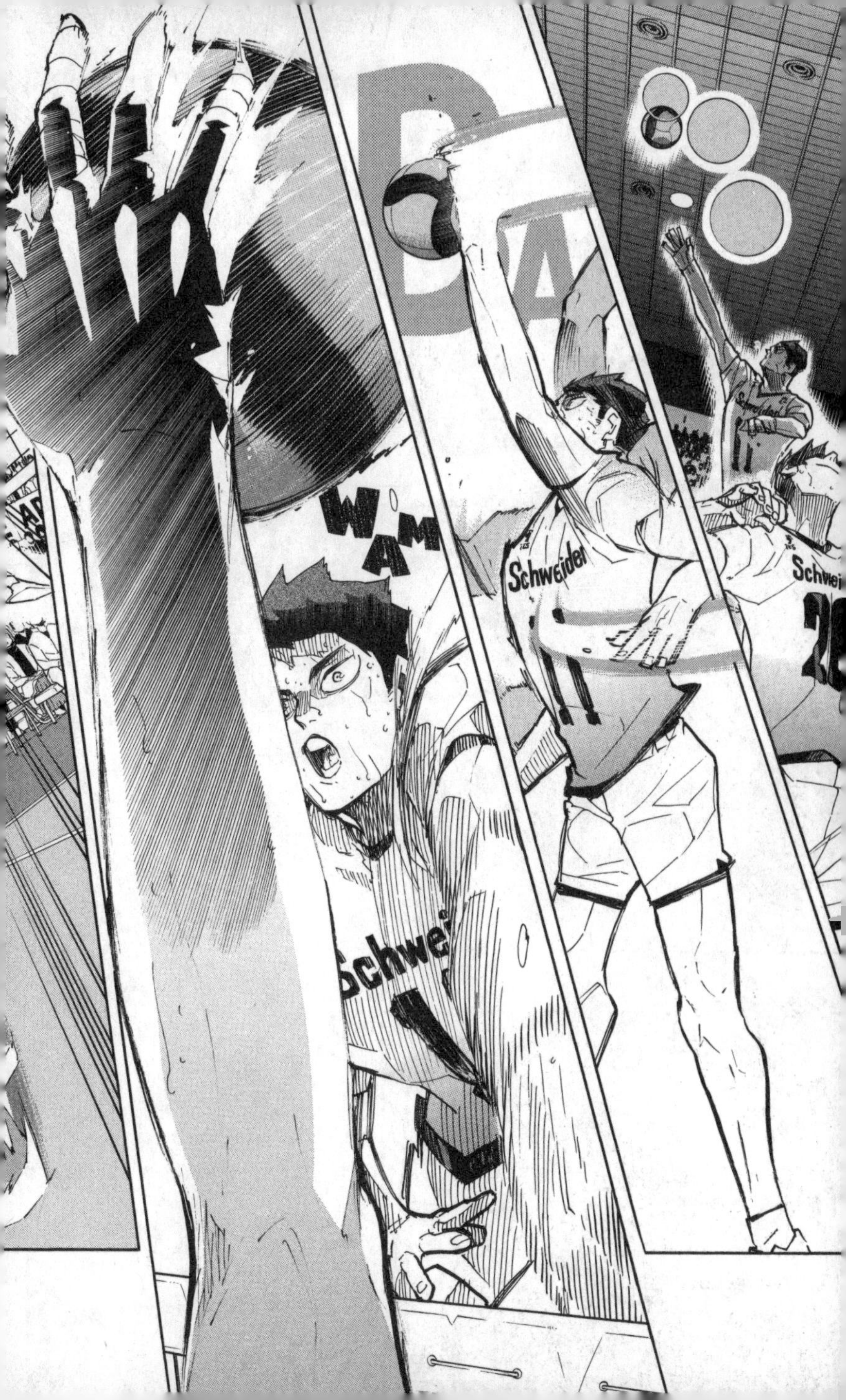
WAM
Schweider

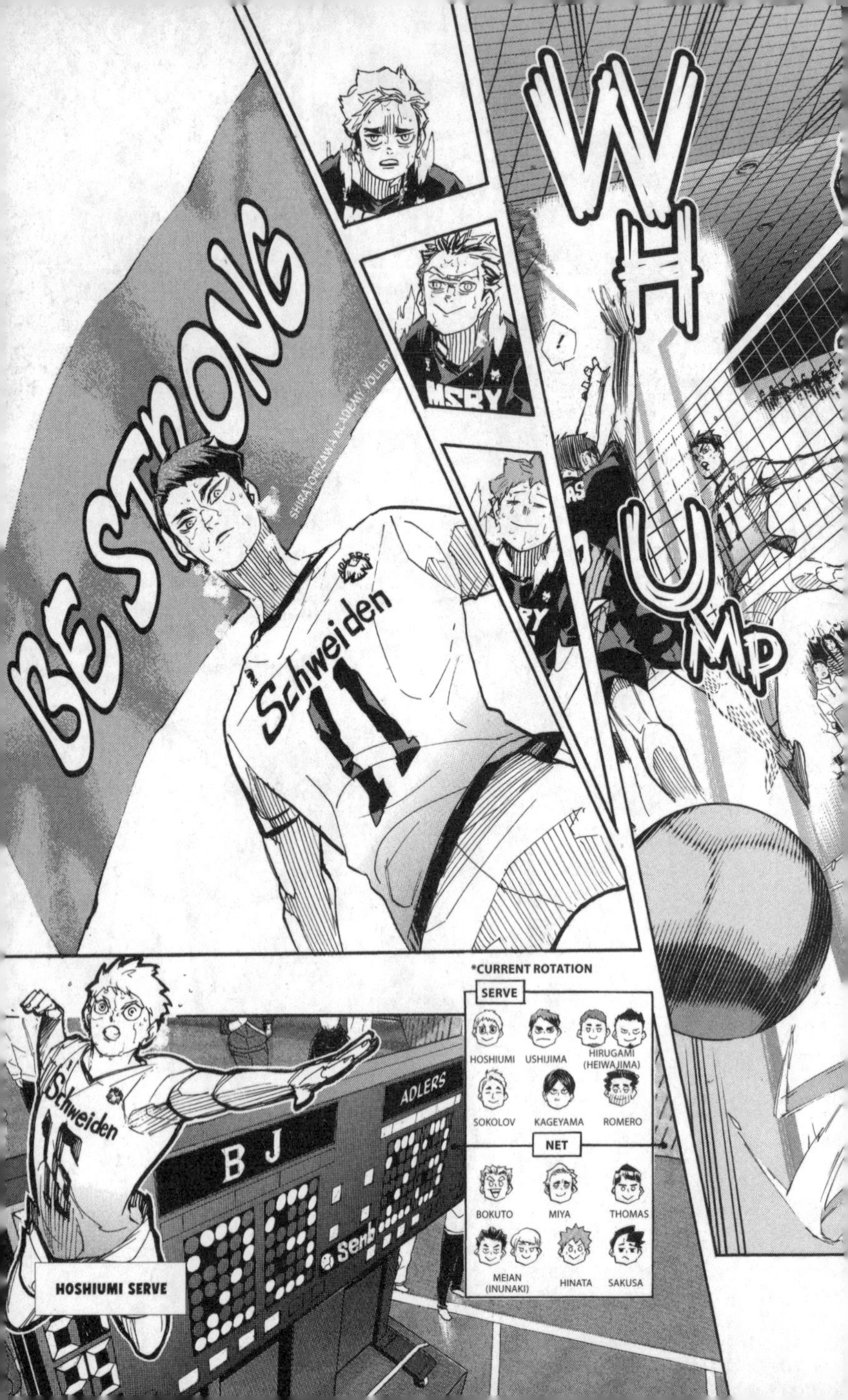
WHUMP
!
BE STRONG
SHIRATORIZAWA ACADEMY VOLLEY
*CURRENT ROTATION
SERVE
HOSHIUMI
USHIJIMA
HIRUGAMI (HEIWAJIMA)
SOKOLOV
KAGEYAMA
ROMERO
NET
BOKUTO
MIYA
THOMAS
MEIAN (INUNAKI)
HINATA
SAKUSA
ADLERS
BJ
HOSHIUMI SERVE

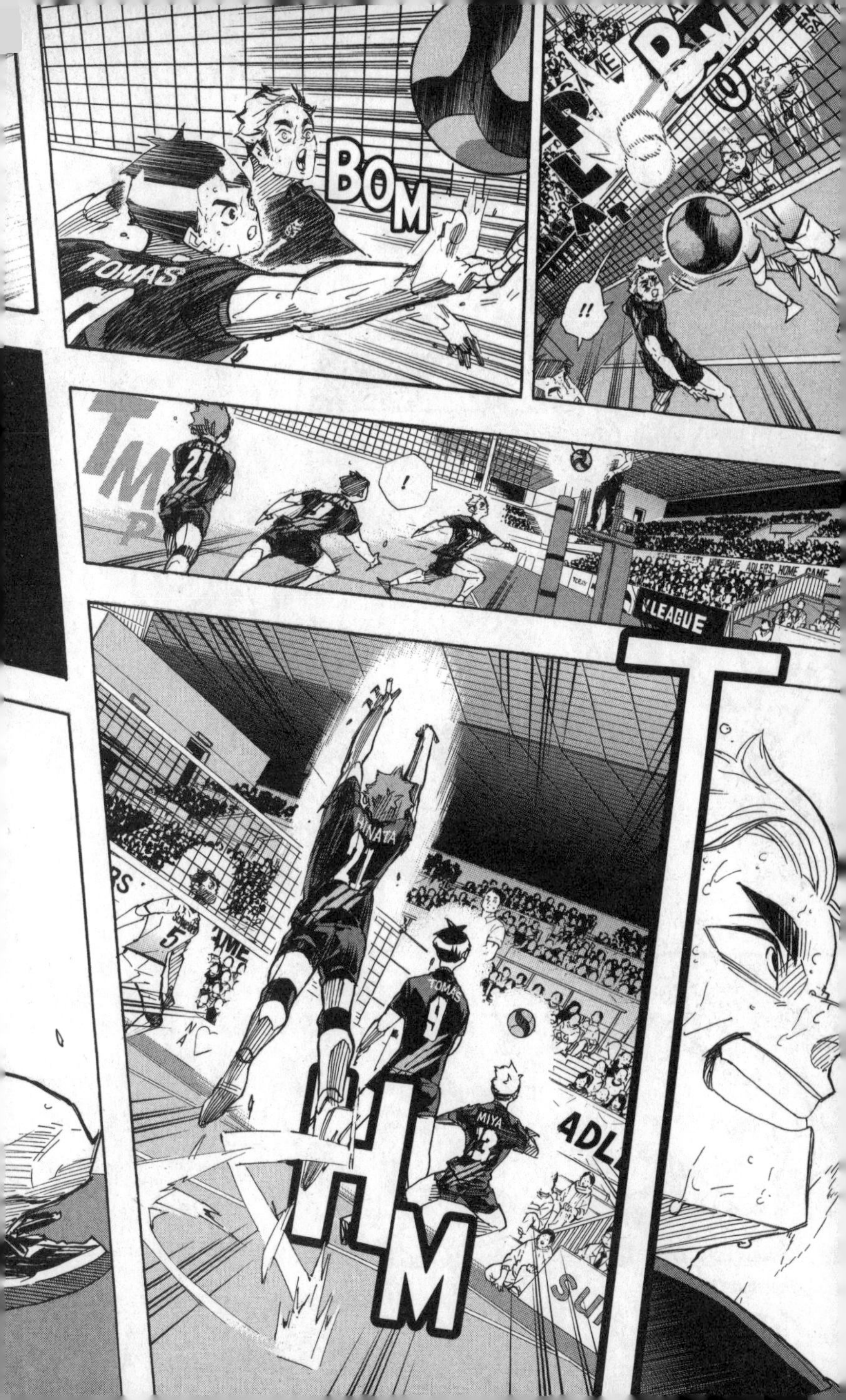

!!
BOM
!
THM

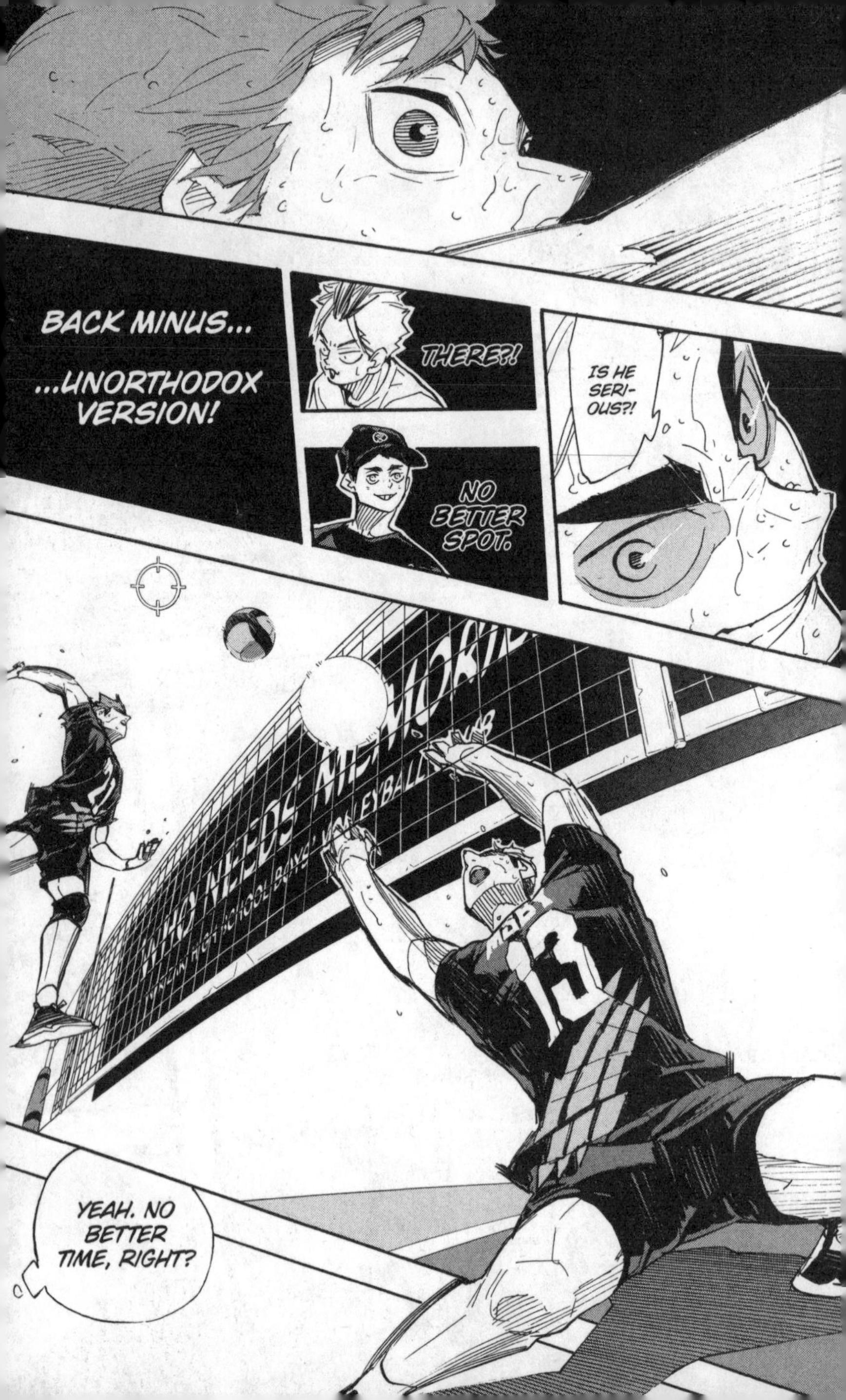
IS HE SERI- OUS?!
THERE?!
NO BETTER SPOT.
BACK MINUS...
...UNORTHODOX VERSION!
YEAH. NO BETTER TIME, RIGHT?

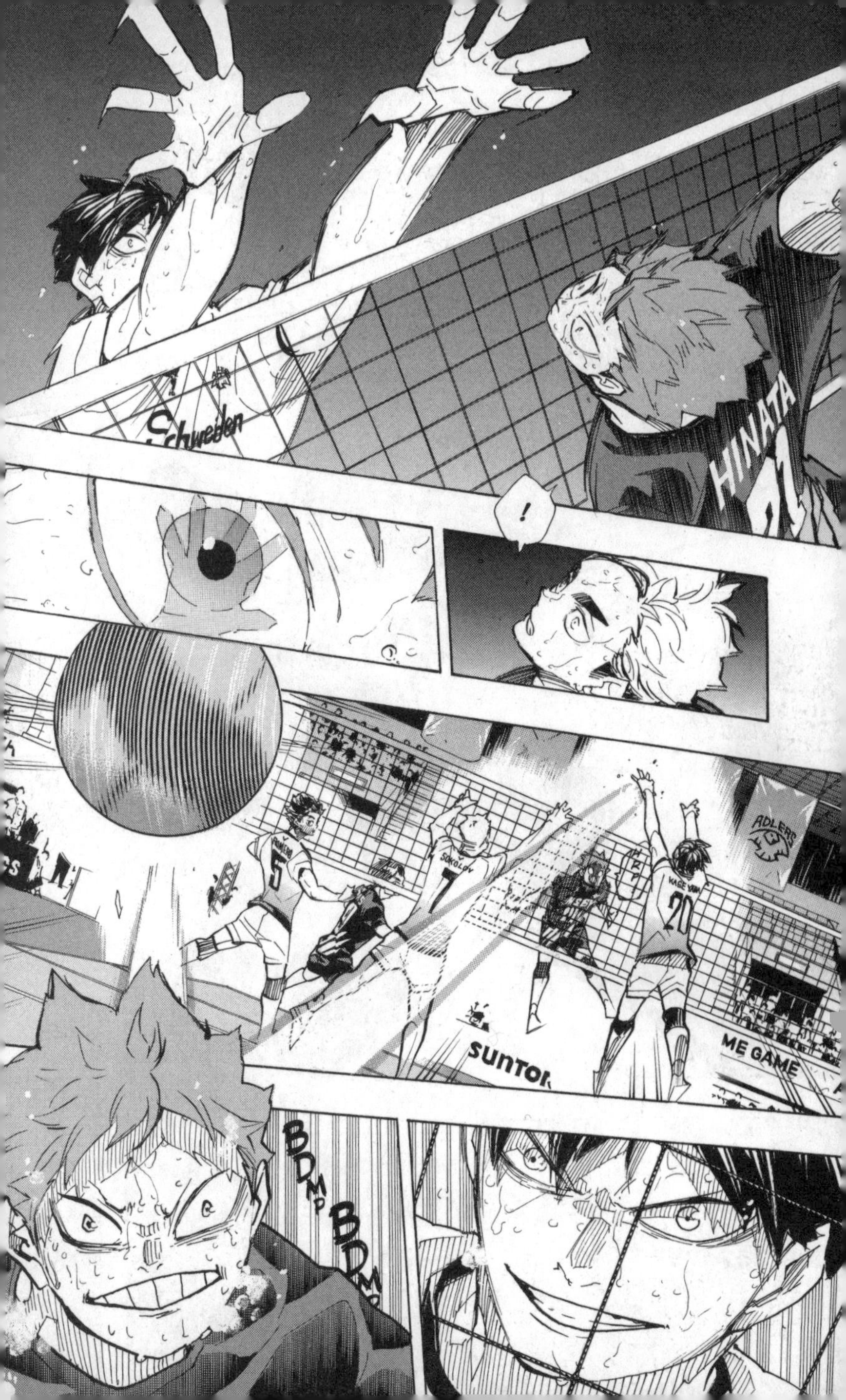
HINATA
Schweiden
!
ADLERS
KAGEYAMA
20
SOKOLOV
7
5
suntory
ME GAME
BDMP
BDMP

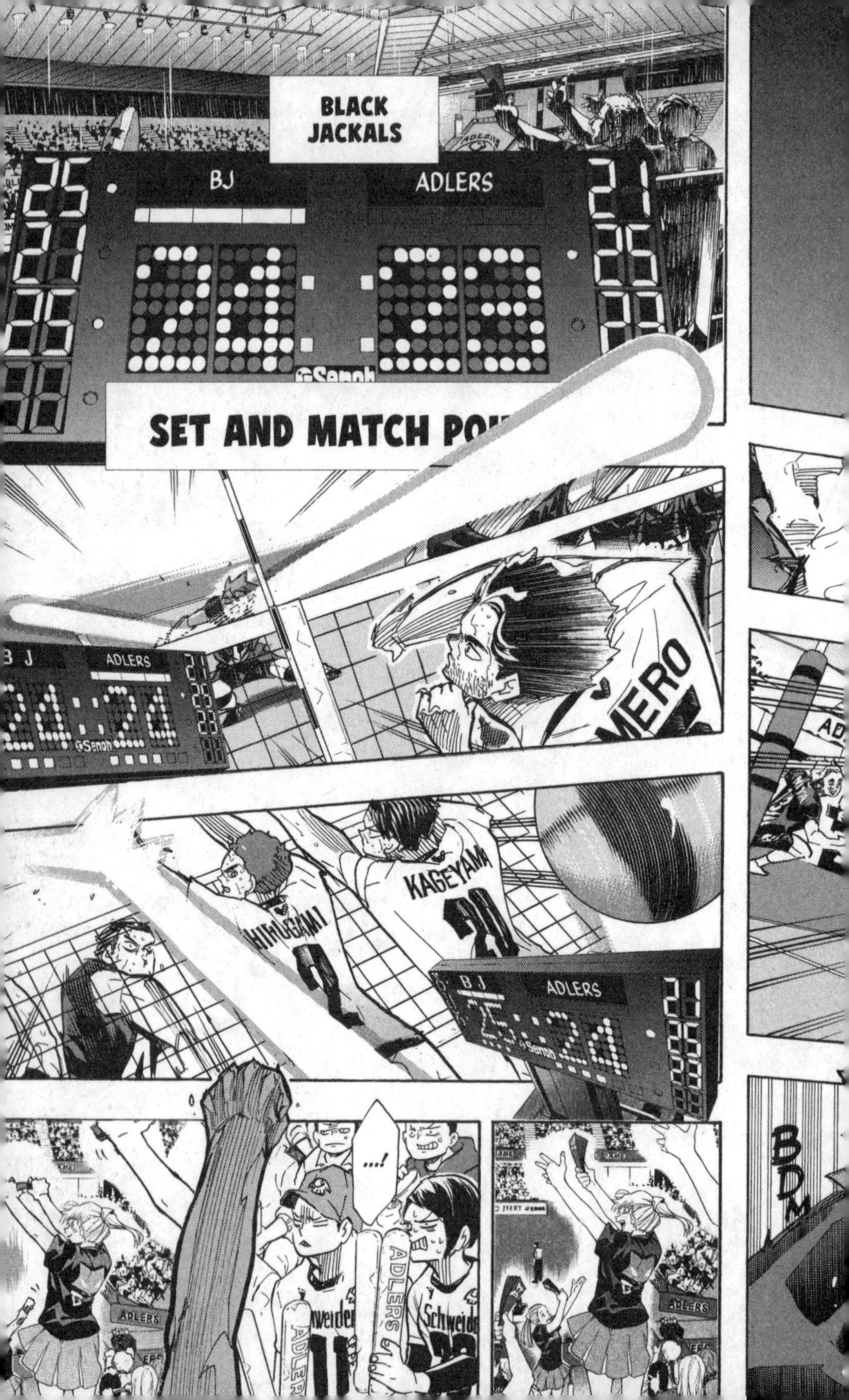
BLACK JACKALS
BJ
ADLERS
SET AND MATCH POI
MERO
KAGEYAMA
HIRUGAMI
...!
ADLERS
Schweiden

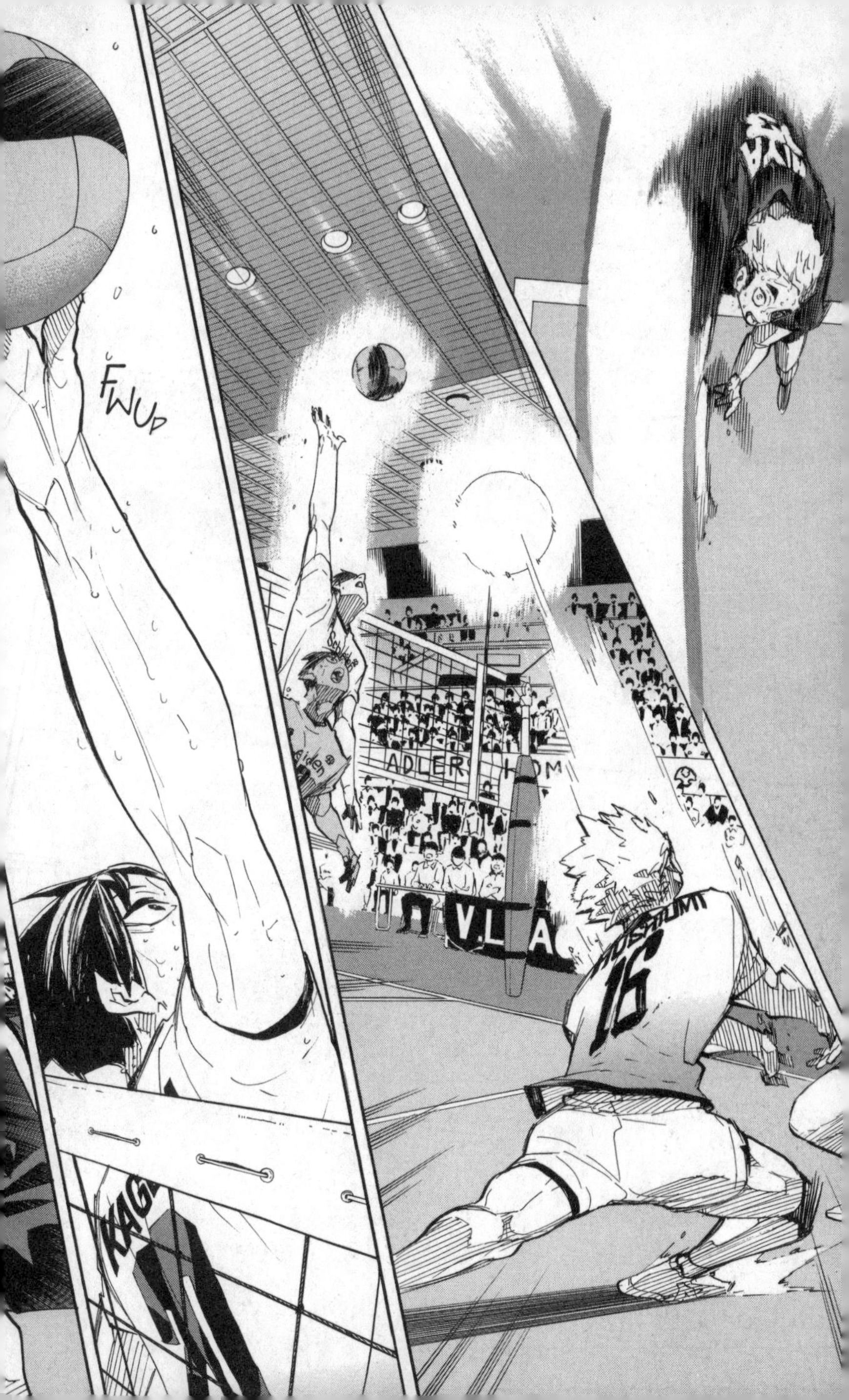
ADLERS
V.L.A
16
FWUP

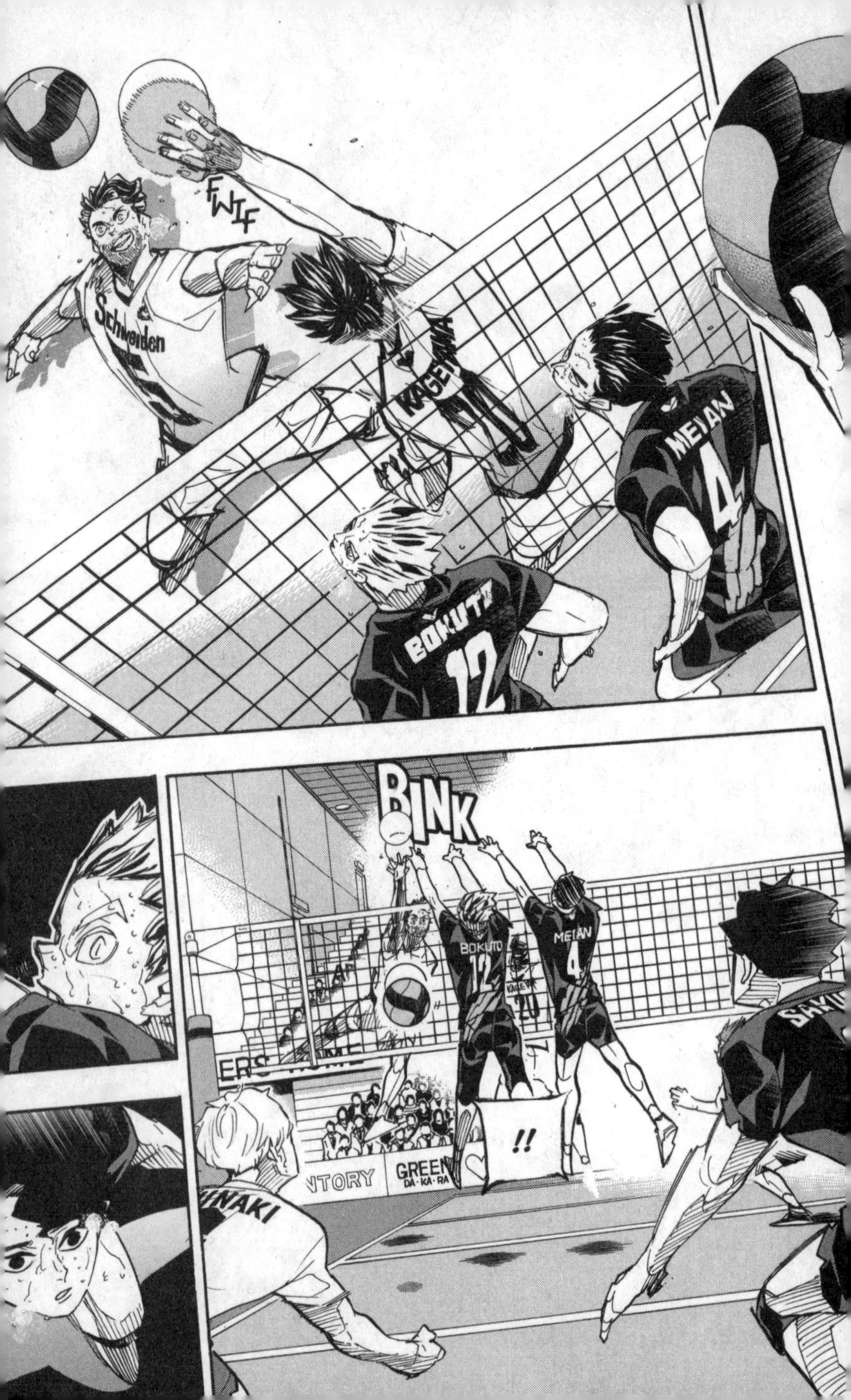
FWIF
BINK
!!
GREEN DA·KA·RA

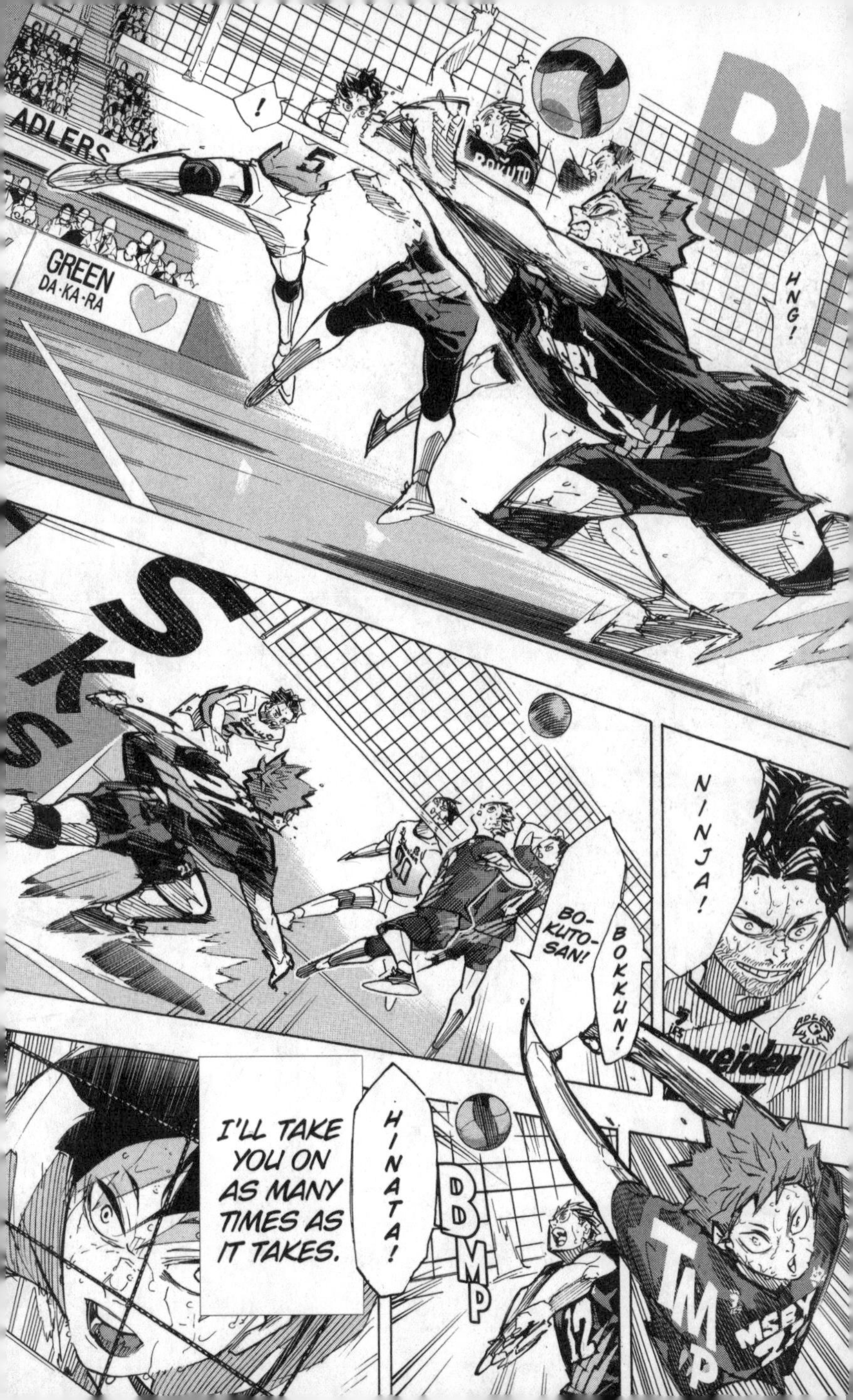
HNG!
!
ADLERS
GREEN
DA-KA-RA
NINJA!
BOKKUN!
BO-KUTO-SAN!
HINATA!
I'LL TAKE YOU ON AS MANY TIMES AS IT TAKES.

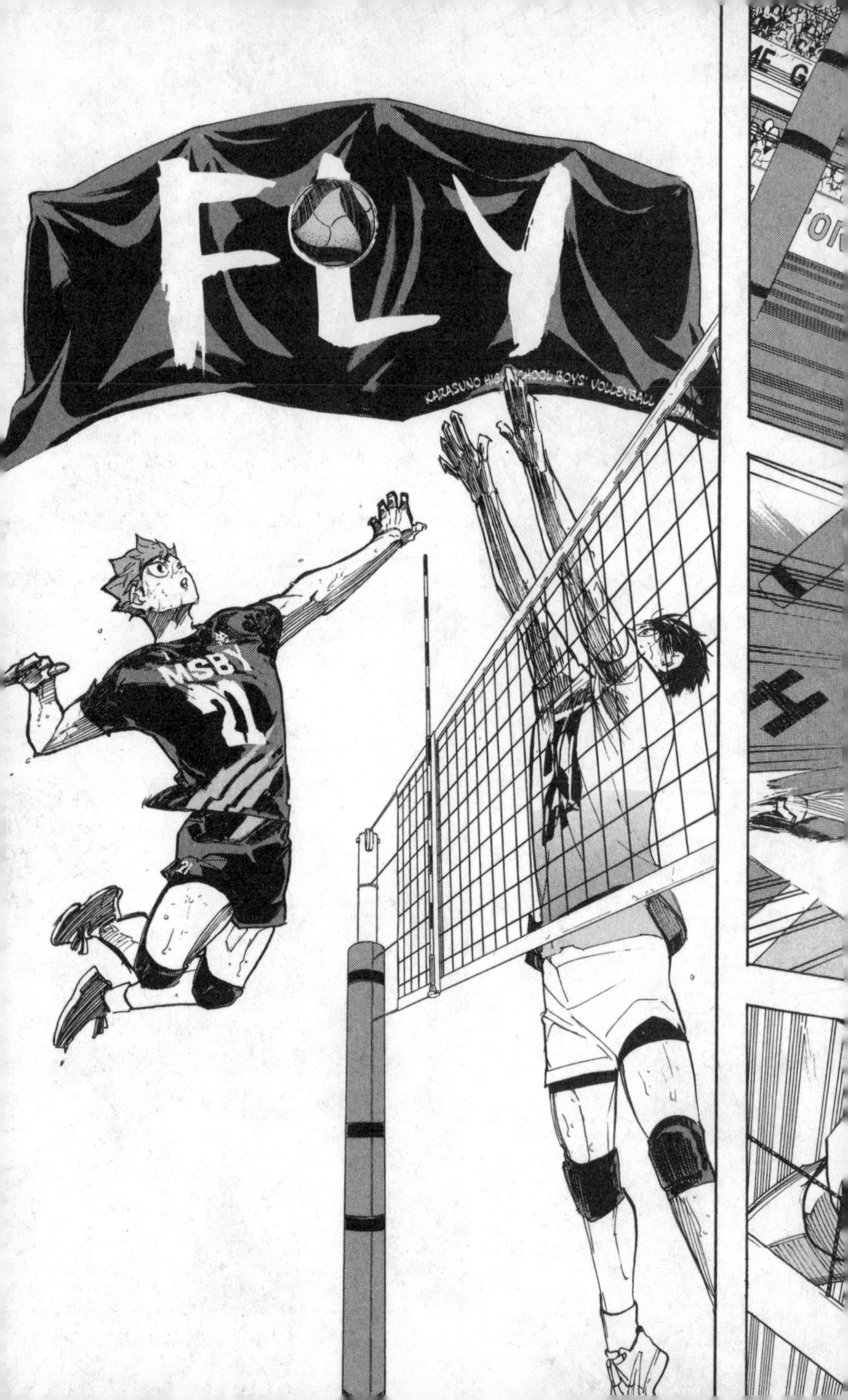
FLY
MSBY
21

CHAPTER 401

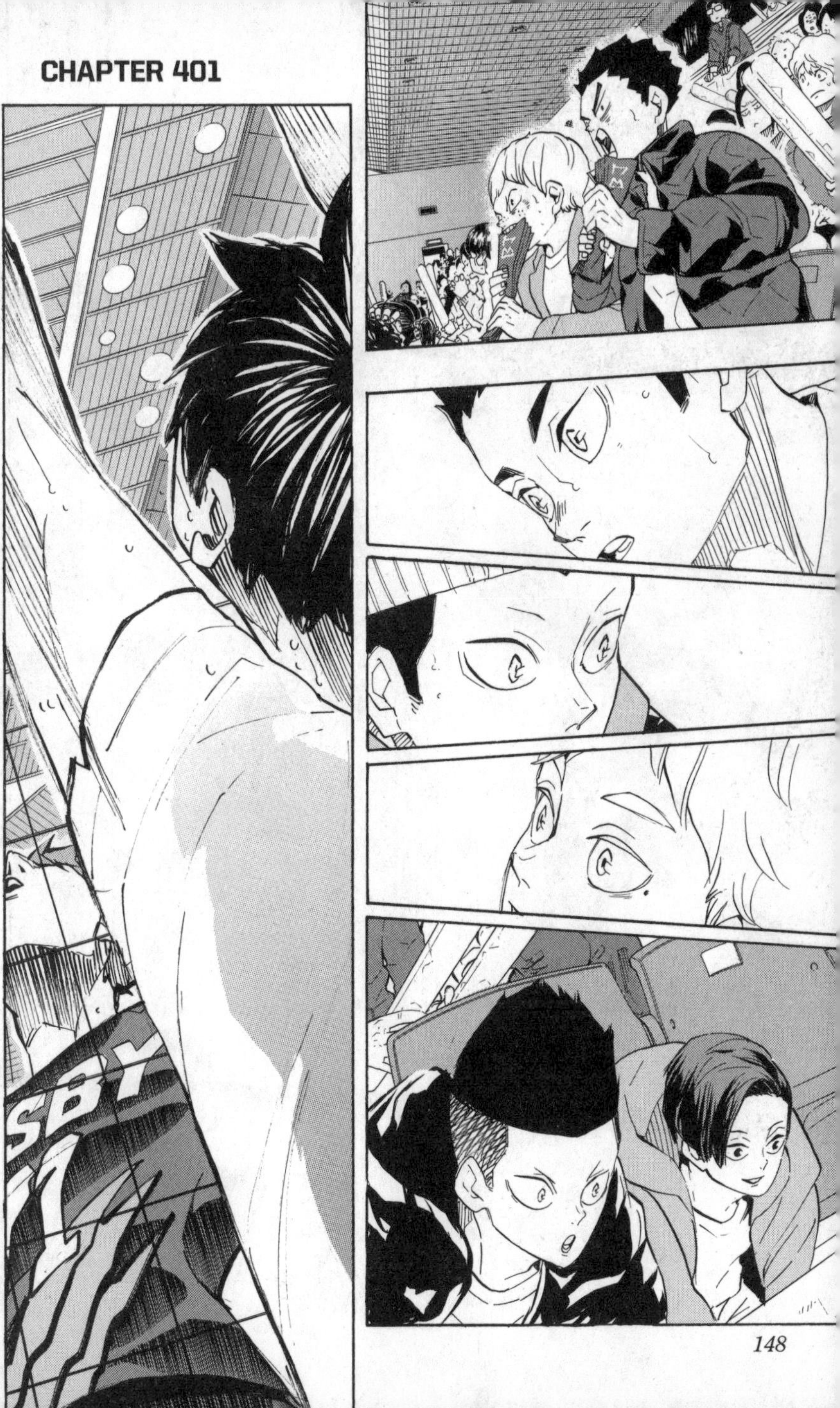

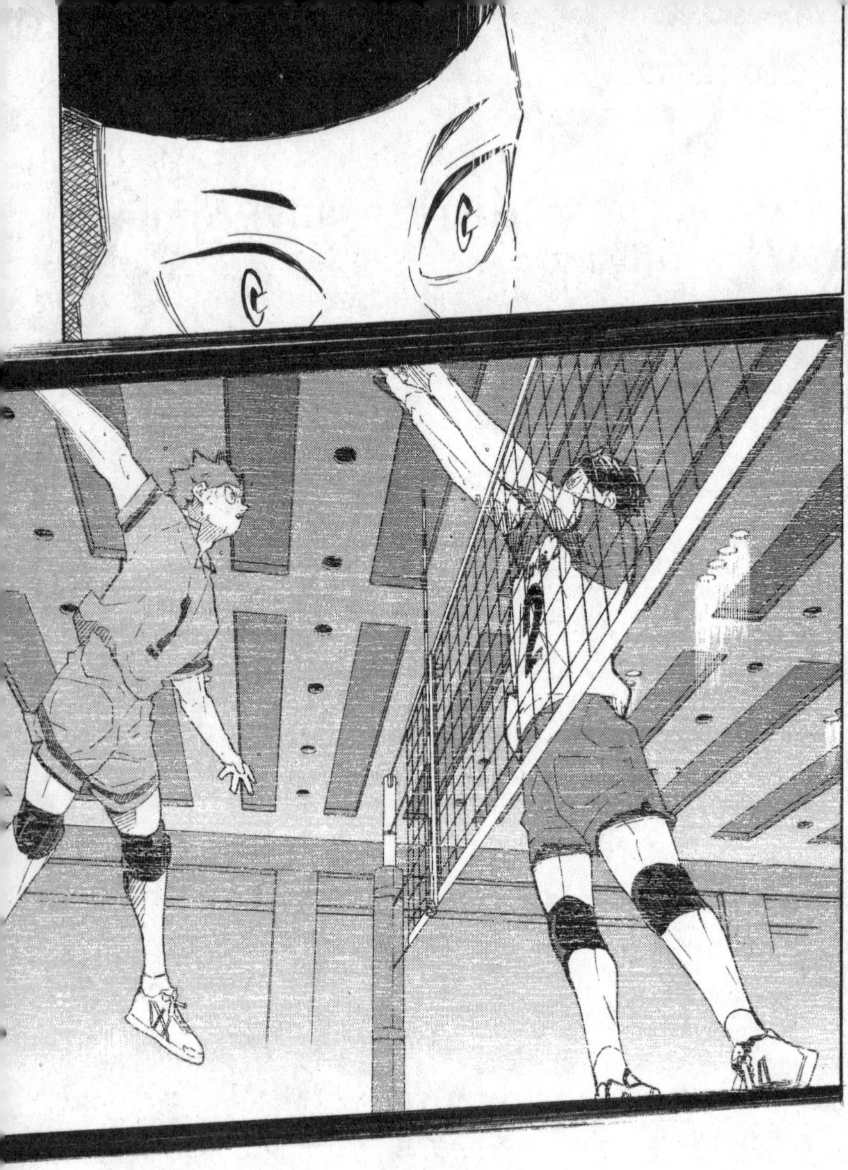

"IF YOU GET REALLY GOOD, I **PROMISE** YOU..."

"...SOMEBODY WHO'S **EVEN BETTER** WILL COME AND FIND YOU."

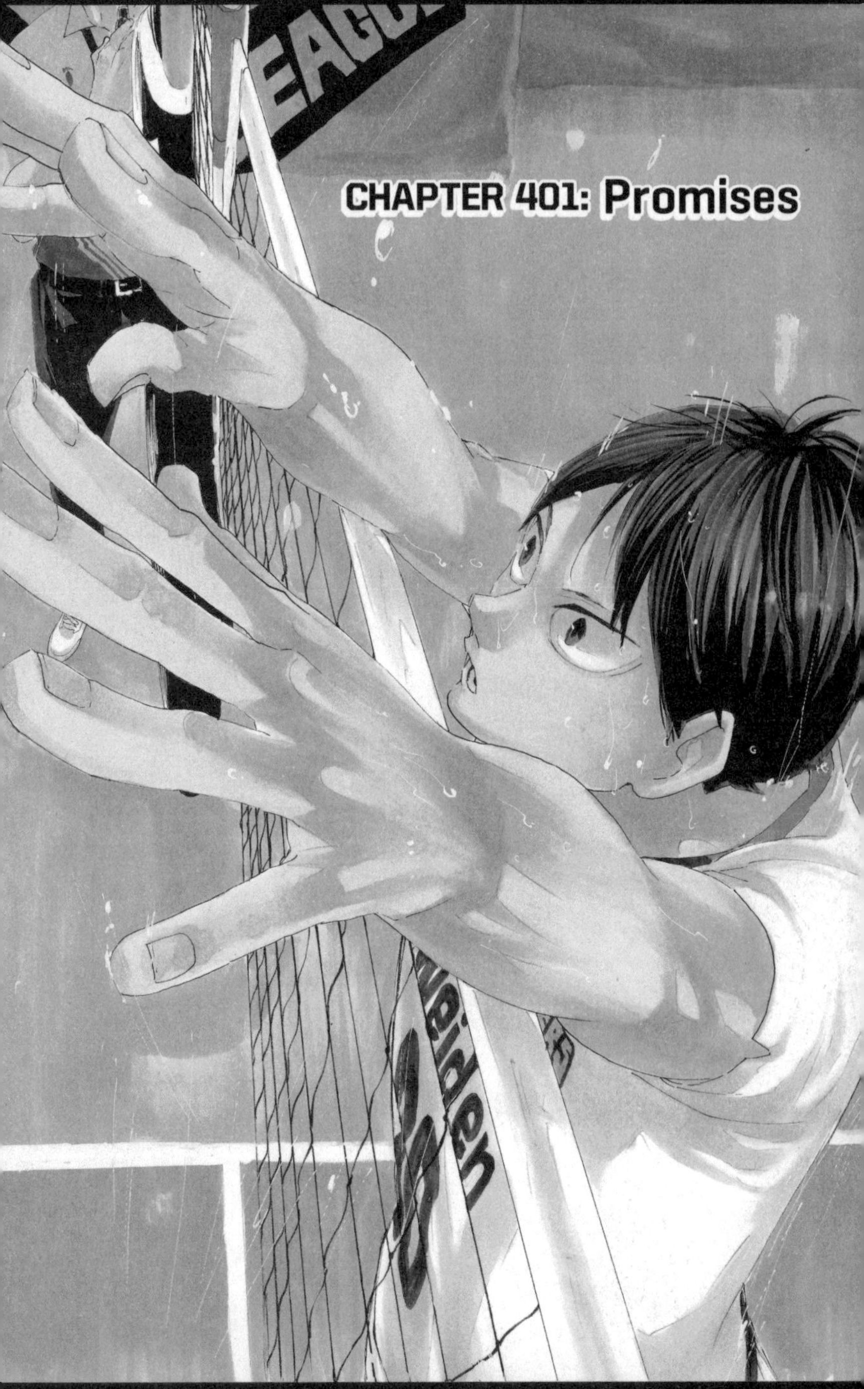
CHAPTER 401: Promises

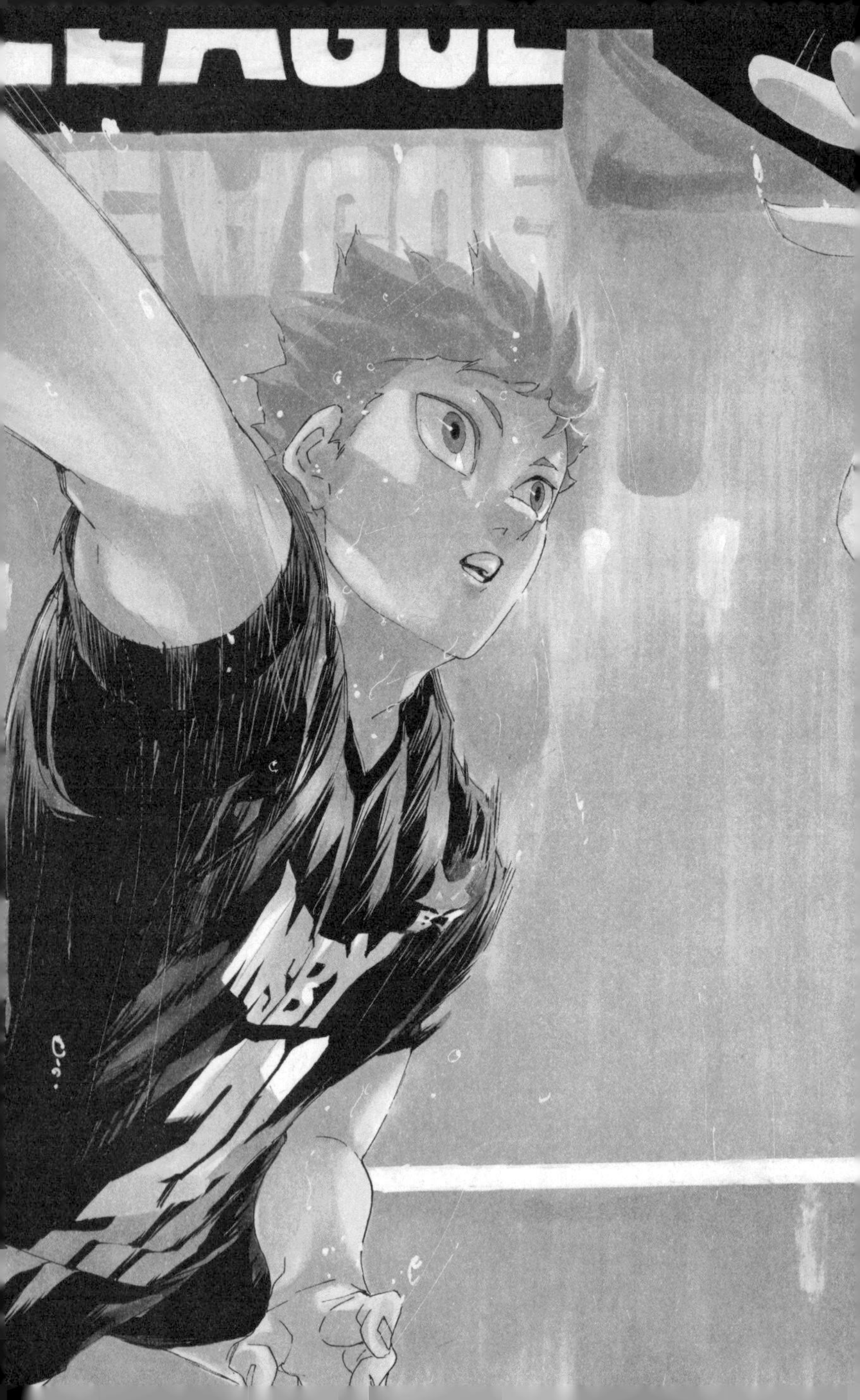

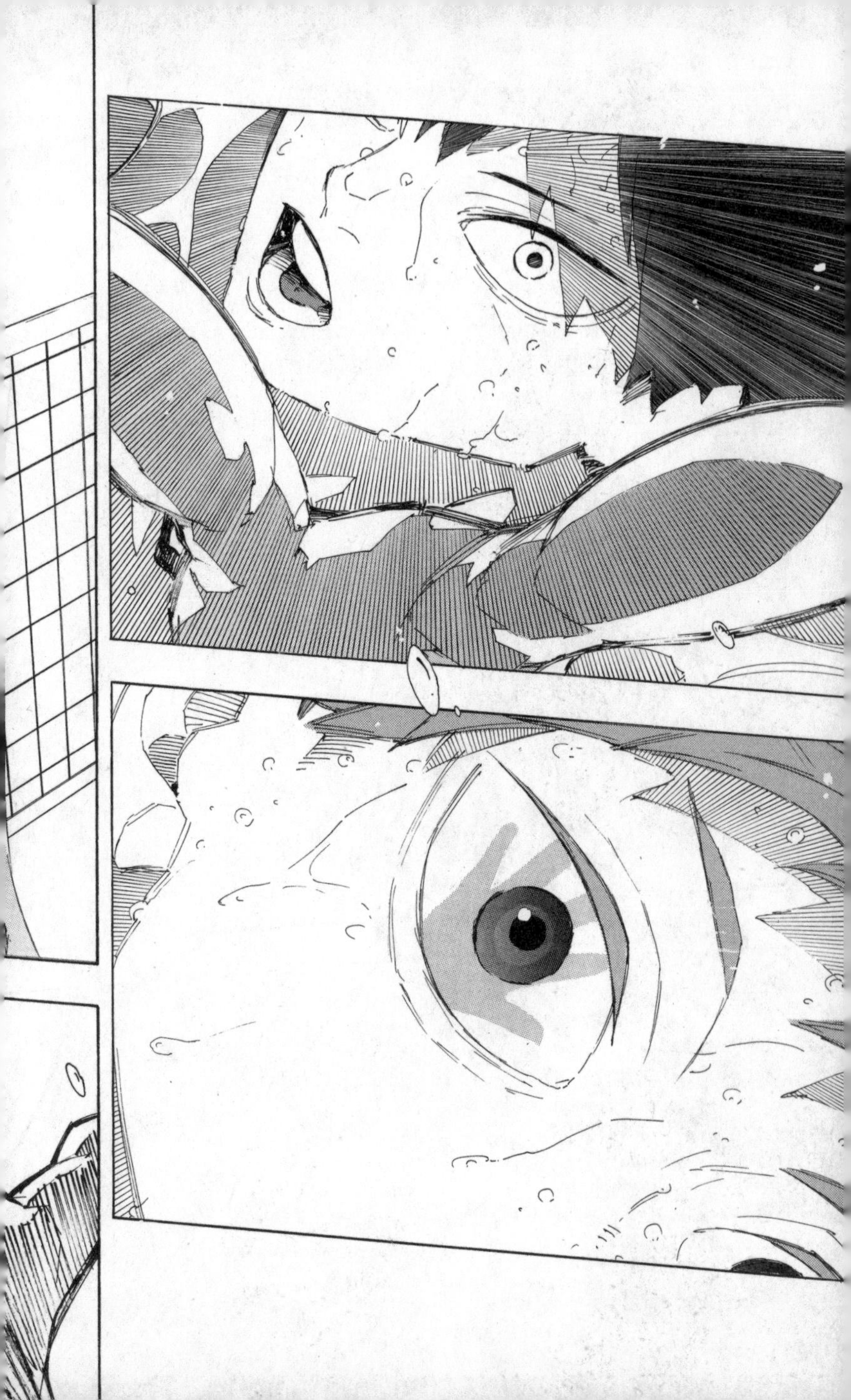

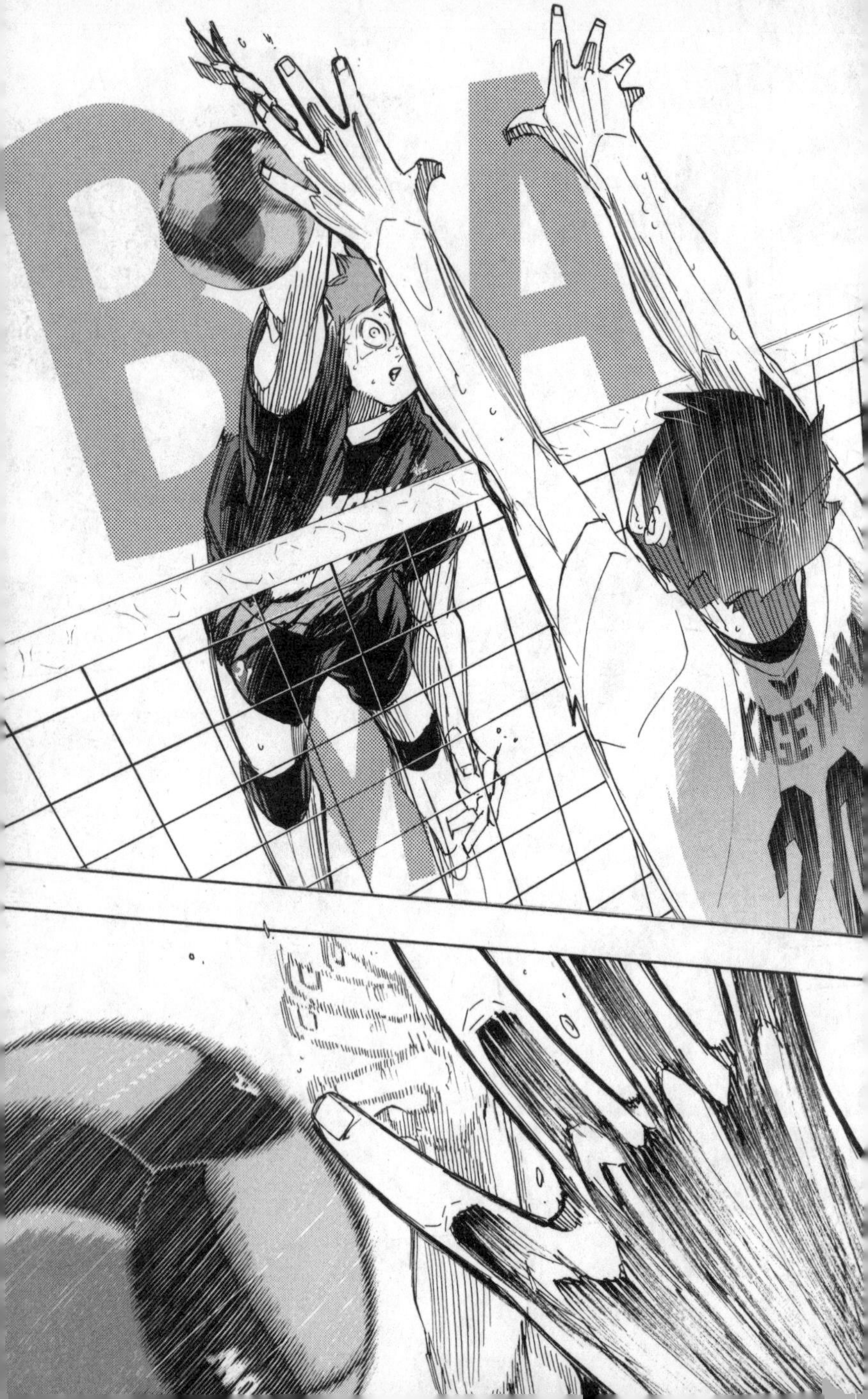
BAM

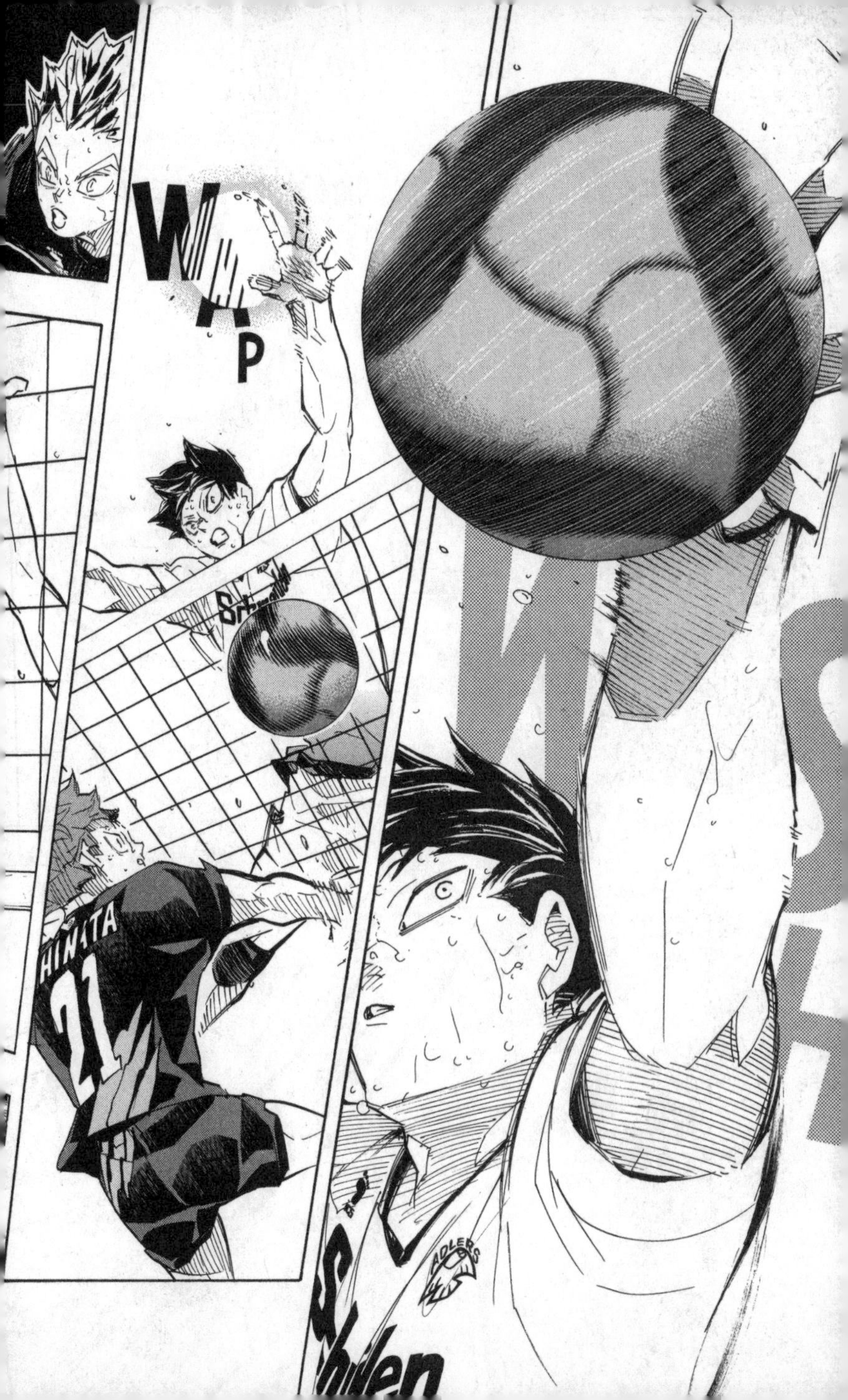
ADLERS
WAP
HINATA
21

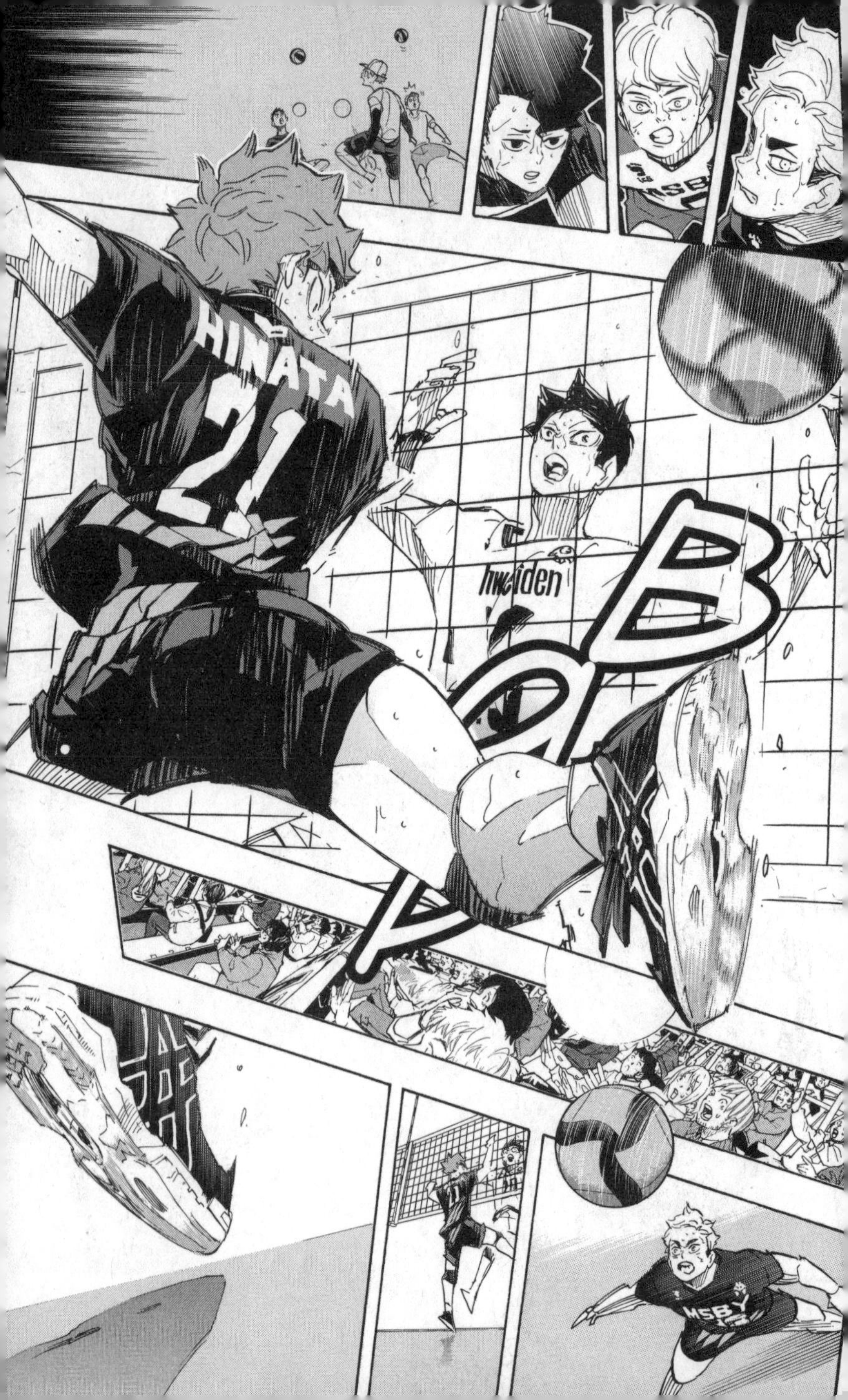
HINATA

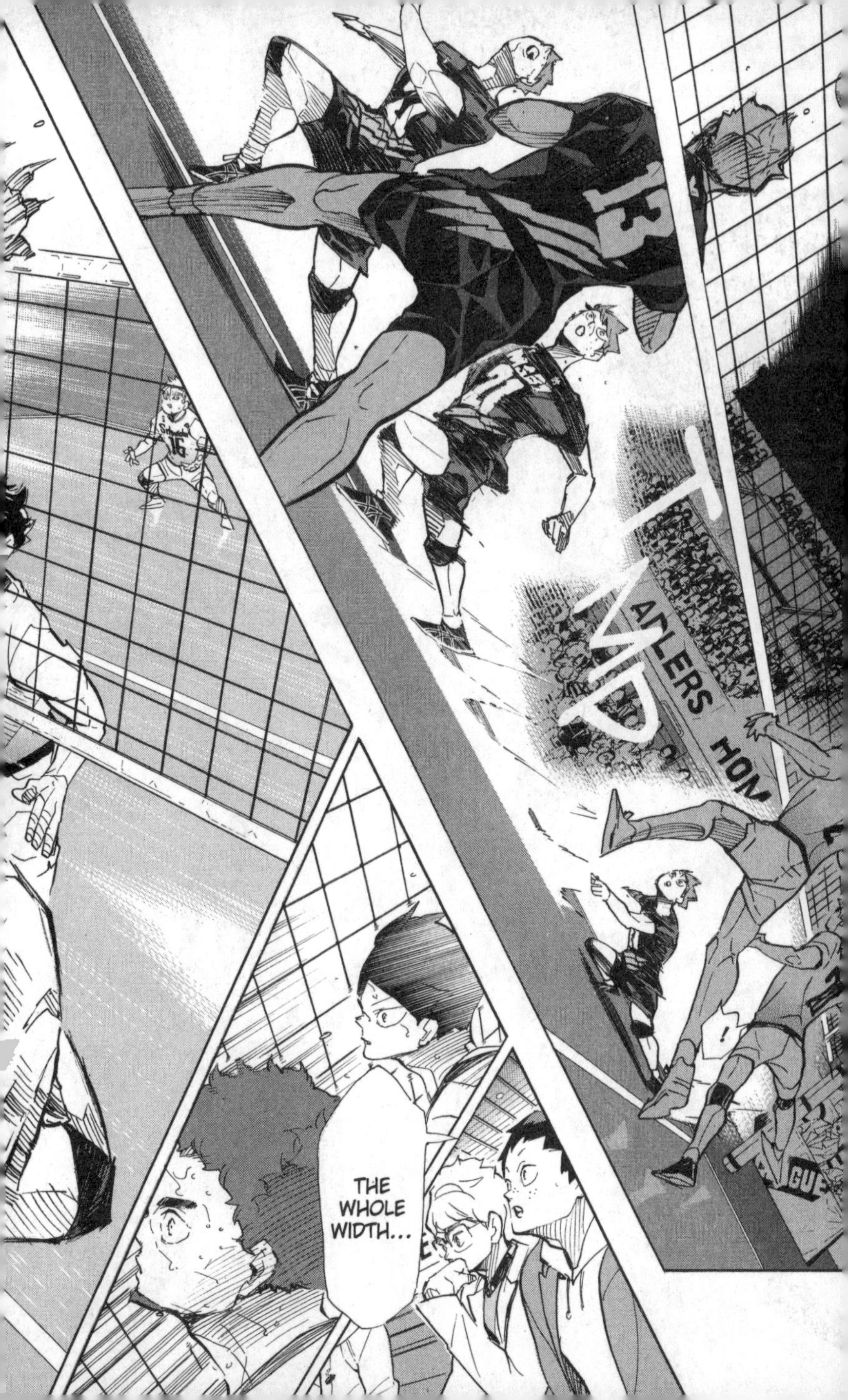
TMP
ADLERS
HOM
THE WHOLE WIDTH...

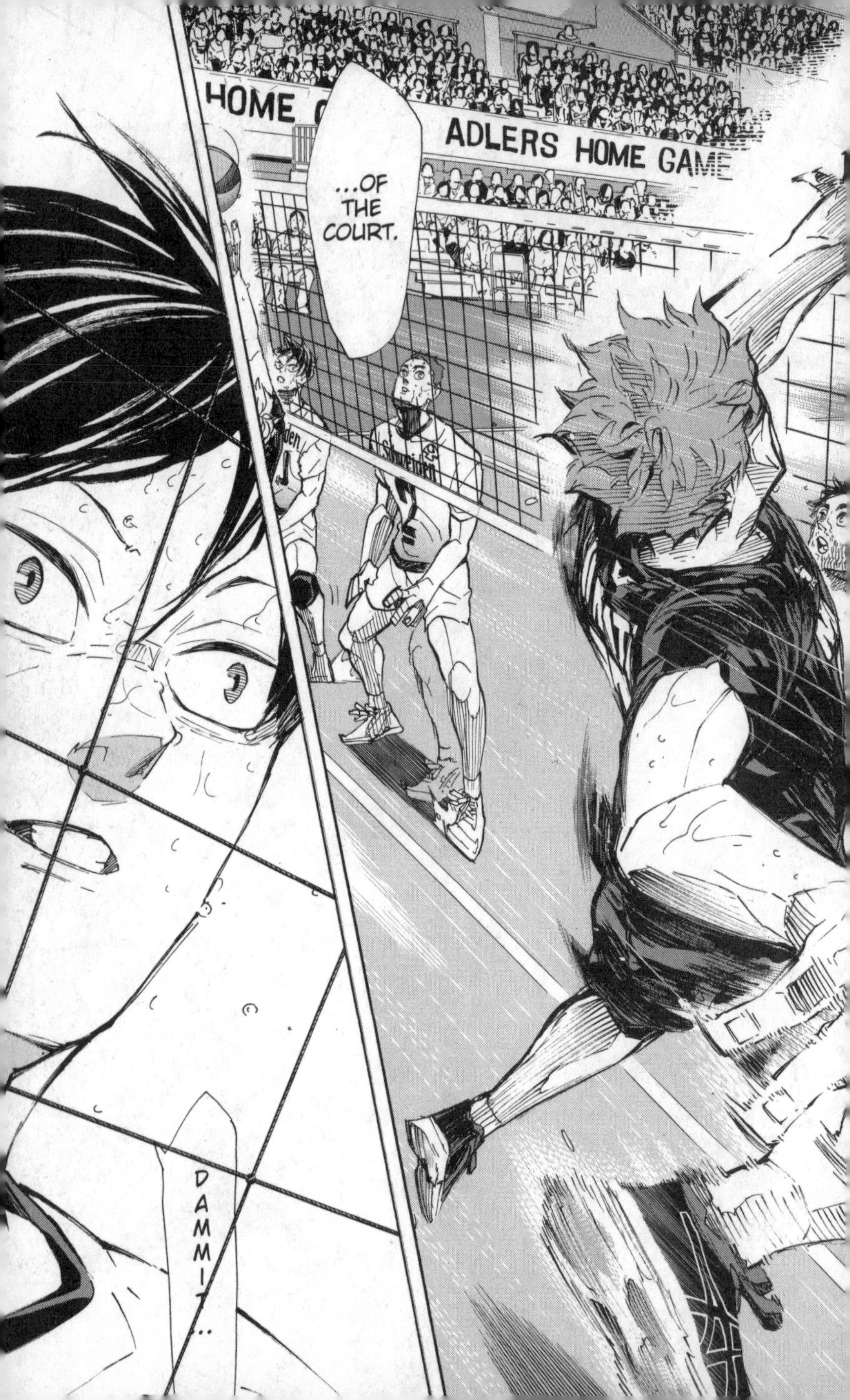
HOME G
ADLERS HOME GAME
...OF THE COURT.
Schweiden
DAMMIT...

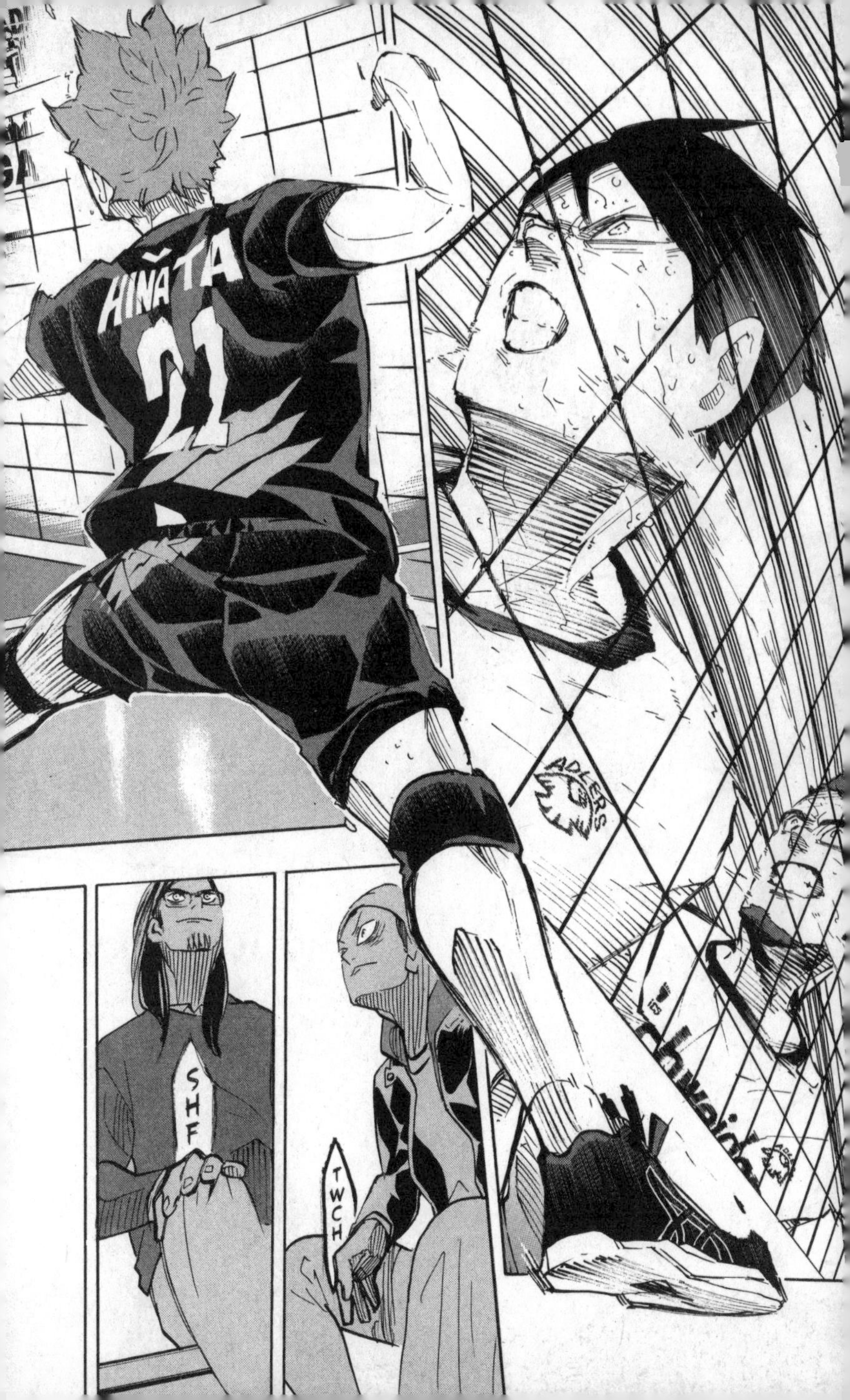
HINATA
21
ADLERS
TWCH
SHF

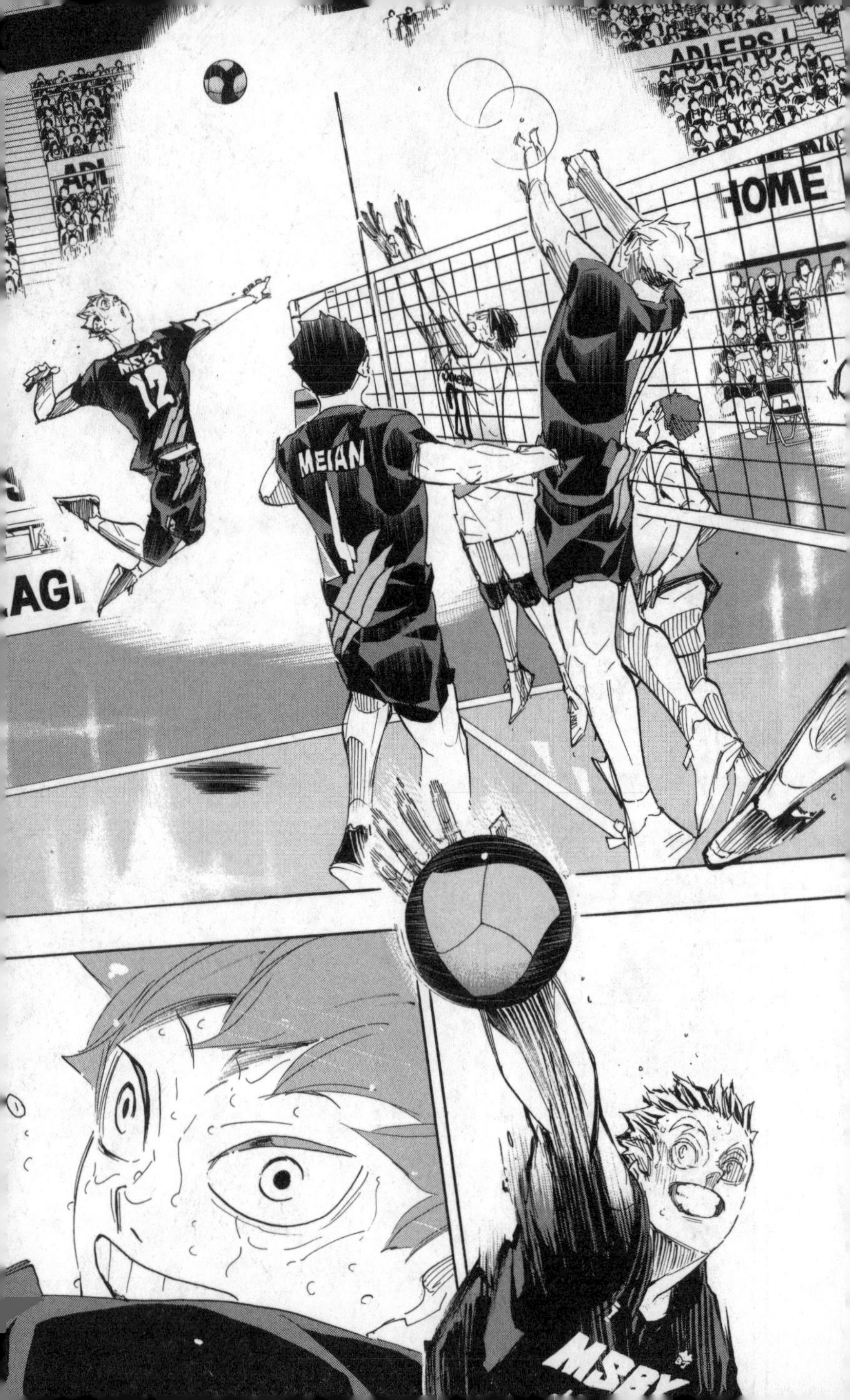
ADLERS
HOME
ADL
MSBY
12
MEIAN
AGI
MSBY

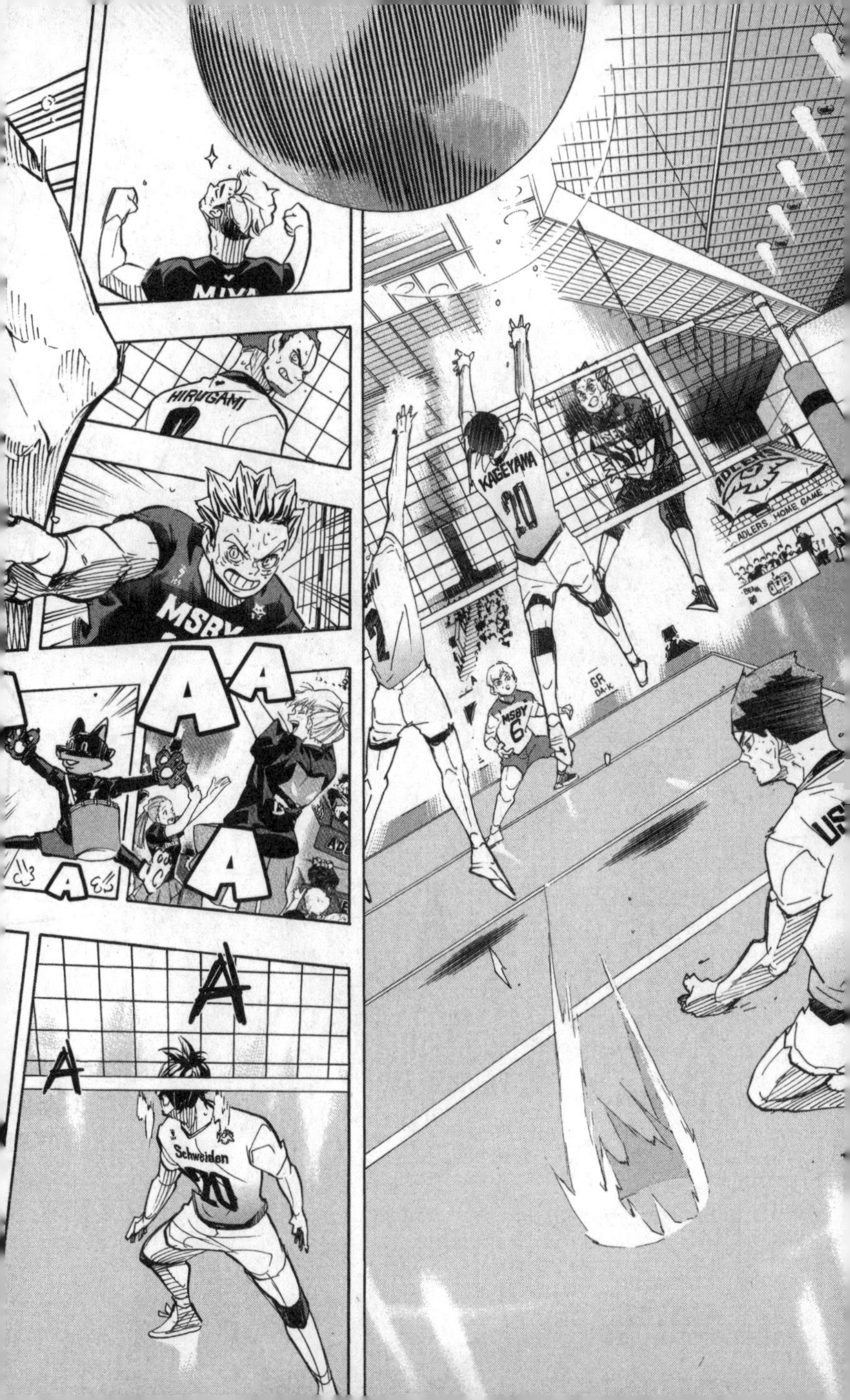
KAGEYAMA
20
MSBY
ADLERS
ADLERS HOME GAME
MSBY
6
MIYA
HIRUGAMI
MSBY
A
A
A
A
A
A
A
Schweiden
20

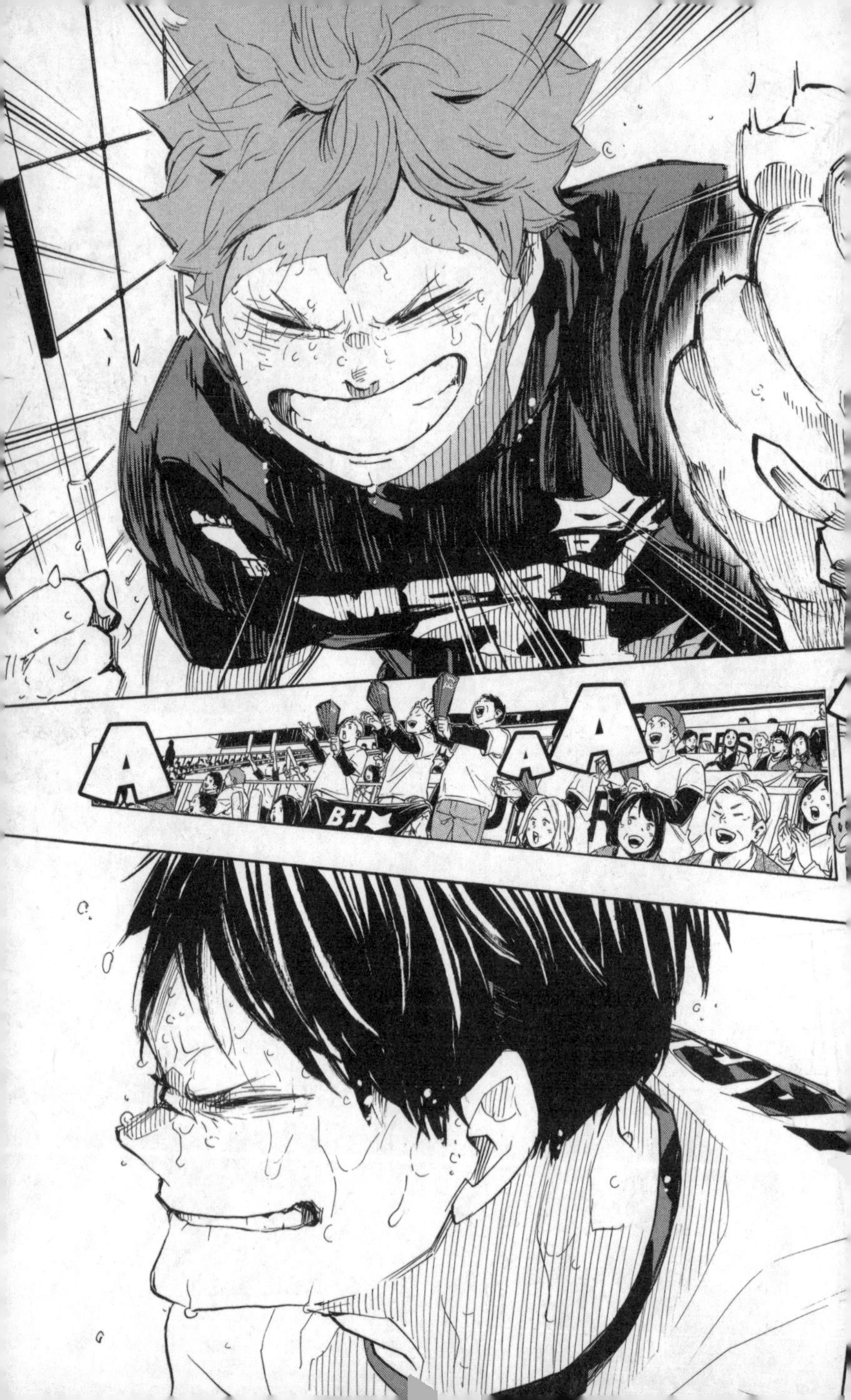
A
A
A
BJ

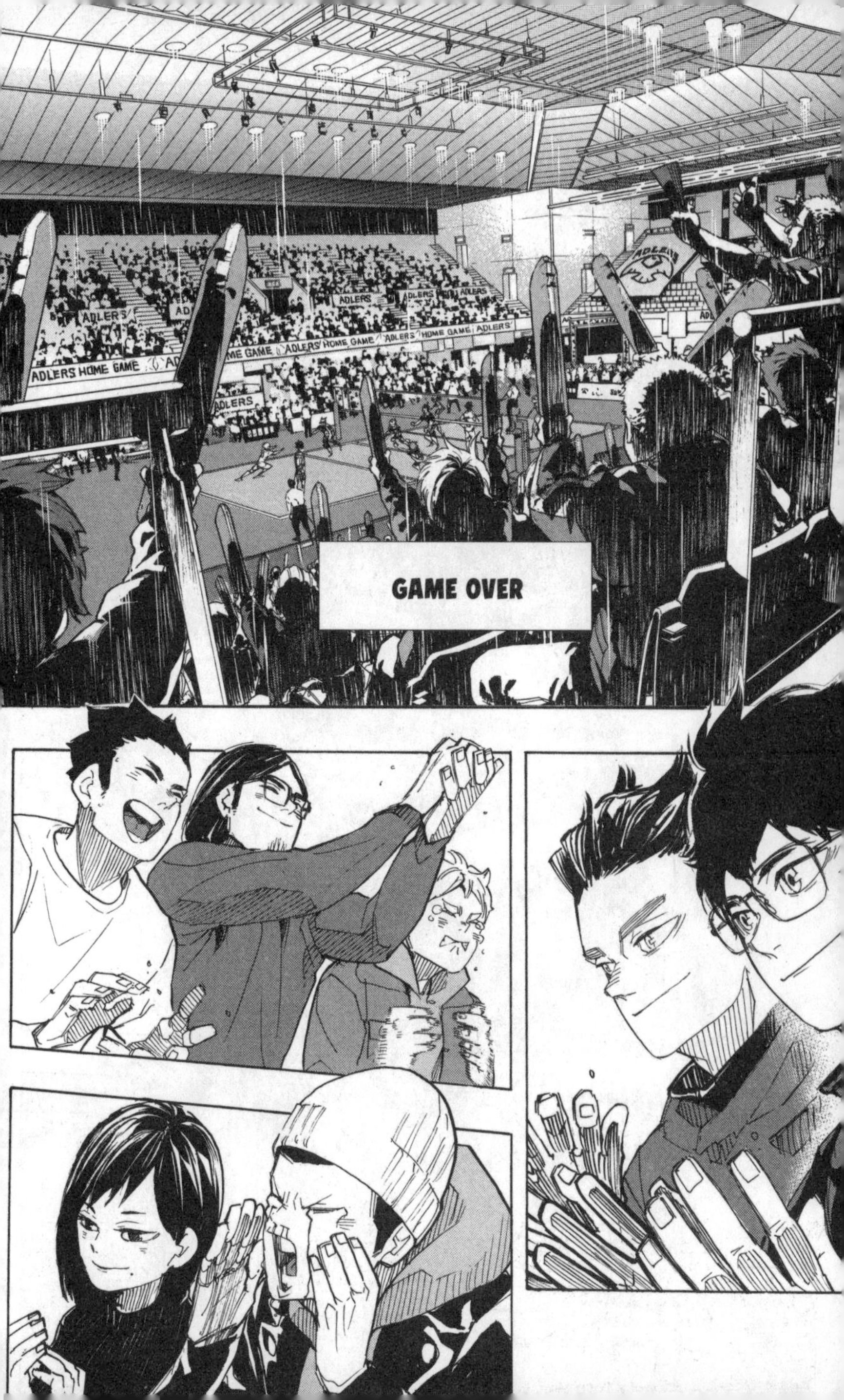
ADLERS HOME GAME
ADLERS' HOME GAME
GAME OVER

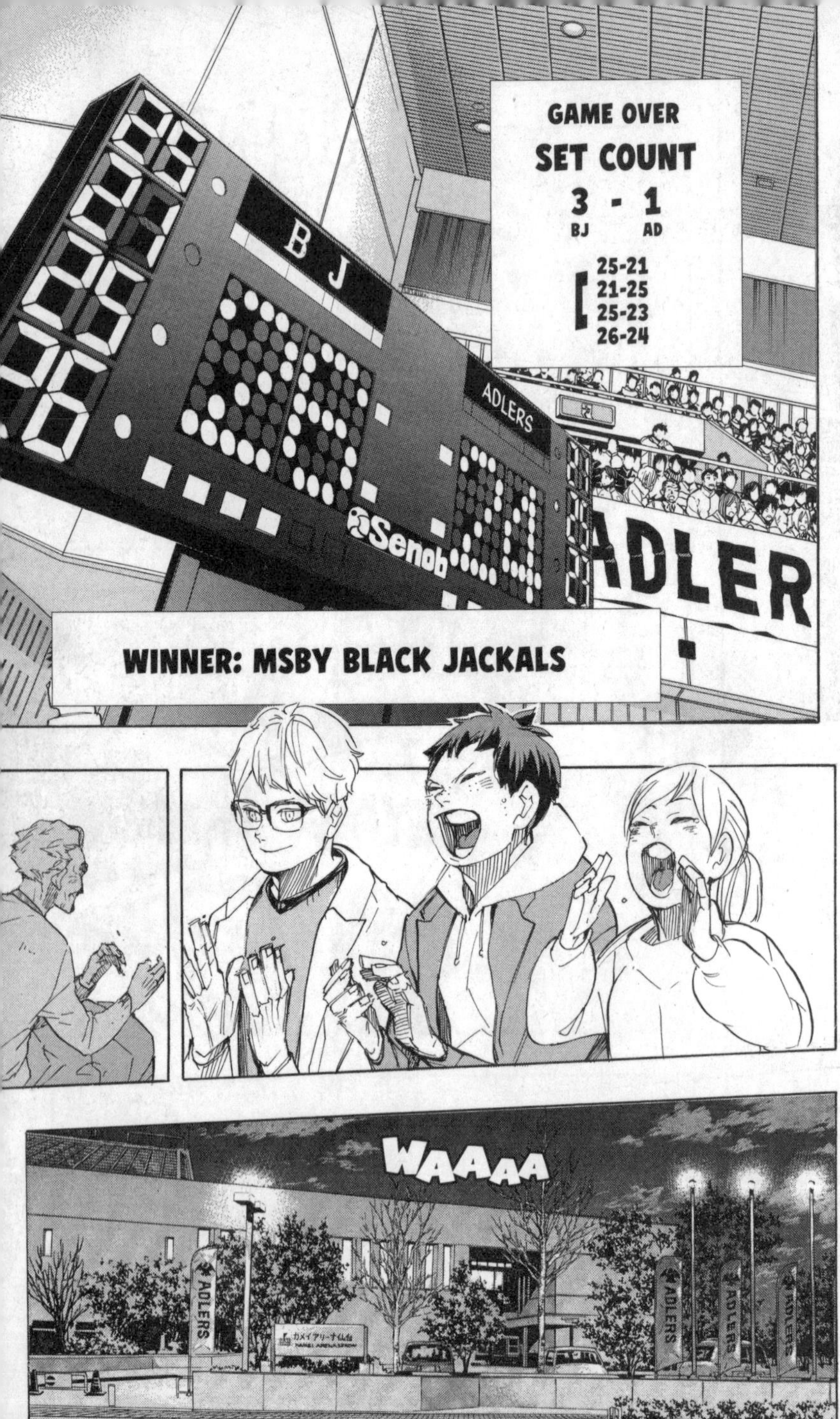
GAME OVER
SET COUNT
3 - 1
BJ AD
25-21
21-25
25-23
26-24
B J
ADLERS
Senob
ADLER
WINNER: MSBY BLACK JACKALS
WAAAA
ADLERS
ADLERS
ADLERS
ADLERS

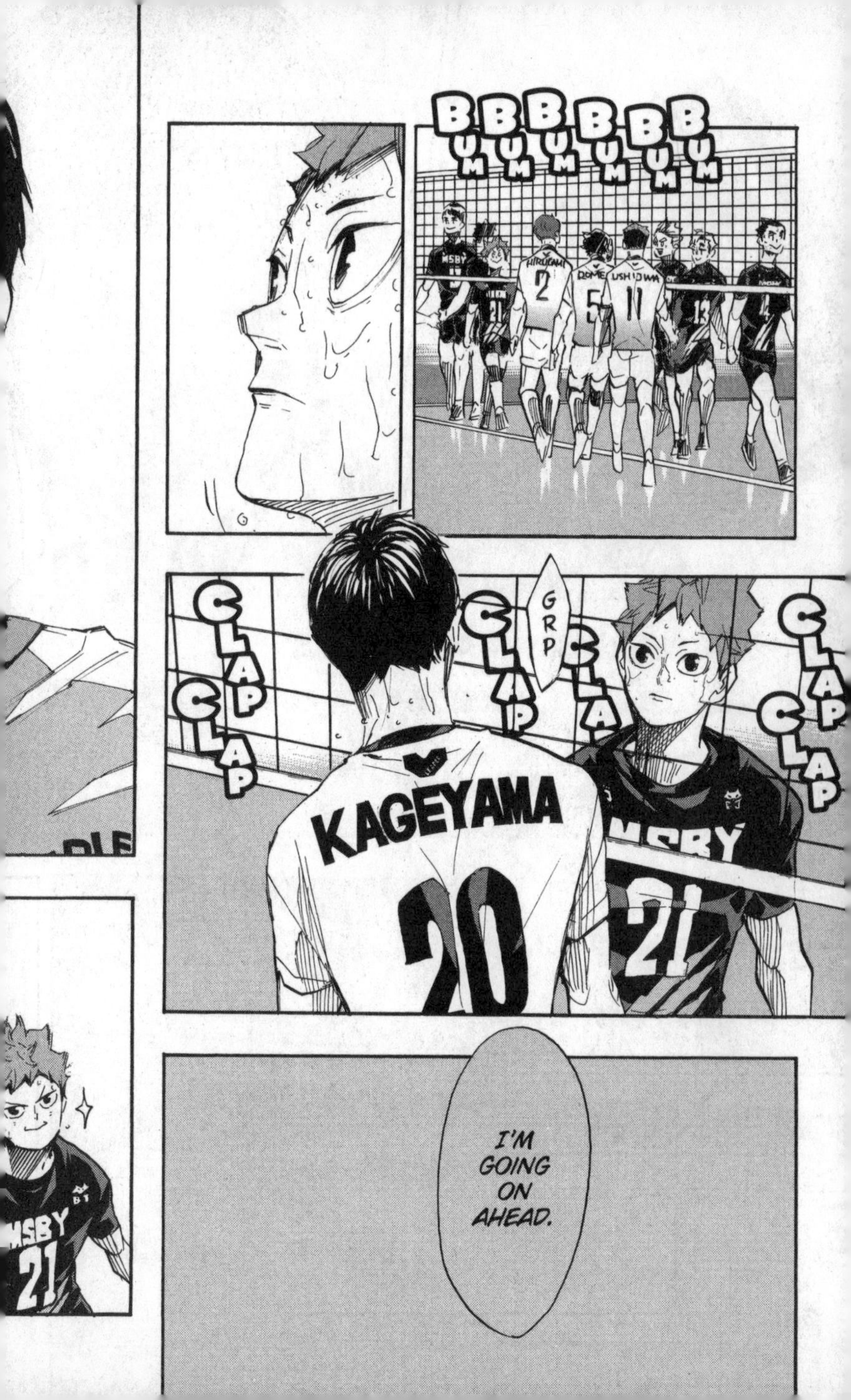

BBBBBBB UUUUUUU MMMMMMM
CLAP CLAP
CLAP
GRP
CLAP
CLAP CLAP
KAGEYAMA
20
MSBY
21
I'M GOING ON AHEAD.

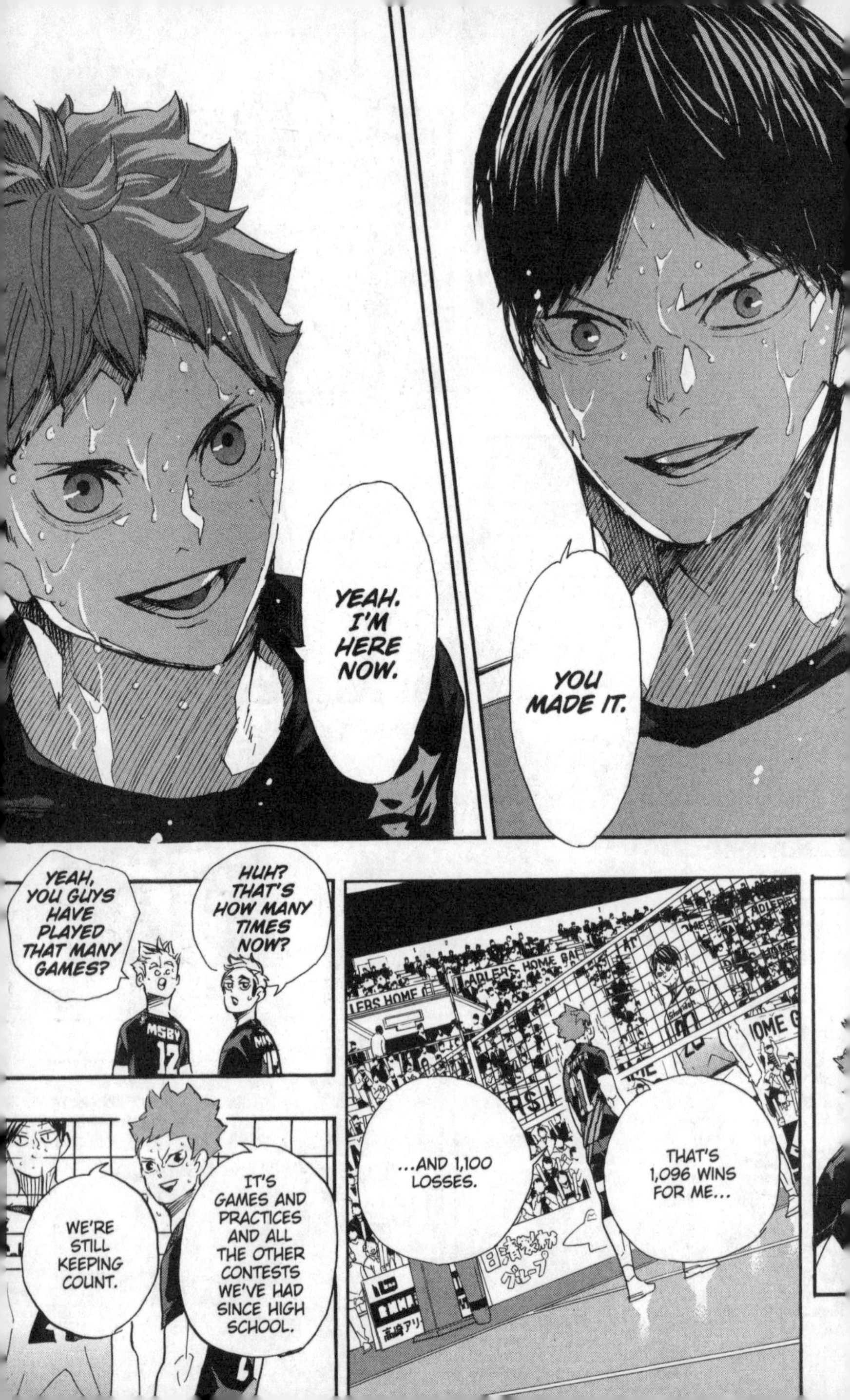
YOU MADE IT.
YEAH. I'M HERE NOW.
THAT'S 1,096 WINS FOR ME...
...AND 1,100 LOSSES.
HUH? THAT'S HOW MANY TIMES NOW?
YEAH, YOU GUYS HAVE PLAYED THAT MANY GAMES?
IT'S GAMES AND PRACTICES AND ALL THE OTHER CONTESTS WE'VE HAD SINCE HIGH SCHOOL.
WE'RE STILL KEEPING COUNT.

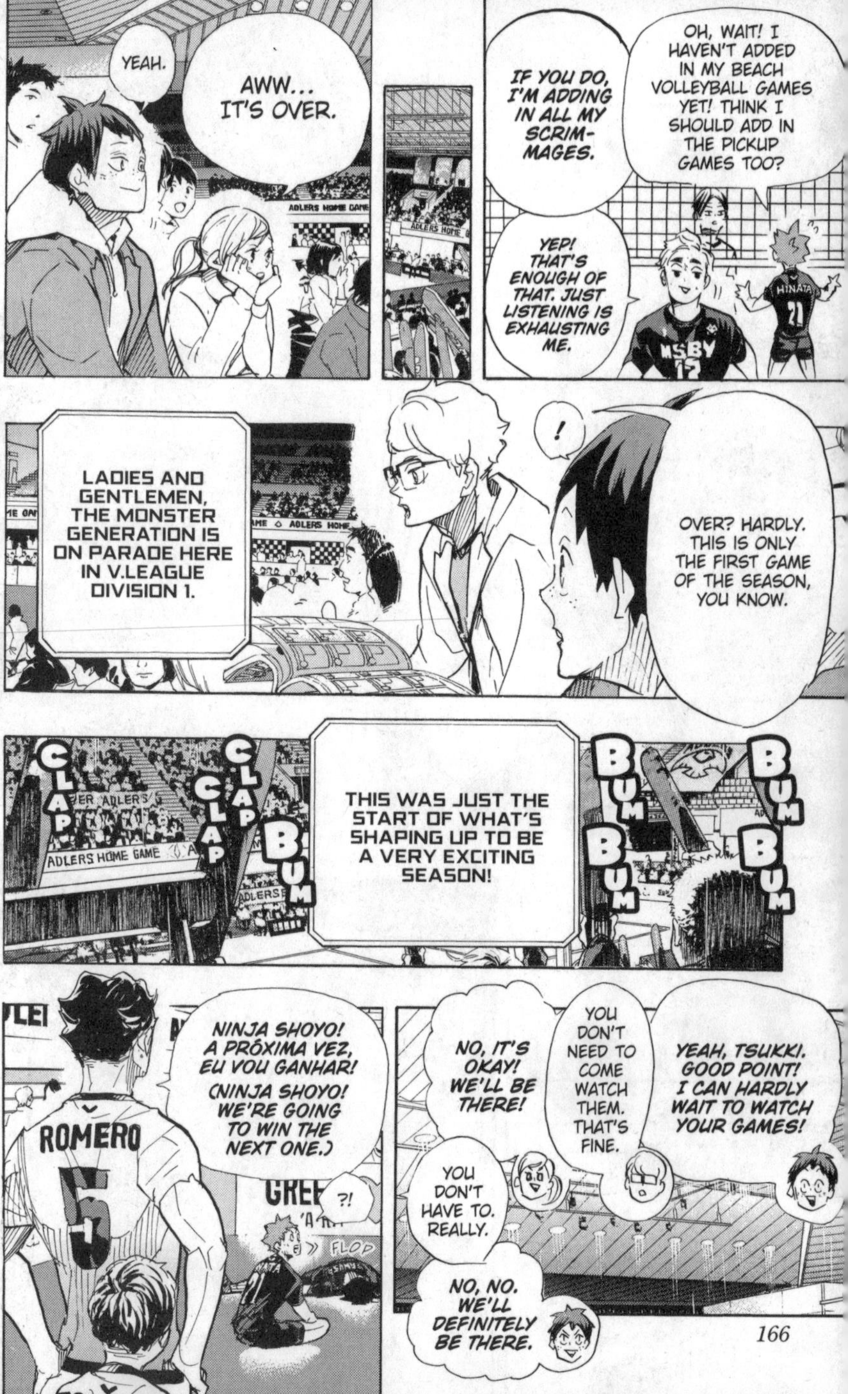
OH, WAIT! I HAVEN'T ADDED IN MY BEACH VOLLEYBALL GAMES YET! THINK I SHOULD ADD IN THE PICKUP GAMES TOO?
IF YOU DO, I'M ADDING IN ALL MY SCRIM-MAGES.
YEP! THAT'S ENOUGH OF THAT. JUST LISTENING IS EXHAUSTING ME.
AWW... IT'S OVER.
YEAH.
OVER? HARDLY. THIS IS ONLY THE FIRST GAME OF THE SEASON, YOU KNOW.
!
LADIES AND GENTLEMEN, THE MONSTER GENERATION IS ON PARADE HERE IN V.LEAGUE DIVISION 1.
BUM BUM
BUM BUM
BUM
THIS WAS JUST THE START OF WHAT'S SHAPING UP TO BE A VERY EXCITING SEASON!
CLAP CLAP
CLAP CLAP
YEAH, TSUKKI. GOOD POINT! I CAN HARDLY WAIT TO WATCH YOUR GAMES!
YOU DON'T NEED TO COME WATCH THEM. THAT'S FINE.
NO, IT'S OKAY! WE'LL BE THERE!
YOU DON'T HAVE TO. REALLY.
NO, NO. WE'LL DEFINITELY BE THERE.
NINJA SHOYO! A PRÓXIMA VEZ, EU VOU GANHAR! (NINJA SHOYO! WE'RE GOING TO WIN THE NEXT ONE.)
?!
FLOP

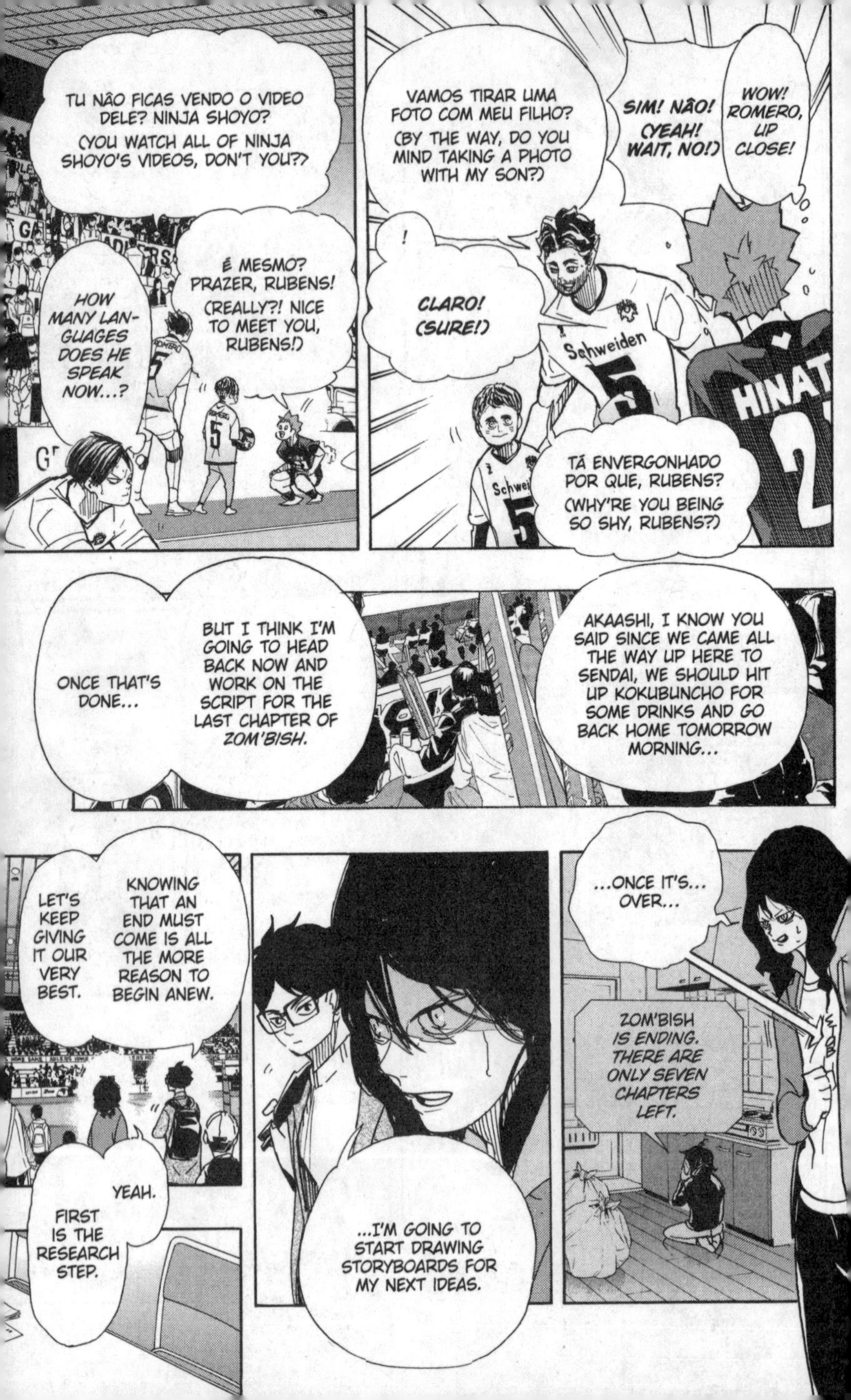
WOW! ROMERO, UP CLOSE!
SIM! NÃO! (YEAH! WAIT, NO!)
VAMOS TIRAR UMA FOTO COM MEU FILHO? (BY THE WAY, DO YOU MIND TAKING A PHOTO WITH MY SON?)
!
CLARO! (SURE!)
TÁ ENVERGONHADO POR QUE, RUBENS? (WHY'RE YOU BEING SO SHY, RUBENS?)
TU NÃO FICAS VENDO O VIDEO DELE? NINJA SHOYO? (YOU WATCH ALL OF NINJA SHOYO'S VIDEOS, DON'T YOU?)
É MESMO? PRAZER, RUBENS! (REALLY?! NICE TO MEET YOU, RUBENS!)
HOW MANY LANGUAGES DOES HE SPEAK NOW...?
AKAASHI, I KNOW YOU SAID SINCE WE CAME ALL THE WAY UP HERE TO SENDAI, WE SHOULD HIT UP KOKUBUNCHO FOR SOME DRINKS AND GO BACK HOME TOMORROW MORNING...
BUT I THINK I'M GOING TO HEAD BACK NOW AND WORK ON THE SCRIPT FOR THE LAST CHAPTER OF ZOM'BISH.
ONCE THAT'S DONE...
...ONCE IT'S... OVER...
ZOM'BISH IS ENDING. THERE ARE ONLY SEVEN CHAPTERS LEFT.
...I'M GOING TO START DRAWING STORYBOARDS FOR MY NEXT IDEAS.
KNOWING THAT AN END MUST COME IS ALL THE MORE REASON TO BEGIN ANEW.
LET'S KEEP GIVING IT OUR VERY BEST.
YEAH.
FIRST IS THE RESEARCH STEP.

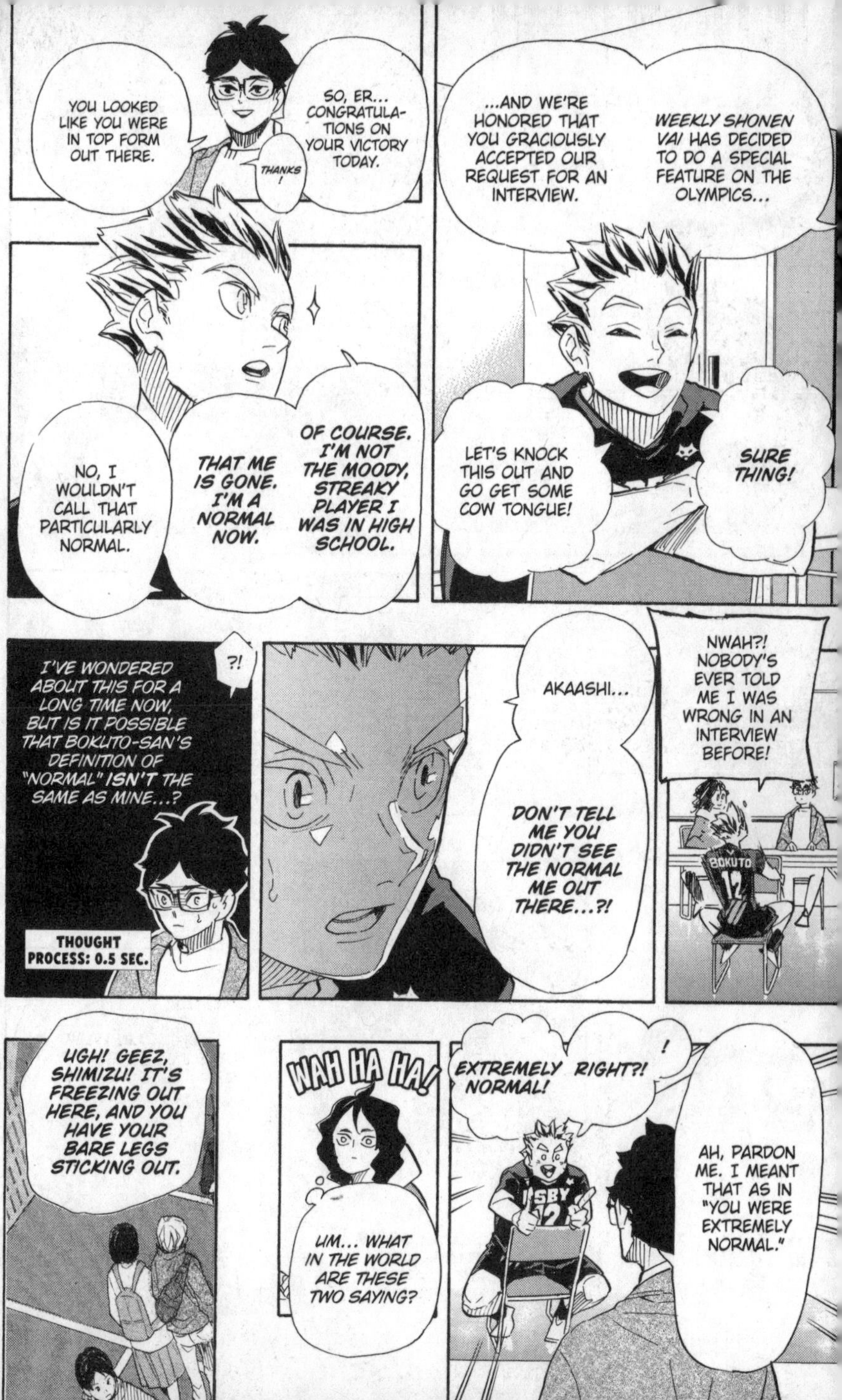
WEEKLY SHONEN VAI HAS DECIDED TO DO A SPECIAL FEATURE ON THE OLYMPICS...
...AND WE'RE HONORED THAT YOU GRACIOUSLY ACCEPTED OUR REQUEST FOR AN INTERVIEW.
SURE THING!
LET'S KNOCK THIS OUT AND GO GET SOME COW TONGUE!
SO, ER... CONGRATULATIONS ON YOUR VICTORY TODAY.
THANKS!
YOU LOOKED LIKE YOU WERE IN TOP FORM OUT THERE.
OF COURSE. I'M NOT THE MOODY, STREAKY PLAYER I WAS IN HIGH SCHOOL.
THAT ME IS GONE. I'M A NORMAL NOW.
NO, I WOULDN'T CALL THAT PARTICULARLY NORMAL.
NWAH?! NOBODY'S EVER TOLD ME I WAS WRONG IN AN INTERVIEW BEFORE!
BOKUTO 12
AKAASHI...
DON'T TELL ME YOU DIDN'T SEE THE NORMAL ME OUT THERE...?!
?!
I'VE WONDERED ABOUT THIS FOR A LONG TIME NOW, BUT IS IT POSSIBLE THAT BOKUTO-SAN'S DEFINITION OF "NORMAL" ISN'T THE SAME AS MINE...?
THOUGHT PROCESS: 0.5 SEC.
!
AH, PARDON ME. I MEANT THAT AS IN "YOU WERE EXTREMELY NORMAL."
RIGHT?!
EXTREMELY NORMAL!
WAH HA HA!
UM... WHAT IN THE WORLD ARE THESE TWO SAYING?
UGH! GEEZ, SHIMIZU! IT'S FREEZING OUT HERE, AND YOU HAVE YOUR BARE LEGS STICKING OUT.

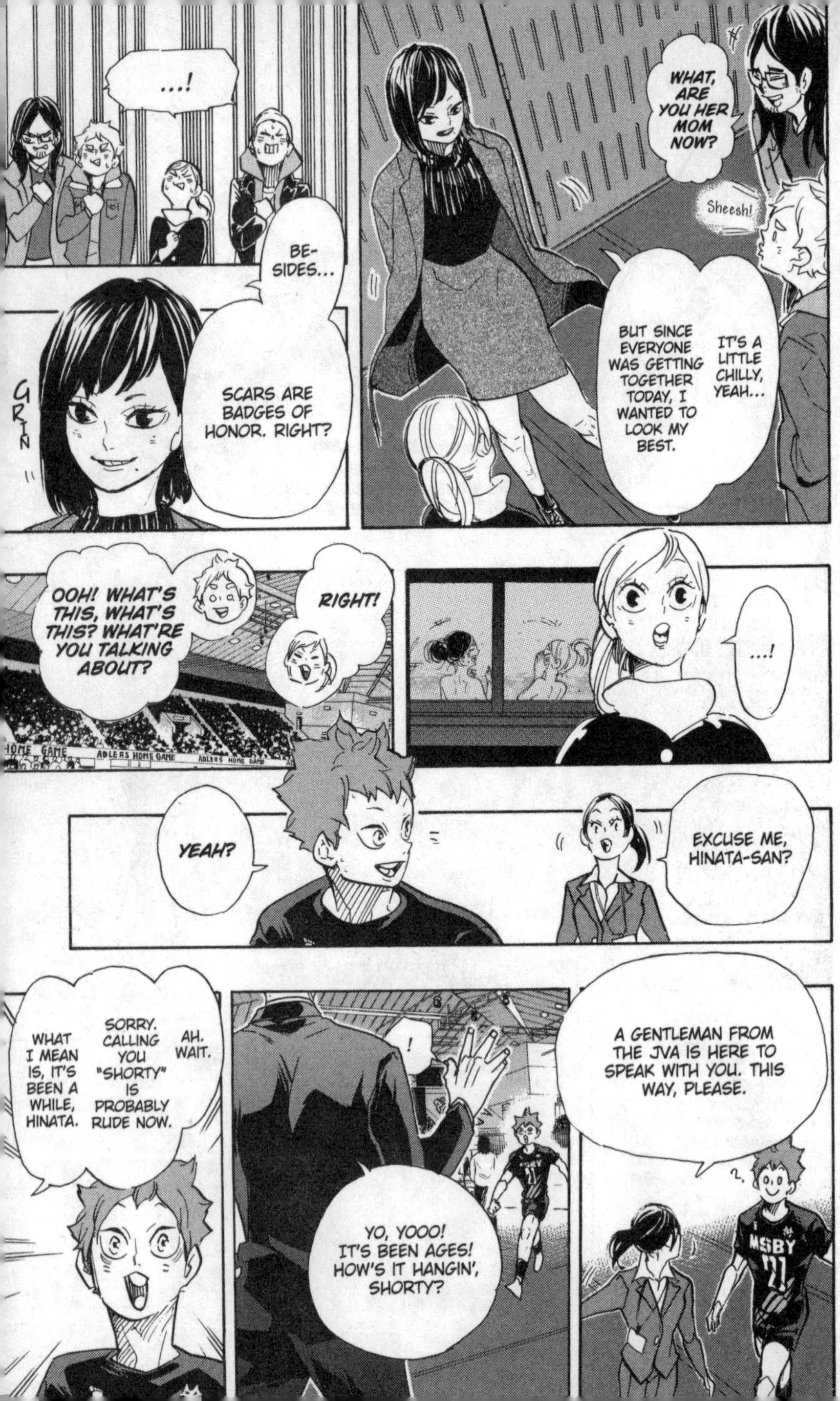
WHAT, ARE YOU HER MOM NOW?
Sheesh!
IT'S A LITTLE CHILLY, YEAH...
BUT SINCE EVERYONE WAS GETTING TOGETHER TODAY, I WANTED TO LOOK MY BEST.
...!
BE-SIDES...
SCARS ARE BADGES OF HONOR. RIGHT?
GRIN
...!
RIGHT!
OOH! WHAT'S THIS, WHAT'S THIS? WHAT'RE YOU TALKING ABOUT?
ADLERS HOME GAME
ADLERS HOME GAME
EXCUSE ME, HINATA-SAN?
YEAH?
A GENTLEMAN FROM THE JVA IS HERE TO SPEAK WITH YOU. THIS WAY, PLEASE.
MSBY
!
YO, YOOO! IT'S BEEN AGES! HOW'S IT HANGIN', SHORTY?
AH. WAIT.
SORRY. CALLING YOU "SHORTY" IS PROBABLY RUDE NOW.
WHAT I MEAN IS, IT'S BEEN A WHILE, HINATA.

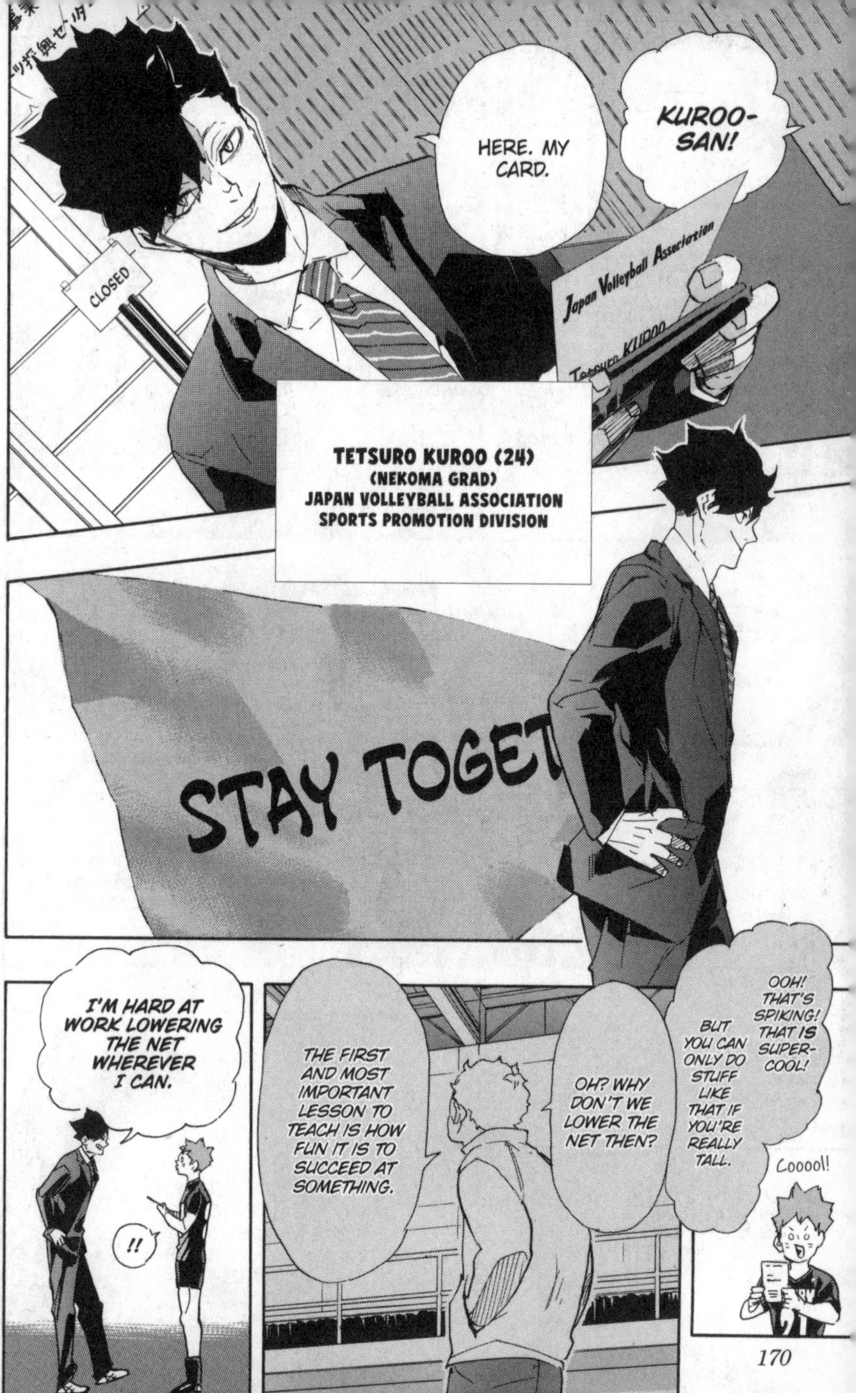
KUROO-SAN!
HERE. MY CARD.
Japan Volleyball Association
Tetsuro KUROO
CLOSED
TETSURO KUROO (24)
(NEKOMA GRAD)
JAPAN VOLLEYBALL ASSOCIATION
SPORTS PROMOTION DIVISION
STAY TOGET
OOH! THAT'S SPIKING! THAT IS SUPER-COOL!
BUT YOU CAN ONLY DO STUFF LIKE THAT IF YOU'RE REALLY TALL.
Coooool!
OH? WHY DON'T WE LOWER THE NET THEN?
THE FIRST AND MOST IMPORTANT LESSON TO TEACH IS HOW FUN IT IS TO SUCCEED AT SOMETHING.
I'M HARD AT WORK LOWERING THE NET WHEREVER I CAN.
!!

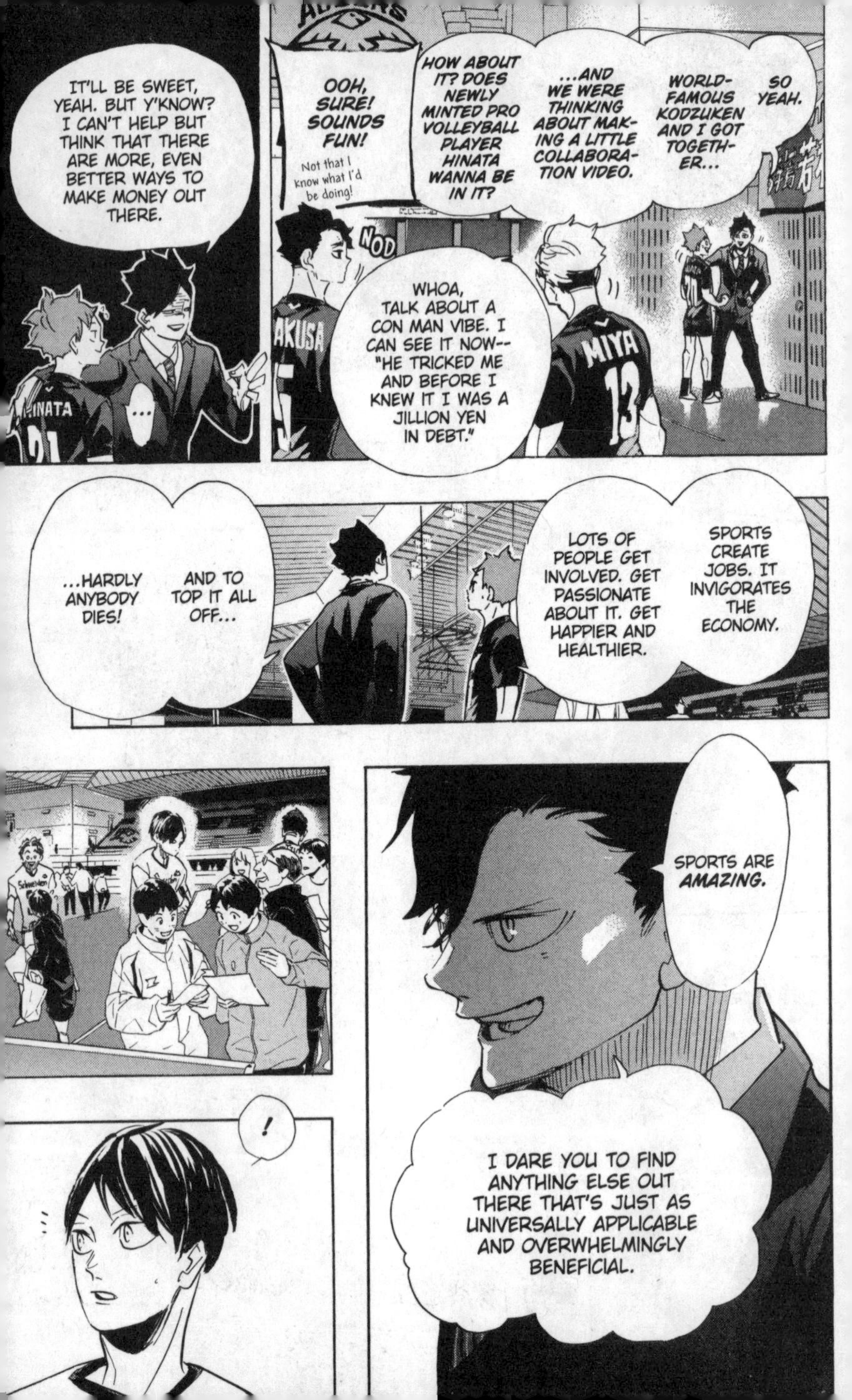
SO YEAH.
WORLD-FAMOUS KODZUKEN AND I GOT TOGETHER...
...AND WE WERE THINKING ABOUT MAKING A LITTLE COLLABORATION VIDEO.
HOW ABOUT IT? DOES NEWLY MINTED PRO VOLLEYBALL PLAYER HINATA WANNA BE IN IT?
OOH, SURE! SOUNDS FUN!
Not that I know what I'd be doing!
NOD
WHOA, TALK ABOUT A CON MAN VIBE. I CAN SEE IT NOW-- "HE TRICKED ME AND BEFORE I KNEW IT I WAS A JILLION YEN IN DEBT."
MIYA 13
IT'LL BE SWEET, YEAH. BUT Y'KNOW? I CAN'T HELP BUT THINK THAT THERE ARE MORE, EVEN BETTER WAYS TO MAKE MONEY OUT THERE.
...
SPORTS CREATE JOBS. IT INVIGORATES THE ECONOMY.
LOTS OF PEOPLE GET INVOLVED. GET PASSIONATE ABOUT IT. GET HAPPIER AND HEALTHIER.
AND TO TOP IT ALL OFF...
...HARDLY ANYBODY DIES!
SPORTS ARE *AMAZING.*
I DARE YOU TO FIND ANYTHING ELSE OUT THERE THAT'S JUST AS UNIVERSALLY APPLICABLE AND OVERWHELMINGLY BENEFICIAL.
!

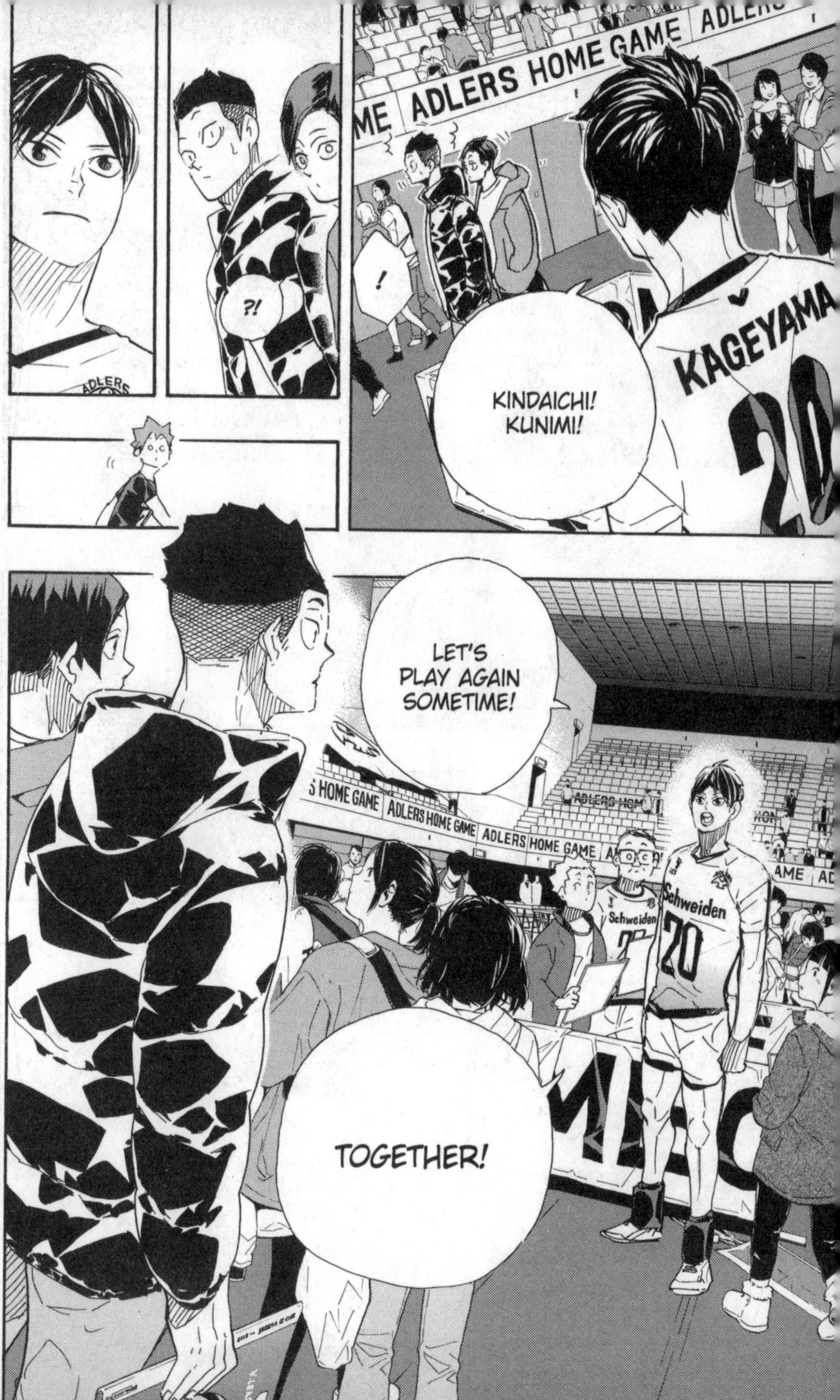
ADLERS HOME GAME
KAGEYAMA
KINDAICHI! KUNIMI!
!
?!
LET'S PLAY AGAIN SOMETIME!
TOGETHER!
ADLERS HOME GAME
Schweiden

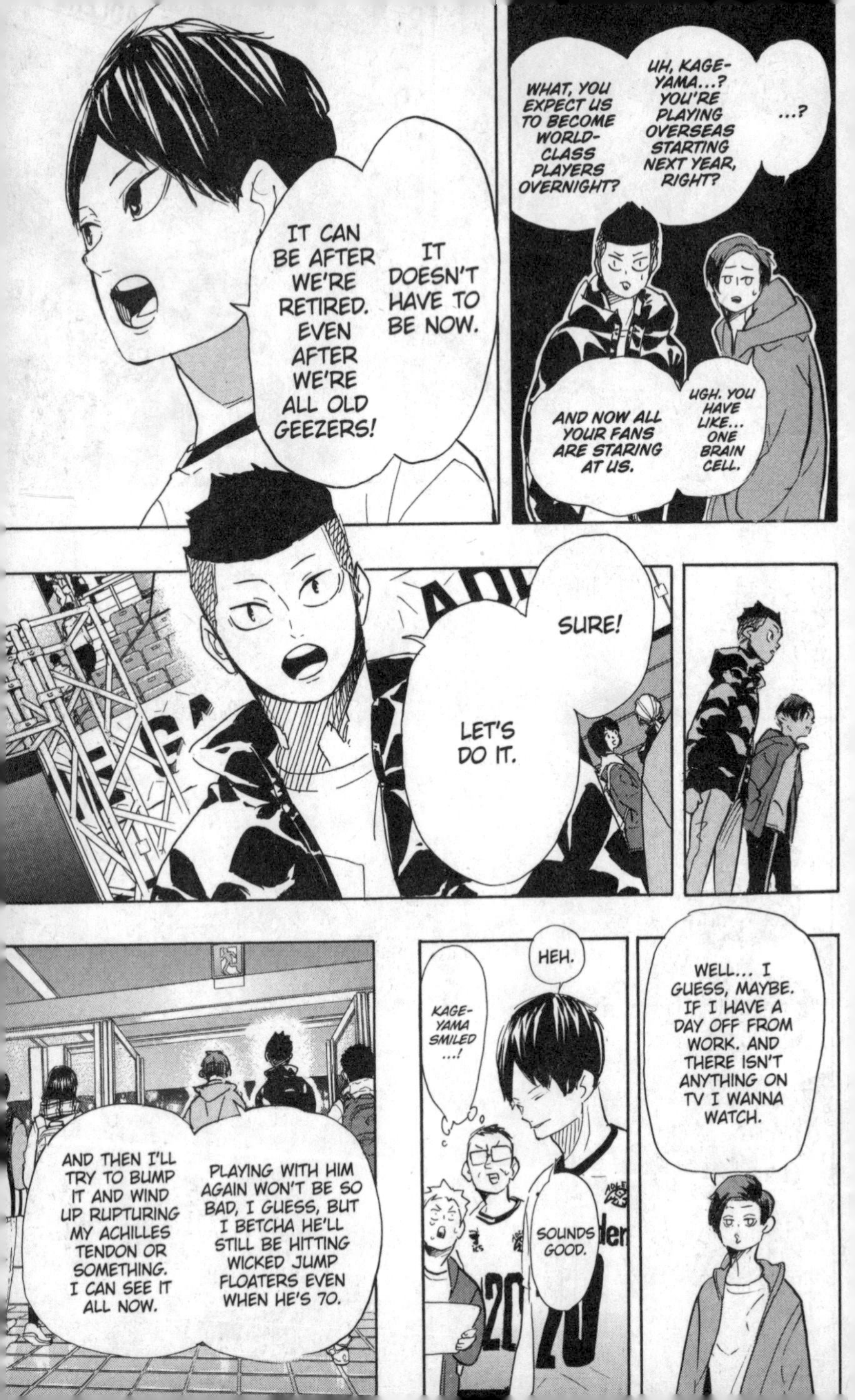
...?
UH, KAGE-YAMA...? YOU'RE PLAYING OVERSEAS STARTING NEXT YEAR, RIGHT?
WHAT, YOU EXPECT US TO BECOME WORLD-CLASS PLAYERS OVERNIGHT?
UGH. YOU HAVE LIKE... ONE BRAIN CELL.
AND NOW ALL YOUR FANS ARE STARING AT US.
IT DOESN'T HAVE TO BE NOW.
IT CAN BE AFTER WE'RE RETIRED. EVEN AFTER WE'RE ALL OLD GEEZERS!
SURE!
LET'S DO IT.
WELL... I GUESS, MAYBE. IF I HAVE A DAY OFF FROM WORK. AND THERE ISN'T ANYTHING ON TV I WANNA WATCH.
HEH.
KAGE-YAMA SMILED ...!
SOUNDS GOOD.
PLAYING WITH HIM AGAIN WON'T BE SO BAD, I GUESS, BUT I BETCHA HE'LL STILL BE HITTING WICKED JUMP FLOATERS EVEN WHEN HE'S 70.
AND THEN I'LL TRY TO BUMP IT AND WIND UP RUPTURING MY ACHILLES TENDON OR SOMETHING. I CAN SEE IT ALL NOW.

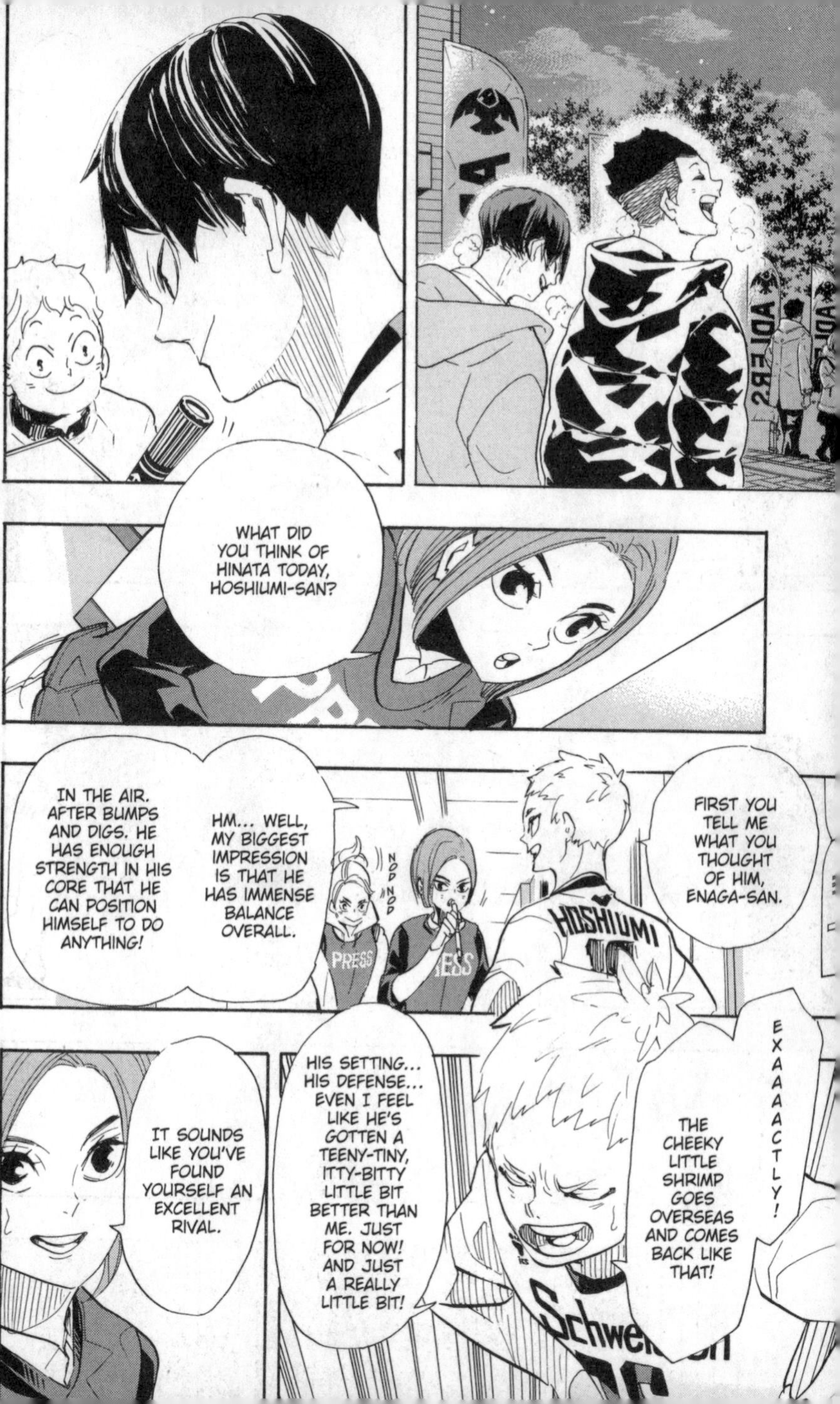
WHAT DID YOU THINK OF HINATA TODAY, HOSHIUMI-SAN?
FIRST YOU TELL ME WHAT YOU THOUGHT OF HIM, ENAGA-SAN.
HOSHIUMI
NOD NOD
PRESS
HM... WELL, MY BIGGEST IMPRESSION IS THAT HE HAS IMMENSE BALANCE OVERALL.
IN THE AIR. AFTER BUMPS AND DIGS. HE HAS ENOUGH STRENGTH IN HIS CORE THAT HE CAN POSITION HIMSELF TO DO ANYTHING!
EXAAAAACTLY!
THE CHEEKY LITTLE SHRIMP GOES OVERSEAS AND COMES BACK LIKE THAT!
HIS SETTING... HIS DEFENSE... EVEN I FEEL LIKE HE'S GOTTEN A TEENY-TINY, ITTY-BITTY LITTLE BIT BETTER THAN ME. JUST FOR NOW! AND JUST A REALLY LITTLE BIT!
IT SOUNDS LIKE YOU'VE FOUND YOURSELF AN EXCELLENT RIVAL.

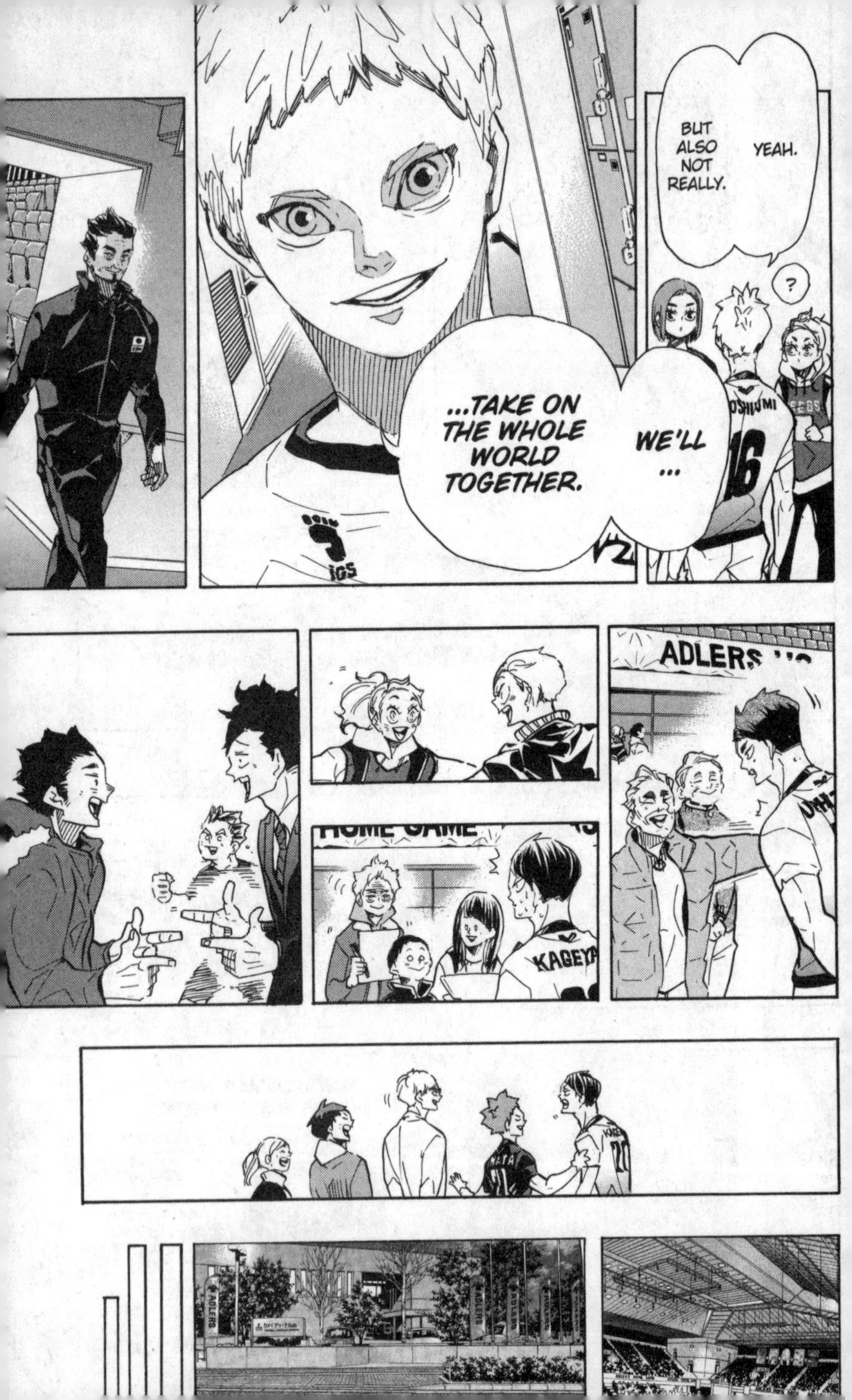
YEAH.
BUT ALSO NOT REALLY.
?
WE'LL ...
...TAKE ON THE WHOLE WORLD TOGETHER.
ADLERS

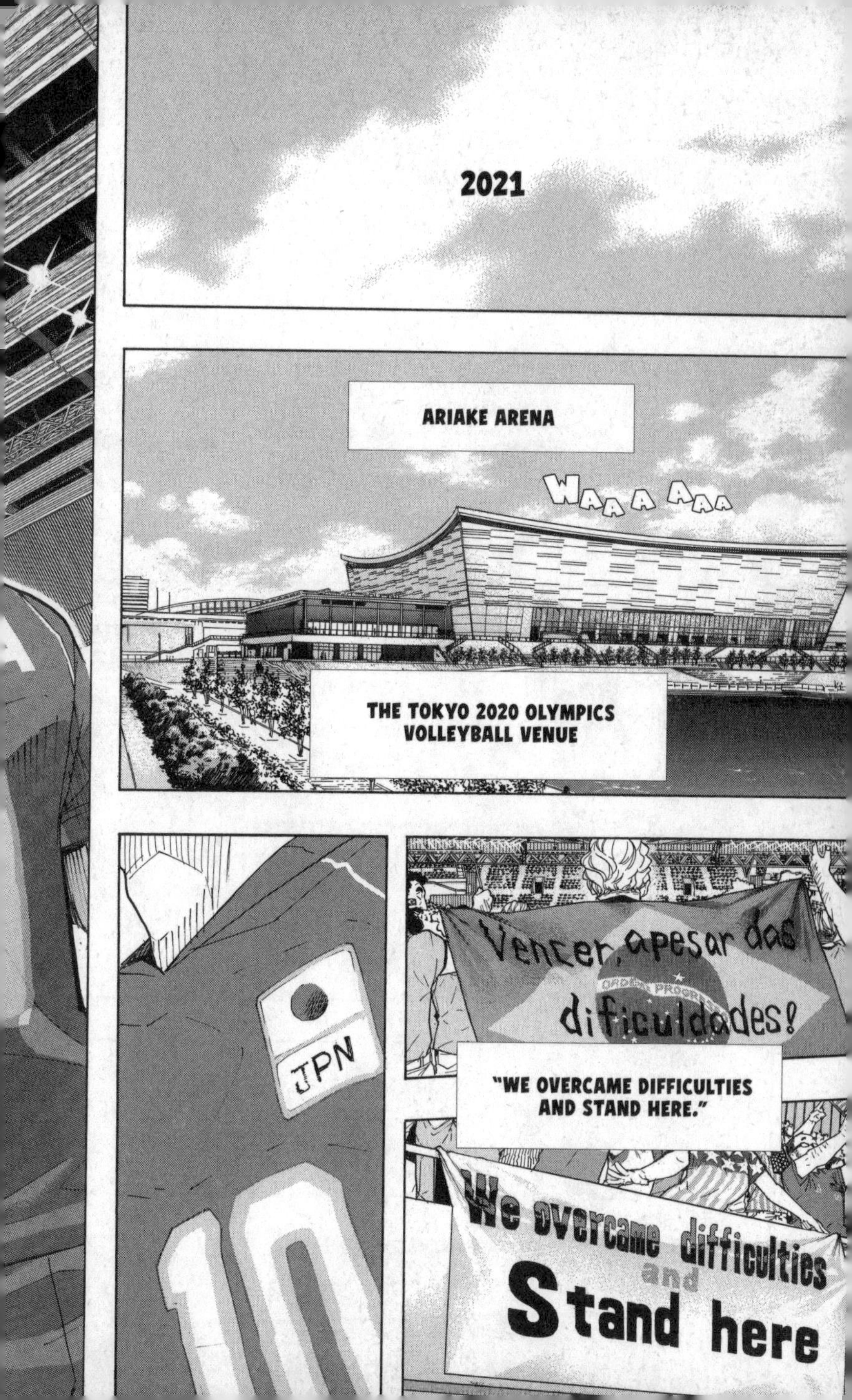
2021
ARIAKE ARENA
WAAA A AAA
THE TOKYO 2020 OLYMPICS VOLLEYBALL VENUE
Vencer, apesar das dificuldades!
"WE OVERCAME DIFFICULTIES AND STAND HERE."
We overcame difficulties and Stand here
JPN
10

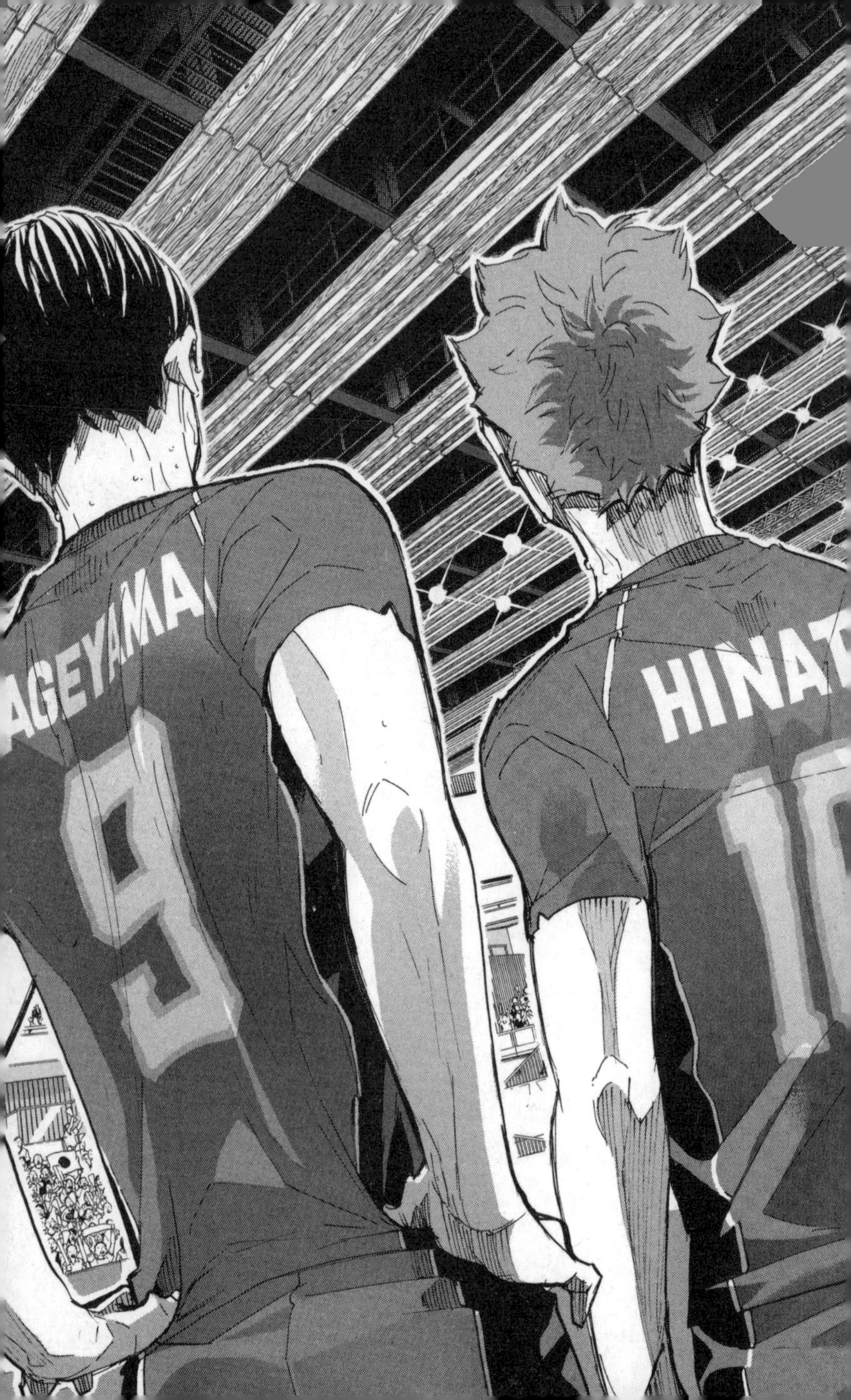
AGEYAMA
9
HINAT

**FINAL
CHAPTER**

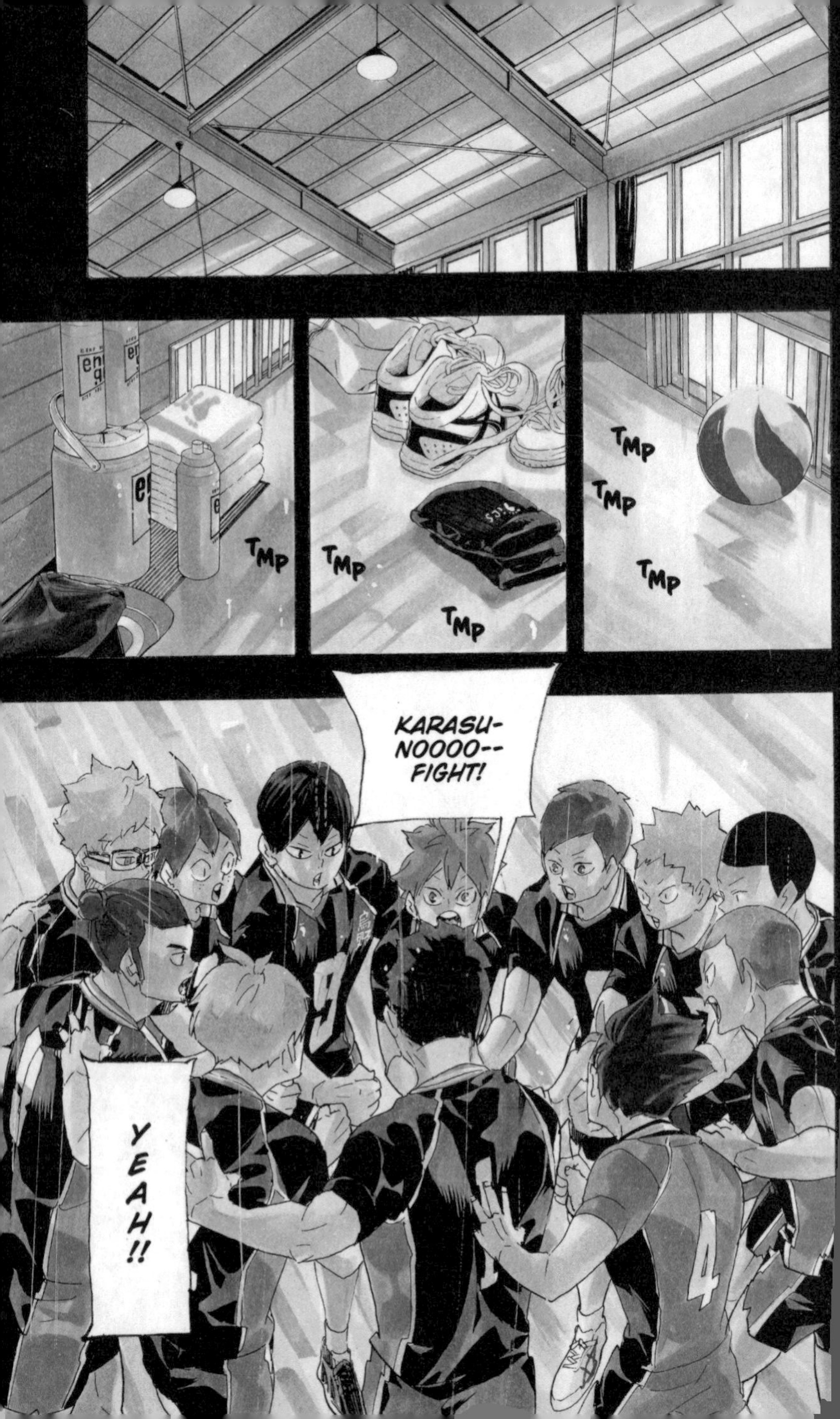
TMP
TMP
TMP
TMP
TMP
TMP
KARASU-NOOOO--FIGHT!
YEAH!!

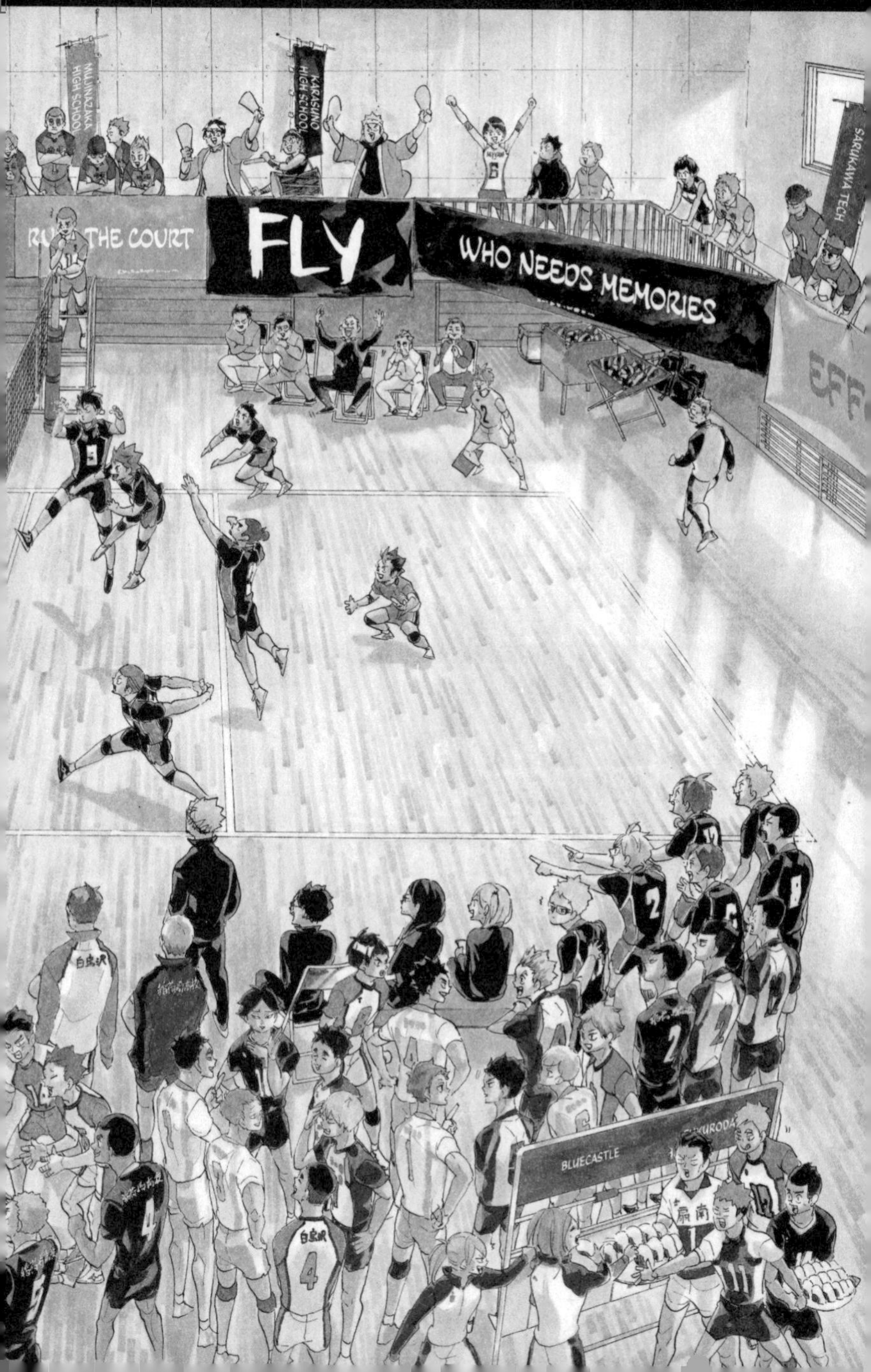
SARUKAWA TECH
KARASUNO HIGH SCHOOL
MUJINAZAKA HIGH SCHOOL
WHO NEEDS MEMORIES
FLY
THE COURT
BLUECASTLE
白鳥沢
扇南

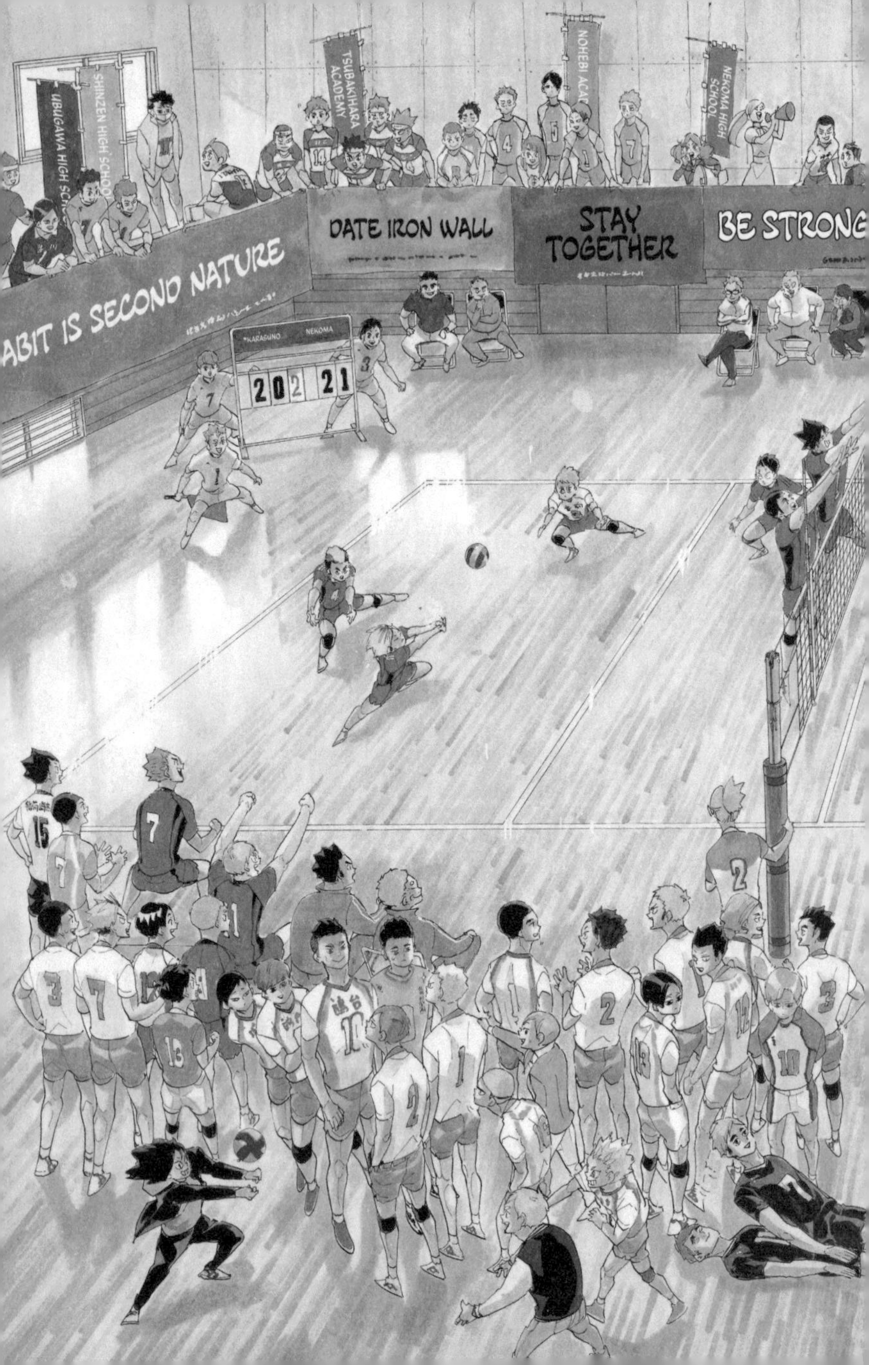
UBUGAWA HIGH SCHO
SHINZEN HIGH SCHOOL
TSUBAKIHARA ACADEMY
NOHEBI ACAD
NEKOMA HIGH SCHOOL
ABIT IS SECOND NATURE
DATE IRON WALL
STAY TOGETHER
BE STRONG
KARASUNO NEKOMA
20 21

2021

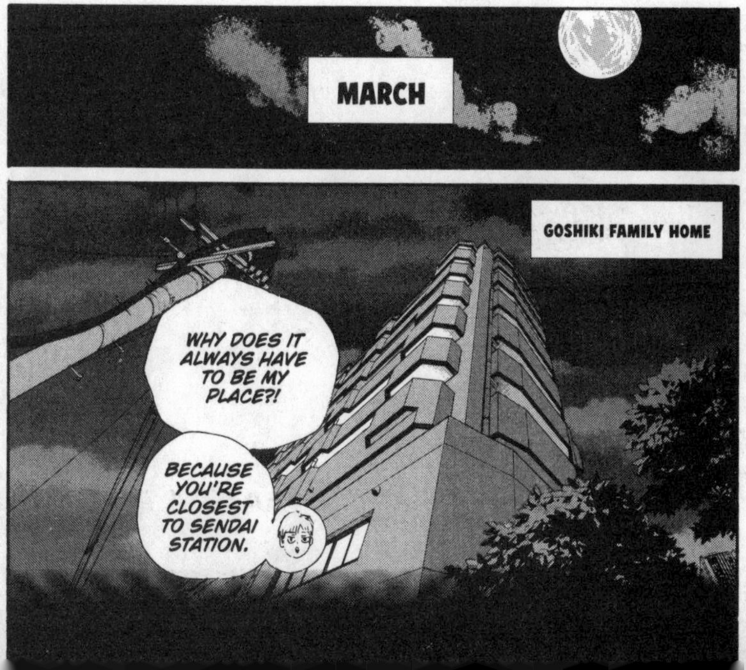
MARCH
GOSHIKI FAMILY HOME
WHY DOES IT ALWAYS HAVE TO BE MY PLACE?!
BECAUSE YOU'RE CLOSEST TO SENDAI STATION.

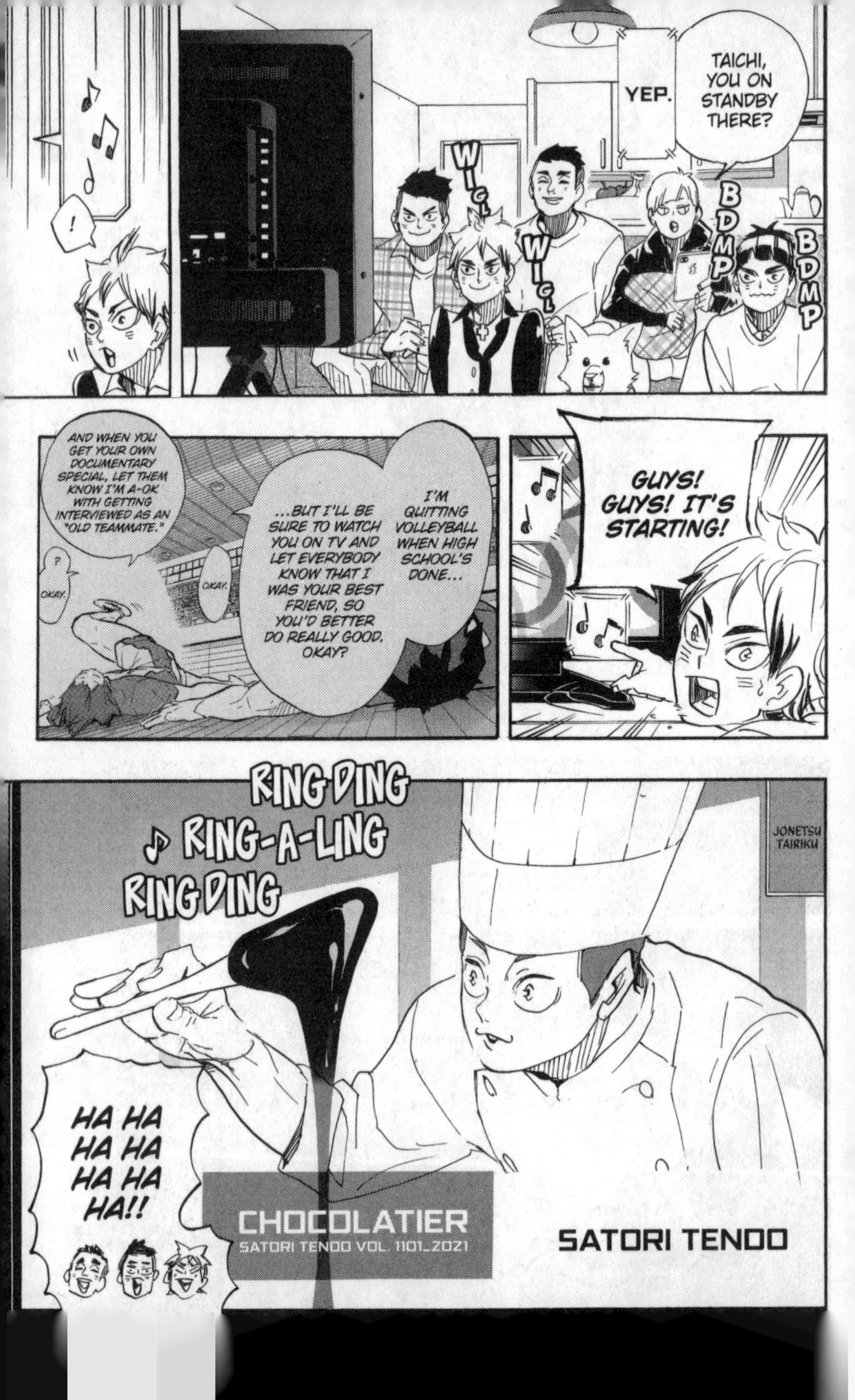
TAICHI, YOU ON STANDBY THERE?
YEP.
BDMP
BDMP
WIGL
WIGL
!
GUYS! GUYS! IT'S STARTING!
I'M QUITTING VOLLEYBALL WHEN HIGH SCHOOL'S DONE...
...BUT I'LL BE SURE TO WATCH YOU ON TV AND LET EVERYBODY KNOW THAT I WAS YOUR BEST FRIEND, SO YOU'D BETTER DO REALLY GOOD. OKAY?
OKAY.
AND WHEN YOU GET YOUR OWN DOCUMENTARY SPECIAL, LET THEM KNOW I'M A-OK WITH GETTING INTERVIEWED AS AN "OLD TEAMMATE."
?
OKAY.
JONETSU TAIRIKU
RING DING
RING-A-LING
RING DING
HA HA HA HA HA HA HA!!
CHOCOLATIER
SATORI TENDO VOL. 1101_2021
SATORI TENDO

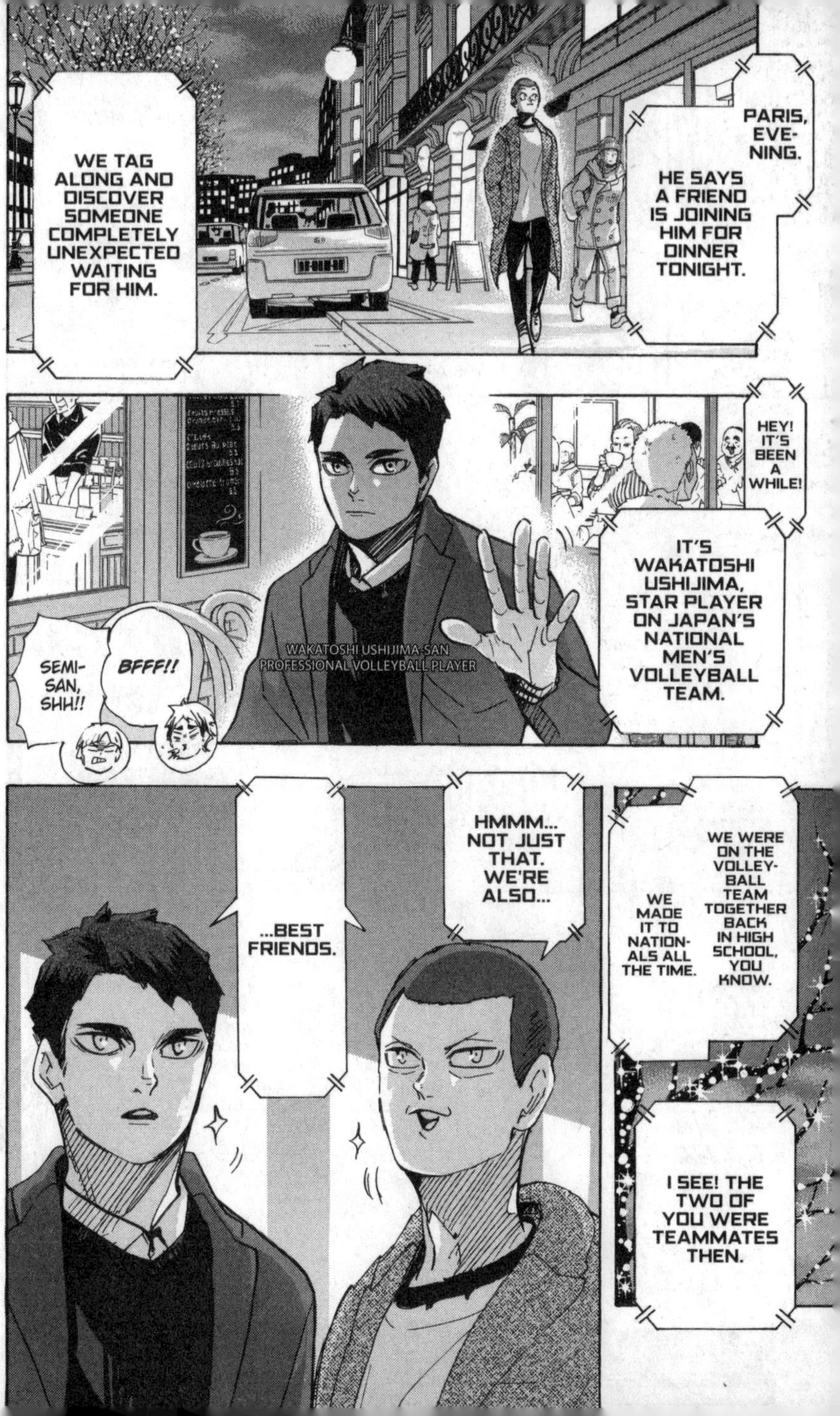
PARIS, EVENING.
HE SAYS A FRIEND IS JOINING HIM FOR DINNER TONIGHT.
WE TAG ALONG AND DISCOVER SOMEONE COMPLETELY UNEXPECTED WAITING FOR HIM.
HEY! IT'S BEEN A WHILE!
IT'S WAKATOSHI USHIJIMA, STAR PLAYER ON JAPAN'S NATIONAL MEN'S VOLLEYBALL TEAM.
WAKATOSHI USHIJIMA-SAN PROFESSIONAL VOLLEYBALL PLAYER
BFFF!!
SEMI-SAN, SHH!!
WE WERE ON THE VOLLEYBALL TEAM TOGETHER BACK IN HIGH SCHOOL, YOU KNOW.
WE MADE IT TO NATIONALS ALL THE TIME.
I SEE! THE TWO OF YOU WERE TEAMMATES THEN.
HMMM... NOT JUST THAT. WE'RE ALSO...
...BEST FRIENDS.

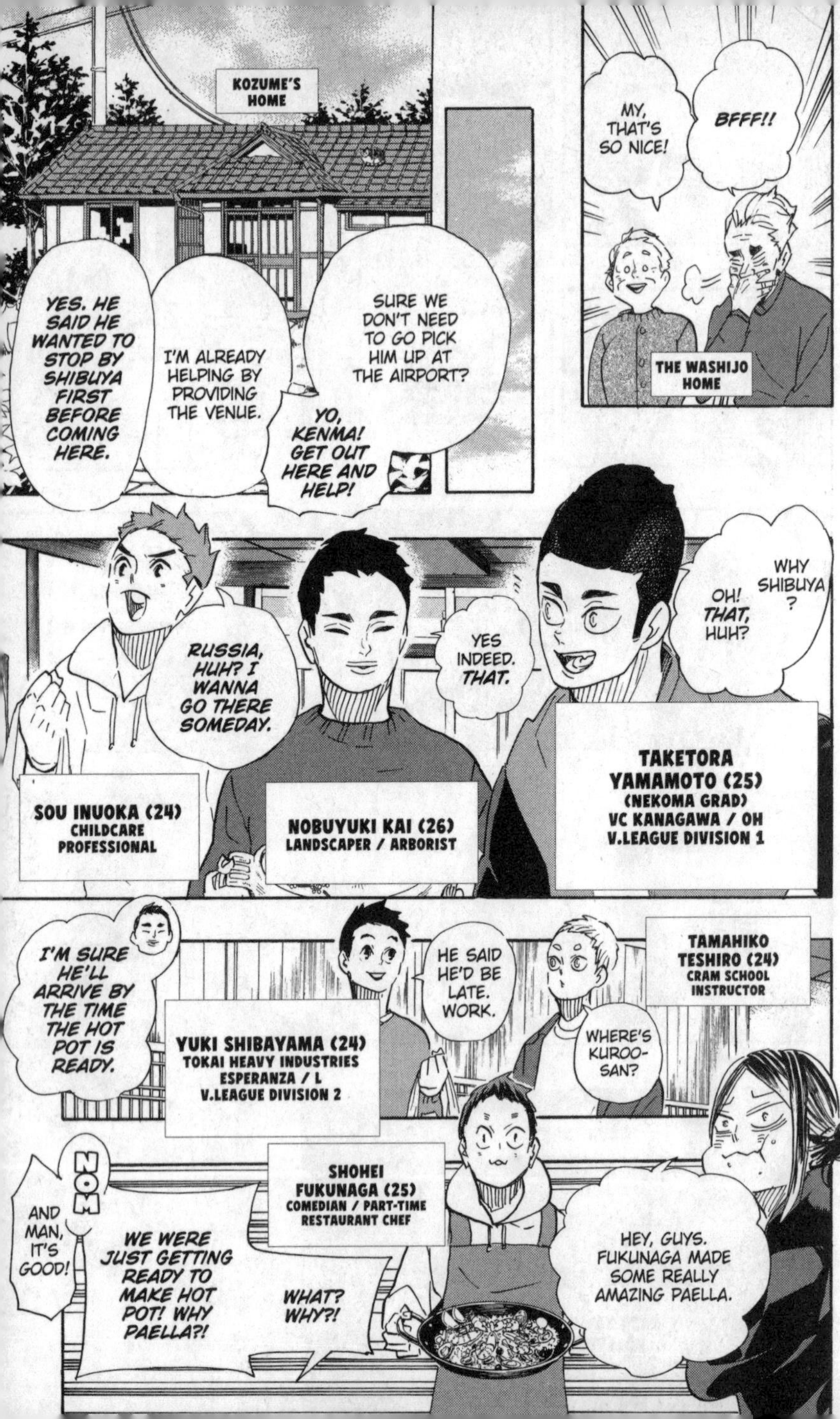
THE WASHIJO HOME
BFFF!!
MY, THAT'S SO NICE!
KOZUME'S HOME
SURE WE DON'T NEED TO GO PICK HIM UP AT THE AIRPORT?
YO, KENMA! GET OUT HERE AND HELP!
I'M ALREADY HELPING BY PROVIDING THE VENUE.
YES. HE SAID HE WANTED TO STOP BY SHIBUYA FIRST BEFORE COMING HERE.
WHY SHIBUYA?
OH! THAT, HUH?
TAKETORA YAMAMOTO (25) (NEKOMA GRAD) VC KANAGAWA / OH V.LEAGUE DIVISION 1
YES INDEED. THAT.
NOBUYUKI KAI (26) LANDSCAPER / ARBORIST
RUSSIA, HUH? I WANNA GO THERE SOMEDAY.
SOU INUOKA (24) CHILDCARE PROFESSIONAL
TAMAHIKO TESHIRO (24) CRAM SCHOOL INSTRUCTOR
WHERE'S KUROO-SAN?
HE SAID HE'D BE LATE. WORK.
YUKI SHIBAYAMA (24) TOKAI HEAVY INDUSTRIES ESPERANZA / L V.LEAGUE DIVISION 2
I'M SURE HE'LL ARRIVE BY THE TIME THE HOT POT IS READY.
HEY, GUYS. FUKUNAGA MADE SOME REALLY AMAZING PAELLA.
SHOHEI FUKUNAGA (25) COMEDIAN / PART-TIME RESTAURANT CHEF
WHAT? WHY?!
WE WERE JUST GETTING READY TO MAKE HOT POT! WHY PAELLA?!
NOM
AND MAN, IT'S GOOD!

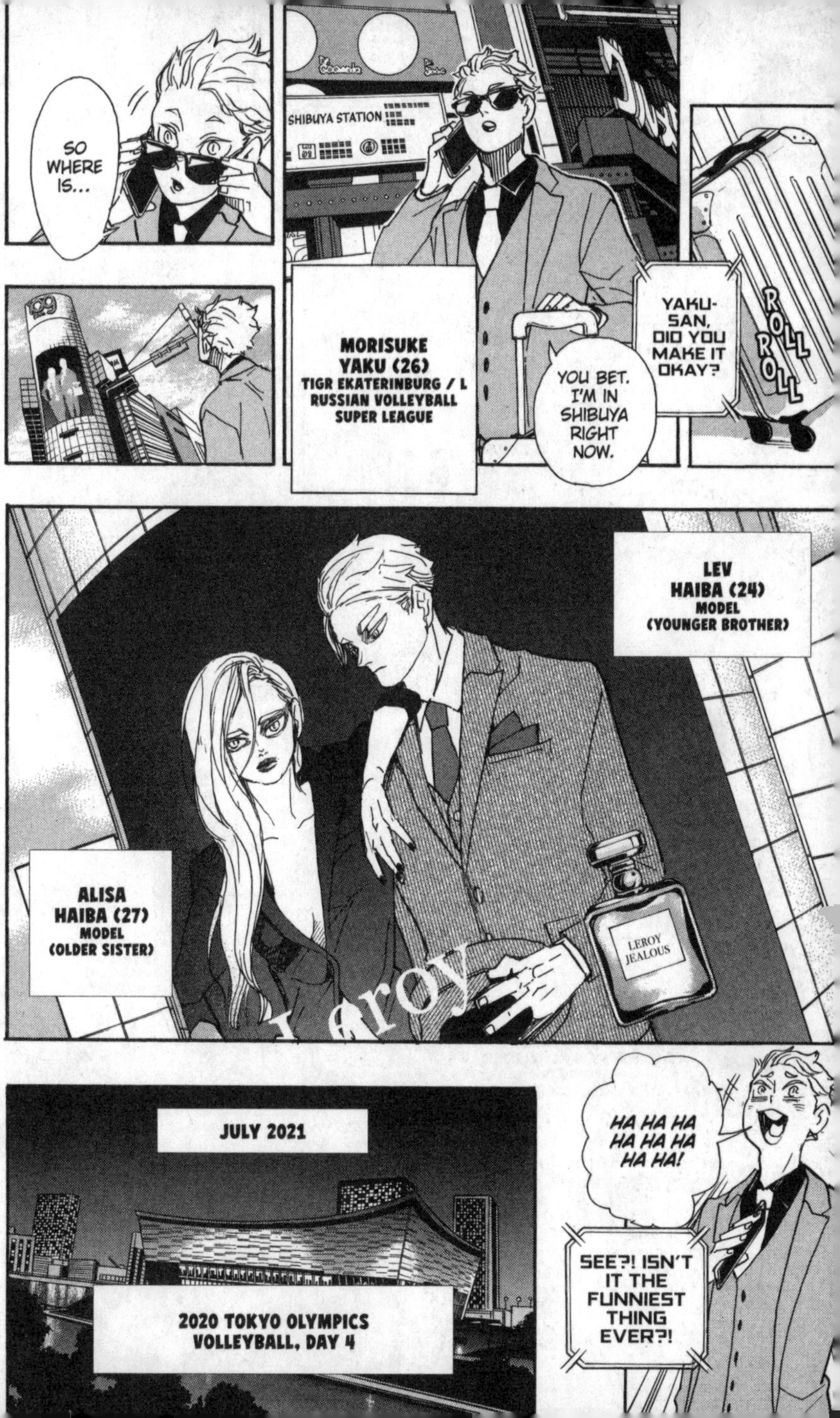
YAKU-SAN, DID YOU MAKE IT OKAY?
ROLL
ROLL
SHIBUYA STATION
YOU BET. I'M IN SHIBUYA RIGHT NOW.
MORISUKE YAKU (26)
TIGR EKATERINBURG / L
RUSSIAN VOLLEYBALL SUPER LEAGUE
SO WHERE IS...
LEV HAIBA (24)
MODEL
(YOUNGER BROTHER)
ALISA HAIBA (27)
MODEL
(OLDER SISTER)
LEROY JEALOUS
Leroy
HA HA HA HA HA HA HA HA!
SEE?! ISN'T IT THE FUNNIEST THING EVER?!
JULY 2021
2020 TOKYO OLYMPICS VOLLEYBALL, DAY 4

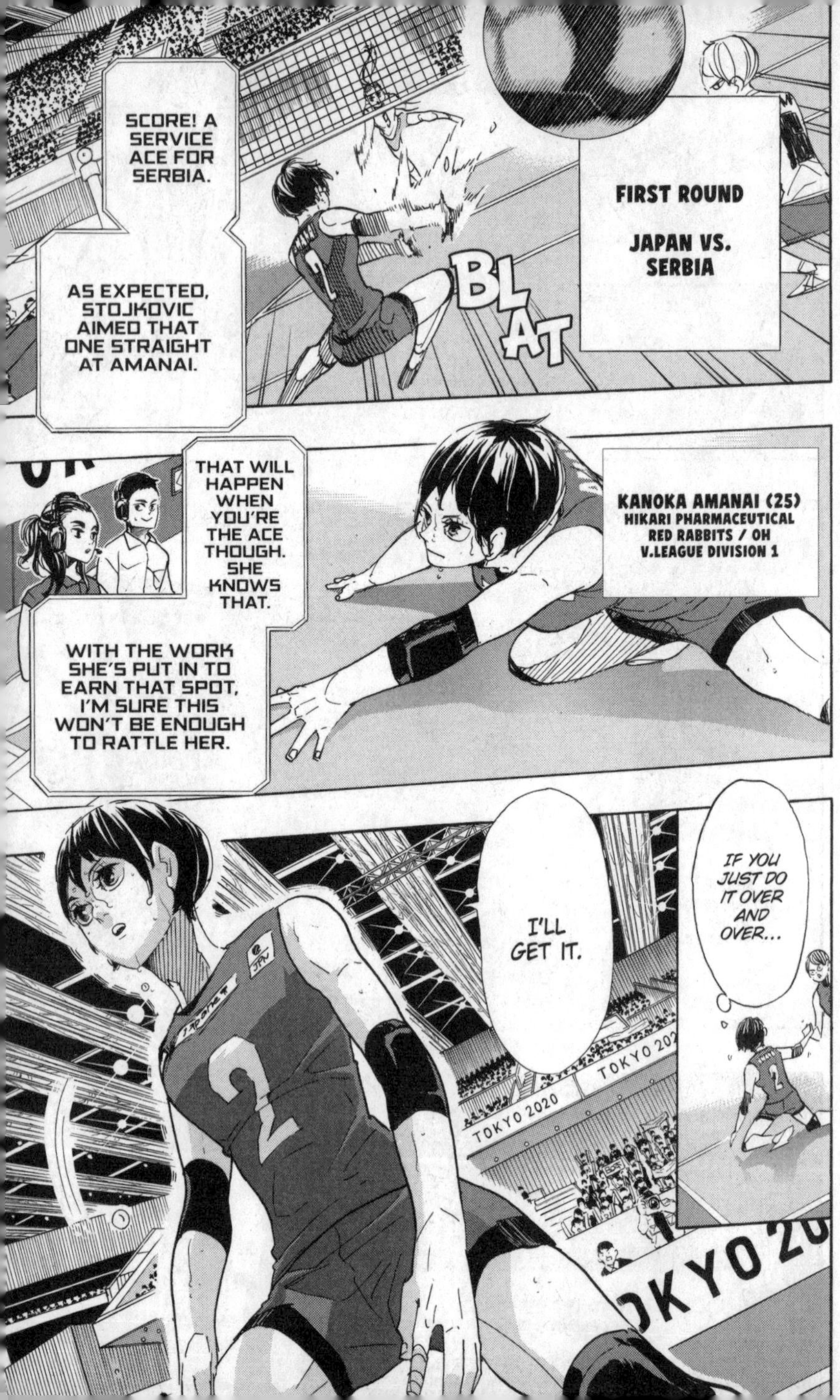
FIRST ROUND
JAPAN VS. SERBIA
BLAT
SCORE! A SERVICE ACE FOR SERBIA.
AS EXPECTED, STOJKOVIC AIMED THAT ONE STRAIGHT AT AMANAI.
KANOKA AMANAI (25)
HIKARI PHARMACEUTICAL RED RABBITS / OH
V.LEAGUE DIVISION 1
THAT WILL HAPPEN WHEN YOU'RE THE ACE THOUGH. SHE KNOWS THAT.
WITH THE WORK SHE'S PUT IN TO EARN THAT SPOT, I'M SURE THIS WON'T BE ENOUGH TO RATTLE HER.
IF YOU JUST DO IT OVER AND OVER...
I'LL GET IT.
TOKYO 2020
TOKYO 2020
OKYO 20

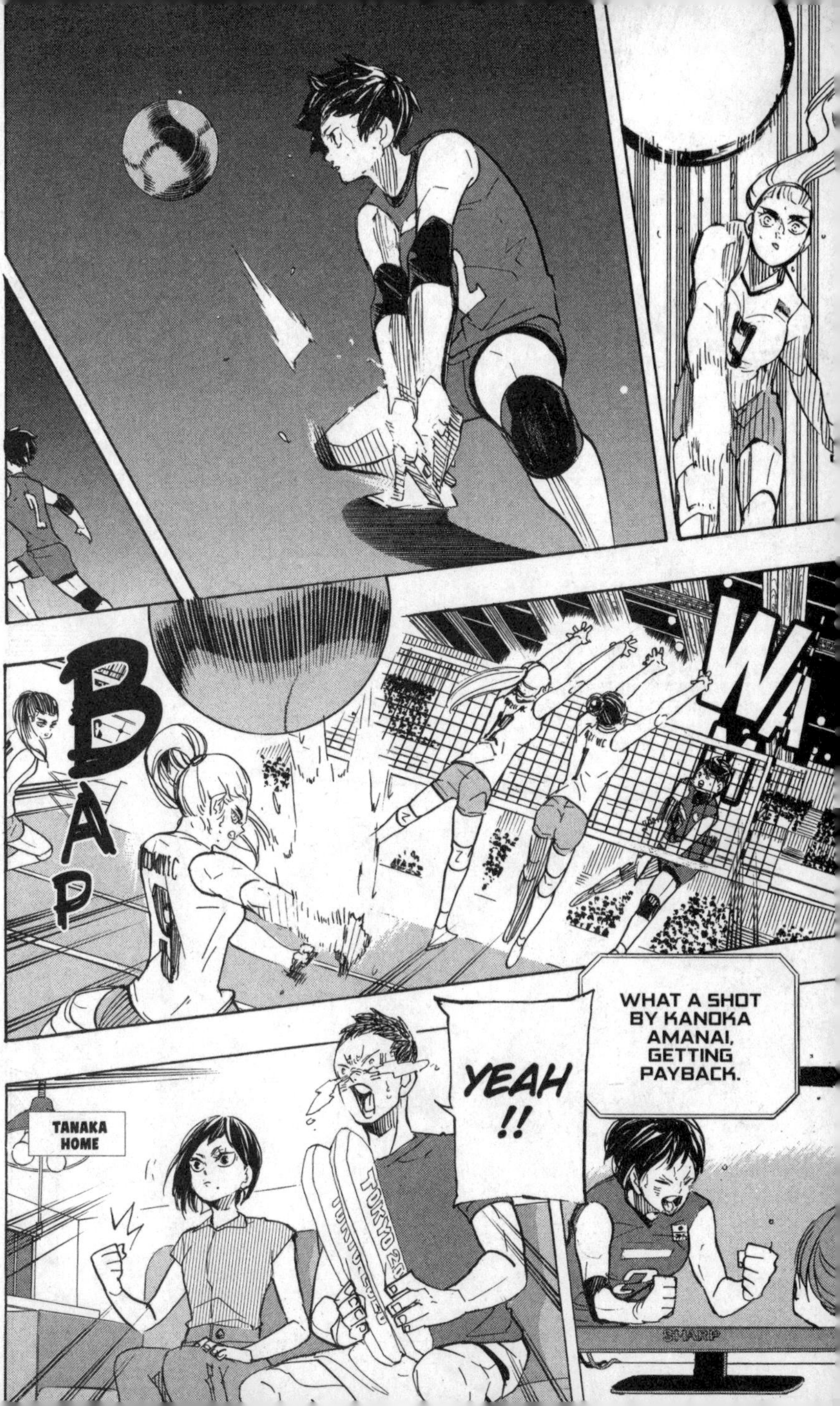
WA
BAP
WHAT A SHOT BY KANOKA AMANAI, GETTING PAYBACK.
YEAH!!
TANAKA HOME

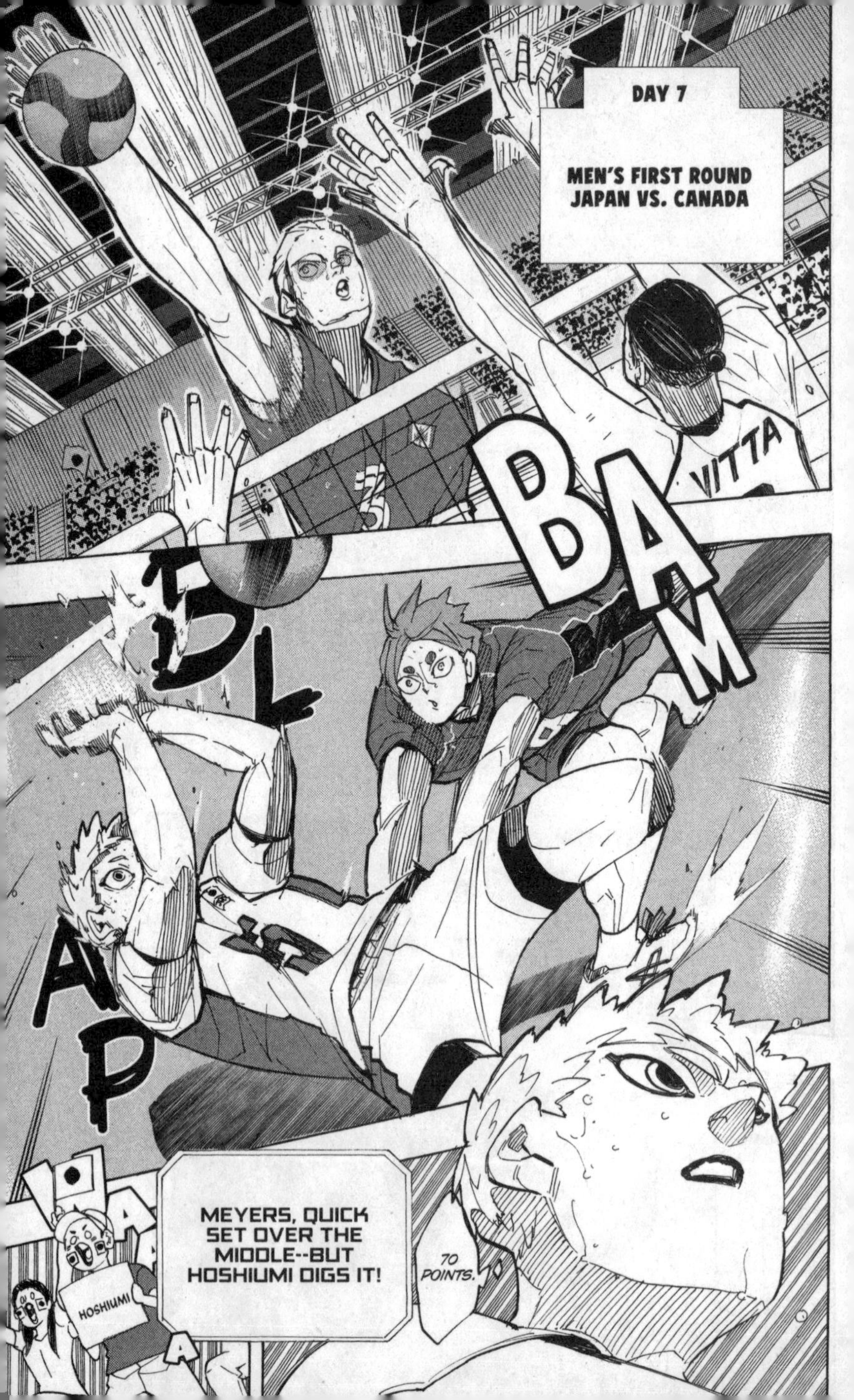
DAY 7
MEN'S FIRST ROUND
JAPAN VS. CANADA
VITTA
BAM
70 POINTS.
MEYERS, QUICK SET OVER THE MIDDLE--BUT HOSHIUMI DIGS IT!
HOSHIUMI

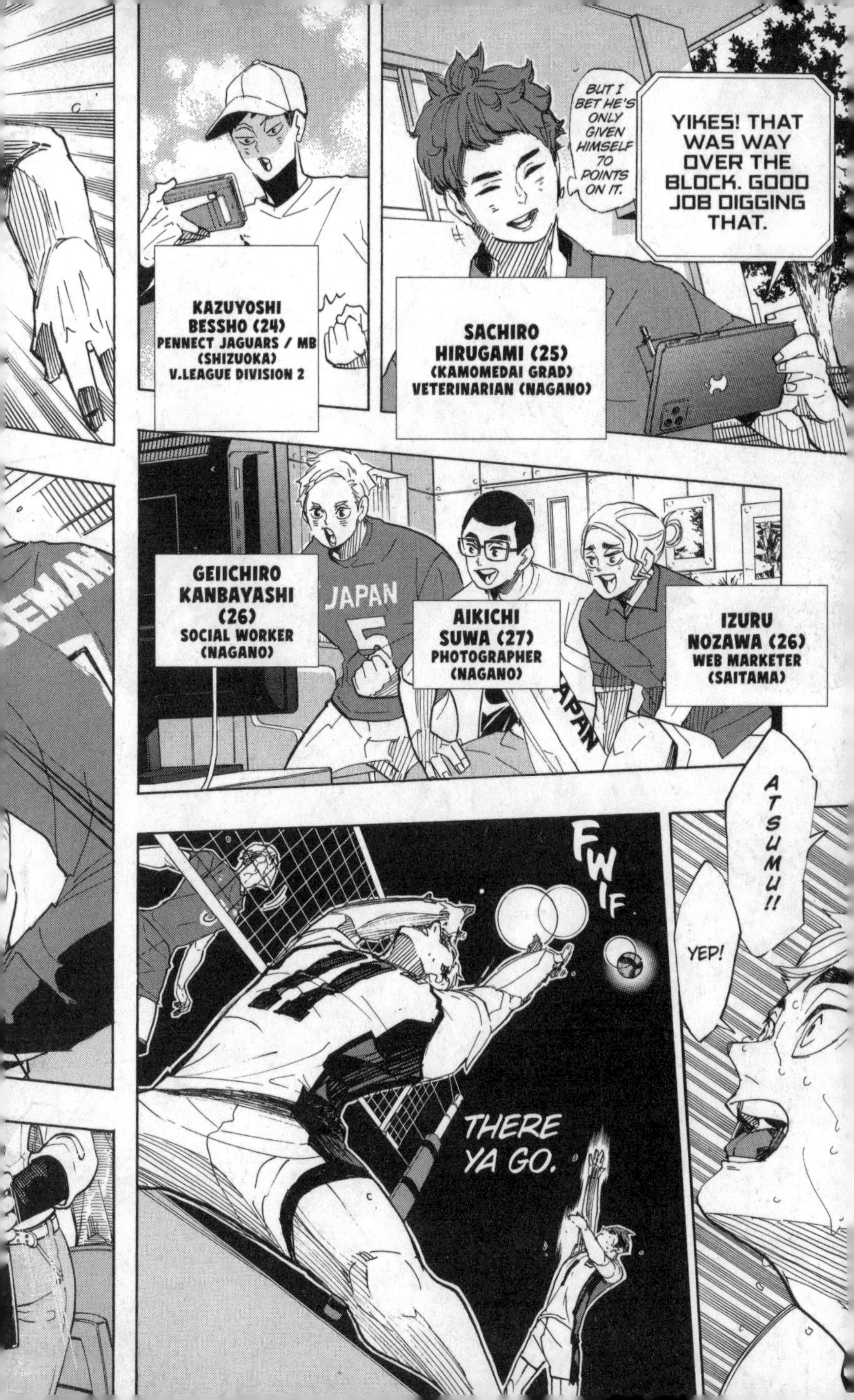
YIKES! THAT WAS WAY OVER THE BLOCK. GOOD JOB DIGGING THAT.
BUT I BET HE'S ONLY GIVEN HIMSELF 70 POINTS ON IT.
SACHIRO HIRUGAMI (25) (KAMOMEDAI GRAD) VETERINARIAN (NAGANO)
KAZUYOSHI BESSHO (24) PENNECT JAGUARS / MB (SHIZUOKA) V.LEAGUE DIVISION 2
IZURU NOZAWA (26) WEB MARKETER (SAITAMA)
AIKICHI SUWA (27) PHOTOGRAPHER (NAGANO)
GEIICHIRO KANBAYASHI (26) SOCIAL WORKER (NAGANO)
JAPAN
ATSUMU!!
YEP!
FWIF
THERE YA GO.

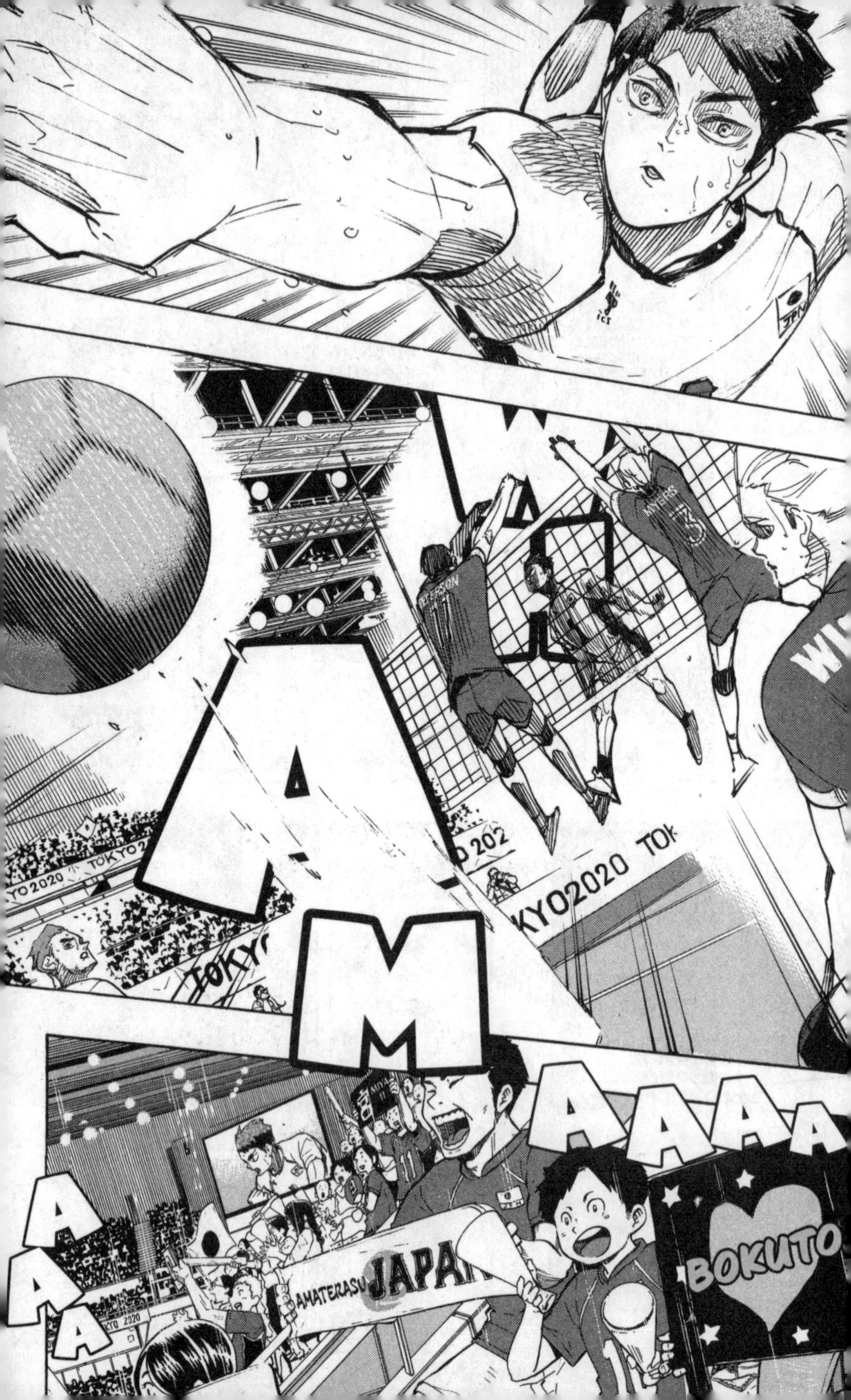

WAAMAAAAAAA
MYERS
PETERSON
TOKYO2020
MIYA
AMATERASU JAPAN
BOKUTO

HOO! I COULD HEAR THAT FROM HERE!
RIGHT?
TOKYO
GRIN
GRIN
?!
AOBA ORTHOPEDICS
WAAAA
HEY NOW, NO GETTING ANY HAPPY FEET JUST YET.
*SHIRT: SHIRATORIZAWA VOLLEYBALL
Chikara Ennoshita
HOW DO GOOD JUMPS START...?
WITH A GOOD APPROACH.
AUGUST
2020 TOKYO OLYMPICS VOLLEYBALL DAY 13
THE PIZZA'S HERE!

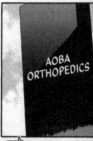

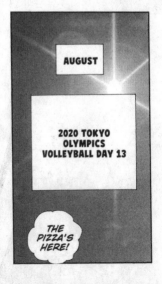

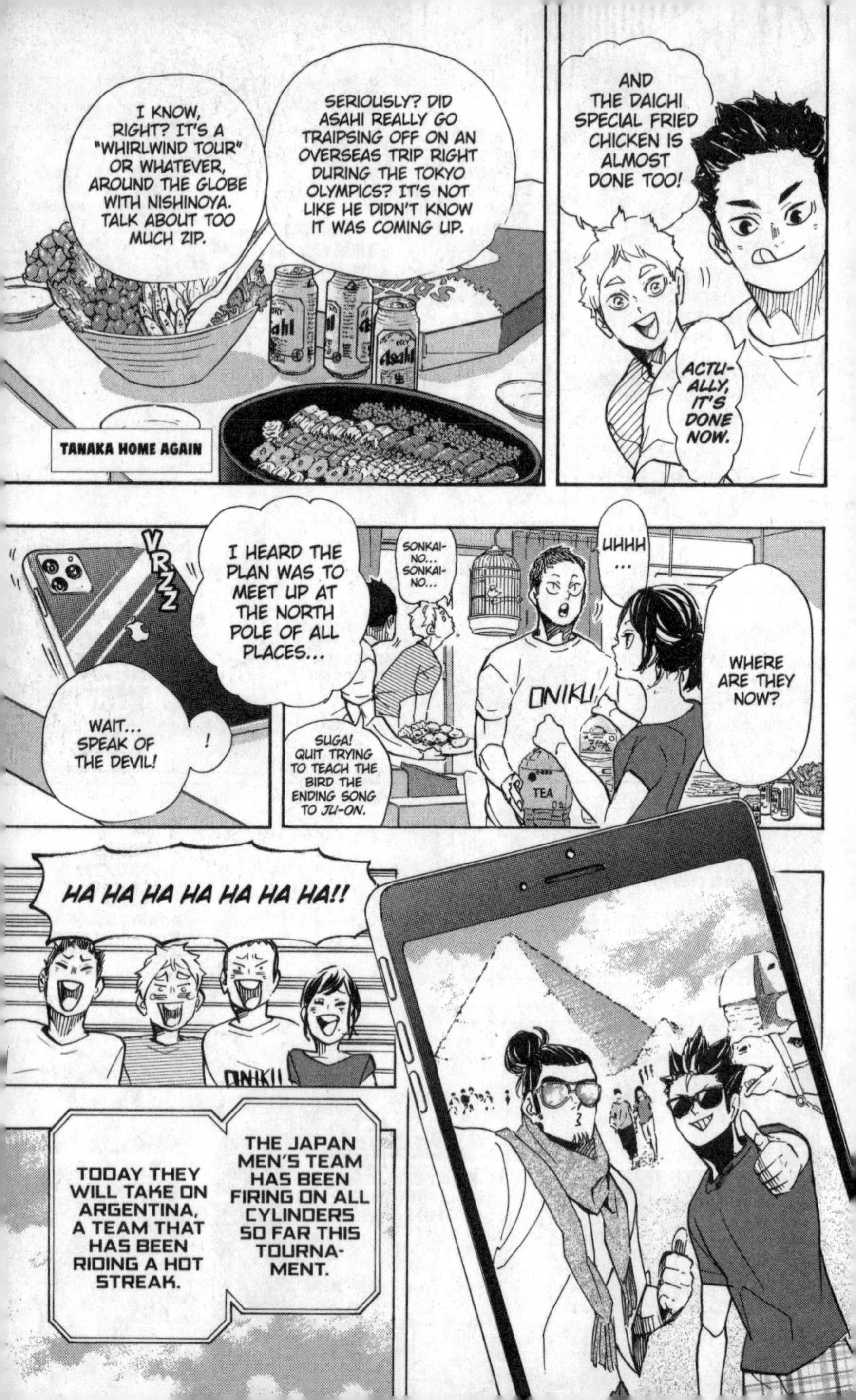
AND THE DAICHI SPECIAL FRIED CHICKEN IS ALMOST DONE TOO!
ACTUALLY, IT'S DONE NOW.
TANAKA HOME AGAIN
SERIOUSLY? DID ASAHI REALLY GO TRAIPSING OFF ON AN OVERSEAS TRIP RIGHT DURING THE TOKYO OLYMPICS? IT'S NOT LIKE HE DIDN'T KNOW IT WAS COMING UP.
I KNOW, RIGHT? IT'S A "WHIRLWIND TOUR" OR WHATEVER, AROUND THE GLOBE WITH NISHINOYA. TALK ABOUT TOO MUCH ZIP.
UHHH...
WHERE ARE THEY NOW?
SONKAI-NO... SONKAI-NO...
ONIKU
TEA
SUGA! QUIT TRYING TO TEACH THE BIRD THE ENDING SONG TO JU-ON.
I HEARD THE PLAN WAS TO MEET UP AT THE NORTH POLE OF ALL PLACES...
VRZZ
!
WAIT... SPEAK OF THE DEVIL!
HA HA HA HA HA HA HA!!
ONIKU
THE JAPAN MEN'S TEAM HAS BEEN FIRING ON ALL CYLINDERS SO FAR THIS TOURNAMENT.
TODAY THEY WILL TAKE ON ARGENTINA, A TEAM THAT HAS BEEN RIDING A HOT STREAK.

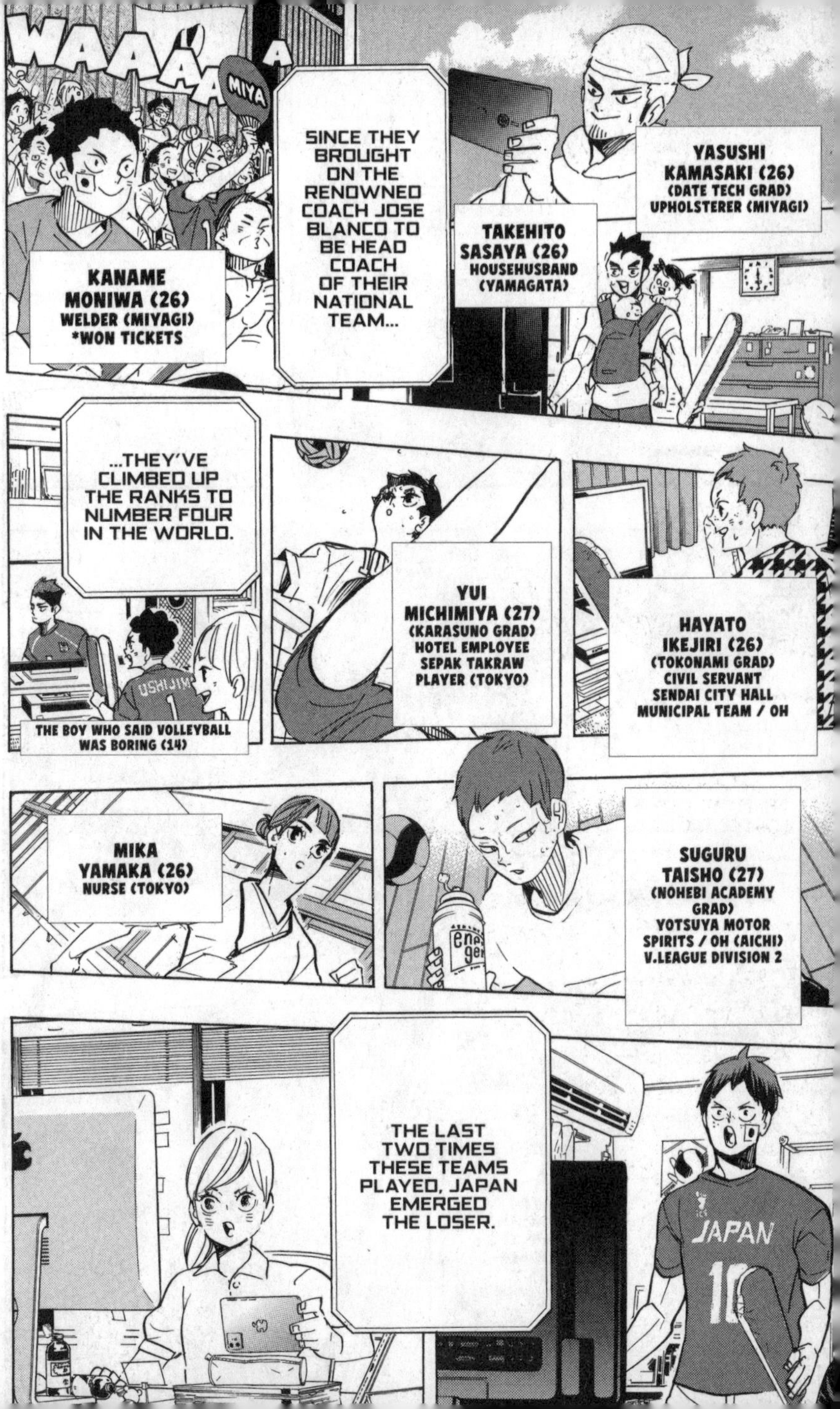
YASUSHI KAMASAKI (26)
(DATE TECH GRAD)
UPHOLSTERER (MIYAGI)
TAKEHITO SASAYA (26)
HOUSEHUSBAND (YAMAGATA)
SINCE THEY BROUGHT ON THE RENOWNED COACH JOSE BLANCO TO BE HEAD COACH OF THEIR NATIONAL TEAM...
WAAAAA
MIYA
KANAME MONIWA (26)
WELDER (MIYAGI)
*WON TICKETS
HAYATO IKEJIRI (26)
(TOKONAMI GRAD)
CIVIL SERVANT
SENDAI CITY HALL MUNICIPAL TEAM / OH
YUI MICHIMIYA (27)
(KARASUNO GRAD)
HOTEL EMPLOYEE
SEPAK TAKRAW PLAYER (TOKYO)
...THEY'VE CLIMBED UP THE RANKS TO NUMBER FOUR IN THE WORLD.
THE BOY WHO SAID VOLLEYBALL WAS BORING (14)
SUGURU TAISHO (27)
(NOHEBI ACADEMY GRAD)
YOTSUYA MOTOR SPIRITS / OH (AICHI)
V.LEAGUE DIVISION 2
MIKA YAMAKA (26)
NURSE (TOKYO)
THE LAST TWO TIMES THESE TEAMS PLAYED, JAPAN EMERGED THE LOSER.
JAPAN
10

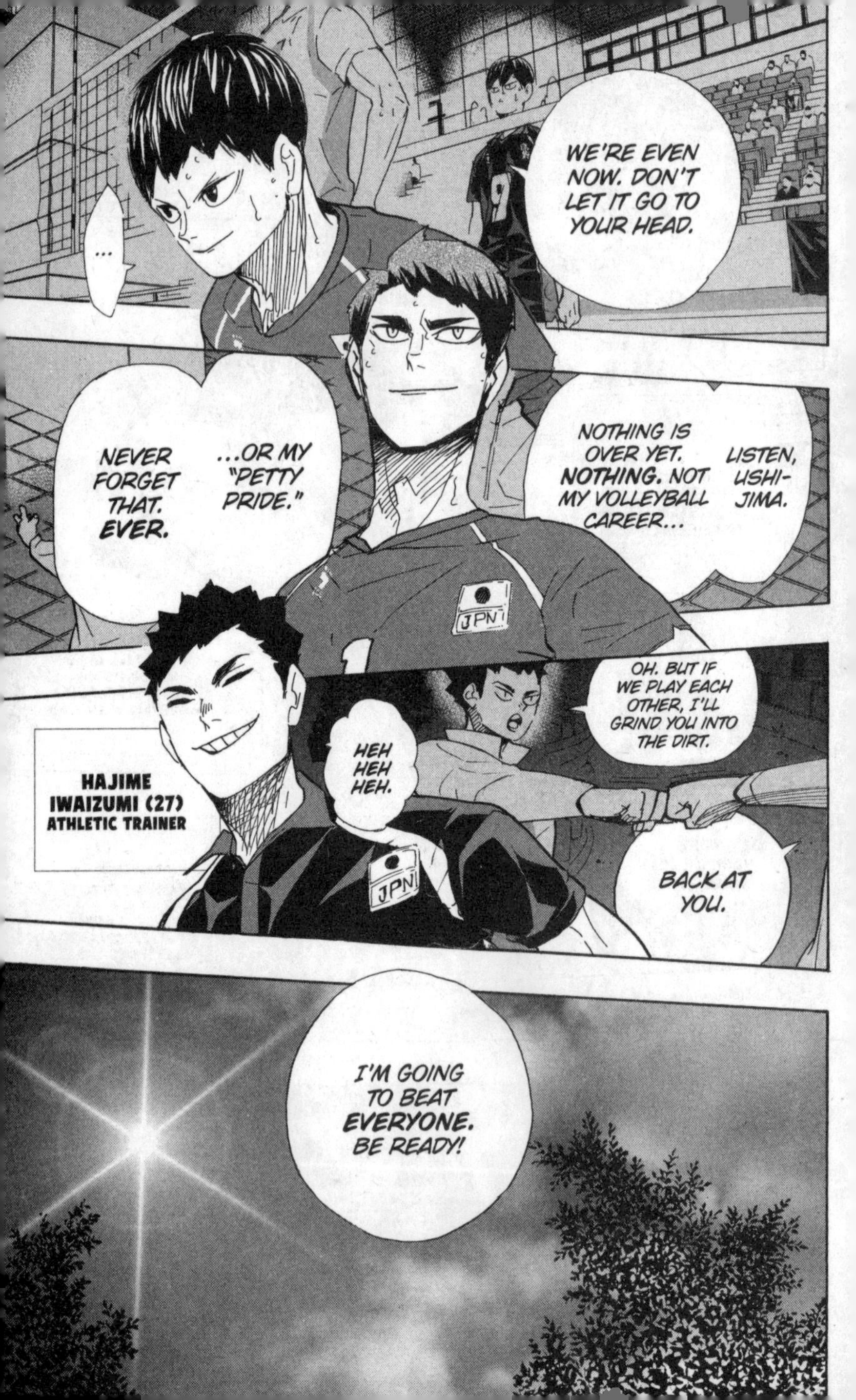
WE'RE EVEN NOW. DON'T LET IT GO TO YOUR HEAD.
...
LISTEN, USHIJIMA.
NOTHING IS OVER YET. NOTHING. NOT MY VOLLEYBALL CAREER...
...OR MY "PETTY PRIDE."
NEVER FORGET THAT. EVER.
OH. BUT IF WE PLAY EACH OTHER, I'LL GRIND YOU INTO THE DIRT.
BACK AT YOU.
HEH HEH HEH.
HAJIME IWAIZUMI (27) ATHLETIC TRAINER
I'M GOING TO BEAT EVERYONE. BE READY!

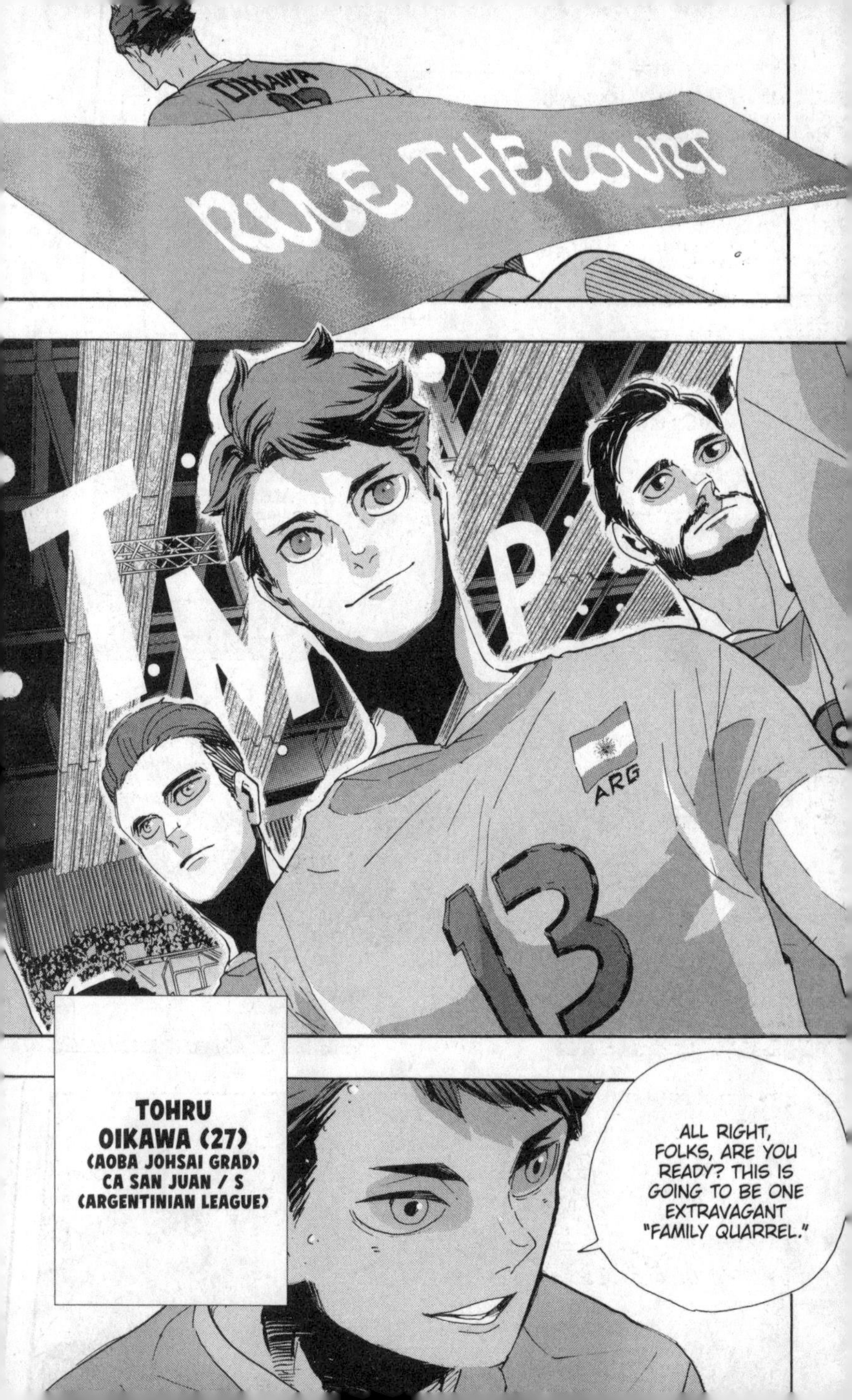
OIKAWA
RULE THE COURT
ARG
13
ALL RIGHT, FOLKS, ARE YOU READY? THIS IS GOING TO BE ONE EXTRAVAGANT "FAMILY QUARREL."
TOHRU OIKAWA (27) (AOBA JOHSAI GRAD) CA SAN JUAN / S (ARGENTINIAN LEAGUE)

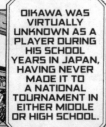

THE BIGGEST TOPIC COMING INTO THIS GAME HAS TO BE ARGENTINA'S STARTING SETTER, TOHRU OIKAWA.
BORN IN JAPAN, HE FOLLOWED HIS MENTOR, COACH BLANCO, TO ARGENTINA AFTER GRADUATION, AND EVENTUALLY BECAME A NATURALIZED ARGENTINIAN CITIZEN.
OIKAWA WAS VIRTUALLY UNKNOWN AS A PLAYER DURING HIS SCHOOL YEARS IN JAPAN, HAVING NEVER MADE IT TO A NATIONAL TOURNAMENT IN EITHER MIDDLE OR HIGH SCHOOL.
TAKAHIRO HANAMAKI (26) CURRENTLY IN BETWEEN JOBS (TOKYO)
OH, SHUT UP.
AND WHAT OF IT, HUH?!
SHIGERU YAHABA (25) SPORTS INSTRUCTOR (MIYAGI)
THERE'S A DIFFERENCE IN SCALE HERE, Y'KNOW. A BIIIG DIFFERENCE.
ISSEI MATSUKAWA (26) FUNERAL HOME EMPLOYEE (MIYAGI)
YEAH. IT'S PRETTY INCREDIBLE.
SHINJI WATARI (26) AQUARIUM EMPLOYEE (KANAGAWA)
LOOK!
Oikawa-san!
Shoyo!!
IT'S NINJA SHOYO AND, UH...
KEN! KEN WATANABE!
GINO AND GABRIEL (BUY ME A BEER BROS)

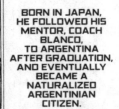

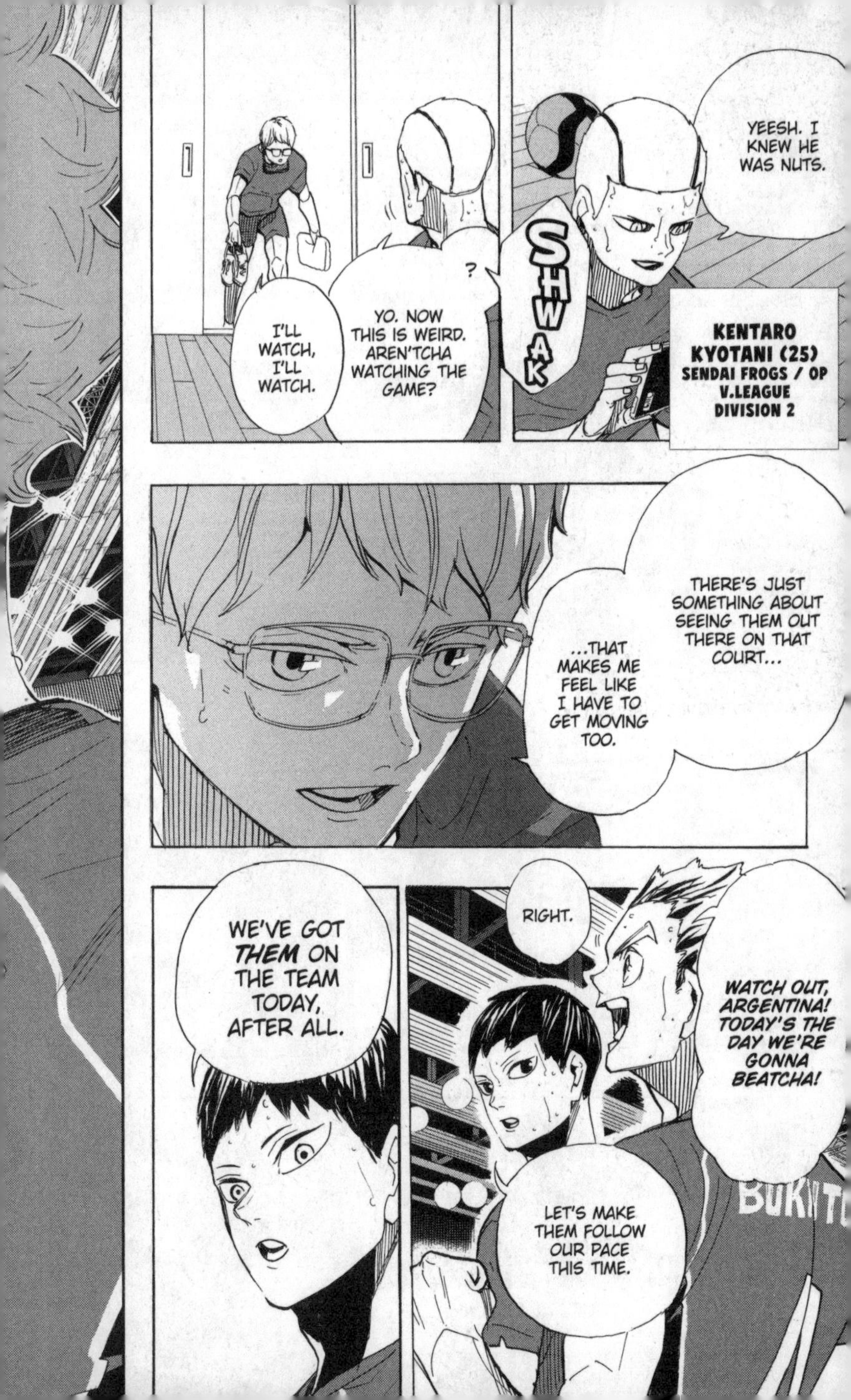
YEESH. I KNEW HE WAS NUTS.
SHWAK
KENTARO KYOTANI (25) SENDAI FROGS / OP V.LEAGUE DIVISION 2
?
YO. NOW THIS IS WEIRD. AREN'TCHA WATCHING THE GAME?
I'LL WATCH, I'LL WATCH.
THERE'S JUST SOMETHING ABOUT SEEING THEM OUT THERE ON THAT COURT...
...THAT MAKES ME FEEL LIKE I HAVE TO GET MOVING TOO.
WATCH OUT, ARGENTINA! TODAY'S THE DAY WE'RE GONNA BEATCHA!
RIGHT.
LET'S MAKE THEM FOLLOW OUR PACE THIS TIME.
WE'VE GOT *THEM* ON THE TEAM TODAY, AFTER ALL.

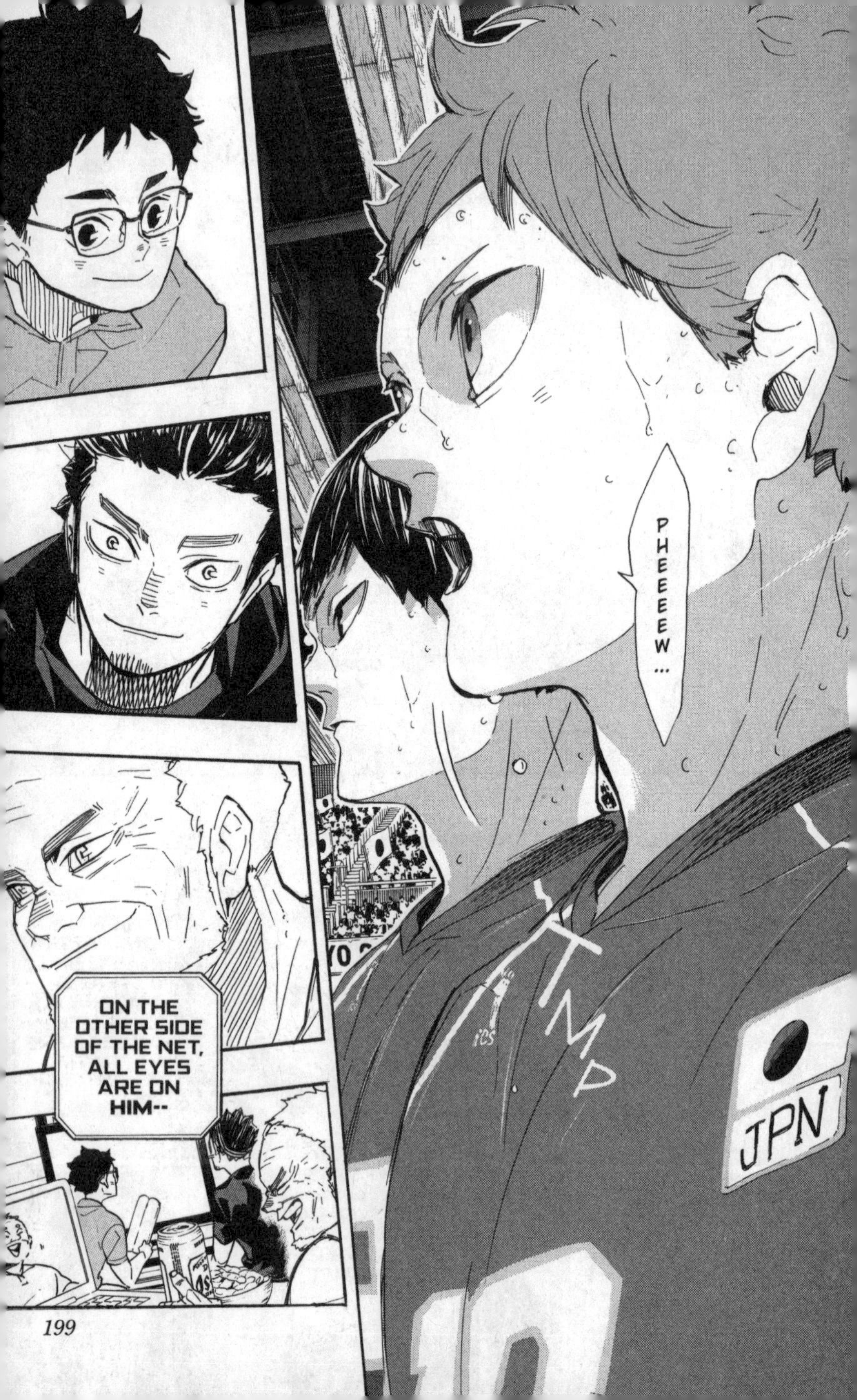
PHEEEEEW...
JPN
ON THE OTHER SIDE OF THE NET, ALL EYES ARE ON HIM--

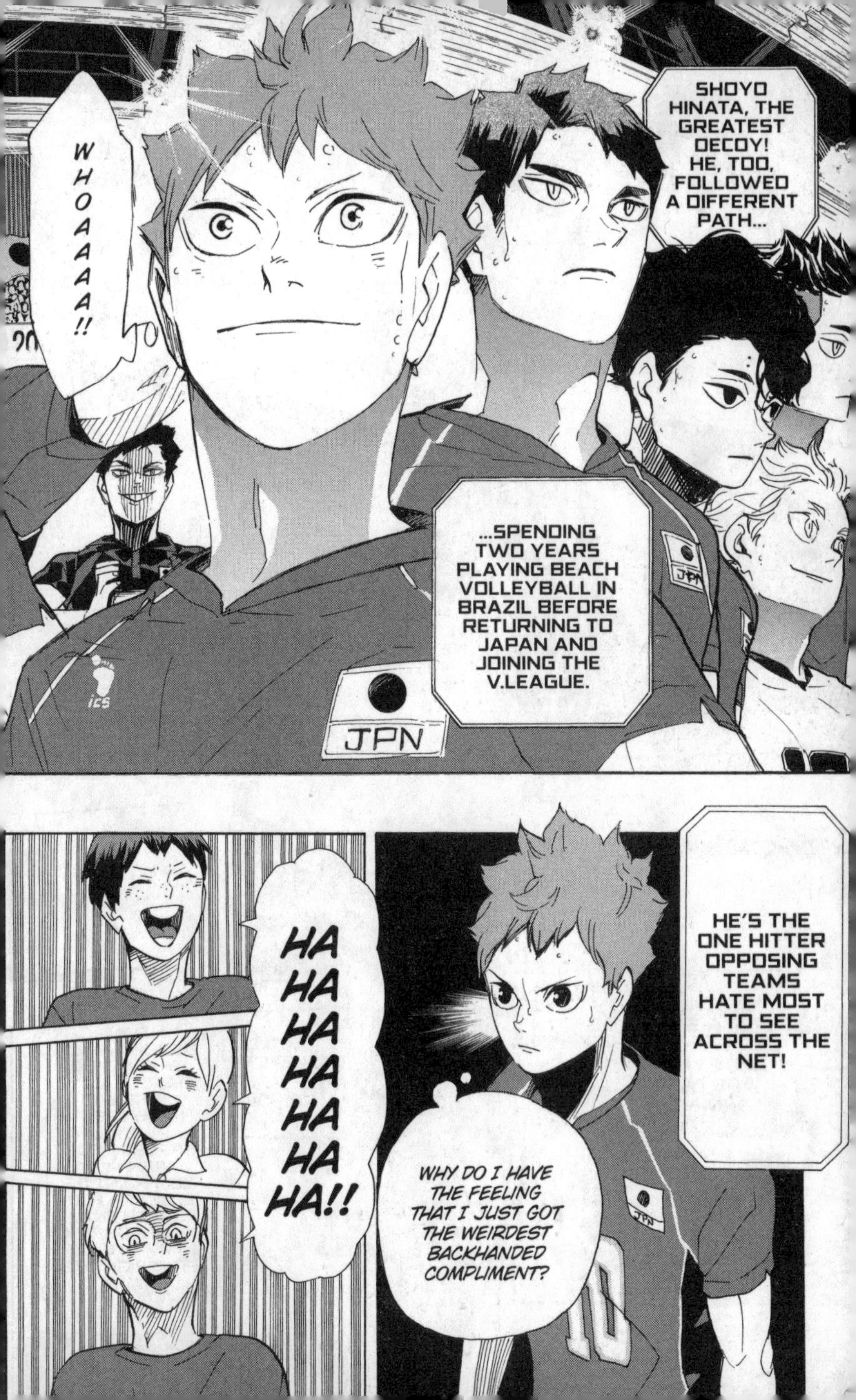
SHOYO HINATA, THE GREATEST DECOY! HE, TOO, FOLLOWED A DIFFERENT PATH...
...SPENDING TWO YEARS PLAYING BEACH VOLLEYBALL IN BRAZIL BEFORE RETURNING TO JAPAN AND JOINING THE V.LEAGUE.
WHOAAAAA!!
JPN
HE'S THE ONE HITTER OPPOSING TEAMS HATE MOST TO SEE ACROSS THE NET!
WHY DO I HAVE THE FEELING THAT I JUST GOT THE WEIRDEST BACKHANDED COMPLIMENT?
HA HA HA HA HA HA HA!!

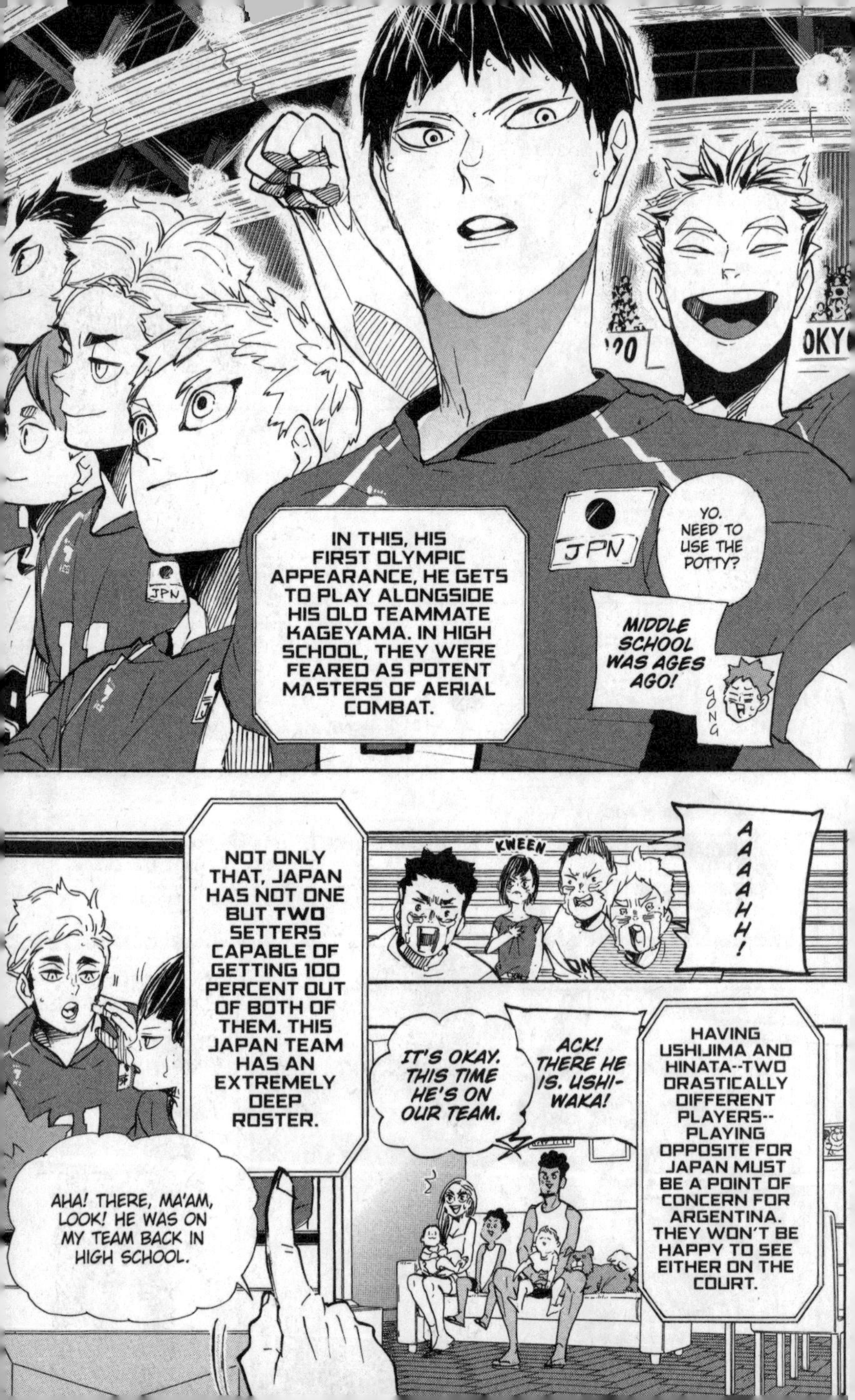
YO. NEED TO USE THE POTTY?
MIDDLE SCHOOL WAS AGES AGO!
GONG
IN THIS, HIS FIRST OLYMPIC APPEARANCE, HE GETS TO PLAY ALONGSIDE HIS OLD TEAMMATE KAGEYAMA. IN HIGH SCHOOL, THEY WERE FEARED AS POTENT MASTERS OF AERIAL COMBAT.
AAAAAH!
KWEEN
HAVING USHIJIMA AND HINATA--TWO DRASTICALLY DIFFERENT PLAYERS--PLAYING OPPOSITE FOR JAPAN MUST BE A POINT OF CONCERN FOR ARGENTINA. THEY WON'T BE HAPPY TO SEE EITHER ON THE COURT.
ACK! THERE HE IS. USHIWAKA!
IT'S OKAY. THIS TIME HE'S ON OUR TEAM.
NOT ONLY THAT, JAPAN HAS NOT ONE BUT TWO SETTERS CAPABLE OF GETTING 100 PERCENT OUT OF BOTH OF THEM. THIS JAPAN TEAM HAS AN EXTREMELY DEEP ROSTER.
AHA! THERE, MA'AM, LOOK! HE WAS ON MY TEAM BACK IN HIGH SCHOOL.

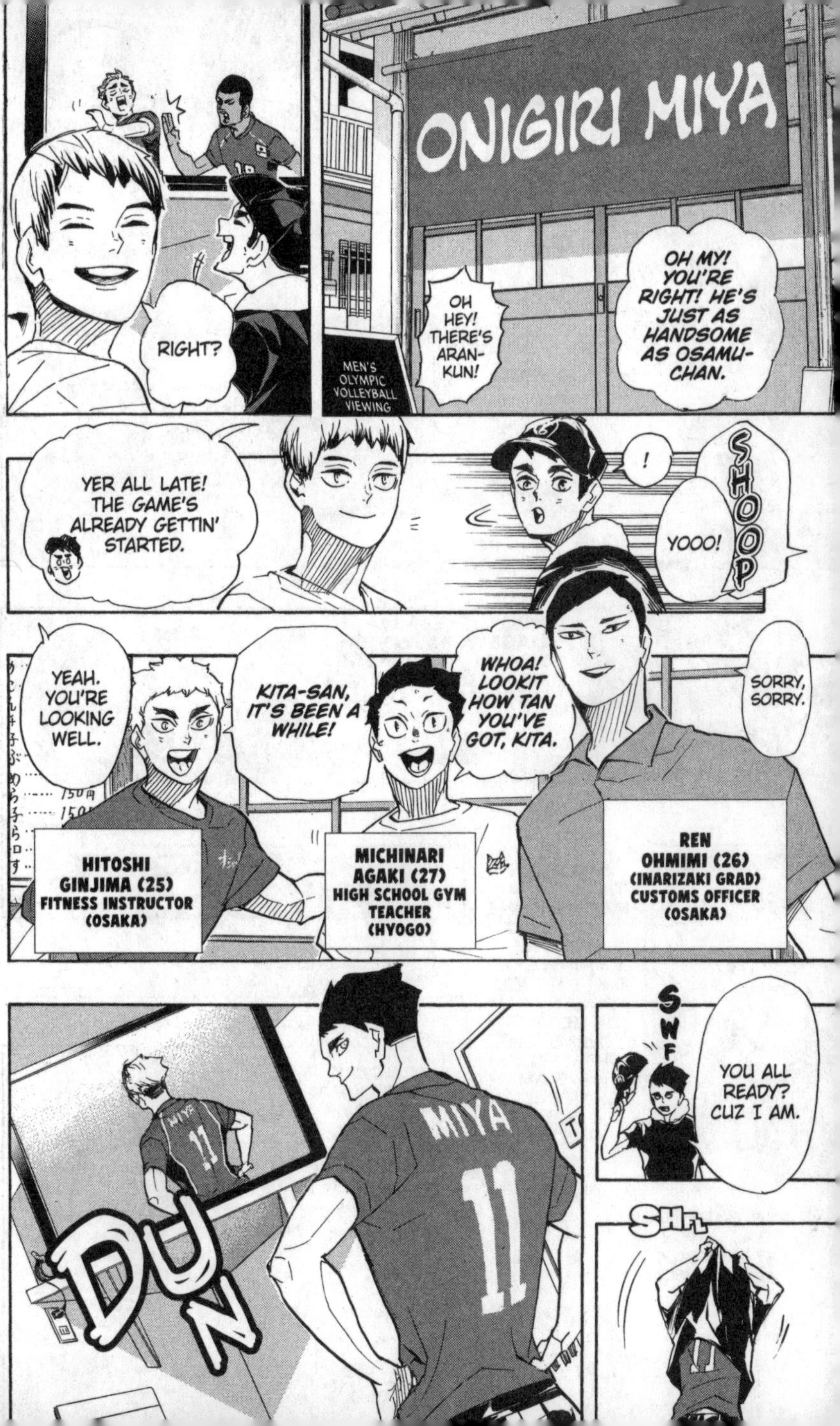
ONIGIRI MIYA
OH MY! YOU'RE RIGHT! HE'S JUST AS HANDSOME AS OSAMU-CHAN.
OH HEY! THERE'S ARAN-KUN!
MEN'S OLYMPIC VOLLEYBALL VIEWING
RIGHT?
SHOOP
YOOO!
!
YER ALL LATE! THE GAME'S ALREADY GETTIN' STARTED.
SORRY, SORRY.
REN OHMIMI (26) (INARIZAKI GRAD) CUSTOMS OFFICER (OSAKA)
WHOA! LOOKIT HOW TAN YOU'VE GOT, KITA.
MICHINARI AGAKI (27) HIGH SCHOOL GYM TEACHER (HYOGO)
KITA-SAN, IT'S BEEN A WHILE!
YEAH. YOU'RE LOOKING WELL.
HITOSHI GINJIMA (25) FITNESS INSTRUCTOR (OSAKA)
SWF
YOU ALL READY? CUZ I AM.
SHFL
MIYA 11
DUN

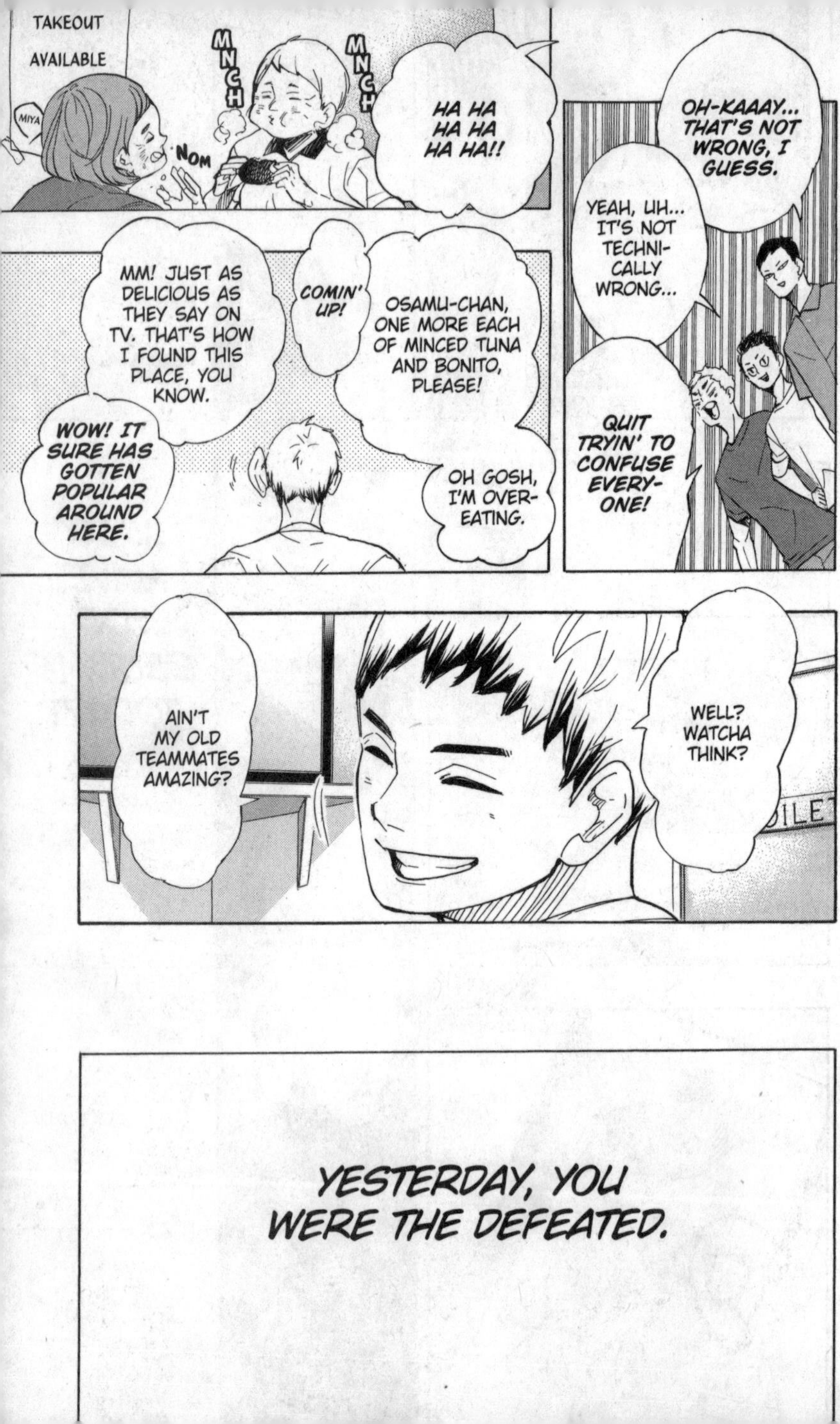
HA HA HA HA HA HA!!
MNCH
MNCH
NOM
MIYA
TAKEOUT AVAILABLE
OH-KAAAY... THAT'S NOT WRONG, I GUESS.
YEAH, UH... IT'S NOT TECHNICALLY WRONG...
QUIT TRYIN' TO CONFUSE EVERYONE!
OSAMU-CHAN, ONE MORE EACH OF MINCED TUNA AND BONITO, PLEASE!
COMIN' UP!
MM! JUST AS DELICIOUS AS THEY SAY ON TV. THAT'S HOW I FOUND THIS PLACE, YOU KNOW.
OH GOSH, I'M OVER-EATING.
WOW! IT SURE HAS GOTTEN POPULAR AROUND HERE.
WELL? WATCHA THINK?
AIN'T MY OLD TEAMMATES AMAZING?
YESTERDAY, YOU WERE THE DEFEATED.

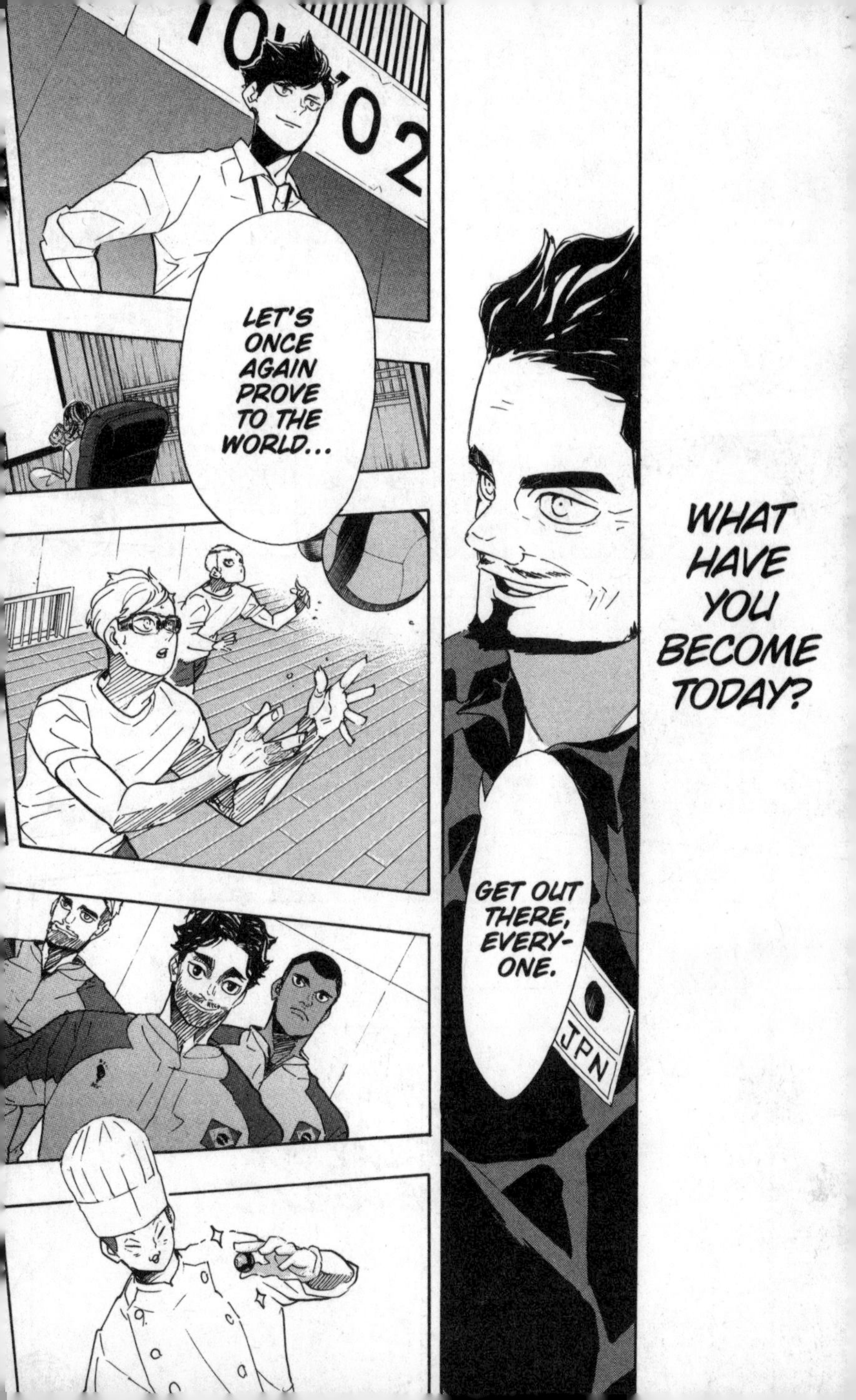
WHAT HAVE YOU BECOME TODAY?
GET OUT THERE, EVERY-ONE.
LET'S ONCE AGAIN PROVE TO THE WORLD...

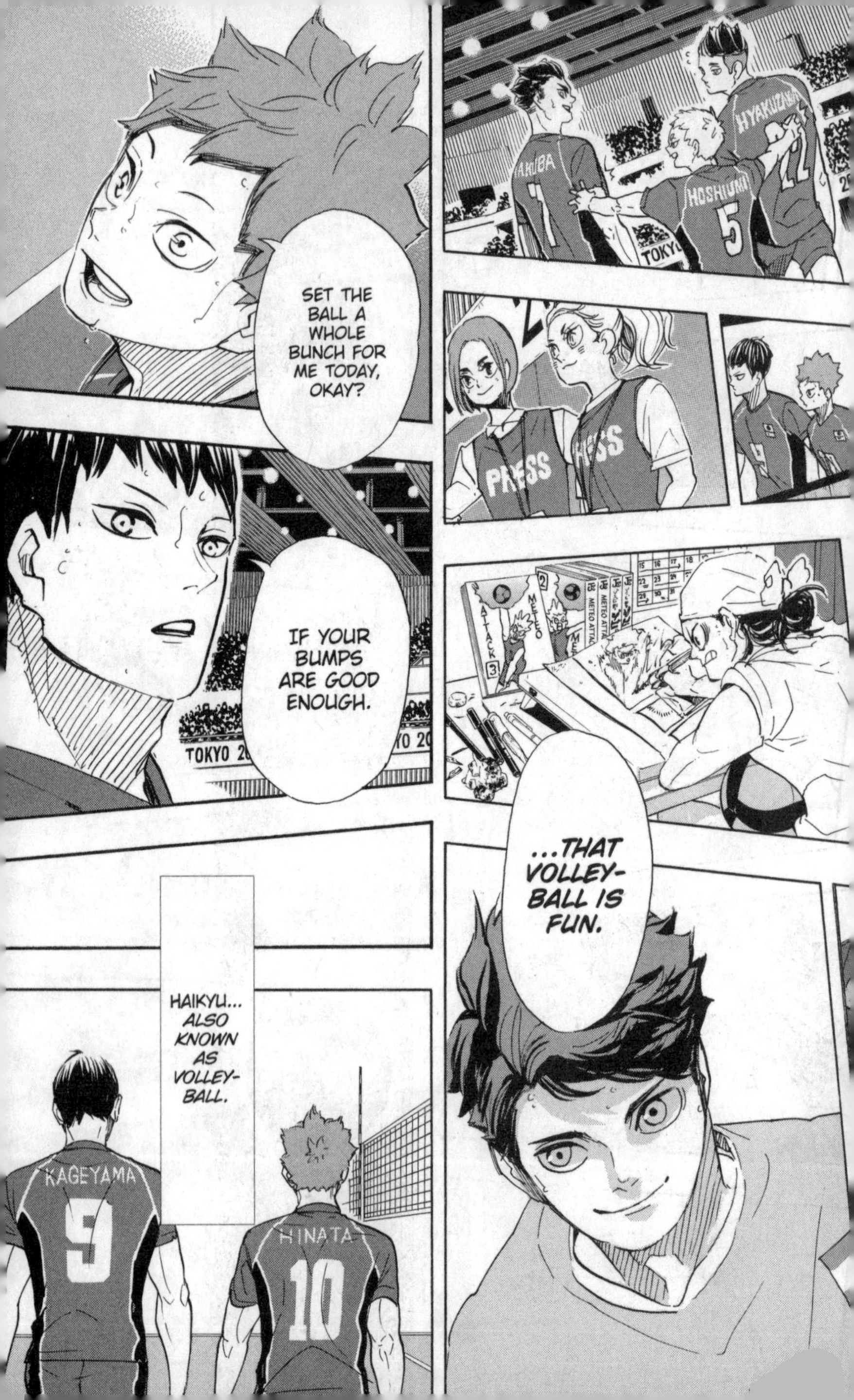
HOSHIUMI
PRESS
SET THE BALL A WHOLE BUNCH FOR ME TODAY, OKAY?
IF YOUR BUMPS ARE GOOD ENOUGH.
...THAT VOLLEYBALL IS FUN.
HAIKYU... ALSO KNOWN AS VOLLEYBALL.
KAGEYAMA
HINATA

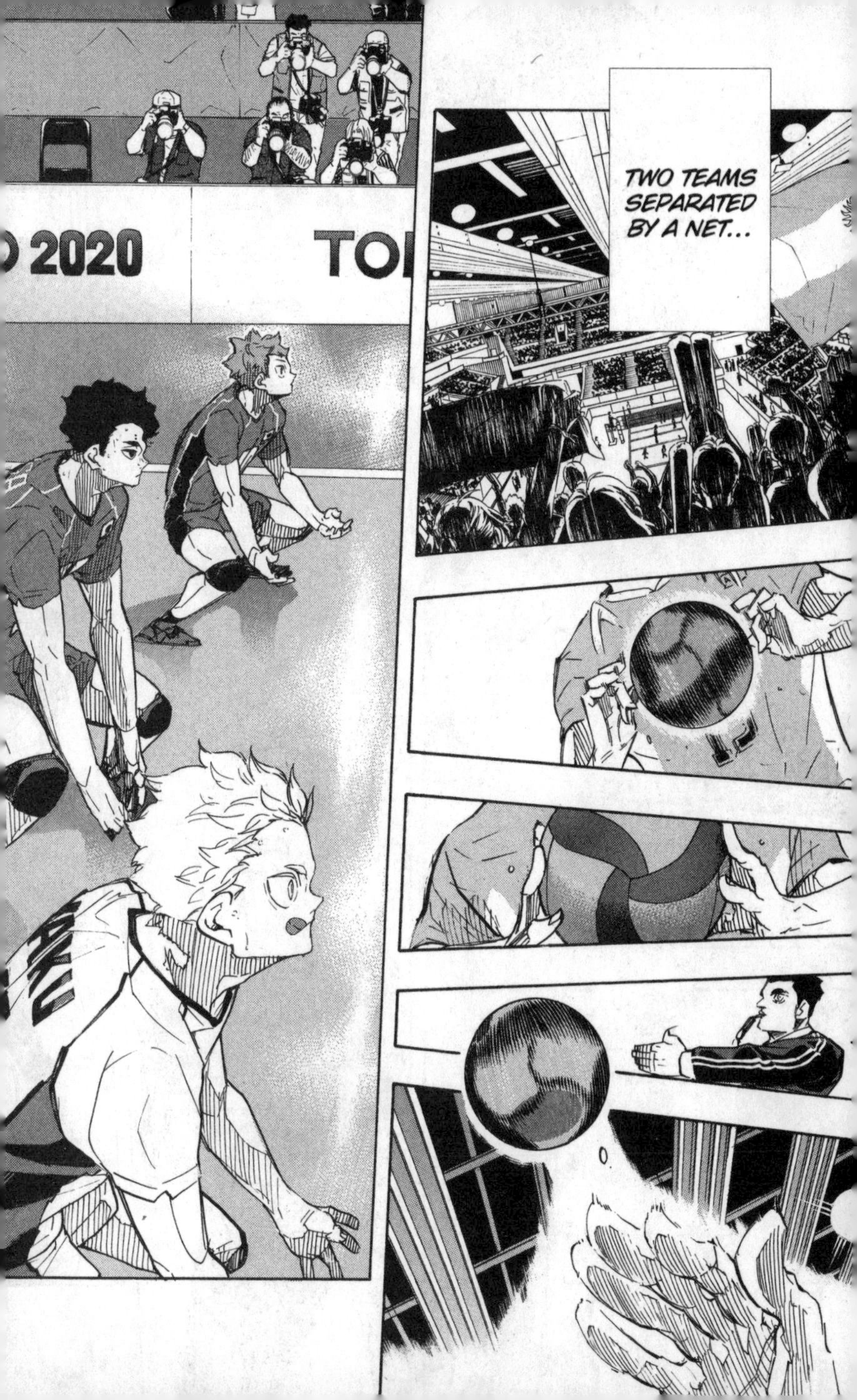
TWO TEAMS SEPARATED BY A NET...

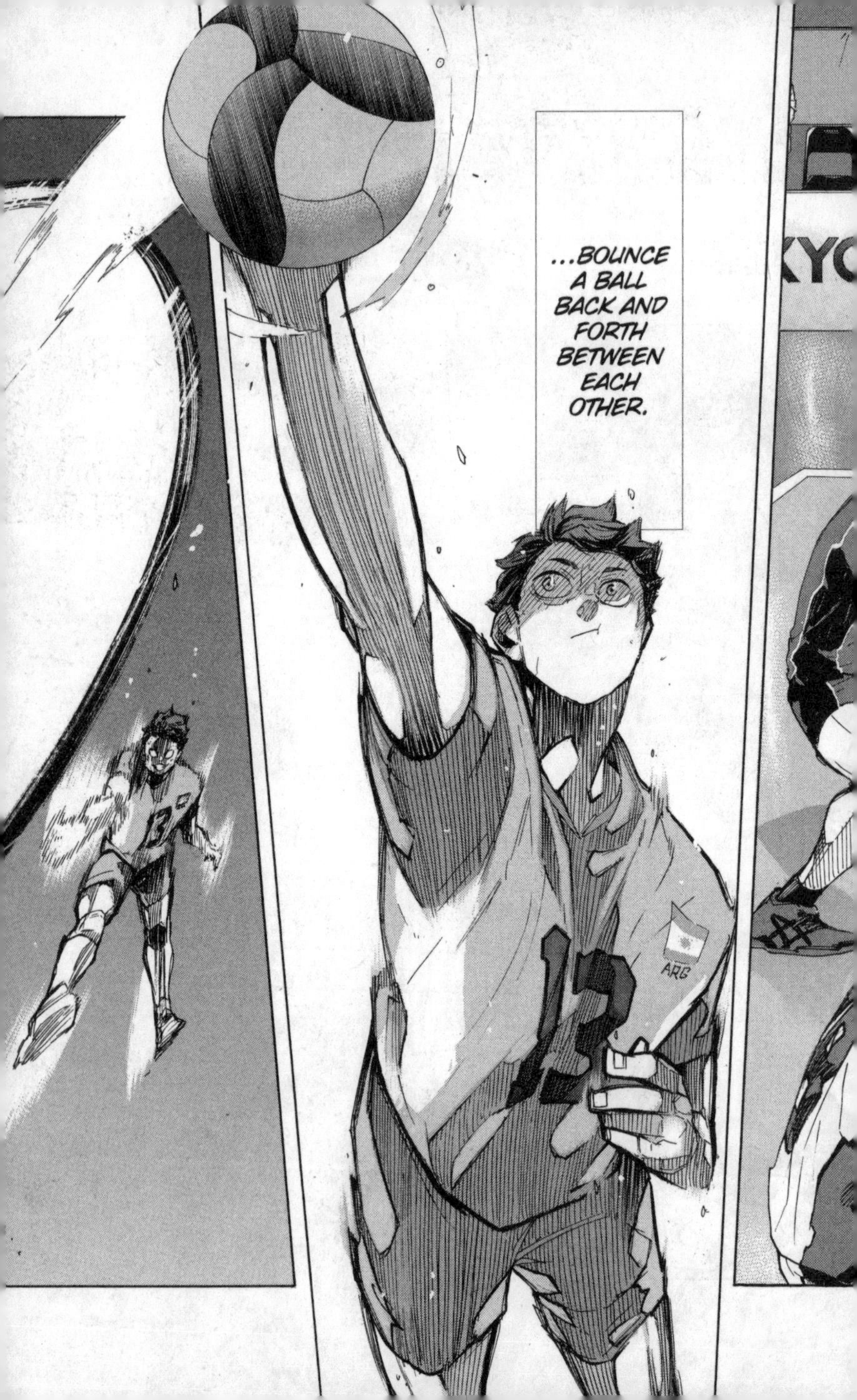
...BOUNCE A BALL BACK AND FORTH BETWEEN EACH OTHER.
ARG

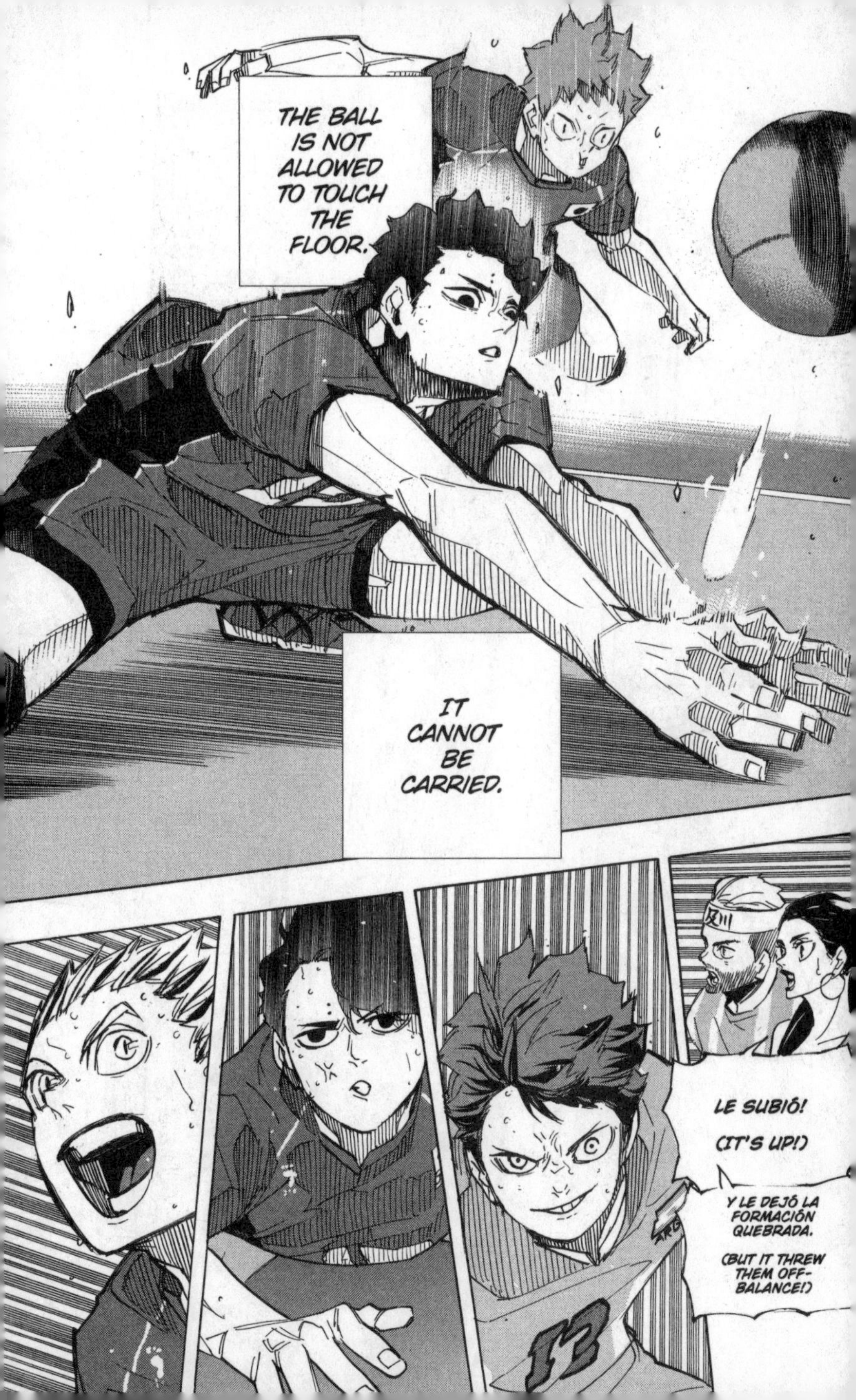
THE BALL IS NOT ALLOWED TO TOUCH THE FLOOR.
IT CANNOT BE CARRIED.
LE SUBIÓ!
(IT'S UP!)
Y LE DEJÓ LA FORMACIÓN QUEBRADA.
(BUT IT THREW THEM OFF-BALANCE!)

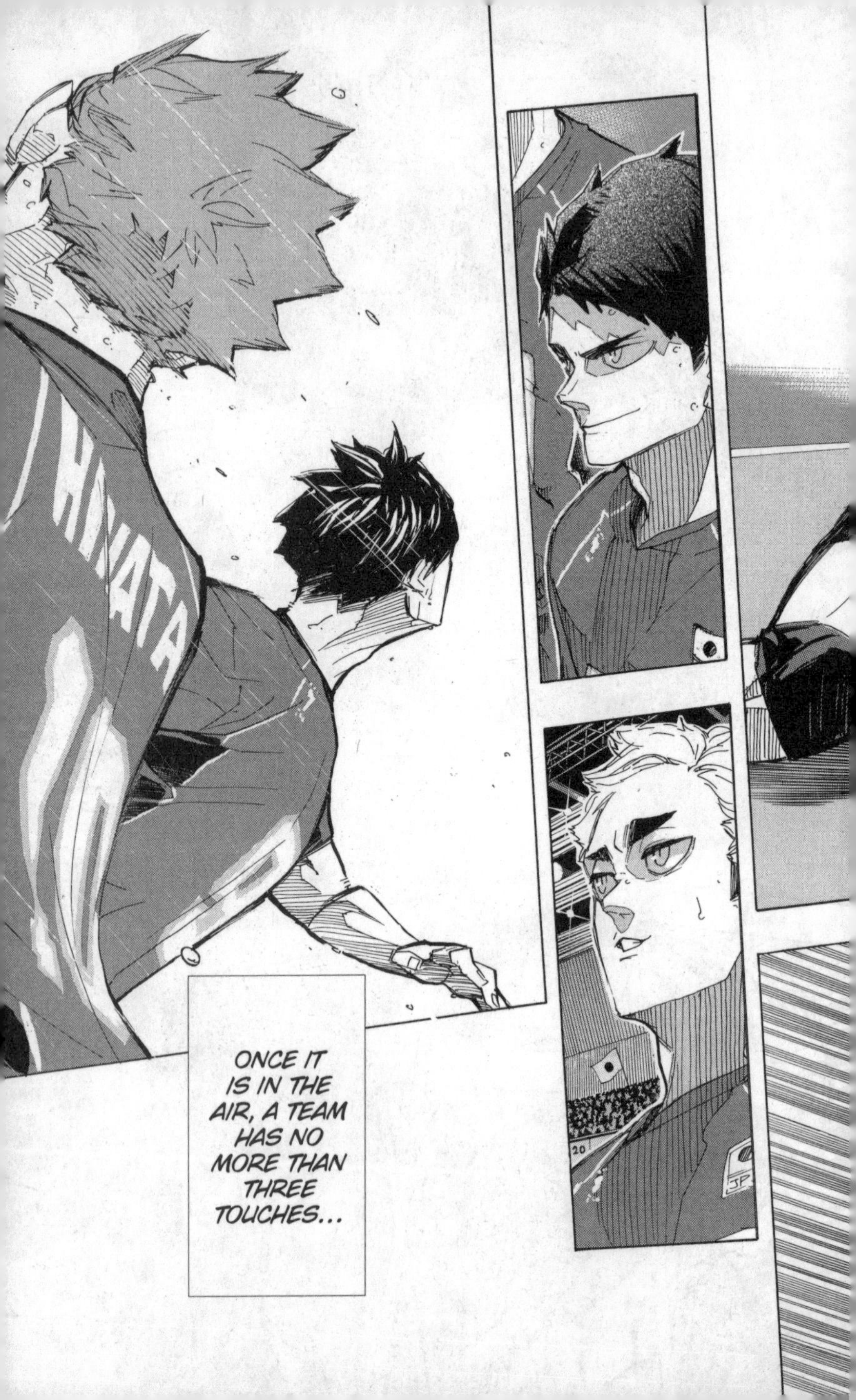
HINATA
ONCE IT IS IN THE AIR, A TEAM HAS NO MORE THAN THREE TOUCHES...
20
JP

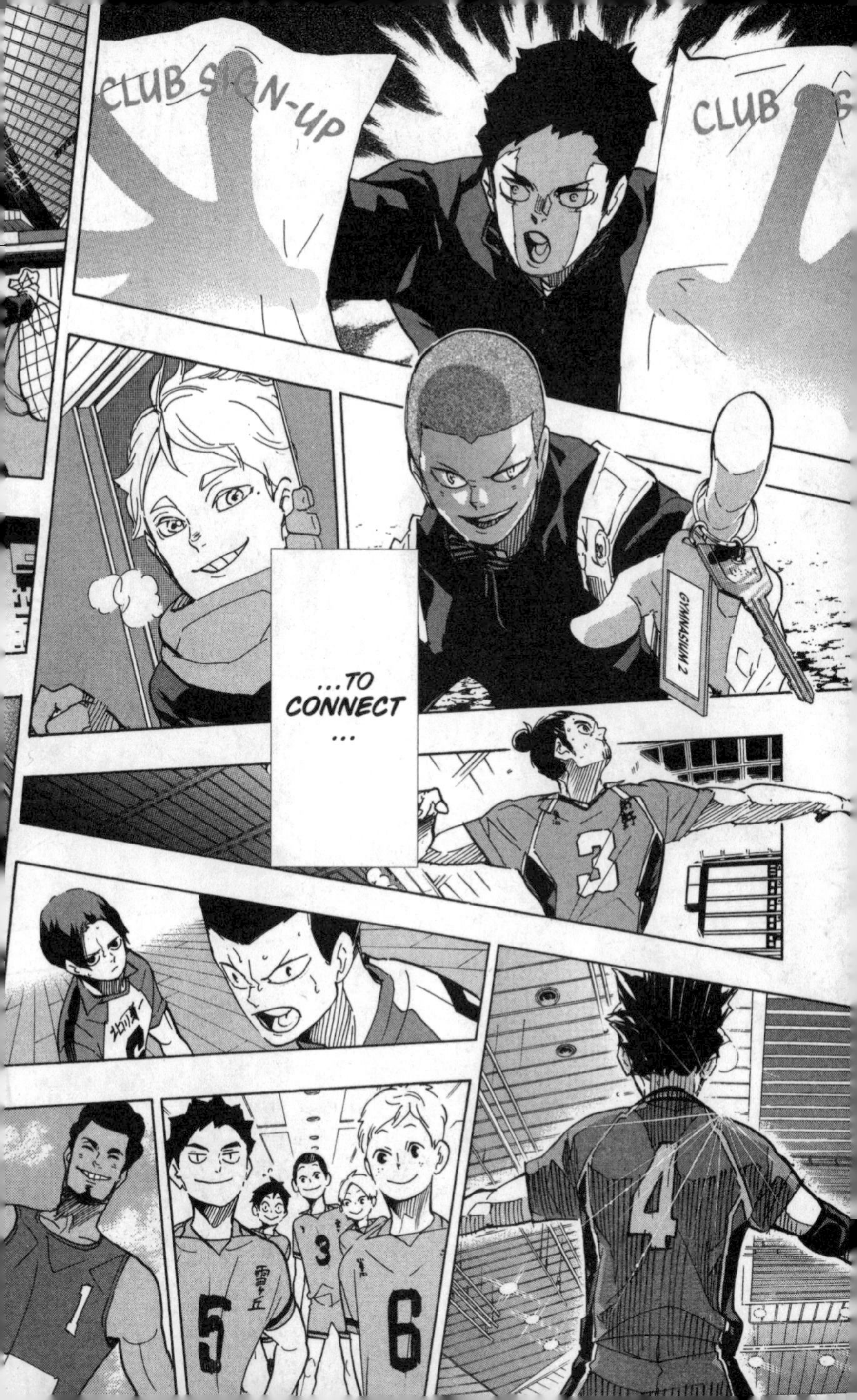

CLUB
CLUB SIGN-UP
GYMNASIUM 2
...TO CONNECT ...

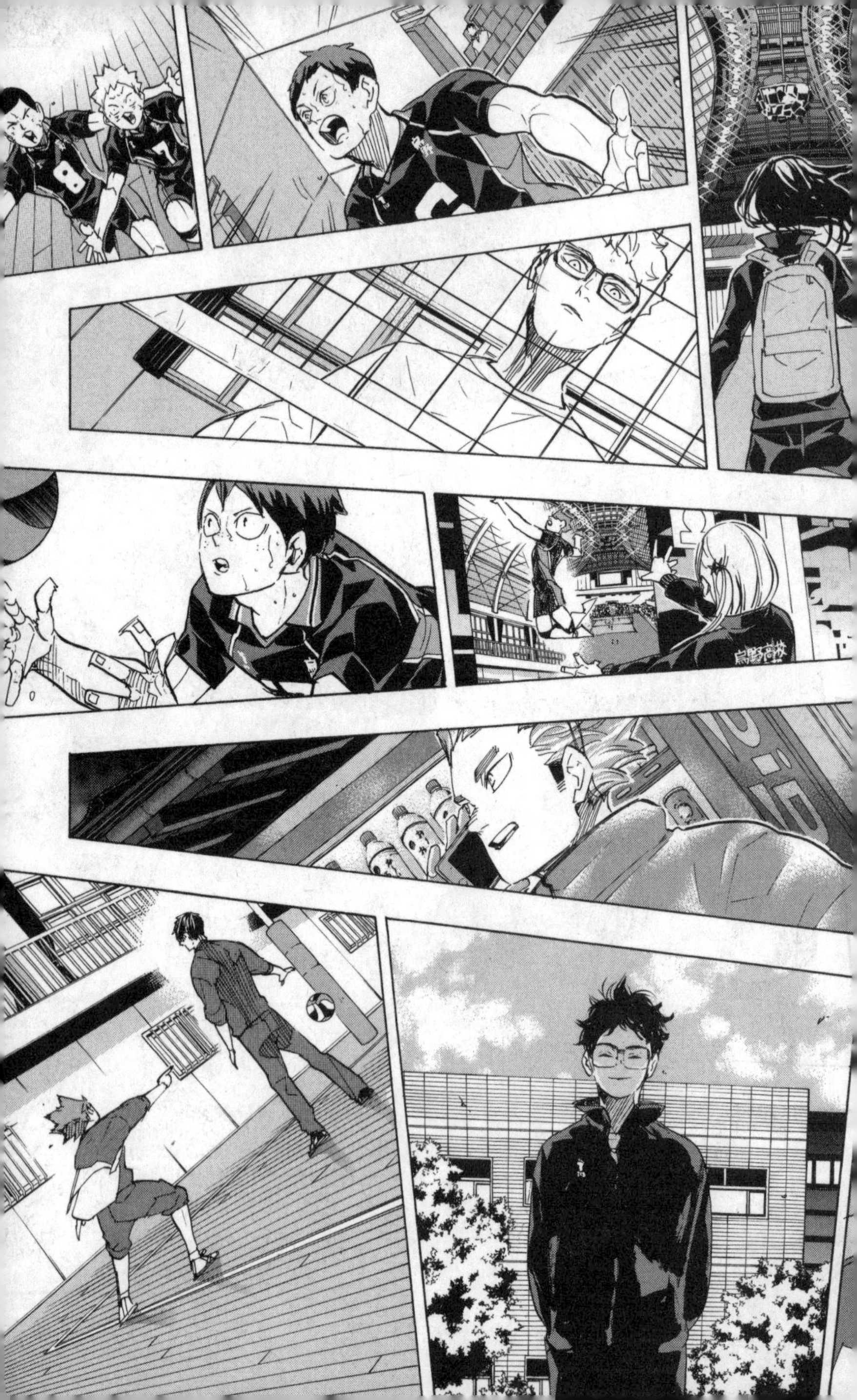
烏野高校

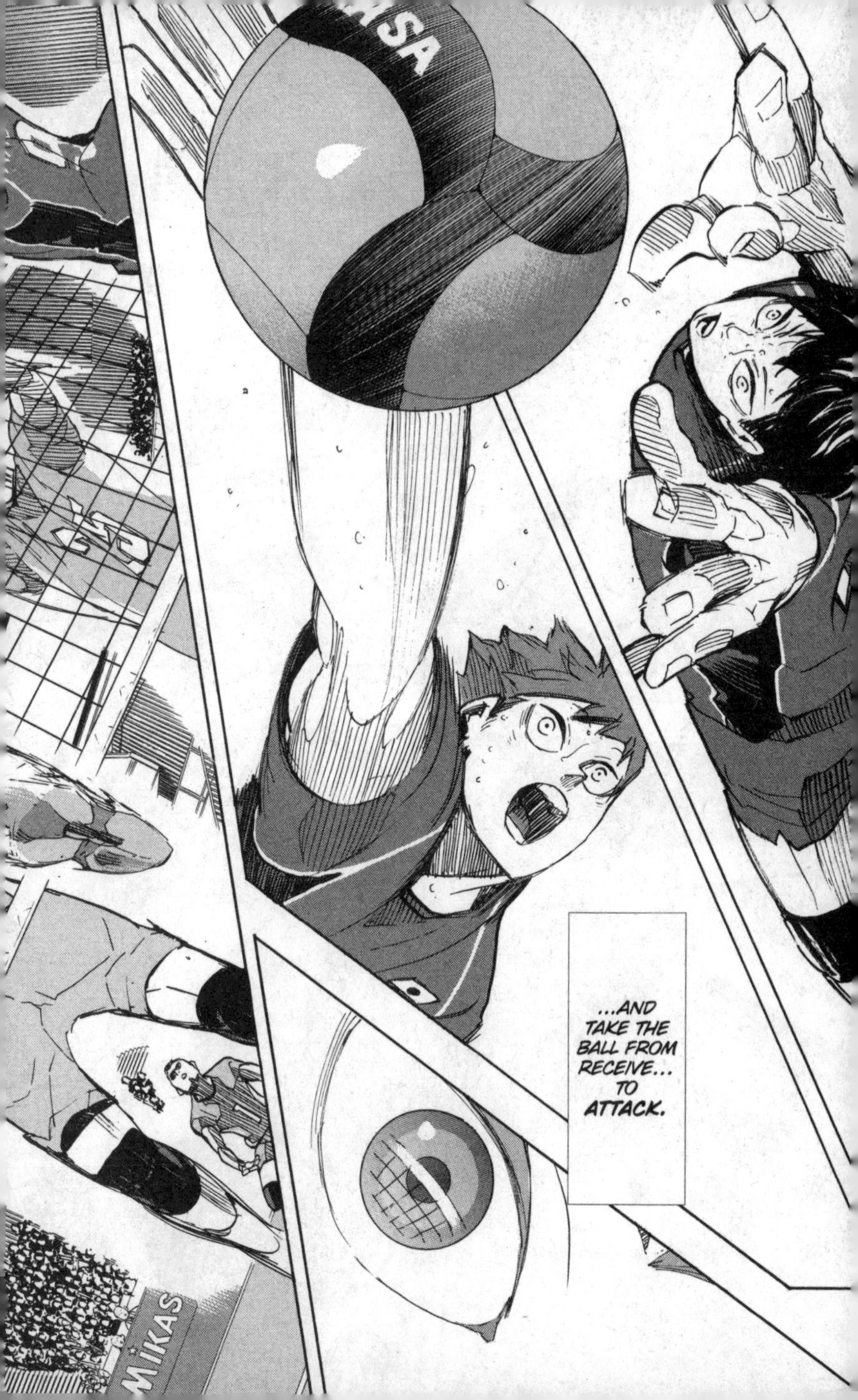
...AND TAKE THE BALL FROM RECEIVE... TO ATTACK.

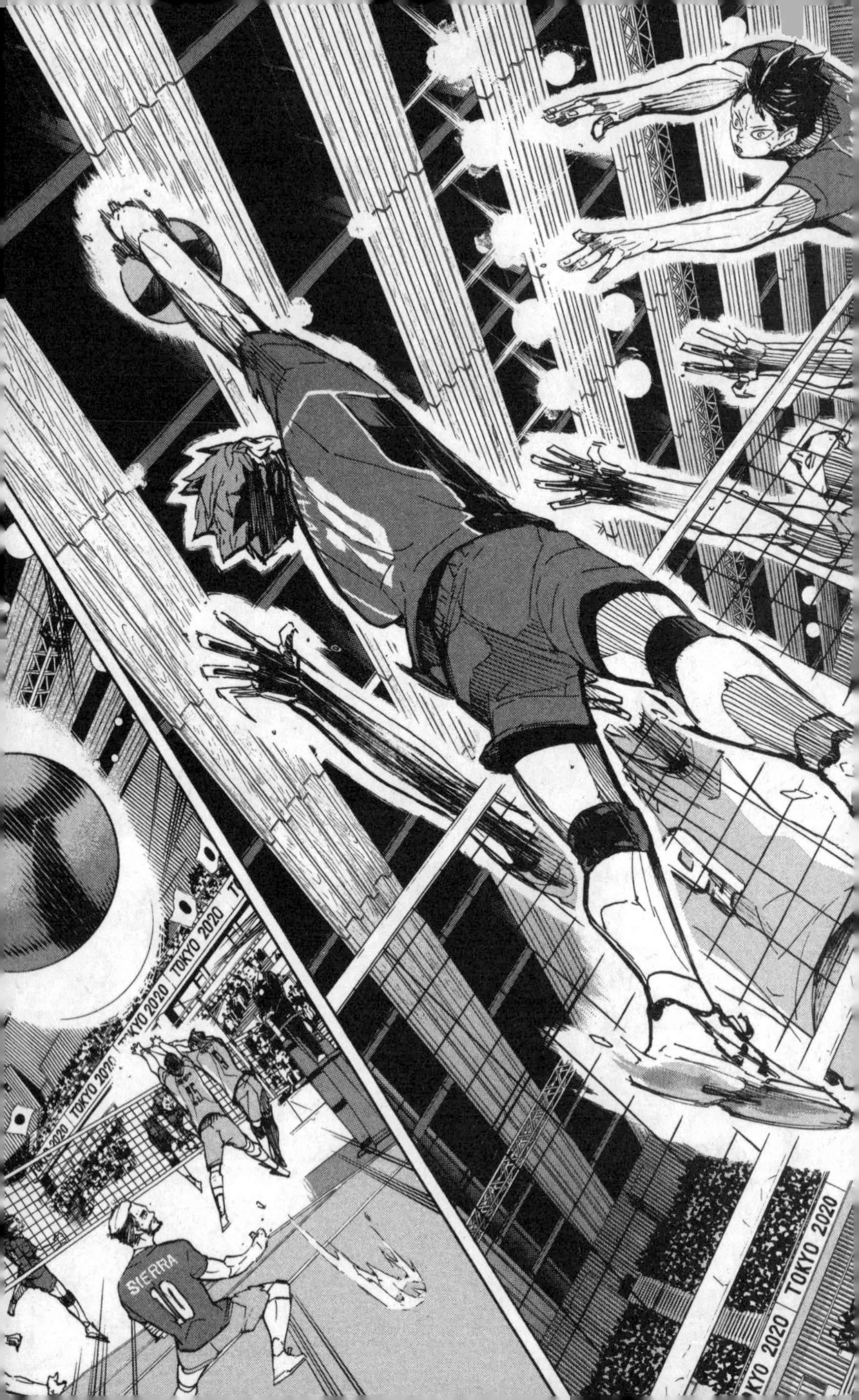
TOKYO 2020
TOKYO 2020
TOKYO 2020
TOKYO 2020
SIERRA
10

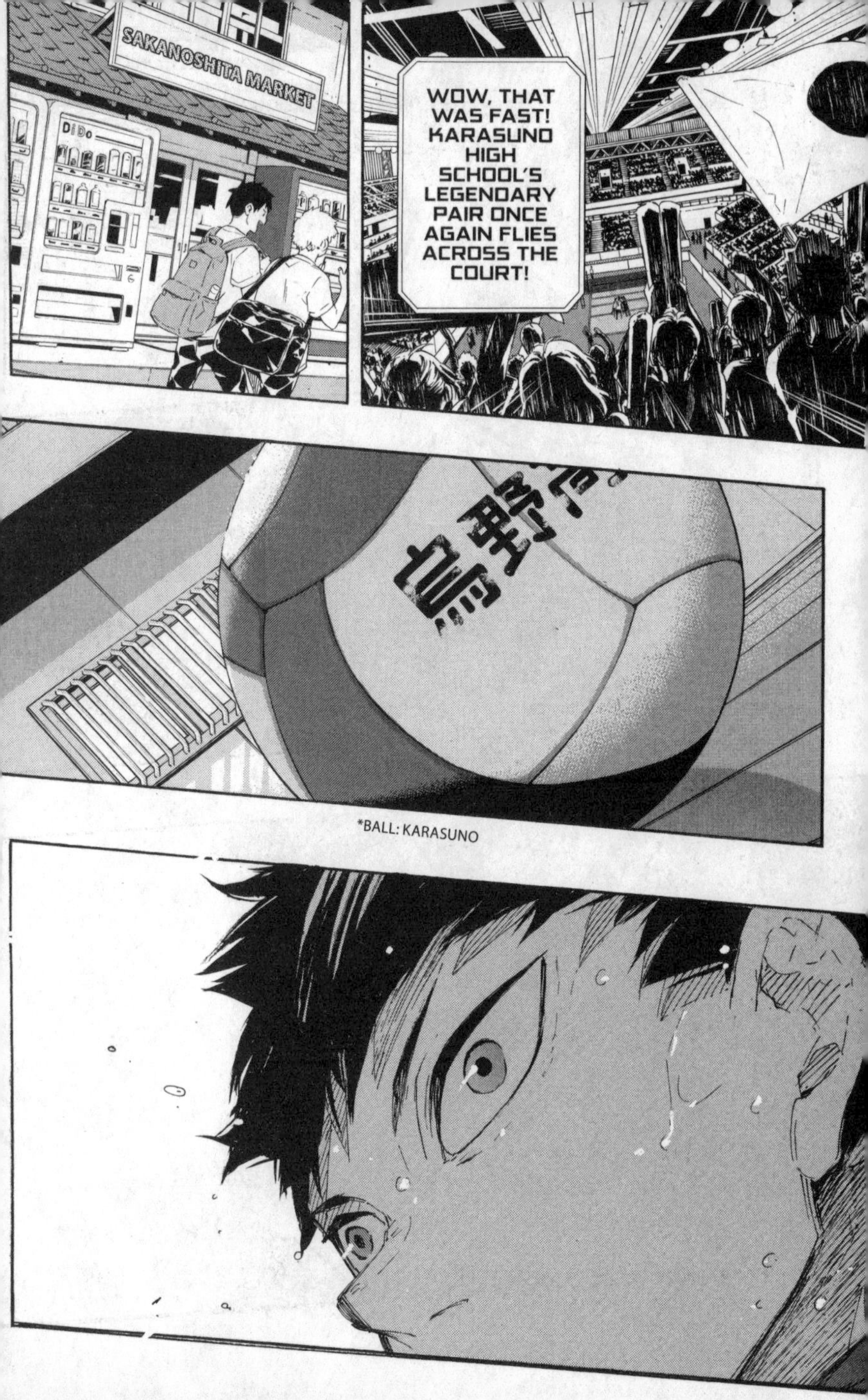
WOW, THAT WAS FAST! KARASUNO HIGH SCHOOL'S LEGENDARY PAIR ONCE AGAIN FLIES ACROSS THE COURT!
SAKANOSHITA MARKET
DiDo
*BALL: KARASUNO

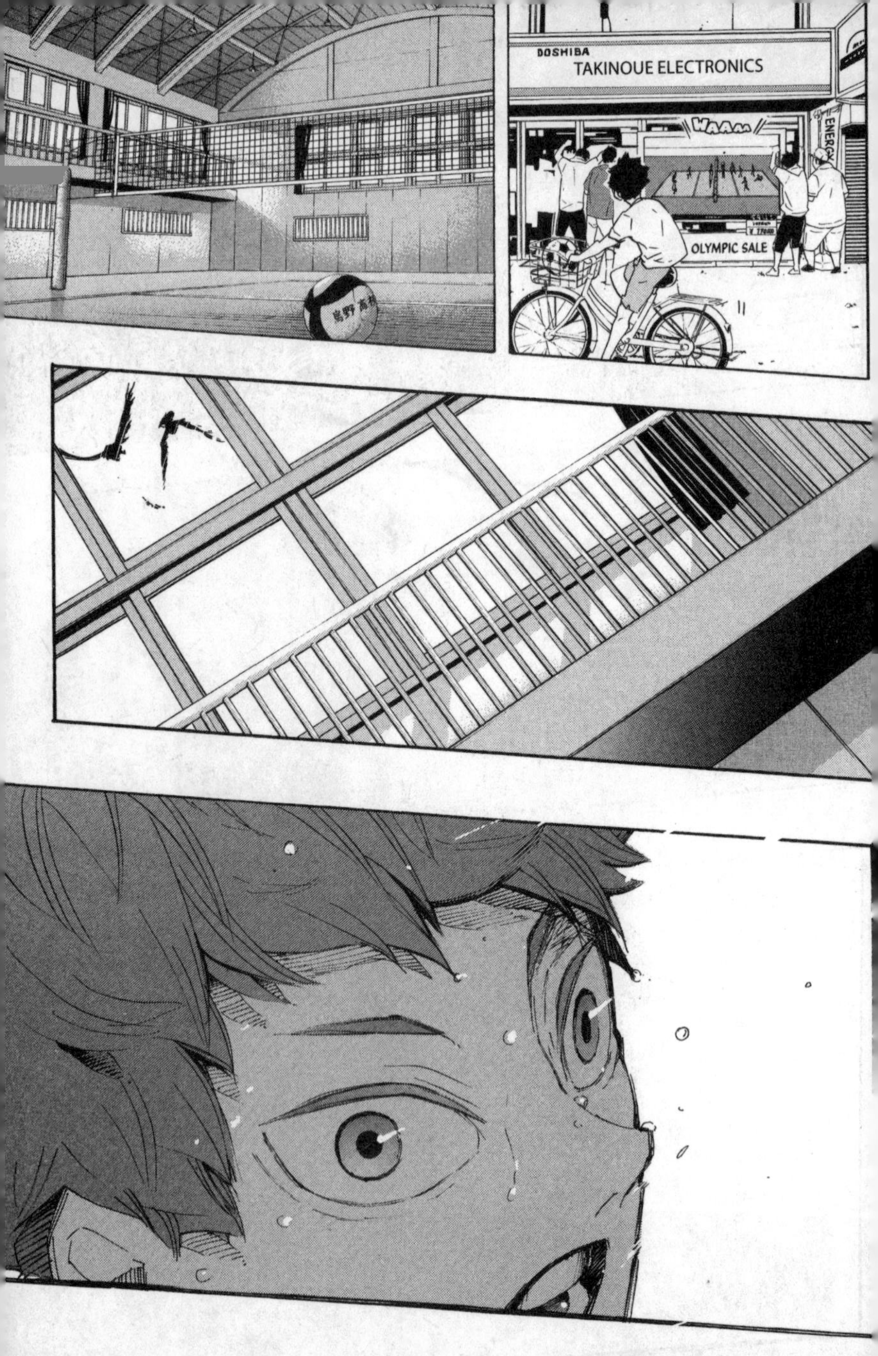
DOSHIBA
TAKINOUE ELECTRONICS
WAAAA
OLYMPIC SALE

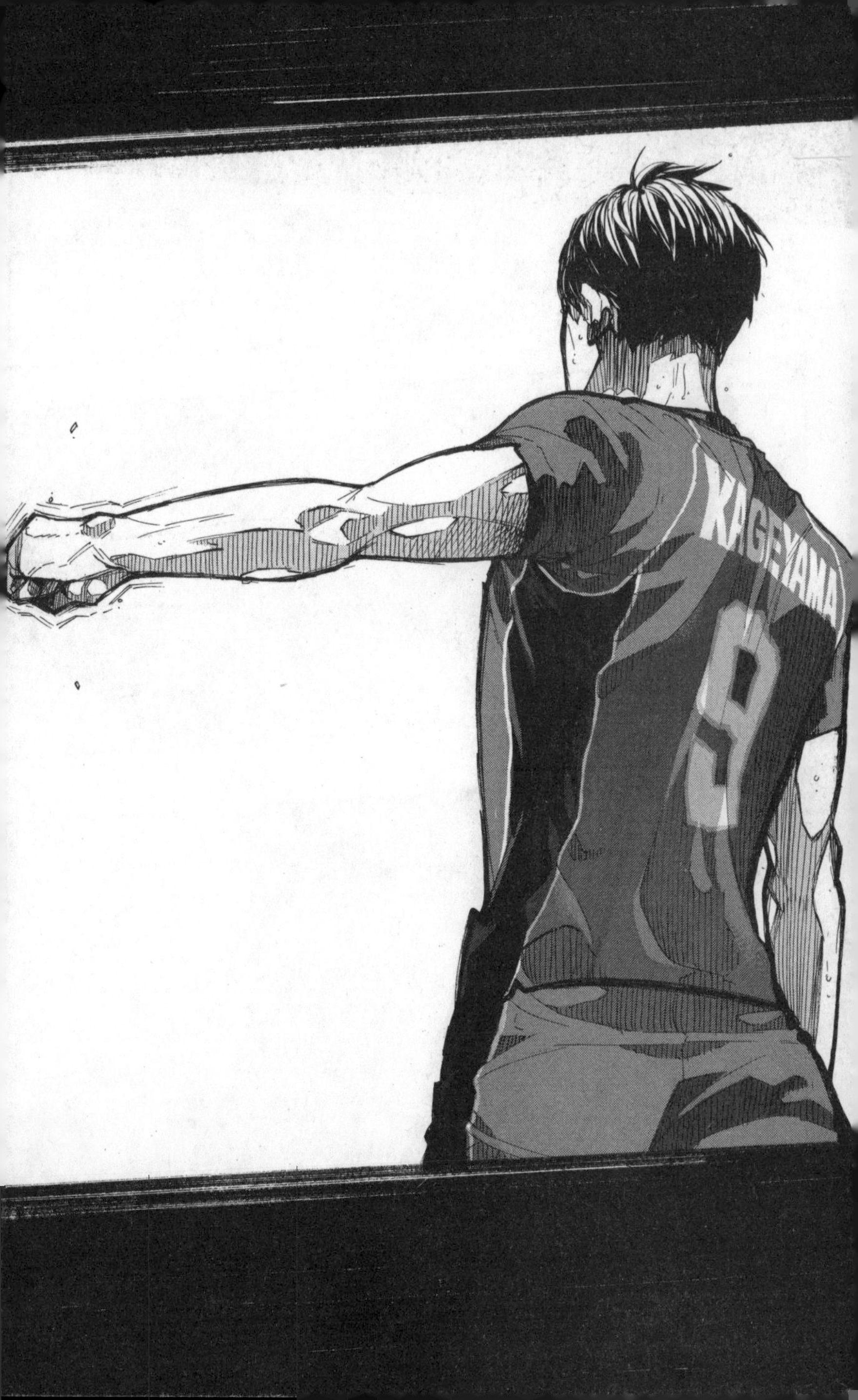
KAGEYAMA
9

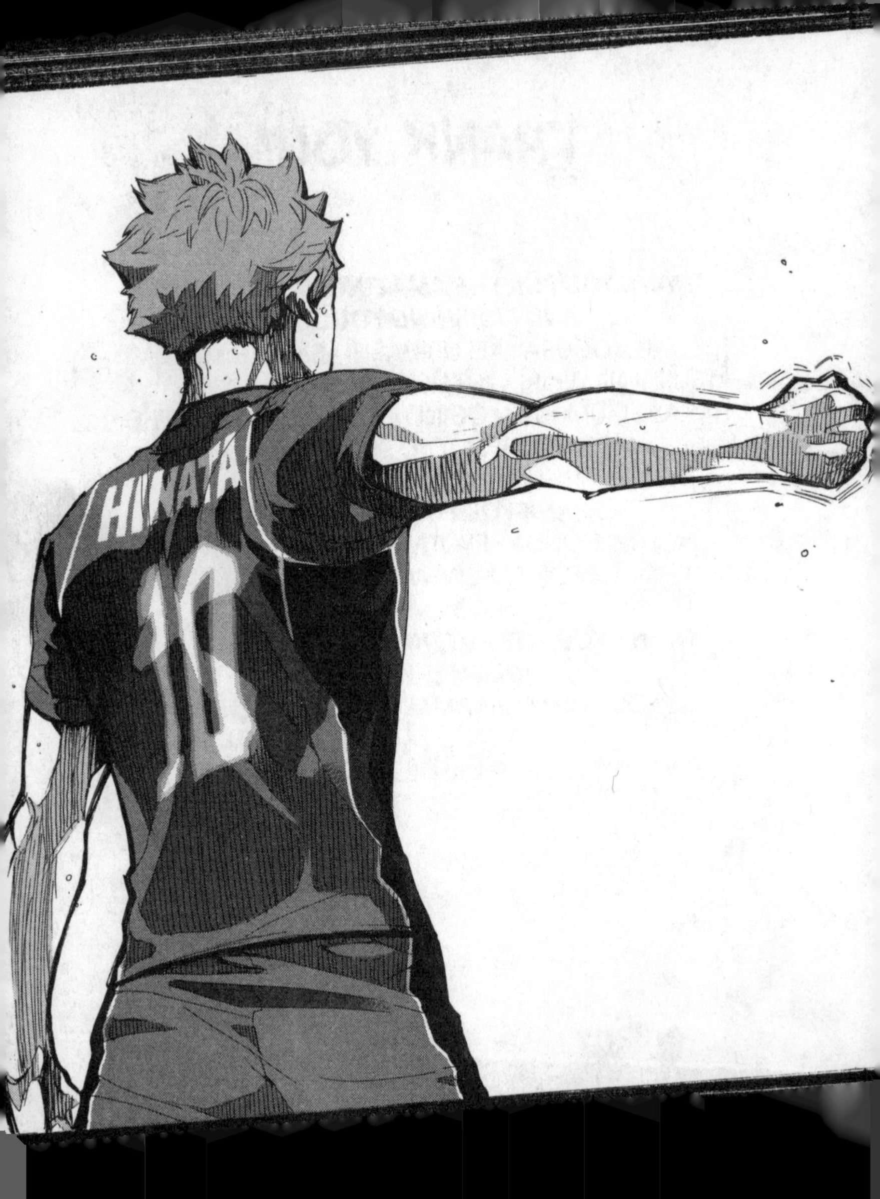
HINATA
10

THANK YOU!

THANK YOU FOR THE AMAZING BACKGROUNDS AND FINISHING TOUCHES.
RYOTARO OGURA • KEI ORIHASHI • SAKUJU KOIZUMI • ATSUSHI NAMIKIRI • YUTAKA AOKI • DAI HOSHIGAWA • HAKASE IZUMI • KEN OGINO • AKI • YUMIYA TASHIRO • MASAYOSHI SATOJO • KOHEI UCHIDA

THANK YOU FOR EVERYTHING.
SUKEYUKI HONDA • RYOTA IKEDA • RITSUKI HIGASHI
(*WEEKLY SHONEN JUMP* EDITORS)

THANK YOU FOR PUTTING TOGETHER MANGA VOLUMES WITH US.
YOSHIHIRO HAKAMADA • RIEKO SUZUKI • KANAKO YANAGIDA
(YUKI DESIGN)

THANK YOU FOR THE COOL DESIGNS.
KAZUKI KATSUMATA • YUKI YAMAMOTO
(FREIHEIT)

**THANK YOU FOR WRITING ARTICLES AND
RELATED MATERIALS.**
SHIZUKA KO (KISOUSHA)

THANK YOU.
YUSUKE SATO (JUMP J BOOKS)
MASASHI NAMBU (PANASONIC PANTHERS
GENERAL MANAGER AND COACH OF JAPAN'S
NATIONAL MEN'S TEAM)

THANKS!
VOLLEYBALL

HARUICHI FURUDATE

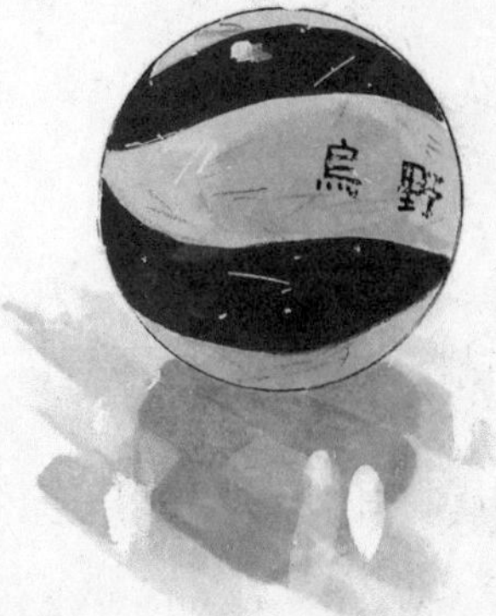
烏野

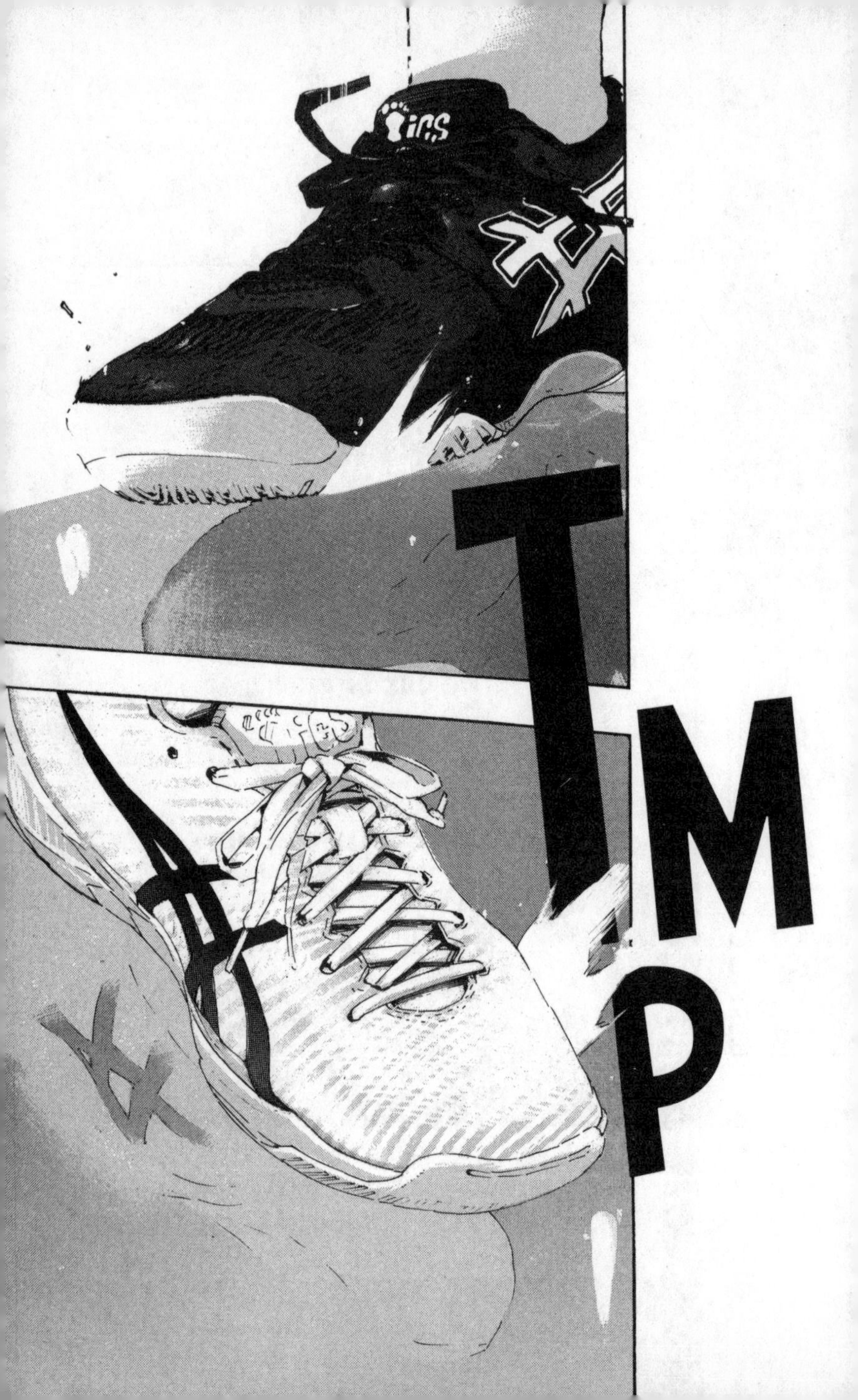
TMP

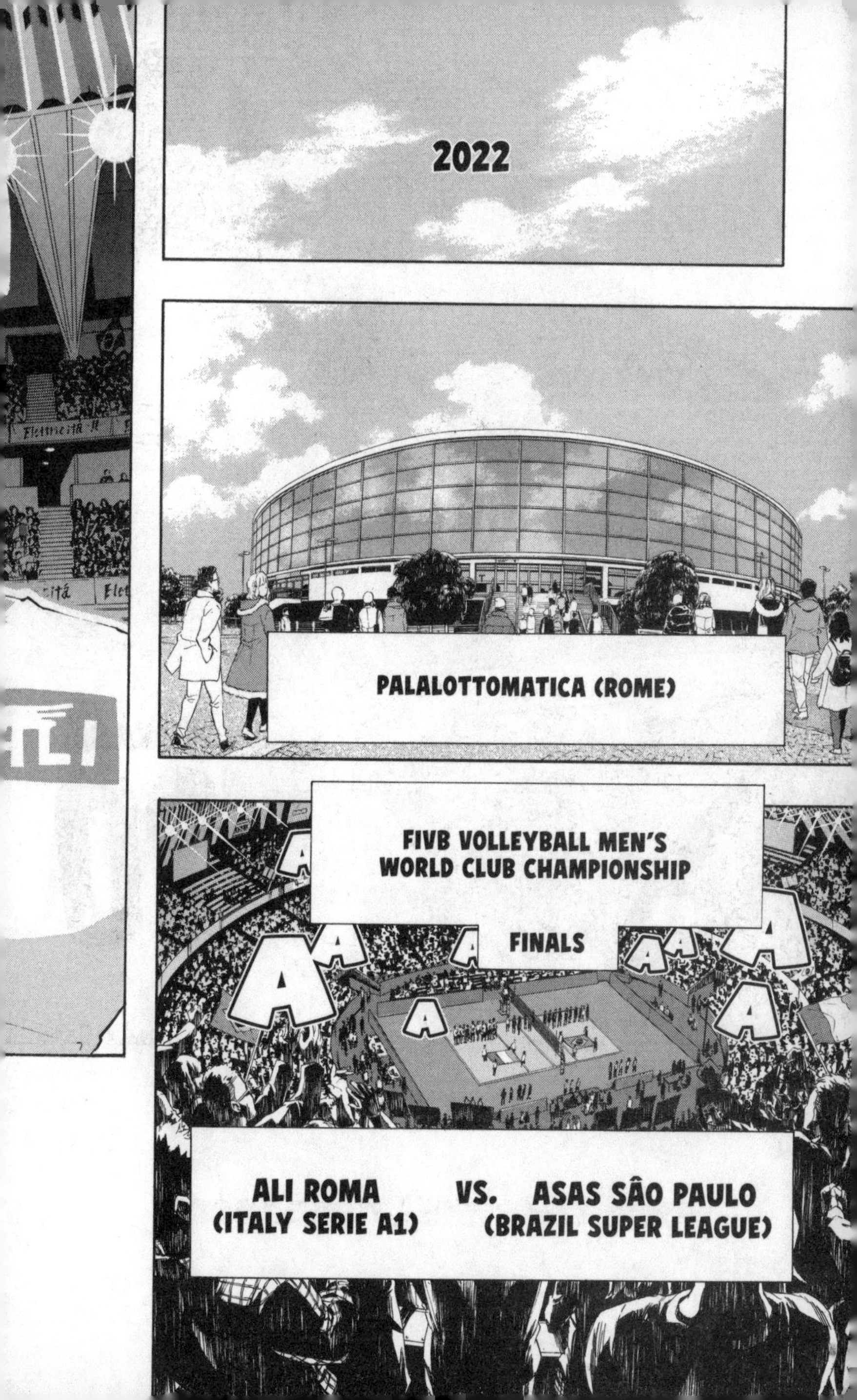
2022
PALALOTTOMATICA (ROME)
FIVB VOLLEYBALL MEN'S WORLD CLUB CHAMPIONSHIP
FINALS
ALI ROMA (ITALY SERIE A1) VS. ASAS SÃO PAULO (BRAZIL SUPER LEAGUE)

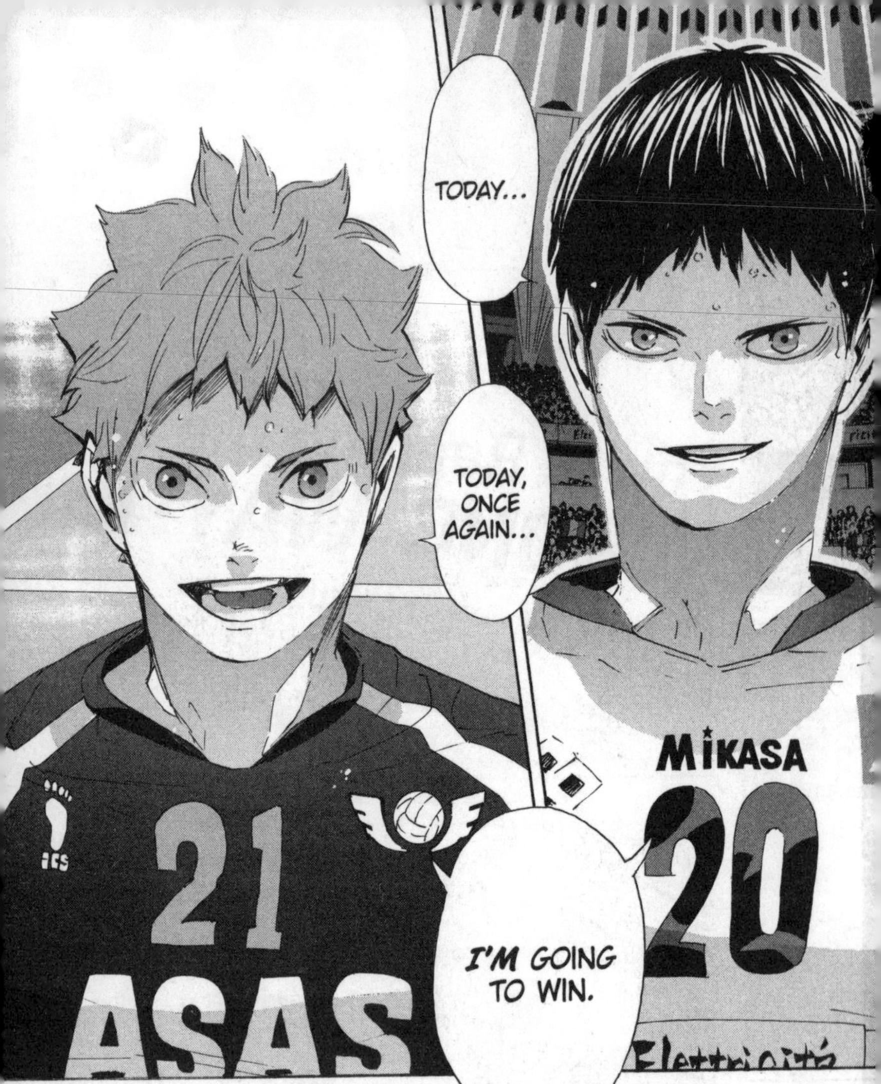
TODAY...
TODAY, ONCE AGAIN...
MIKASA
I'M GOING TO WIN.

FINAL CHAPTER: **Challengers**

THE END!

You're Reading the
WRONG WAY!

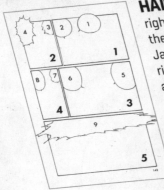

HAIKYU!! reads from right to left, starting in the upper-right corner. Japanese is read from right to left, meaning that action, sound effects and word-balloon order are completely reversed from English order.